The Impact of Algorithmic Technologies on Healthcare

Scrivener Publishing
100 Cummings Center, Suite 541J
Beverly, MA 01915-6106

Machine Learning in Biomedical Science and Healthcare Informatics

Series Editors: Vishal Jain (mailto:drvishaljain83@gmail.com) and Jyotir Moy Chatterjee (mailto:jyotirchatterjee@gmail.com)

In this series, an attempt has been made to capture the scope of various applications of machine learning in the biomedical engineering and healthcare fields, with a special emphasis on the most representative machine learning techniques, namely deep learning-based approaches. Machine learning tasks are typically classified into two broad categories depending on whether there is a learning 'label' or 'feedback' available to a learning system: supervised learning and unsupervised learning. This series also introduces various types of machine learning tasks in the biomedical engineering field from classification (supervised learning) to clustering (unsupervised learning). The objective of the series is to compile all aspects of biomedical science and healthcare informatics, from fundamental principles to current advanced concepts.

Publishers at Scrivener
Martin Scrivener (martin@scrivenerpublishing.com)
Phillip Carmical (pcarmical@scrivenerpublishing.com)

The Impact of Algorithmic Technologies on Healthcare

Edited by

Parul Dubey

Symbiosis Institute of Technology, Nagpur Campus, Symbiosis International (Deemed University), Pune, India

Mangala Madankar

Dept. of Artificial Intelligence, G H Raisoni College of Engineering, Nagpur, India

Pushkar Dubey

Pandit Sundarlal Sharma (Open) University, Chhattisgarh, India

and

Bui Thanh Hung

Faculty of Information Technology, Industrial University of Ho Chi Minh City, Vietnam

Scrivener Publishing

WILEY

This edition first published 2025 by John Wiley & Sons, Inc., 111 River Street, Hoboken, NJ 07030, USA and Scrivener Publishing LLC, 100 Cummings Center, Suite 541J, Beverly, MA 01915, USA

For more information about Scrivener publications please visit www.scrivenerpublishing.com.

Wiley Global Headquarters
111 River Street, Hoboken, NJ 07030, USA

For details of our global editorial offices, customer services, and more information about Wiley products visit us at www.wiley.com.

Library of Congress Cataloging-in-Publication Data

ISBN 978-1-394-30546-9

Front cover images courtesy of Wikimedia Commons
Cover design by Russell Richardson

Set in size of 11pt and Minion Pro by Manila Typesetting Company, Makati, Philippines

Printed in the USA

10 9 8 7 6 5 4 3 2 1

Contents

Preface

A new age of efficiency and creativity has dawned on the healthcare industry with the emergence of algorithmic technology. Entitled "The Impact of Algorithmic Technologies on Healthcare," this book showcases the many ways AI, ML, and the IoT have revolutionized healthcare. From digital twins to blockchain technology's potential use in healthcare systems, this work covers a wide range of subjects in its nineteen well-written chapters. As a significant resource for healthcare professionals, researchers, and students, each chapter examines a particular area of interest, showcasing both theoretical foundations and practical applications.

After introducing digital twins and discussing how they can improve healthcare delivery, the book moves on to discuss the larger effects of digital technology on the healthcare system. Chapters that follow include topics such as medical imaging innovations, predictive analytics for better patient outcomes, and deep learning algorithms for brain tumor detection. Additonal topics include generative adversarial networks (GANs) and convolutional neural networks (CNNs). Smart wearables for remote patient monitoring, effective Internet of Things solutions, telemedicine developments, and blockchain security for healthcare systems are all covered in the book. Integrating biometric systems driven by artificial intelligence, securing cyber-physical systems in healthcare, and digitizing wellness via EHRs and EMRs are all covered as well. The book concludes with a thorough case study and contrasts the effects of different healthcare apps, shedding light on the subject and encouraging further study and development in this dynamic area.

Our objective with this book is that the collection will help readers better grasp how these technologies may be used to boost efficiency, improve patient care, and improve healthcare outcomes.

Parul Dubey
Chief Editor
November 2024

1

Introduction to Algorithmic Health: Exploring Healthcare Through Digital Twins

A.S. Vinay Raj[1], N. Gopinath[2*], R. Anandh[3], M. Mohammed Jalaluddin[4] and Lyndsay R. Buckingham[5]

[1]*Information Science and Engineering, Global Academy of Technology, Bangalore, India*
[2]*Department of CINTEL, SRM Institute of Science and Technology, Kattankulathur, Tamil Nadu, India*
[3]*Department of CSE, Vel Tech Rangarajan Dr. Sagunthala R&D Institute of Science and Technology, Chennai, India*
[4]*Department of Computer Applications, B.S. Abdur Rahman Crescent Institute of Science and Technology, Vandalur, Chennai, India*
[5]*Universidad Pontificia Comillas, Mandrid, Spain*

Abstract

Components from several industries can be connected over the Internet thanks to a new communication paradigm called the Internet of Things (IoT). One of the most exciting applications of IoT technology is in contemporary healthcare as the social resource requirements, such as physicians, hospital, and health monitoring devices, in the traditional healthcare system are increasing. This paper covers the development of a tiny, wearable sensor that may be used to monitor electrocardiograms, photo plethysmography, and body temperature. The anticipated sensor can constantly evaluate blood pressure (BP) and relies on the pulse arrival time devoid of needing excess devices/wires as the PPG and ECG sensors are merged into a single device. Vital sign monitoring is done using the three sensors on the sensor. A power board handles battery charging and energy supply, and a centerboard handles signal processing and acquisition. For remote health monitoring applications, affixing all components to the human body is simple, thanks to its rigid–flex structure. The centerboard's sensors can be taken out to save energy and be used

**Corresponding author*: gopinathit14@gmail.com

Parul Dubey, Mangala Madankar, Pushkar Dubey and Bui Thanh Hung (eds.) The Impact of Algorithmic Technologies on Healthcare, (1–26) © 2025 Scrivener Publishing LLC

for specialized physiological signal assessments such as the ECG. The usefulness of the suggested sensor is tested through experiments, and performance is compared to a commercial reference device.

Keywords: Healthcare, Internet of Things, remote sensing, sensors, human body

1.1 Introduction

Many scientific fields have shown great interest in the Internet of Things (IoT). IoT technologies allow many components from many locations to be connected so that resources and information can be shared without being limited by time or space. The current healthcare industry is one of the most enticing uses of IoT [1]. Chronic illnesses are one of the leading global health concerns for people as life expectancy rises. Early detection and management of chronic diseases and improving people's health depend on continuously monitoring human vital indicators such as body temperature for an extended period, breathing rate, heart rate, and blood pressure. When considering hospital beds, medical equipment, physicians, and nurses, the traditional healthcare system has fewer social resources than the aging population. One intriguing answer to the need for ongoing health monitoring is the creation of wearable technology, which is a project for the future incorporating IoT technologies [2].

A tiny, low-power, wearable sensor is suggested for vital sign monitoring with Internet of Things-connected healthcare applications. The sensor comprises three sensors, a power board, and a centerboard. Flexible, flat cables connect the sensors to the boards. Consequently, removing any unnecessary sensors from the system is simple to minimize its overall size and power usage. To measure physiological parameters, including body temperature, PPG, and ECG, the sensor rigid–flex construction makes using biocompatible tapes to secure it to the chest simple. Without additional preparations, continuous blood pressure calculation on the suggested sensor is possible with the combination of PPG and ECG sensors [3]. The sensor data will be sent to a gateway, desktop computers, or mobile through a Bluetooth module. To safeguard subjects' confidentiality and privacy during transmission, AES-128 encryption is used. Each health data set will have a timestamp added before the gateway transfer data to a cloud server for further processing and preservation. The trade-off approach for monitoring users with movement requirements is to use a smartphone as a mobile gateway, although mobility is not the main emphasis of this study.

1.2 Related Works

Generally, three primary components are typically found in an IoT-connected healthcare system as follows: (1) wearable sensors to monitor health indicators, (2) an Internet gateway to link wearables to wearables, and (3) a cloud server for storing and processing data after they have been collected. Wearable sensors are essential for a healthcare platform with Internet of Things connectivity for remote health monitoring [4]. At the same time, gateways and cloud servers comprise the fundamental IoT infrastructure. The body's vital signs can provide insight into an individual's health. Scientists have suggested numerous wearable sensors to measure health data. Comprehensive wearable sensor reviews for remote healthcare applications, comprising Galvanic Skin Response (GSR), body temperature and activity, blood oxygen saturation (SpO2), and cardiovascular monitoring are described. For instance, a ring-shaped wearable sensor that measures heart rate is proposed. It is based on photoplethysmography (PPG), which examines clinical and technological problems during long-term continuous HR monitoring. In an intelligent assisted living home, wearable motion sensors identify behavioral anomalies in senior citizens. The suggested probabilistic framework is designed to enhance the quality of life for senior citizens by utilizing wearable sensors to detect abnormalities in their everyday routines. In ref. [5], RR and the duration of apnea during sleep are measured using a tiny magnetometer-based sensor. They are transferring the sensor data to a smartphone gateway to contrast it to an airflow sensor sold commercially. As for blood pressure readings, the wearable BP-monitoring system cannot use the bulky, cuff-equipped standard sphygmomanometer because of its short measurement intervals. Several intriguing wearable blood pressure monitoring techniques have recently been developed, all based on pulse transit time (PTT) and pulse arrival time (PAT) [6].

Most wearable BP estimation systems in long-term monitoring cases could be more user friendly since they use separate devices to measure PPG (finger/earlobe) and ECG (on the body). A wristwatch design for blood pressure readings is proposed. To acquire the ECG and PPG signals, the user must wear a watch on his left wrist and contact the electrode over the right hand [7]. A suitable regression model built using the PAT's collected ECG and PPG data can be used to determine the related BP values. Even though the bio-watch's hardware design is more straightforward because it requires two hands to take a reading, it cannot continuously measure long-term blood pressure numbers. Since the given work integrates PPG and ECG sensors, it can be applied to a chest-based sensor for continuous, long-term blood pressure estimation. In contrast to conventional wearables based on the wrist and finger, the suggested chest-based sensor is covert enough to be worn under clothing without interfering with daily activities [8].

1.2.1 Reviews on Wearable Sensors

One important method for tying wearable sensors and IoT gateways together is wireless communication. Many wireless protocols, including Zigbee, 6LowPAN, BLE, and others, have been proposed for short- and long-range data transmission (LoRaWan, Sigfox, etc.). For IoT-connected healthcare applications, researchers have put forth several wearable health monitoring devices. For example, the Health-IoT platform incorporates an intelligent medication box and non-intrusive bio-sensors [9]. Developing a wearable biosensor for body temperature and ECG monitoring coexists with integrating RFID technology into the medicine box to facilitate patient identification and prescription reminders. The author in ref. [10] describes an inexpensive wearable SN for the IoT healthcare system. The SN can gather and send body temperature, respiration rate, and ECG data to a gateway that can send emergency alerts. A wearable ECG monitor that may be customized is displayed next to an IoT architecture. The heart rate variability (HRV) and heart rate (HR) can be evaluated when ECG data are transferred to the smartphone using a Bluetooth module. The author used mobile phone accessories to set up a wireless health-monitoring system. The ECG signals are recorded and collected using the dry electrodes. A smartphone application can then analyze and predict a patient using these data. Unfortunately, it cannot record continuous ECG data because both hands are needed to record the signal. A wearable medical gadget with IoT capabilities for measuring several physiological parameters, including HR, HRV, and RR, is presented [11]. The primary gateway for storing local data and sending it to the Internet cloud is chosen to be an Android phone. However, since the smartphone could be needed for other everyday tasks, there are better options than utilizing it as the only gateway. To obtain physiological measurements, health data can be transferred via the Internet to a cloud and kept in a local database; this work uses both a mobile and a fixed gateway.

Because of the widespread use of IoT platforms and devices, security concerns about IoT today face unique obstacles outside of the conventional information technology framework. A comprehensive analysis of IoT security, including several security tiers, protocols, standards, solutions,

Table 1.1 Comparison of various existing approaches.

Ref	[4]	[6]	[8]
Sensors	Heart pulse and temperature sensor	Pulse oximeter and temperature sensor	Accelerometer, pulse oximeter, temperature sensor
Data	Heart rate and temperature sensor	Oxygen, blood, heart rate, and temperature level	Acceleration, blood oxygen level, heart rate, and temperature
Battery	Li ion	Li ion	Super-capacitors
Energy consumption	PVC controller	Two PVC controllers	PVC, DC–DC boost converter
Power consumption (mW)	4.9	20.2	2.1
Lifetime	137	33.2	1.9
Sensor charging time	14.6	11.7	0.04
Times/h	15	60	3
Sleep and wake up	15	1	20
Active time/day	880	5	10
Sleep time/ period	9.3	50	1190
Sustainability factor	Bluetooth 100 m	2.8	Bluetooth 100 m
Wireless technology	Wrist sensor	Wi-Fi	Wrist
Wear ability	Finger	Upper arm	Fingers
Data monitoring	Android phone	Server	Android phone

and potential blockchain applications, is provided. A variety of lightweight encryption algorithms, including BCC, LEA, Twine, Skipjack, and AES, are invented or upgraded to meet new needs as a result of resource limits on IoT sensor nodes (energy, latency, and processing power). Owing to its minimal processing needs, low latency, and inexpensive electricity, the BLE module's integrated AES-128 encryption engine is used in ref. [12]. Moreover, as the suggested sensor measures ECG, biometric ECG authentication may help maintain privacy. The movement of the user must be considered by a wearable healthcare infrastructure connected to the IoT to allow for ongoing health monitoring.

A framework for the design of a wearable health-monitoring system that supports mobility is detailed. There is a comparison and discussion of several conceptual and technological approaches. Mobility-supported healthcare systems are described with two examples of needs and solutions being a handover mechanism and a coordinator node. Since the suggested wearable healthcare system is outside this article's purview, it uses a smartphone or mobile gateway as a workaround to satisfy the mobility criterion. The health data are stored in an intermittent buffer to maintain the connection when the mobile gateway's sensor is removed and put back on the stationary gateway. The wearable sensor will be connected to many mobility-supported gateways via the received signal strength index (RSSI) [13] allowing researchers to investigate possible localization applications. Table 1.1 depicts the comparison of diverse existing wearable sensor systems.

1.3 Hardware Description

Wearable biomedical sensors are flexible and lightweight to painlessly cling to the human body. Given the challenges associated with cable-based wearable sensor connections to external healthcare devices, wireless data transmission is a fundamental necessity. Power usage must also be considered when long-term health monitoring is required. A wearable wireless sensor that is presented in this study for monitoring vital signs is shown in ref. [14]. Flexible, flat wires link the centerboard to other sensor boards. The biocompatible tapes, which can easily adhere to the sensor's architecture, are rigid-flexible and attached to the chest. The suggested wearable sensor consists of three sensors for body temperature, PPG, and ECG readings, power board for the energy supply, and a centerboard for signal processing and transmission [15].

1.3.1 Sensor Board

The centerboard's design is depicted in Figure 1.1, which links the other sensor boards to process and acquire signals. The Simblee® RFD77101, a professional-grade, high-performance Bluetooth 4.0 transceiver, also known as a BLE module, is the central component of the center board. It has an inbuilt antenna and an ARM Cortex M0 processor in a small volume measuring (11 mm × 8 mm × 3 mm). First, signal processing, which includes low-pass filtering, real-time DC removal, and band-pass filtering, will be carried out by the integrated microcontroller (MCU) on the physiological data that has been acquired [16]. The BLE module transmits the measured vital signs to a gateway to store the data for remote health monitoring and additional analysis. Because of its tiny form factor and low power requirements, the chosen BLE module is appropriate for wearable technology. Its ultra-low-power sleep mode uses less than 4 μA of current, whereas 8 mA is its maximum transmission current. An integrated circuit for the analog front end (AFE), called AD8232, and a buck-boost converter for voltage control, called RT6150A, and ECG signal acquisition make up the remaining portion of the centerboard.

Figure 1.1 Simblee® RFD77101.

1.3.2 Power Requirements

A separate board is constructed to power the wearable sensor. An LIR2450 (Multicomp®) 120-mAh rechargeable battery can be installed on the back side of the power board. An economical, effective buck-boost converter, the Richtek® RT6150A, maintains a steady voltage of 3.3 V. Rechargeable batteries are designed to last longer when a Microchip® linear charge controller, product number MCP73831, is used to control the battery's charging state. When the battery's capacity is nearly depleted, it starts with a constant current quick charging mode. At a preset time, the controller will begin charging the battery with a variable current at a fixed voltage. On the middle board, the MCU analog-to-digital converter (ADC) is connected to the battery to monitor its voltage. Given that there's a chance the battery voltage will exceed the 3.3-V MCU reference value, this low-power voltage divider circuit is employed [17]. This voltage divider is not like the traditional two-resistor voltage divider in that it is only functional when the "enable" signal (Bat-EN) is sent by the MCU, which helps protect you from accidentally draining the battery. After reading the battery voltage, the MCU will activate the P-channel MOSFET using the conventional voltage divider's output (Bat-ADC). When a battery measurement is unnecessary, the resistors usually never drain current because of the P-MOSFET's high impedance (open circuit) state when the MCU pulls down the Bat-EN [18].

1.3.3 ECG Sensor Measurements

The ECG sensor cannot function without the AFE circuit, which collects ECG data. ECG data are recorded in this work using an off-the-shelf Analog Devices® AD8232 ECG AFE chip. A wholly integrated signal conditioning block for ECG and other physiological measurements is called AD8232. It gathers, enhances, and filters tiny bio-potential signals [19]. Its low current is 170 μA, and it can work between 2 and 3.5 V. It is appropriate for wearable healthcare applications because of its inexpensive cost, small size, and low power consumption. To reduce the distortion of the ECG signal, some filters are 0.5-Hz high pass and 40-Hz low pass. To improve the display of the ECG waveform, the integrated operational amplifier is used to amplify further the biopotential signals collected from electrodes.

Three flexible PCB-based dry copper electrodes are made and mounted for ECG biopotential capture rather than conventional wet gel electrodes. Printed copper that is dried electrodes are more economical and environmentally beneficial than throwaway wet electrodes because they may

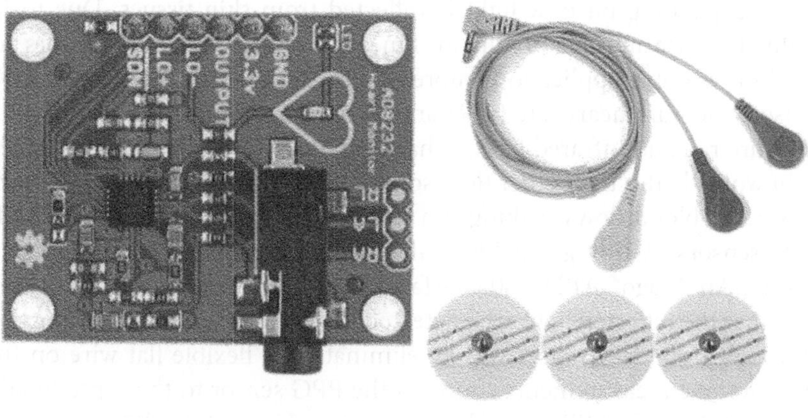

Figure 1.2 ECG sensor measurements using an AD8232 AFE chip.

be reused several times. Weak ECG signals can be sufficiently gathered thanks to the dry copper electrodes in the ECG AFE circuit [20]. Using a Tektronix® DPO7104 oscilloscope, a 28-year-old male participant's raw ECG sensor measurement data are shown in Figure 1.2. The T and P waves in the ST segment and the QRS complex are among the essential components of ECG signals that are easily recognizable, as shown in Figure 1.2. Upon gathering the ECG signal, it undergoes additional processing before being wirelessly sent and seen in real time. Data are stored on the IoT-cloud for future analysis.

1.3.4 PPG Sensor

Another popular wearable application involves the PPG sensor, which monitors human health, and the ECG sensor. A non-invasive optical method called photoplethysmography measures fluctuations in the amount of blood at the tissues' subcutaneous microvascular bed. A PPG sensor's fundamental idea is to highlight skin tissues using a light source. Subcutaneous tissues and blood vessels reflect light, and a photodiode (PD) is used to measure changes in light intensity that are transmitted through or reflected. Several chemicals found in skin tissues can alter the intensity of light that is transmitted or reflected, but periodic blood flows are the source of the most dynamic variation. The variation in light intensity picked up by the PD coincides with the heart rate since the diastolic and systolic stages of a heartbeat cause variations in the blood volume in arteries. PPG sensors are classified as transmission or reflectance mode depending on how light is reflected from skin tissues. Due to its ability to sense any area of human skin, reflectance mode PPG sensors are used in wearable applications more often [21]. Transmission-mode PPG sensors measure heart rate (HR) and oxygen saturation typically used to measure red and infrared light. It has been discovered recently that green light works better than other light sources for the detection of fluctuations in surface blood flows making it a superior choice for reflectance-mode PPG sensors. A tiny green LED takes measurements and lights up skin tissues. An Avago® APDS9008 surface-mounted photodiode (PD) is used to gather the reflected light. The detected PPG signals' amplitude will grow, and high-frequency noises will be eliminated. A flexible flat wire on the chest to take measurements connects the PPG sensor to the centerboard. An individual's first PPG signals are shown in Figure 1.3, where they were recorded on his chest while he was stationary for 1 min. After the DC components are eliminated, the PPG data's spectrum is examined using fast Fourier transform (FFT) [22].

The time interval between PPG peaks can be used to measure heart rate. It is also possible to compute the respiration rate since breathing causes a chest movement that acts as a DC component signal with a low frequency. The rear of the PPG board has a high-accuracy temperature sensor for measuring body temperature, the Silicon Labs® Si7051. The central board is connected to all the sensors and dry electrodes using flexible flat wires, which is a handy and comfortable way to attach the suggested sensor and its rigid–flex structure to the chest for health monitoring [23]. Furthermore, removing them from the sensor configuration is a straightforward process. When there is no need for ECG monitoring, for instance, the sensor can be made smaller by removing the electrodes. Consequently, based on the user's needs, the sensor can be tailored to measure the required physiological parameters [24].

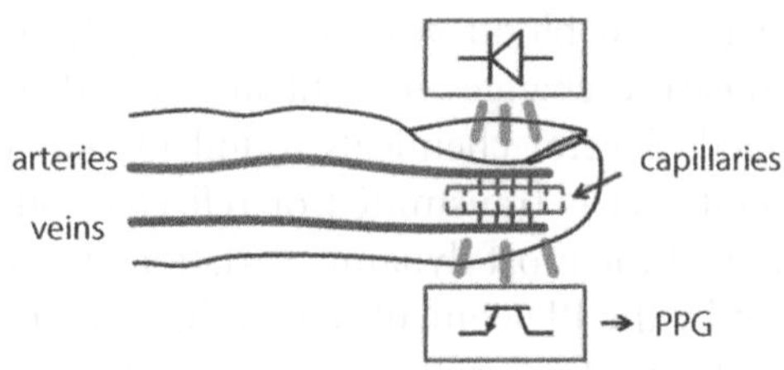

Figure 1.3 PPG working principle.

1.3.5 Power Consumption

Low power consumption is a crucial prerequisite for wearable sensor operation over an extended period. Here, low-power circuits are used to implement the suggested sensor. The individual sensor, BLE, and MCU power consumption are displayed in Table 1.2. Several operating modes for tailored healthcare applications can be set for the sensor to minimize power consumption further as follows: (1) All signals are continuously measured and transmitted, (2) cycles of computed vital sign transmission and continuous observations of specific signals, and (3) cycles of physiological parameter readings and transmission [25]. For continuous collection and transmission of the stated sensor, it is advised to use a maximum power of 44.57 mW (average current: 13.51 mA) for all sensor signals used for the BP estimate over the gateway. The sensor has an 8.88-h operating battery life in this mode when using a 120-mAh cell. The consumption of electricity will be lower when only one sensor is necessary. Assuming PPG is the sole HR monitoring tool, HR data are transmitted to the gateway once every minute. If so, the average current of 5.46 mA can lower the power consumption to 18.03 mW, for instance (BLE data transfer takes less than a second). Consequently, when powered, the sensor may run for 21.98 h on the same battery. The sensor may be set to operate in two cycles, lasting 1 min each for regular operation and 4 min for sleep (which can be adjusted based on various needs). This will further extend its lifespan [26]. In this 5-min cycled operation mode, the sensor can run on the 120-mAh battery for over 100 h. Table 1.2 shows the power consumed by sensor nodes.

Table 1.2 Power consumed by sensor nodes.

Item	Current	Power
PPG sensor	1.3 mA	4..3 mW
ECG sensor	176 μA	0.58 mW
Temperature sensor (1 Hz sample rate)	195 nA	0.64 uW
BLE transmission @ dBm	8 mA	26 mW
Micro-controller	4 mA	13 mW
Micro-controller at sleeping mode	7 μA	23 uW

1.4 Methodology

1.4.1 Healthcare Monitoring System

The various physiological markers of the human body serve as fundamental indicators of an individual's state of health. Periodically recording physiological data is essential mainly targeting the elderly demographic. The development of wireless communication and low-power miniature electronics capabilities has led to the proposal of numerous wearable or implantable biomedical sensors to monitor people's health for medical reasons. This study suggests that wearable sensors can measure body temperature, PPG, and ECG [27]. The appropriate signal-processing algorithms are utilized to determine blood pressure and pulse rate in light of the PPG and ECG readings.

1.4.2 Heart Rate Monitoring with ECG

Since cardiovascular diseases (CVDs) account for a large portion of catastrophic mortality, the ECG signal is one of the physiological characteristics that is monitored the most frequently among the other parameters. Enhancing patients' health condition can be significantly aided by early detection and management of CVDs. To prevent CVDs, it is crucial to monitor ECG in real time and over an extended period. Through wireless data transmission to Internet cloud healthcare centers, remote ECG monitoring has become possible with the advent of IoT technology. The recommended sensor collects ECG signals by attaching dry electrodes to the subject's chest and using them to power the AFE circuit. The ECG data will be sent through the gateway and the wireless network to an Internet cloud after the ECG signals have been sent to the center board's BLE module. The wireless network and gateway deployment will be the primary subjects of discussion during the presentation [28].

Future analysis will be facilitated by having the ECG data saved in the cloud center. The cloud center enables medical practitioners to review patients' ECG data remotely. The wearable sensor system is depicted in Figure 1.4, where the ECG waveform can be accessed online. The gateway receives data from the BLE module shown on the real-time ECG display. Python/MATLAB 2020a can construct a graphical user interface (GUI) on a computer that displays ECG signals. A PC linked to a BLE network can serve as the gateway. A different gateway concept is based on a smartphone that uses an app created on the Evothings® platform to display the

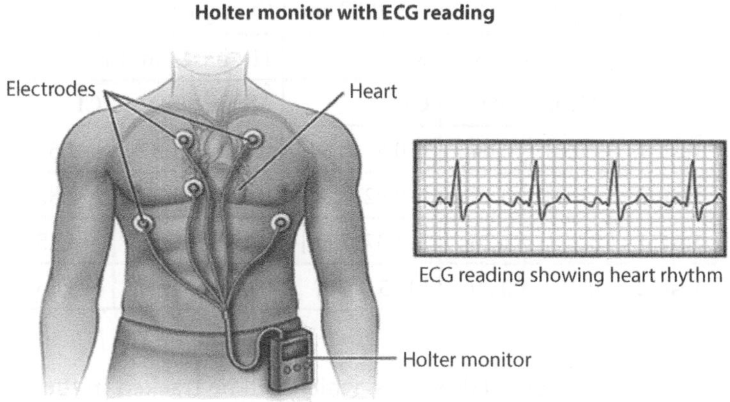

Figure 1.4 ECG signal monitoring using a Holter monitor.

ECG waveform. A smartphone app screenshot for real-time tracking of ECG waveforms is shown in ref. [29].

1.4.3 Heart Rate Analysis

One of the most crucial organs is the heart because it pumps blood filled with oxygen and other nutrients throughout the body functioning as a circulatory system pump. Heart rate refers to the speed at which the heart contracts and relaxes. As a standalone risk factor for CVDs, HR is one of the body's key indicators. The duration of the PPG signal between its peaks or the R-R intervals found in ECG data can be used to compute HR. A three-lead ECG module on the Finapres® NOVA, HR data from the suggested wearable sensor are compared with HR data from a commercial health-monitoring gadget [30]. The wearable PPG and ECG sensors are used to assess heart rate. Table 1.3 compares the HR readings from the PPG, ECG, and reference gadgets. The identical patient uses the reference device and related sensor for 10 min.

The individual works up a sweat for 3 min while seated on a stationary bike. The table illustrates a significant correlation (more than 98%) between the HR readings on the sensor of the PPG and ECG sensors and the reference device's HR. Two male participants (S1 and S2) undergo the same experiment twice. A comparison between the reference HR and the calculated HR from the sensor is shown in Table 1.3. The experiment's outcomes show that the suggested wearable sensor ECG and PPG can produce

Table 1.3 HR computation based on PPG and ECG signal.

		HR based on ECG			HR based on PPG		
		Mean	**SD**	**CI**	**Mean**	**SD**	**CI**
S1	**Test_1**	−0.01	0.045	[−0.87, 0.87]	0.05	1.37	[−2.67, 2.74]
	Test_2	−0.01	0.45	[−0.92, 0.92]	0.04	1.47	[−2.87, 2.93]
S2	**Test_1**	0.1	1.26	[−2.37, 2.60]	0.15	2.35	[−4.45, 4.75]
	Test_2	0.01	0.39	[0.75, 0.76]	0.03	1.90	[−3.66, 3.75]

accurate and dependable HR values, which will be tracked in the Internet of Medical Devices system.

1.4.4 BP Analysis

The blood flowing force through a blood vessel pressing against its walls is called blood pressure, another essential bodily indicator. The two numbers used to express blood pressure are two blood pressure readings: the systolic (SBP), which is the peak value recorded, and the diastolic (DBP), which is the lowest number detected during a pulse. One of the main risk factors for CVDs, which can result in impairment or even death, is persistently high blood pressure or hypertension. Regretfully, less than 46% of cases of hypertension are diagnosed since the early signs are no always evident. The sphygmomanometer uses an arm cuff to take traditional blood pressure readings [31]. Because of its enormous bulk and low measurement frequency, long-term, constant BP monitoring is a better option than this. In situations where long-term, constant BP monitoring is required, researchers have recently developed several noninvasive blood pressure estimate techniques. One of the possible methods relies on the PAT, which has an inverse connection with blood pressure (BP). The pulse wave propagation time from the heart to the peripheral arteries via the arterial tree is measured, which is the time interval between the PPG signals' maximum inclination point. It can be computed using the ECG signals' R peak. Applying the ECG data from the recommended wearable sensor yields the PAT. A regression approach is given for the real-time BP estimate to convert the PAT into BP data [32].

In addition to the PAT, there is a correlation between BP and HR since rising BP causes HR to rise in an attempt to enhance cardiac output. Consequently, the HR and PAT are combined into a linear regression model by the BP estimation methodology:

$$BP = a * PAT + b * HR + c \tag{1.1}$$

The linear least square approach can be used to calculate the model parameters that are individual to each subject, the coefficients (a, b, and c), about the reference blood pressure data obtained from commercial beat-to-beat blood pressure monitor. Two healthy male individuals are used in a 5-day experiment to ascertain the parameters of the BP estimate model in a laboratory setting with a 25°C regulated temperature. The sensor is secured to collect ECG and PPG signals on the subject's chest. The BLE module then sends these signals to the computer, where they are processed in real-time [33]. The Finarpes® NOVA noninvasive blood pressure-monitoring device is used for reference blood pressure readings. After an arm-cuff unit performs an initial BP calibration procedure, it can give you real-time, beat-to-beat blood pressure readings by employing a middle finger cuff. Five days are dedicated to gathering the subjects' data. The participant must complete two 15-min training sessions and 10-min daily validation session to adjust the coefficients of the BP estimation model.

Every session is followed by a 10-minute rest period. The training consists of two 3-min activities to raise the subject's blood pressure, while he sits on a stationary bicycle. Before and after the workout, he takes a one 3-min break to get his blood pressure to normal. The coefficients are computed and updated following the two training sessions and will be used in place of the BP estimate model. The BP estimate model's accuracy is verified in real time against the reference BP monitoring equipment through a validation session. Table 1.4 summarizes the overall RMSE for both subjects and the estimated blood pressure (BP) and blood pressure (BP) reference for every day of the experiment [34]. According to the results, the commercial gadget and the BP estimate model exhibit good agreement. Figure 1.5 displays the real-time SBP results with a significant correlation

Table 1.4 RMSE evaluation.

		Days							
Sample	**Pressure**	**1**	**2**	**3**	**4**	**5**	**6**	**7**	**Overall**
S1	**Systolic pressure**	9.1	6.0	6.1	7.4	4.4	4.3	4.1	6.6
	Diastolic pressure	3.1	2.5	2.9	5.9	5.5	5.6	5.5	4.0
S2	**Systolic pressure**	6.8	5.7	7.6	5.0	6.9	6.8	6.7	6.4
	Diastolic pressure	5.4	7.5	7.2	5.8	4.4	4.3	4.2	6.1

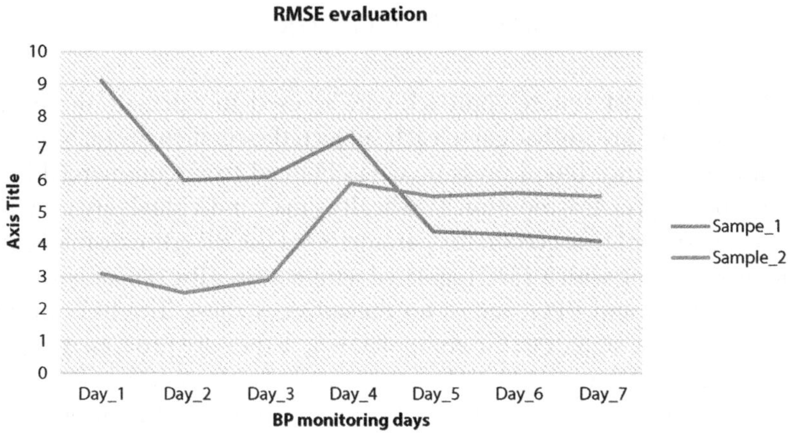

Figure 1.5 RMSE evaluation.

of 0.82 compared to the reference SBP values. The experiment results demonstrate that wearable sensors and real-time blood pressure monitoring with a reliable estimation model are possible with suitable methods for calibration. Long-term, continuous remote blood pressure monitoring throughout business operations is feasible.

1.4.5 Human Body Temperature Analysis

Body temperature, which falls between 36.2°C and 37.5°C, is typically considered the first vital sign. The body goes through a complicated series of operations to maintain a steady body temperature, which allows all other bodily functions to work as usual. A fever or illness is usually indicated by an elevated body temperature, which is the body's defensive response to disease-causing stimuli. Thus, taking your body temperature regularly is critical to identify any potential illnesses early. To periodically measure body temperature, the Si7051, the wearable sensor, makes use of a tiny Silicon Labs® digital temperature sensor. Over the whole measurement range of 36°C to 41°C, the sensor has a high accuracy of 0.1°C. It is appropriate for wearable applications because of its power consumption, which is among the lowest in the industry, with a sampling rate of 1 Hz and an average of 195 nA. The sensor measures body temperature every 30 s, and the results are relayed to, and stored on, a cloud server. The sensor system's website or a smartphone application can show real-time temperature data [35].

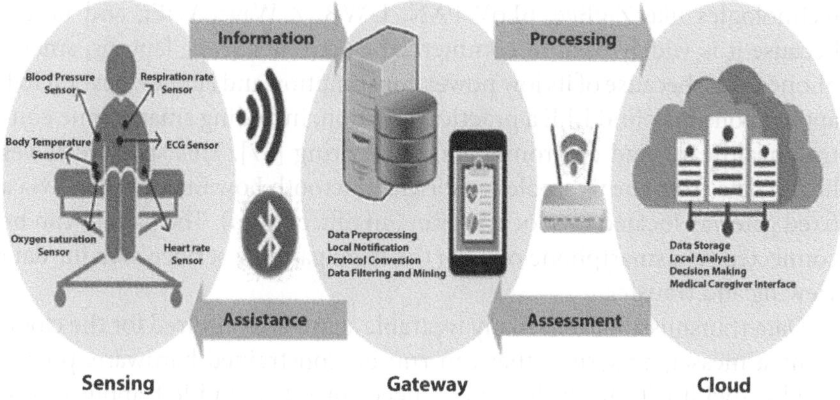

Figure 1.6 Generic architecture of IoT-based remote monitoring system.

1.4.6 IoT-Based Remote Monitoring System

To monitor their health state, multiple wearable sensors are applied to various subjects in IoT-connected healthcare applications. In Figure 1.6, a wireless sensor network comprises a gateway, and the information is sent over the BLE module from each sensor. The sensor data will be sent to an Internet cloud by a fixed gateway with a WiFi connection using the lightweight messaging protocol Message Queuing Telemetry Transport (MQTT). In remote healthcare settings, medical staff can review patients' health data through a cloud user interface (UI) or a local user interface (UI) on the gateway [36]. The user can utilize a smartphone as the mobile gateway and the stationary gateway linked to the sensor of each participant. A personalized smartphone application may show the user's health information, which can be transferred to a cloud server. All sensor data are visible for users to access the cloud database. The health information of several subjects will be kept on the cloud server for backup and future research needs.

1.4.7 Network Connectivity

BLE modules are used in the wireless sensor network's implementation to transfer local information to the gateway, which then uses the MQTT protocol to transport data to the Internet cloud. The Bluetooth Group is responsible for developing and marketing Bluetooth Low Energy, a new wireless technology. BLE's short-range, low-latency data transmission is its intended use (0–100 m) with efficiency and low power consumption. The use of BLE is increasing despite the existence of alternative wireless technologies like ZigBee, 6LoWPAN, UWB, Z-Wave, WiFi, and others because it is widely used in commercial electronics (cars, laptops, smartphones, etc.) because of its low power consumption and latency. Several IoT applications may find BLE a practical solution, including smart home control, healthcare, and environmental monitoring [37]. This study retrieves health data from the wearable sensor via Bluetooth Low Energy (BLE) via a fixed gateway located in a local region (an office room). The patient can be connected to a smartphone outside the fixed gateway service area for data viewing and transfer.

Data transmission from many wearable sensors is required for the cloud using a messaging system that can run on constrained hardware, power, and bandwidth. To meet the unique needs of WSNs and IoT applications, the CoAP and MQTT protocol have been suggested. Conversely, CoAP is predicated on a protocol that facilitates a one-to-one state data exchange among the server and client. MQTT is a many-to-many communication protocol that enables data transmission between several brokers and customers at the same time. This explains why the cloud and gateway in this effort are using MQTT. TCP/IP networks are used to publish/subscribe to the MQTT messaging protocol. It is intended to be a very lightweight, low-complexity messaging protocol for sensors with little power, high latency, and bandwidth, among other applications with limited resources. Customers and brokers make up the typical MQTT; brokers oversee client relationships, and customers can publish and subscribe to communications on various subjects [38]. The deployment of the wireless network connecting the cloud, IoT gateway, and wearable sensor is depicted in Figure 1.7. The gateway can utilize the distinct MAC address of every wearable sensor to differentiate data from various predefined frame types. BLE modules are used to send the sensor health data that are sent to the IoT gateway. The gateway will acknowledge the data as soon as it receives it from the sensor. Data from various gateways can be synchronized using the timestamp attached to each piece of information after the gateway gets it. The local IoT gateway acts as a bridge to connect to a cloud MQTT broker. For data visualization, the local area network's local user interface may receive access to the health data. Similarly, remote health monitoring is possible through the cloud UI with a cloud MQTT subscription.

1.4.8 Network Gateway

As illustrated in Figure 1.7, the Simblee® BLE module in this study is linked to the Raspberry Pi, the fixed gateway via USB ports. The Pi's built-in BLE

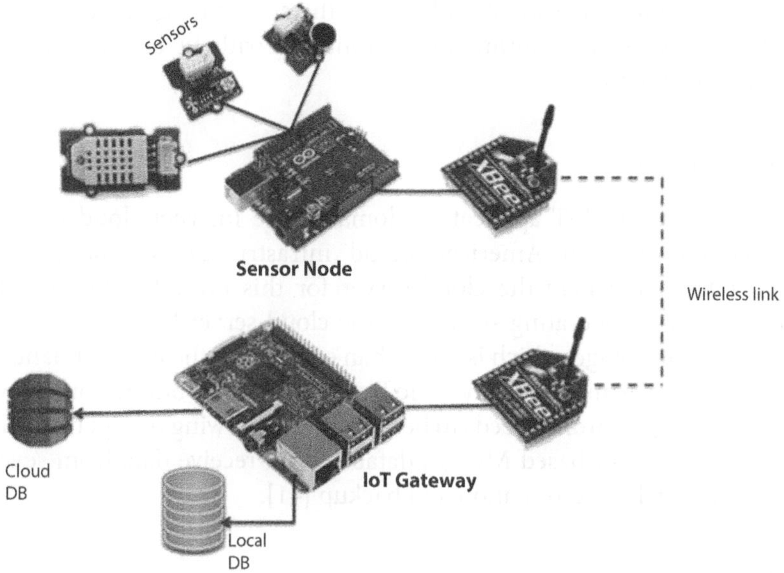

Figure 1.7 IoT gateway.

module is replaced by a standalone BLE module that gathers health data from numerous SNs, which would complicate the software programming processes needed for edge computing. The Raspbian system has a MySQL database loaded to save data on the gateway. This makes it possible to backup and retrieve health data from several subjects as needed. Data are forwarded to the cloud server over the Internet connection via the Pi's WiFi module. The Raspberry Pi is equipped with MQTT; it acts as a mechanism for messaging between the cloud and the gateway [38]. A minimal online user interface (UI) built on Node.js is set up for local users, smartphone cellphones, and local area network-connected web browsers to access. Suppose the person wearing the sensor cannot connect to it as an alternative to the fixed gateway (out of service); a smartphone's built-in mobile gateway can receive and send data to the cloud. Viewing sensor data is possible with the web-based smartphone application built on the Evothings® platform. It is used to develop mobile applications using HTML5, CSS, and JavaScript rather than the operating system's platform-specific APIs for Android and iOS. Bluetooth Low Energy (BLE) connects wearable sensors and smartphones [39]. Sensor data, such as the ID of the subject, physiological data, and battery level can be shown using the built application on a smartphone running the Evothings® Viewer installed on it.

With the mobile gateway in addition to the stationary gateway, patients' health status can be continuously monitored without being limited by physical location [40].

1.4.9 Server

In many different IoT application domains, the Internet cloud is a crucial component. An American cloud infrastructure company called DigitalOcean is where the cloud server for this project is located. The Ubuntu 16.04.5 operating system on the cloud server has 2 GB of RAM and 25 GB of storage, which is more than enough for the needs at hand. To enable data transmission from the IoT gateway to the Ubuntu cloud server, the cloud MQTT broker needs to be deployed. Following receipt by the IoT gateway, the cloud-based MySQL database will receive data from several sensor for further examination and backup [41].

1.4.10 Database

Since two gateways—one fixed and one mobile—are used in this job, data integrity must be ensured by synchronizing the data from the two cloud gateways and keeping the local database current. As previously stated, upon receipt by the gateway, every set of RF data is accompanied by a timestamp. The cloud server and the gateway can use the timestamp to synchronize the database [42].

1.4.11 Security

By transforming data into cypher text, one of the most popular techniques for safeguarding private information is encryption. The data can only be decrypted by those who share the same key. The same information can, therefore, be ciphered and deciphered by sensors and gateways using the same key. An integrated AES encryption engine powers the advanced BLE module Simblee. The gateways and wearable data connection are encrypted in our study using the industry standard AES-128-bit encryption because security is not our main area of interest. AES-128's low memory and computational requirements make it a good choice for wearables with limited resources [43].

1.5 Performance Analysis

Multiple participants are tested using three wearable sensors to verify the functionality and viability of the IoT-connected healthcare system. A small lab room with 25°C temperature is utilized to conduct experiments. The Wi-Fi-connected Internet of Things gateway is positioned to collect data in the middle of the space. Three subjects, seated at various room corners, have sensors on their chests. This experiment removes the ECG electrodes from the sensor because blood pressure and ECG readings need active continuous data transmission to be verified. The temperature sensors and PPG record three patients' body and heart rates. The sensor data are transmitted to the cloud server from the IoT gateway. The data are validated each time it is sent from the sensor to the gateways; if not, it is sent three times. A missending counter will be created and added to the next sending cycle if the receiving acknowledgement is not received [44].

To ensure that every piece of data is successfully transferred to the cloud at least once, the quality of service is set to level 1 (at least once) for the MQTT protocol data exchanged amid the cloud server and the gateways. For remote health monitoring, each patient's temperature and heart rate can be seen in real time on the cloud-based user interface webpage. The sensor may be expanded using electrodes to monitor blood pressure and ECG when necessary for severe cases. Researchers worldwide have put out many wearable device designs with IoT applications in recent years to monitor essential indicators, including heart rate, blood pressure, temperature of the body, and respiration rate. An extensive overview and comparative analysis of current wearable healthcare systems are provided. The majority of the gadgets have attachment points on the hand or chest. On the other hand, regular movements can easily affect devices worn on hands. While the belt around the belly is not the best option because of comfort concerns, the authors of ref. [45] suggest a chest-based sensor. This study suggests a rigid–flex sensor for wearers' chests that may be quickly and readily placed without causing too much disruption to day-to-day activities. Low-power circuitry and cyclic operation loops are required in sensor design to increase wearable device operating times. A wearable device's operating duration typically ranges from a few hours to several days. A small rechargeable coin battery (120 mAh) that can run for 100 h in a 5-min operating cycle is employed as the power source for this project.

Most medical experts focus on the cardiorespiratory system regarding healthcare applications. Standard devices that are capable of measuring respiration rate, heart rate, and heart rate variability are ECG/PPG sensors, which come in many designs. The suggested sensor proven effective in earlier research is integrated with ECG and PPG sensors in this work. The PPG and ECG sensors can be quickly removed and put back together in various monitoring situations to minimize power consumption and maximize comfort. Moreover, adopting ECG and PPG yields an additional crucial insight: blood pressure is estimated using the pulse transit time. Our earlier work presents the procedures for gathering data, analyzing it, and assessing our blood pressure estimation technique [46]. Wireless communication is crucial for remote health monitoring scenarios in IoT-connected healthcare applications. Because of its ubiquitous usage in electronic products and low battery consumption, BLE is the widely used wireless technology for wearable medical devices. Since BLE can only transmit data at a distance of 100 m, several gateways are suggested for long-distance data transfer. For fixed gateways, numerous mobile computers, like the Raspberry Pi is utilized in refs. [47] and [48] select cell phones as their mobile gateways. In this work, short- and long-range data transfer on cellphones and portable PCs are accomplished via BLE and WiFi, respectively. Both gateways use the MQTT protocol, a subscribe messaging system perfect for IoT applications with low power and data rate needs [49, 50]. There is a smartphone application for medical professionals and a web application for customers to see the tracked health data.

1.6 Conclusion

This study presents a novel wearable sensor for long-term healthcare monitoring in Internet of Things contexts. Three primary parts comprise the sensor system as follows: many sensors for physiological parameter measurement; a central board for the reception, processing, and transmission of signals; and a power board for the battery charger and energy source. Because of the rigid–flex structure that connects these parts, the sensor can monitor body temperature, heart rate, PPG, and ECG. Combining the ECG and PPG on one device allows continuous blood pressure estimation using the PAT technique without needing extra connections or hardware setups. The suggested sensor effectiveness is shown through experimental findings compared to a commercial medical reference piece of equipment. In IoT-connected healthcare applications, health data are transferred from the sensor to an IoT gateway via a BLE module. The gateway sends the data to a cloud server on the Internet for processing and archiving. The development of mobile (smartphone) and stationary (Raspberry Pi) gateways enables the sensor to function constantly indoors and outdoors. In the cloud, timestamping guarantees data integrity and synchronization, while data encryption protects privacy in both the sensor and the gateway. A cloud website can display real-time physiological information for remote healthcare applications. Future development will concentrate on creating additional edge computing features on the gateway to improve the IoT-connected healthcare platform.

References

1. Yeh, L.Y., Chiang, P.Y., Tsai, Y.L., Huang, J.L., Cloud-based fine-grained health information access control framework for lightweight IoT devices with dynamic auditing and attribute revocation. *IEEE Trans. Cloud Comput.*, PP, 99, 1–13, 2015.
2. Porambage, P., Braeken, A., Gurtov, A., Ylianttila, M., Spinsante, S., Secure end to end communication for constrained devices in IoT-enabled ambient assisted living systems, in: *IEEE 2nd world forum on internet of things*, Milan, pp. 711–714, 2015.
3. Banka, S., Madan, I., Saranya, S.S., Smart healthcare monitoring using IoT. *Int. J. Appl. Eng. Res.*, 13, 15, 11984–11989, 2018, ISSN 0973-4562.
4. Perumal, K. and Manohar, M., A survey on internet of things: case studies, applications, and future directions, in: *Internet of things: novel advances and envisioned applications*, pp. 281–297, 2017.
5. Guadagni, Y. *et al.*, RISK: a random optimization interactivesystem based on kernel learning for predicting breast cancerdisease progression, in: *Proceedings of the 5th International Work-Conference, IWBBIO*, Spain, Granada, 2017, April 26–28, pp. 189–196, 2017.
6. Ambrogio, A.D., Gaudio, P., Gelfusa, M., Luglio, M., Malizia, A., Roseti, C., Marsella, S., Use of integrated technologies for fire monitoring and first alert, in: *Proceedings of the International Conference of Information andCommunication Technologies, AICT 2016*, p. 15, 2017.
7. Boella, G., Di Caro, L., Humphreys, L., Robaldo, L., Rossi, P., van der Torre, L., Eunomos, a legal document and knowledgemanagement system for the Web to provide relevant, reliable and upto-date information on the law. *Artif. Intell. Law*, 24, 3, 245–283, 2016.
8. Gopinath, N. and Shyry, S.P., Secured: quantum key distribution (SQKD) for solving side-channel attack to enhance security, based on shifting and binary conversion for securing data (SBSD) frameworks. *Soft Comput.*, 27, 18, 13365–13372, 2023.

9. Abiodun, M.K., Awotunde, J.B., Ogundokun, R.O., Misra, S., Adeniyi, E.A., Arowolo, M.O., Jaglan, V., Cloud and big data: a mutual benefit for organization development. *J. Phys. Conf. Ser.*, 1767, 1, 012020, 2021.
10. Adebiyi, M.O., Arowolo, M.O., Olugbara, O., A genetic algorithm for prediction of RNA-seq malaria vector gene expression data classification using SVM kernels. *Bull. Elect. Eng. Informat.*, 10, 2, 1071–9, 2021.
11. Mutlag, A. *et al.*, Enabling technologies for fog computing in healthcare IoT systems. *Fut. Generat. Comput. Syst.*, 90, 62–78, 2019.
12. Jara, A.J., Zamora, M.A., Skarmeta, A.F., Drug identification and interaction checker based on IoT to minimize adverse drug reactions and improve drug compliance. *Pers. Ubiquit. Comput.*, 18, 1, 5–17, 2014.
13. Chiuchisan, G., An approach of a decision support and home monitoring system for patients with neurological disorders using internet of things concepts. *WSEAS Trans. Syst.*, 13.1, 460–469, 2014.
14. Santos, J. *et al.*, An IoT-based mobile gateway for intelligent personal assistants on mobile health environments. *J. Netw. Comput. Appl.*, 71, 194–204, 2016.
15. Shamim Hossain, M. and Ghulam, M., Cloud-assisted industrial internet of things (iiot)-enabled framework for health monitoring. *Comput. Netw.*, 101, 192–202, 2016.
16. Bhatia, M. and Sood, S.K., Temporal informative analysis in smart-ICU monitoring: M-HealthCare perspective. *J. Med. Syst.*, 40, 8, 1–15, 2016.
17. Gupta, S., Lipika, G., Abhay, K.A., A novel framework of health monitoring systems. *Int. J. Big Data Anal. Healthcare (IJBDAH)*, 6.1, 1–14, 2021.
18. Uddin, M.S., Jannat, B.A., Suraiya, B., Real time patient monitoring system based on Internet of Things, in: *2017 4th International Conference on Advances in Electrical Engineering (ICAEE)*, IEEE, 2017.
19. Dey, N., Ashour, A.S., Bhatt, C., Internet of things driven connected healthcare, in: *Internet of things and big data technologies for next generation healthcare*, pp. 3–12, Springer, Cham, 2017.
20. Rahmani, A.M. *et al.*, Exploiting smart e-Health gateways at the edge of healthcare Internet-of-Things: a fog computing approach. *Future Gener. Comput. Syst.*, 78, 641–58, 2018.
21. Arowolo, M.O., Adebiyi, M.O., Adebiyi, A.A., Olugbara, O., Optimized hybrid investigative based dimensionality reduction methods for malaria vector using KNN classifier. *J. Big Data*, 8, 1, 1–14, 2021.
22. Vahidi Farashah, M., Etebarian, A., Azmi, R. *et al.*, An analytics model for TelecoVAS customers' basket clustering using ensemble learning approach. *J. Big Data*, 8, 36, 2021.
23. Vahidi Farashah, M., Etebarian, A., Azmi, R. *et al.*, A hybrid recommender system based-on link prediction for movie baskets analysis. *J. Big Data*, 8, 32, 2021.

24. Xiao, F.F. *et al.*, Artificial neural networks forecasting of PM2. 5 pollution using air mass trajectory based geographic model and wavelet transformation. *Atmos. Environ.*, 107, 118–28, 2015.
25. Al-Khafajiy, M., Webster, L., Baker, T., Waraich, A., Towards Fog Driven IoT Healthcare: Challenges and Framework of Fog Computing in Healthcare. *ICFNDS'18*, Amman, Jordan, June 26–27, 2018.
26. Anand, P., Pinjari, H., Hong, W.H., Seo, H.C., Rho, S., Fog Computing-Based IoT for Health Monitoring System. *J. Sens.*, 2018, 11, 2018, Article ID 1386470.
27. George, A., Dhanasekaran, H., Chittiappa, J.P., Challagundla, L.A., Nikkam, S.S., A., O., Internet of Things in health care using fog computing. *2018 IEEE Long Island Systems, Applications and Technology Conference (LISAT)*, 2018, 10.1109/LISAT.2018.8378012.
28. Mutlag, A.A., Ghani, K.A.M., N., A., Mohammed, M.A., M., O., Enabling technologies for fog computing in healthcare IoT systems. *Future Gener. Comput. Syst.*, 90, 62–78, Jan. 2019.
29. Negash, B., Gia, T.N., Anjanpour, A., Azimi, I., Jiang, M., Westerlund, T., Rahmani, A.M., Liljeberg, P., Tenhunen, H., Leveraging Fog Computing for Healthcare IoT, in: *Fog Computing in the Internet of Things*, A. Rahmani, P. Liljeberg, J.S. Preden, A. Jantsch (Eds.), Springer, Cham, 2017.
30. Ullah, K., Shah, M.A., Zhang, S., Effective ways to use Internet of Things in the field of medical and smart health care, in: *2016 International Conference on Intelligent Systems Engineering (ICISE)*, 2016, pp. 372–379, 2016.
31. Cedillo, C., Sanchez, Campos, K., Bermeo, A., A systematic literature review on devices and systems for ambient assisted living: Solutions and trends from different user perspectives. *Int. Conf. eDemocracy eGovernment (ICEDEG)*, vol. 1, pp. 59–66, 2018.
32. Gopinath, N. and Prayla Shyry, S., Enhancing the cloud security using side channel attack free QKD with entangled fuzzy logic. *J. Intell. Fuzzy Syst.*, 43.6, 8359–8369, 2022.
33. Woo, M.W., Lee, J., Park, K., A reliable IoT system for personal healthcare devices. *Futur. Gener. Comput. Syst.*, 78, 626–640, 2018.
34. Aktas, F., Ceken, C., Erdemli, Y.E., IoT-based healthcare framework for biomedical applications. *J. Med. Biol. Eng.*, 15, 1–12, 2017.
35. Guo, W., Xiong, N., Vasilakos, A.V., Chen, G., Cheng, H., Multi-source temporal data aggregation in wireless sensor networks. *Wirel. Pers. Commun.*, 56, 3, 359–370, 2018.
36. Wan, J., O'Grady, M., li, M., Alaqi, M., Time-bouned Activity Recognition for Ambient Assisted Living. *IEEE Trans. Emerg. Top. Comput.*, 3, 1, 1–14, 2018.
37. Hallfors, N.G., Alhawari, M., Abi Jaoude, M., Kifle, Y., Saleh, H., Liao, K., Ismail, M., Isakovic, A.F., Graphene oxide: Nylon ECG sensors for wearable IoT healthcare—nanomaterial and SOC interface. *Analog Integr. Circ. Sig. Process.*, 1, 1–8, 2018.

38. Varatharajan, Manogaran, G., Priyan, M.K., Sundarasekar, R., Wearable sensor devices for early detection of alzheimer disease using dynamic time warping algorithm. *Clust. Comput.*, 6, 1–10, 2017.
39. Romero, L.E., Chatterjee, P., Armentano, R.L., An IoT approach for integration of computational intelligence and wearable sensors for Parkinson's disease diagnosis and monitoring. *Health Technol.*, 6, 3, 167–172, 2016.
40. Özgür, Bromuri, S., Sindlar, M., van derWeide, T., Pelaez, E.A., Schaechtle, U., Alves, B., Zufferey, D., Rodriguez-Villegas, E., Schumacher, M.I., Stathis, K., COMMODITY $_{12}$: A smart e-health environment for diabetes management. *J. Ambient Intell. Smart Environ.*, 5, 5, 479–502, 2013.
41. Xia, Zhu, Y., Sun, X., Qin, Z., Ren, K., Towards privacy-preserving content-based image retrieval in cloud computing. *IEEE Trans. Cloud Comput.*, 6, 1, 276–286, 2018.
42. Xia, Xiong, N.N., Vasilakos, A.V., Sun, X., Epcbir: An efficient and privacy-preserving content-based image retrieval scheme in cloud computing. *Inf. Sci.*, 387, 195–204, 2017.
43. Mendes, A., daSilva, I.C.M., Ramires, V.V., Reichert, F.F., Martins, R.C., Tomasi, E., Calibration of raw accelerometer data to measure physical activity: A systematic review. *Gait Posture*, 61, 98–110, 2018.
44. Wu, C.R., Zapevalova, E., Chen, Y.W., Li, F., Time optimization of multiple knowledge transfers in the big data environment. *Comput. Mater. Continua*, 54, 269–285, 2018.
45. Garcia-Ceja, Galvn-Tejada, C.E., Brena, R., Multi-view stacking for activity recognition with sound and accelerometer data. *Inf. Fusion*, 40, 45–56, 2018.
46. Lee, and Kwan, M.-P., Physical activity classification in free-living conditions using smartphone accelerometer data and exploration of predicted results. *Comput. Environ. Urban Syst.*, 67, 124–131, 2018.
47. Hui, and Zhongmin, W., Compressed sensing method for human activity recognition using tri-axis accelerometer on mobile phone. *J. China Univ. Posts Telecommun.*, 24, 2, 31–71, 2017.
48. Cheng, Feng, D., Shi, X., Chen, C., Data quality analysis and cleaning strategy for wireless sensor networks. *EURASIP J. Wirel. Commun. Netw.*, 61, 1–11, 2018.
49. Cheng, Su, Z., Xiong, N., Xiao, Y., Energy-efficient node scheduling algorithms for wireless sensor networks. *Inf. Sci.*, 329, 2, 461–477, 2016.
50. Cheng, Xiong, N., Vasilakos, A.V., Yangy, L.T., Chen, G., Nodes organization for channel assignment with topology preservation in multi-radio wireless mesh networks. *Ad Hoc Netw.*, 10, 5, 760–773, 2012.

2

The Digital Revolution in Healthcare

Devanand Bhonsle[1]*, Rama Shukla[2], Deepshikha Sahu[3], Tanuja Kashyap[4], Monika Dewangan[5] and Seema Mishra[5]

[1]*Electrical Engineering, Shri Shankaracharya Technical Campus, Bhilai, India*
[2]*Electrical Engineering, AKS University, Satna, India*
[3]*Human Resource Management, Jain University, Bangluru, India*
[4]*Electronics and Telecommunication, Bhilai Institute of Technology, Durg, India*
[5]*Electrical Engineering, RSR Rungta College of Engineering and Technology, Bhilai, India*

Abstract
In the era of digital revolution; various industries reach new heights by leveraging technological advancements. Among these sectors, healthcare adopted digital technologies, and there is a transition from mechtronics to the fast digital electronic devices. Nowadays, digital technologies have become an integral part of healthcare. It facilitates tasks such as robust clinical support, accessing medicine knowledge resources, and enhanced monitoring of patient. This chapter explores the influence of technologies on the healthcare sector and also addresses privacy and security issues associated with the implementation of digitalization in the healthcare sector.

***Keywords*:** Healthcare, IoMT, remote monitoring, sensors, wearable device

2.1 Introduction

The current scenarios are reshaping the global financial system and offer new avenues for business model development by globalization and digitization. Businesses utilize digital channels for communication both internally and externally among organizations and customers, respectively. Digitization improved the efficiency of many companies' target prompt

**Corresponding author*: devanandbhonsle@sstc.ac.in

Parul Dubey, Mangala Madankar, Pushkar Dubey and Bui Thanh Hung (eds.) The Impact of Algorithmic Technologies on Healthcare, (27–44) © 2025 Scrivener Publishing LLC

responses, which yield to enhance adaptability and increasing sales. Digital technology has mitigated these costs enabling multinational operations to localize certain functions through remote collaboration and swift communication. Digitalization has made it feasible for companies to operate with minimal physical presence abroad focusing instead on key markets or digital sales channels. This shift underscores the transformative potential of digitization known as the 4th Industrial Revolution. In general; it is also referred to as Industry 4.0 [1], which fosters innovation and growth across sectors. The healthcare industry has been at the forefront of integrating comprehensive, equitable, and integrated models to adapt to these changes [2]. Digitalization plays a very important role to enhance clinical support, quality care, and facilitate tasks such as disease monitoring and vaccine distribution. Technologies like block chain [3], cloud computing, and Artificial Intelligence (AI) are revolutionizing healthcare by enabling the analysis of a large number of patients' data leading to improved outcomes and personalized care. Data management allows effective integration and analysis of patient information across healthcare providers [4]. This integration enhances care coordination and enables healthcare professionals to derive actionable insights from patient data. Despite the benefits, ensuring data security and privacy remains a significant challenge in the healthcare sector, with data breaches posing substantial risks and financial costs [5]. Despite these challenges, the healthcare sector is poised for a digital transformation that promises to revolutionize patient care and operational efficiency [6].

2.1.1 Challenges

Digital technologies in the healthcare system introduced several challenges in which cyber security is a primary concern. These threats may impose significant financial burdens, excessive user permissions, and authentication deficiencies, which are most common vulnerabilities in healthcare systems [7]. Additionally, the introduction of the Internet of Medical Things (IoMT) increases data security risks as IoMT devices are susceptible to compromising data security and privacy [8, 9]. One of the cyber security issues in healthcare is ransomware attacks [10], which underscore their severity and impact on patient data privacy and security [11, 12]. Data privacy and protection are basic rights, especially in healthcare, where sensitive patient information is collected and stored [13]. A breach in data security compromises patients' personal and medical details undermining the purpose of digitalization in healthcare [3]. Therefore, effective data protection measures are essential to secure patient information and maintain trust in healthcare sector [14]. Electronic health records and information exchanges are essential digital tools to exchange patient information. However, these activities are suffered from data security risks. Addressing these risks and raising awareness among healthcare stakeholders is crucial to ensure the secure implementation of digital technologies in healthcare [1].

2.1.2 Motivation

The integration of digital technology and healthcare brought tremendous improvements. Introduction of new technologies viz. AI, machine learning [15], and blockchain brought the revolution in healthcare system [16]. However, digital transformation requires vast amounts of patient data, which may introduce significant risks to data privacy. Hence, it is important to know about the security and privacy concerns, which may arise from digitalization in healthcare [17]. This study aims to investigate and address security and privacy challenges. The contributions of this research include analyzing the impact of digital technologies in healthcare sector and identify specific security and privacy concerns within the healthcare sector [18]. Digitalization has become integral to industrial growth, and the healthcare sector has embraced it to enhance service capacity, efficiency, and overall performance [19]. However, ensuring appropriate data protection is crucial before integrating digital technologies into any business sector, with a particular emphasis on healthcare due to its sensitive nature. This research highlights on the context and necessity of digitalization in healthcare and various applications of digital technologies and challenges in maintaining data security and privacy [20, 21]. Various techniques and strategies may be useful to reduce the chances of cyber-attacks to provide security to patients' data. This study empowers healthcare sectors to take necessary and effective measures to prevent confidential data [22]. Moreover, this study helps to understand the impact of digitalization in healthcare sectors and can guide for further research to improve patient care [8]. With the increasing dependency on digital technologies in the healthcare sector, security and privacy are the prime concerns. It is important to ensure the integrity and trustworthiness of healthcare systems [9]. In the modern era, cyberspace has rendered the international borders irrelevant. As a result, digital technologies are adoptable by leading businesses across the world, which transforms their business models. Digitalization has taken businesses to new heights, including the healthcare sector [11]. Healthcare digitalization involves interactions among healthcare professionals, which enables quicker treatment decisions. It is facilitated by the seamless exchange of medical data [22–24]. Technologies, like smart phone with android applications, optimized the medical services, which includes enhancing patient outcomes, reducing costs, and minimizing errors. Data integration facilitates the exchange of electronic information, streamlining medical processes and reducing complexities associated with interfacing among different systems. However, integration of IoMT introduced several new challenges in which data privacy and security are the prime concern, which must be addressed in digitalization of the healthcare sector.

2.2 Digital Technologies in the Healthcare Sector

It is interesting how medical advancements have reached several achievements and each era bringing new breakthroughs. The integration of digital technology has revolutionized the healthcare sector. Innovation in networking and computer has enhanced the scope of modern medical therapies. In the present scenario, in the healthcare sector, security and privacy are the main objectives, which protect patient information, improve confidentiality, and ensure integrity of healthcare systems [22]. These objectives are essential to maintain the trust between patients and healthcare providers and upholding the ethical standards and legal requirements. To meet these security objectives is required to ensure the protection of patient information and building trust in this technology.

2.2.1 Electronic Health Record

The use of Electronic Health Record (EHR) devices are increasing in healthcare sector day by day. They enhanced access to the doctors and sharing of patients' medical records. Computers and tablets are ubiquitous as traditional medical tools, like stethoscopes, which reflect the integration of technology into daily healthcare practices. This technological evolution streamlines medical workflows and improves the efficacy of communication and collaboration among healthcare professionals [25].

2.2.2 Remote Patient Monitoring

The utilization of Remote Patient Monitoring (RPM) helps medical professionals to monitor their patients remotely. It shortens the reaction times and reduces expenses. It has become a valuable complement to telemedicine by alleviating the burdens of travel for patients. It enables continuous monitoring and proactive intervention, hence, improving the overall healthcare efficiency [18, 26].

2.2.3 Artificial Intelligence

In the modern era, AI is utilized in the healthcare sector, where its algorithms mimic human reasoning to create intelligent systems [27]. These AI systems are able to analyze huge amounts of medical data and assist healthcare professionals in various tasks like diagnosis of abnormalities, planning for the treatment, and patient management [28]. AI improves the efficiency, accuracy and outcomes.

2.2.4 Telemedicine

During COVID-19, telemedicine made significant advancements [23]. At the time of pandemic when people were not allowed to go out, telemedicine helped everyone a lot. It uses a smart phone to connect with the doctors. IT restricted physical contact, which helped to reduce infection. Regulatory restrictions on telemedicine have been relaxed as the industry evolved.

2.2.5 Federated Learning

Federated learning provides security and privacy-protective techniques to share ML models across various devices in IoMT [3]. These devices are equipped with modern sensors and various components for data generation. They are connected to a central server to leverage federated learning for IoMT. The server trains an ML model using data from these devices and then distributes it back to each device for utilization.

2.3 Evolution of Digitalization in Business

There is still a debate among entrepreneurs to choose between traditional and digital business models. Traditional businesses typically operate through the retail outlets, while digital businesses take the advantages of modern technology to enhance customer experiences. But in the present scenario, traditional businesses are also adopting digitization strategies to streamline operations and enhance customer value. Digital technology has been adopted in almost all the industries.

Digitization is a revolutionary step, and its widespread adoption has reshaped global business landscapes. It affects almost all the business activities necessitating significant adaptations within existing business models. However, businesses are often faced with many novel challenges in crafting digital strategies.

2.3.1 Industry 4.0 and Business Intelligence

The growth in the internet technology enabled the tech firms to access huge data in real time. However; it is a complex technology, and it challenges traditional software. Hence updation in the software is required from time to time. New algorithms help for better decision making for the uncovered patterns. These advancements enhance the product quality and distribution. Industry 4.0 is driven by new technologies viz. AI, IoT, cloud computing, BI, etc. [1]. These technologies are used as tools for better customer data management, streamline design processes, and enhance data management efficiency [2].

2.3.2 New Opportunities to Traditional Management

Digital entrepreneurship is different from the traditional one in various aspects such as product and service digitization, characterization, delivery, and business model implementation. Advanced information systems reshaped the traditional management control concepts. It involves planning, supervising, creating conducive environments, and measuring performance across dimensions like customer experience and profitability. Managers must prioritize fairness, social justice, and equality to ensure business sustainability with the advancements and expanding digitalization.

2.3.3 Role of Digitalization in Healthcare

Digital technology plays a pivotal role for healthcare innovation. However, it faces very severe challenges. This is the early stage of digitization in various sectors. Centralized information storage and improved data accessibility exhibit a very promising role, but many integration obstacles are reported. Technologies enhance the efficiency of various sectors in terms of efficiency, cost reduction, etc. But simultaneously, many barriers obstruct its performances. Addressing these challenges is crucial for the advancement in digitized healthcare system effectively.

2.3.4 Industry 4.0 in Healthcare Sector

Healthcare sector is a part of Industry 4.0, which leverages modern technologies viz. AI, IoT, machine learning [15], human psychology, and big data mining. These techniques enhance user comfort. However, as it moves toward Industry 5.0, it will face challenges especially in privacy and security concerns. It is crucial to address the complexity in industry readiness. Key factors for developing smart environments include cost, accessibility, and resource consumption. Businesses embracing Industry 4.0 can provide real-time solutions for various issues [1]. Integration of digital diagnostic systems has notably improved in CT scan, MRI, and other imaging techniques, which enable retrospective diagnosis of patient healthcare data [29, 30].

2.4 Role of IoMT in Healthcare

The advancement in the IoT provided interactive cloud setups and data-driven costs. Healthcare providers can get patient data during emergencies. IoT has enabled quality healthcare services in rural areas also. It becomes possible using data analytics and telemedicine. Several countries have utilized IoMT alongside other strategies to fight against COVID-19 [24] for the safety of frontline workers while reducing mortality rates. The widespread adoption of IoMT led to significant advancements in applications, technology, and security measures. Integration with AI, Block chain, and big data further enhances capabilities of IoMT.

2.4.1 Internet of Medical Things Architecture

The IoMTs are used to interconnect smart sensors, gadgets, and wearable devices linked to the internet to collect, store, and analyze the data [3]. Its architecture has four layers viz. Perception layer, Edge layer, Networking layer, and Cloud Computing layer. These layers work together to integrate health-related data. Below is the description of their role in the IoMT architecture. Figure 2.1 shows the architecture of IoMT.

(a) Perception Layer

The Perception Layer is the first layer of IoHT architecture. It is responsible of collecting health-related data from using smart wearable sensors and medical devices. Some of the most useful sensors are heart rate monitors, blood pressure monitors, oxygen level monitors, and glucose detectors.

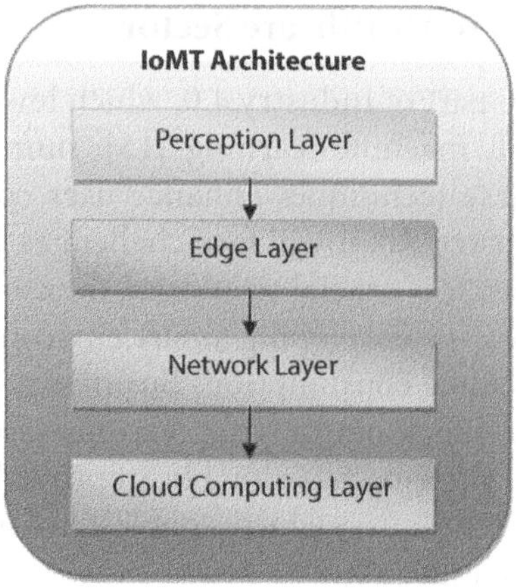

Figure 2.1 IoMT architecture.

Once the data are collected by these sensors, it is transferred to the Edge Layer for processing.

(b) Edge Layer

The second layer of the IoHT layer is called the Edge Layer. It is the intermediate layer, and it bridges the Perception Layer and the Networking Layer. It is responsible for real-time data processing from sensors. These data are converted into a suitable format for transmission through the internet. It is designed in such a manner that it can handle a large data volume.

(c) Network Layer

The third layer of the IoHT architecture is the Network Layer which is responsible of transmitting data from Perception to the Cloud Computing Layer. It has various networking protocols and technologies like Bluetooth, ZigBee, and Wi-Fi, which are used to transfer the data over the internet. The Network Layer ensures a reliable, fast, and secure data transmission.

(d) Cloud Computing Layer

The fourth and last layer of the IoHT architecture is the Cloud Computing Layer. It handles the storage and analysis of data collected and received from the Perception Layer. This layer is responsible for proving access to researchers and healthcare providers to use data so that it can be used to develop new therapies and treatments for different medical conditions.

2.5 Internet of Medical Things Devices

IoMTs are used to connect healthcare devices to the internet to improve patient health outcomes [3]. With the expansion of the Internet of Things (IoT) technology, IoMT has become an accessible and cost-effective tool in the era of healthcare services [37]. IoT devices are capable of being connected to the internet and enable collecting real-time data, which are stored and analyzed to enhance healthcare services. This section focuses on various IoMT devices, characteristics, and their impact on healthcare services.

2.5.1 Wearable Devices

The most common IoT wearable devices are smart watches, fitness trackers, and smart clothes. They are designed to be worn on the body. They track various health metrics such as blood pressure, temperature, heart rate, sleep patterns, and physical activity. These devices facilitate real-time monitoring of a patient's health and can communicate data to healthcare providers. For example, if a wearable device detects abnormal blood pressure levels, it can alert patients to take necessary action or consult healthcare providers.

2.5.2 Smart Medical Devices

IoT-based medical devices are also referred to as smart medical devices. They are built to provide medical support. They can track health indicators, for example, oxygen and glucose, body temperatures, etc. They can make direct communication with the healthcare professionals which enables real-time monitoring of patients' health. For example, a smart insulin pump can adjust insulin levels on the basis of glucose readings. It can minimize the risk of both low and high sugar levels.

2.5.3 Telemedicine Devices

Telemedicine is an IoT technology that allows individuals to receive medical treatment from their homes. It includes remote monitoring systems, video conferencing, mobile health programs, etc. It provides the facility to access healthcare for rural areas hence reduce the need for physical clinic visits. Using these devices. Patients may consult healthcare professionals via video conferencing and eliminate unnecessary travel.

2.5.4 Smart Home Devices

Smart home devices are used at home to improve convenience, comfort, privacy and security. Some of the most common smart home devices are smart thermostats, locks, and lights. Smart home devices can transform healthcare delivery by monitoring patient health. It can alert healthcare providers when required. For example, a smart bed can monitor sleep patterns and alert healthcare providers for any deviation.

2.6 Security and Privacy in the Healthcare Sector

Security and privacy are the prime concern in the healthcare sector. Below is the discussion of security and privacy solutions:

1. Mutual Authentication Solution
Chen *et al.* [31] developed a security protocol to provide security in the healthcare IoT system. It is a three-factor IoT-based protocol, which ensures privacy and access control by integrating authentication and key negotiation. Additionally, biometrics is used enhance user experience. Asymmetric encryption and decryption are used, which further enhance security. After comparative analysis against similar protocols, it is demonstrated that the proposed protocol performs significantly, reduces computational cost, and increases time efficiency and security properties.

2. Authentication and Key Agreement Solution
Yu *et al.* [32] described a security scheme that leverages block chain and physically unclonable functions. It provides data integrity, robust physical security, and transparency. This scheme effectively prevents security attacks like impersonation, forgery and session key disclosure. It gives the guarantee for mutual authentication.

3. Lightweight Authentication Solution
Kumar *et al.* [33] introduced Robust Authentication Protocol for IoMT to boost the security and privacy of Health Infrastructure in IoMT applications. It establishes authentication and key agreement between patients, cloud servers, and doctors to form session keys without storing data in a cloud database system. This technique is better than many existing techniques against various security threats.

4. RFID Security Authentication Solution
Wang *et al.* [34] investigated the integration of Radio Frequency Identification (RFID) technology in smart healthcare. It helps in patient management, cost reduction, and care enhancement. The risks associated with improper RFID tag use is also discussed.

5. Block Chain-Based Solution
Singh *et al.* [8] proposed a decentralized healthcare finance system. This system is based on block chain technology. This system minimizes communication costs using lightweight cryptographic algorithms. Initially, it was designed for micro-level healthcare finance system. It is fast and performs work within milliseconds.

6. Homomorphic Encryption-Based Solution
Othman *et al.* [35] addressed the challenges associated with the implementation of IoT in healthcare specially for energy consumption and security concerns. Wireless medical devices lead to increased energy usage and security vulnerabilities. To mitigate these problems, a new scheme is introduced, which preserves privacy by leveraging homomorphic encryption.

7. Lightweight Cryptographic Primitive-Based Solution
Das *et al.* [36] presented a mutual authentication scheme for privacy concerns in IoT-based healthcare systems. The scheme used efficient cryptographic techniques based on ex-oring operator, concatenation, and hash operations. It establishes a secure connection between authorized devices and a gateway. It prevents unauthorized access to the healthcare system.

8. Data Aggregation-Based Solution
Bhowmik *et al.* [12] proposed the Edge-Enabled Efficient Privacy-Preserving Data Aggregation (EEPPDA) solution to protect healthcare-related information. The technique utilizes homomorphic encryption to secure information, which is then aggregated on an edge server before transmitting to a cloud server. This scheme reduces computational complexity and communication overhead significantly.

2.7 Eliminating Security and Privacy Concerns of Digitalization of the Healthcare Sector

The rapid involvement and fast growth of digitization in modern business can overwhelm the healthcare management system, and they may strive to keep up with digital transformation. It is necessary to integrate new technologies, but compromise cannot be done with privacy and security of patients and stakeholders. Hence, effective management is very important in medicine for the safety of patients' information. One of the aims of ongoing research is to assess the security of manufacturing medical devices with the development of international standards for their production.

2.7.1 Threats to the Healthcare Sector

The healthcare sector is more vulnerable to cyber threats compared to other industries. Interconnected healthcare devices offer several benefits, like remote monitoring and increased efficiency, but simultaneously, there are significant cyber security risks due to weak security measures. Healthcare providers struggle to protect against increasingly sophisticated cyber attacks. Most of the cyber attacks are financially motivated, and future cyber threats could have even more serious consequences, which may affect medical devices and compromising patient safety. Hence, it is the crucial and alarming situation that will make the system robust to fulfill cyber security measures so that patient data can be secured.

2.7.2 Developing Medical Equipment Management Programs

One of the challenges is detecting cyber attacks that are not detected or reported previously. Medical Equipment Management Programs (MEMP) play an important role to ensure the privacy and security of medical devices, which may prevent cyber threats. The involvement of communication technology has increased the risk of security breaches in medical devices both internally and externally. To mitigate the threats, MEMPs identify and safeguard critical systems; however, there is a need for more investigations to optimize safety, cost, and reliability in medical equipment service.

2.7.3 How are Medical Data Stored in Software Like EHR?

EHRs are very useful in determining which health-related data can be accessed more easily. However, cyber security measures may be the cause in making them insufficient in providing secured access. Hence, healthcare sectors need sufficient security so that confidentiality and integrity of medical information can be assured. EHRs are distributed across multiple locations, which make them more vulnerable to unauthorized access and potential manipulation.

2.8 Discussion

The introduction of big data, cloud computing, and AI in the 21st century, made almost all the sectors very advanced technically by accelerating digital transformation. Intelligent technologies, like AI and ML, enabled to create intelligent systems, and they are reshaping businesses. Cloud computing technology offers several benefits viz. reduced storage costs, improved data archiving, enhanced collaboration, etc. Big data processing, along with AI and ML, makes the system intelligent, and they reduce the cost in the healthcare sector. Introduction of ML improved patients' care. Below is a brief discussion of the role of digital revolution in the healthcare field:

- By using digital assistants, healthcare workers may connect with patients, and they can provide them with more focused service for their benefit.
- Clinical decision support plays an important role in assisting healthcare workers in making decisions viz. forecasting of medical outcomes including mortality, length of stay, or readmissions.
- ML-enabled NLP helps in understanding complex scientific language into simple and understandable language.
- ML-enabled clinical information retrieval systems offer high-quality knowledge from clinical narratives.
- Automated billing and invoicing make the system very precise, smooth, and very fast, which saves the time of patients' caretaker and healthcare service provider workers. Automated billing system also stops the chance of frauds or any human errors.

2.9 Future Works

2.9.1 Research on Privacy and Security in the Healthcare Sector for the Better

Research for the improvement in privacy and security regulations is one of the most valuable tasks. It is very important to understand the current landscape of the effectiveness of regulations, which may help the researchers to understand the gaps that can provide insights into areas for improvement and innovation. Emerging technologies may be introduced for best practices for compliance with these regulations so that patient data protection can be enhanced. Furthermore, exploring the impact of regulatory changes and advancements in encryption technology improved the data security in the healthcare organizations. Overall, this research area holds significant importance to ensure the confidentiality and integrity of patient information in the healthcare sector.

2.9.2 Understanding the Impact of Digitization

The impact of digitization significantly affected patient outcomes in the healthcare sector. Adoption of EHRs enabled healthcare providers to access patient medical history accurately, which is helpful in improving the diagnosis processes and treatments. Telemedicine enhanced patient outcomes as it enabled remote consultations. It reduces personal visits, and as a result, there is no physical contact. It also saves money and time for both patients and healthcare adviser. Moreover, big data and machine learning [38] facilitate the analysis of huge datasets and identify patterns, which makes the healthcare system more effective. Overall, digitization improves the efficacy of the healthcare system by improving accuracy and accessibility. In the present scenario, there is still room for further improvement in the digitization of the healthcare sector.

2.9.3 Investigation of Privacy and Security Risks Associated with Wearable Technology

In the present era, many people use smart wearable devices. They are advanced and secure, but there is a chance of hacking by the intruders. Many devices ask for the updates, which should be done by a secured network only. But digital advancement also allows the hackers too. Hence, it is necessary to investigate privacy and security risks linked with wearable technology.

2.9.4 Analysis of Role of AI in Healthcare

Virtual assistants and AI-powered chatbots may provide medical information to patients simply by asking a question. NLP assists an AI-based system to understand and interpret a query and gives the best output accordingly. AI helps the patients to access medical information and enhances communication with a healthcare service provider. Medical images can be analyzed more effectively using AI-based imaging techniques. However, there are many scopes in the future to understand the imaging technique effectively so that better service can be delivered, which may enhance patient outcomes.

2.9.5 Understand the Role of Block Chain Technology in Healthcare

Block chain technology has the potential to revolutionize the healthcare sector as it offers transparent, secure, and decentralized techniques for sharing and storing patients' data. EMRs use the block chain platforms to enable secure and efficient sharing of information among healthcare providers. It is also helpful for automatic claims and reimbursement done by the insurance companies. Block chain technology can enhance supply chain management of drugs and medical devices. Hence, more use of block chain in healthcare can significantly improve the efficiency and security of healthcare sectors.

2.9.6 Study on the Role of Patient Engagement in Privacy and Security

Patient engagement plays a vital role to secure data. Patients should be aware of their rights and responsibilities, and they may contribute to protect their personal information and medical records. This is possible only by educating patients on securing personal information and confidential data. Empowering patients may enhance overall healthcare privacy and security.

2.10 Conclusion

Digitalization is necessary for the advancement of healthcare practices, regulations, and activities. Healthcare professionals' digital capability ensures patient safety and successful integration of digitalization into professional environments. In developing economies, digital healthcare systems and other health information technologies are increasing day by day, and they would be very effective replacements of outdated paper-based record systems. Digitization made healthcare system not only paperless but also confirms the privacy and security of the patients' health information. However, the digital system may be affected by unauthorized intruders, which may harm the whole system and get access to the data. In most of the cases, the hackers' goal is fanatical benefits. Hence, it is obvious to make the system robust and secure completely.

References

1. Manogaran, G., Thota, C., Lopez, D., Sundarasekar, R., Big data security intelligence for healthcare industry 4.0, in: *Cybersecurity for Industry 4.0*, pp. 103–126, Springer, New York city, USA, 2017.
2. Popov, V.V., Kudryavtseva, E.V., Kumar Katiyar, N., Shishkin, A., Stepanov, S.I., Goel, S., Industry 4.0 and digitalisation in healthcare. *Materials*, 15, 6, 2140, 2022.
3. Girardi, F., De Gennaro, G., Colizzi, L., Convertini, N., Improving the healthcare effectiveness: The possible role of EHR, IoMT and blockchain. *Electronics*, 9, 6, 884, 2020.
4. Kruse, C.S., Frederick, B., Jacobson, T., Monticone, D.K., Cybersecurity in healthcare: A systematic review of modern threats and trends. *Technol. Health Care*, 25, 1, 1–10, 2017.
5. Bhonsle, D., Baksi, S., Pillai, A.G., Rahangdale, R., Verma, C., Khan, M.H.M., A review on a sensor based brain–computer interface and its applications, in: *Cognitive Sensors, Applications in smart healthcare*, vol. 2, pp. 6–1, 2023.
6. Bhonsle, D., Bhale, Y., Pillai, A.G., Tiwari, S., Moyal, V., Fan, C.P., Applications and challenges of IoT based smart healthcare systems cognitive sensors: an overview, in: *Cognitive Sensors Intelligent sensing, sensor data analysis and applications*, vol. 1, pp. 7–1, 2022.
7. Sharma, D.K., Chakravarthi, D.S., Shaikh, A.A., Ahmed, A.A.A., Jaiswal, S., Naved, M., The aspect of vast data management problem in healthcare sector and implementation of cloud computing technique. *Mater. Today: Proc.*, 80, 7, 1–6, 2021.
8. Singh, R., Dwivedi, A.D., Srivastava, G., Chatterjee, P., Lin, J.C.W., A privacy preserving internet of things smart healthcare financial system. *IEEE Internet Things J.*, 10, 21, 18452–18460, 2023.
9. Das, S. and Namasudra, S., Lightweight and efficient privacy-preserving mutual authentication scheme to secure internet of things-based smart healthcare. *Trans. Emerg. Telecommun. Technol.*, 31, 11, e4716, 2023.
10. Kim, D.W., Choi, J.Y., Han, K.H., Medical device safety management using cyber security risk analysis. *IEEE Access*, 8, 115370–115382, 2020.
11. Othman, S.B., Almalki, F.A., Chakraborty, C., Sakli, H., Privacy preserving aware data aggregation for IoT-based healthcare with green computing technologies. *Comput. Electr. Eng.*, 101, 08025, 2022.
12. Bhowmik, T. and Banerjee, I., EEPPDA—Edge-enabled efficient privacypreserving data aggregation in smart healthcare internet of things network. *Int. J. Netw. Manage.*, 33, 1, e2216, 2023.

13. Kwiatkowska, E.M. and Skorzewska-Amberg, M., Digitalisation of healthcare and the problem of digital exclusion. *Cent. Eur. Manage. J.*, 27, 48–63, 2019.
14. Jiang, F., Jiang, Y., Zhi, H., Dong, Y., Li, H., Ma, S., Wang, Y., Dong, Q., Shen, H., Wang, Y., Artificial intelligence in healthcare: past, present and future. *Stroke Vasc. Neurol.*, 2, 4, 230–243, 2017.
15. Sriram, G.S., Reddy, G.L., Babu, P., Bachanna, S.C., Gurpreet, V., Moyal, V., Bhonsle, D., Chamato, F.A., A smart solution for cancer patient monitoring based on internet of medical things using machine learning approach. *Evid. Based Complement. Alternat. Med.*, 2022, 1, 1–6, 2022.
16. Rahman, M.A., Hossain, M.S., Islam, M.S., Alrajeh, N.A., Muhammad, G., Secure and provenance enhanced internet of health things framework: A block chain managed federated learning approach. *IEEE Access*, 8, 205071–205087, 2020.
17. Martin, G., Martin, P., Hankin, C., Darzi, A., Kinross, J., Cybersecurity and healthcare: how safe are we? *BMJ*, 358, 1–6, 2017.
18. Ahmed, M.I. and Kannan, G., Secure and lightweight privacy preserving internet of things integration for remote patient monitoring. *J. King Saud Univ. Comput. Inf. Sci.*, 34, 9, 6895–6908, 2022.
19. Roski, J., Bo-Linn, G.W., Andrews, T.A., Creating value in health care through big data: opportunities and policy implications. *Health Aff.*, 33, 7, 1115–1122, 2014.
20. Abouelmehdi, K., Beni-Hssane, A., Khaloufi, H., Saadi, M., Big data security and privacy in healthcare: A review. *Procedia Comput. Sci.*, 113, 73–80, 2017.
21. Kshatri, S.S., Bhonsle, D., Verma, R., Pillai, A.G., Moyal, V., Crime Detection Approach Using Big Data Analytics and Machine Learning. *NeuroQuantology*, 20, 8, 1480, 2022.
22. Cowie, M.R., Blomster, J.I., Curtis, L.H., Duclaux, S., Ford, I., Fritz, F., Goldman, S., Janmohamed, S., Kreuzer, J., Leenay, M. *et al.*, Electronic health records to facilitate clinical research. *Clin. Res. Cardiol.*, 106, 1, 1–9, 2017.
23. Rizvi, T., Bhonsle, D., Uzma, R., Analysis and comparison of psychological constraints among various countries during COVID-19, in: *Computational Intelligence and Applications for Pandemics and Healthcare*, pp. 248–268, IGI Global, Hershey, Pennsylvania, USA, 2022.
24. Rizvi, T., Bhonsle, D., Rahangdale, R., Bagga, J., A survey on behavioral change during the COVID-19 outbreak in India, in: *Computational Intelligence and Applications for Pandemics and Healthcare*, pp. 184–203, IGI Global, Hershey, Pennsylvania, USA, 2022.
25. Wang, W., Li, X., Qiu, X., Zhang, X., Zhao, J., Brusic, V., A privacy preserving framework for federated learning in smart healthcare systems. *Inf. Process. Manage.*, 60, 1, 103167, 2023.
26. Chau, K.Y., Lam, M.H.S., Cheung, M.L., Tso, E.K.H., Flint, S.W., Broom, D.R., Tse, G., Lee, K.Y., Smart technology for healthcare: Exploring the

antecedents of adoption intention of healthcare wearable technology. *Health Psychol. Res.*, 7, 1, 33–39, 2019.
27. Coventry, L. and Branley, D., Cybersecurity in healthcare: A narrative review of trends, threats and ways forward. *Maturitas*, 113, 48–52, 2018.
28. Herrmann, M., Boehme, P., Mondritzki, T., Ehlers, J.P., Kavadias, S., Truebel, H. *et al.*, Digital transformation and disruption of the health care sector: internet-based observational study. *J. Med. Internet Res.*, 20, 3, e9498, 2018.
29. Bhonsle, D., Chandra, V.K., Sinha, G.R., Medical image denoising using bilateral filter. *Int. J. Image Graph. Signal Process.*, 4, 6, 36, 2012.
30. Bhonsle, D., Chandra, V.K., Sinha, G.R., An optimized framework using adaptive wavelet thresholding and total variation technique for de-noising medical images. *J. Adv. Res. Dyn. Control. Syst.*, 10, 953–965, 2018.
31. Chen, C.M., Chen, Z., Kumari, S., Lin, M.-C., LAP-IoHT: A lightweight authentication protocol for the internet of health things. *Sensors*, 22, 14, 5401, 2022.
32. Yu, S. and Park, Y., A robust authentication protocol for wireless medical sensor networks using blockchain and physically unclonable functions. *IEEE Internet Things J.*, 9, 20, 20214–20228, 2022.
33. Kumar, V., Mahmoud, M.S., Alkhayyat, A., Srinivas, J., Ahmad, M., Kumari, A., RAPCHI: Robust authentication protocol for IoMT based cloud-healthcare infrastructure. *J. Supercomput.*, 78, 14, 16167–16196, 2022.
34. Wang, X., Fan, K., Yang, K., Cheng, X., Dong, Q., Li, H., Yang, Y., A new RFID ultra-lightweight authentication protocol for medical privacy protection in smart living. *Comput. Commun.*, 186, 121–132, 2022.
35. Othman, S.B., Almalki, F.A., Chakraborty, C., Sakli, H., Privacy preserving aware data aggregation for IoT-based healthcare with green computing technologies. *Comput. Electr. Eng.*, 101, 108025, 2022.
36. Das, S. and Namasudra, S., Lightweight and efficient privacy-preserving mutual authentication scheme to secure internet of things-based smart healthcare. *Trans. Emerg. Telecommun. Technol.*, 34, 11, e4716, 2023.
37. Rizvi, T., Mishra, R., Chopkar, P.N., Gomkale, A., Upadhye, P., Bhonsle, D., Internet of Things-based cognitive wireless sensor networks: applications, merits, and demerits, in: *Cognitive Sensors, Intelligent sensing, sensor data analysis and applications*, vol. 1, pp. 2–1, IOP Publishing, Bristol, UK, 2022.

3

Data-Driven Diagnostics: Deep Learning for Brain Tumor Classification

Astha Pathak[1]* and Lalita Panika[2]

[1]*Department of Computer Science and Engineering, Shri Shankaracharya Technical Campus Bhilai, Durg, India*

[2]*Department of Computer Science and Engineering, Bhilai Institute of Technology, Raipur, India*

Abstract

One cannot stress how crucial early brain tumors diagnosis is to prolonging patients' lives. Because there are so many magnetic resonance imaging (MRI) pictures available, radiologists find it challenging to diagnose patients quickly and accurately. Through the use of database image resources and MRI pictures from the Kaggle Public database, several forms of brain tumors have been classified. Pre-processing has been done on the data for feature selection and noise reduction. The architecture of convolutional neural networks (CNNs) has been applied to classification. The results were validated using a 10-fold cross-validation approach. Comparing the suggested lightweight design to current classification methods, experiments showed that it achieved an optimal classification accuracy of 86.28%.

Keywords: Convolutional Neural Network (CNN), Deep Learning (DL), Magnetic Resolution Images (MRI)

3.1 Introduction

Brain cancer is one of the leading causes of mortality worldwide [1]. Worldwide, there are 250,000 cases of primary brain tumors, including in children under the age of 15 years. Since the brain is a complex organ, it

**Corresponding author*: asthapathak1806@gmail.com

Parul Dubey, Mangala Madankar, Pushkar Dubey and Bui Thanh Hung (eds.) The Impact of Algorithmic Technologies on Healthcare, (45–60) © 2025 Scrivener Publishing LLC

is impossible to determine whether a person has a brain tumor until they exhibit potentially fatal symptoms like seizures or memory loss. The etiology of brain tumors is unknown, and each variety carries unique hazards that may lead to death in the end. Both the tumor's growth rate and location may have an impact on how well the nervous system works, which may result in headaches, seizures, balance issues, memory loss, and other symptoms [2]. The body is in charge of producing billions of tissues and cells. An imbalance like this can result in irregular or unanticipated aberrant growth, which can eventually lead to the creation of a tumor. This type of tumor is known as brain tumor when it forms in the brain. Brain tumors are among the worst diseases in the world, impacting patients' lives in a neurological, physical, and psychological manner. Typically, there are three stages of a tumor: benign, pre-malignant, and malignant [3]. So its early diagnosis and categorization of brain tumors is an essential study area since it helps patients choose the best course of therapy [4, 5]. A subgenre of machine learning called "deep learning" (DL) is utilized in many different applications, most notably in the medical industry, to solve complex problems requiring incredibly high sensitivity and accuracy. To classify normal and abnormal brain tumors, segment tumor regions (edema, enhancing and non-enhancing regions), and other uses, DL is mostly used in brain image analysis [6, 7]. Conversely, convolution neural network is a kind of DL model that is frequently used for medical picture classification and segmentation. This investigation will be carried out in accordance with this concept. Through the use of deep learning, it seeks to support radiologists in their final selection process and aid in the development of dependable, accurate, and quick analysis [4]. Convolution is a statistical method that the network uses, as suggested by its name, CNN. Limited application exists for CNN, which takes the position of convolution in one of the network's layers for the conventional matrix multiplication. CNN requires fewer parameters and connections during training than standard feedforward neural networks. It consists of one or more output layers, one or more convolution layers, numerous fully joined layers, and subsampling layers. The convolutional and fully connected layers of CNN, which include the parametric, pooling, and nonlinearity layers, employ the input matrix as input. Gliomas, meningiomas, pituitary tumors, and other tumor classifications are among the multiple output classes that are created from the analysis of the input matrix by these layers. The assessment layer uses the accuracy score of detection to measure how well the classification worked. If an example does not satisfy the required learning standards, it retrains itself [5].

When it comes to identifying brain tumors, professionals most frequently employ magnetic resonance imaging, or MRI. Diseased tissues are easily visible on magnetic resonance imaging (MR) pictures, which also allow for the detection of any tissue degradation in the brain [8].

The suggested approach uses the public Kaggle dataset to collect recordings of the symptoms that patients with brain cancer experience. In the suggested paradigm, the layers of a CNN architecture shift to reveal its intermediate layers. The goal of this study is to train the model to produce the best possible result. There are eight sections in this paper. In Section 3.2, a few earlier works are briefly discussed. In Section 3.3, the suggested model is given together with an outline of the performance assessment and a description of the dataset. Section 3.5 contains the conclusion, and Section 3.4 provides a summary of the results.

3.2 Literature Review

Adithya *et al.* [9] presented a study in which they classified MRI brain pictures using state-of-the-art deep learning methods such as CNN, AlexNet, ResNets, and VGG-16. The objective is to diagnose brain cancer at a premature stage tackling the problem of absent or ambiguous symptoms. For precise brain area isolation, they use a strong pre-processing pipeline that includes thresholding, Gaussian blurring, gray scale conversion, and art fact removal. To enhance MRI analysis, sophisticated image augmentation methods, including edge-based segmentation and clustering, are used. Our deep learning-based solution relieves radiologists of some of their workload by automating tumor diagnosis and segmentation. Data augmentation has been used to address class imbalance with over 2,750 MRI pictures resulting in an amazing 98% test accuracy.

To eliminate the sounds that are present in the Associate in Nursing master data, Jaiwant Singh Raghav *et al.* [10] often pre-process the victimization of the morphological gap during this investigation. After that, tumor regions may be accurately identified using binary threshold and neural network segmentation approaches. Square measurements are applied to datasets during training, testing, and validation.

Berlin Shaheema *et al.* [11] suggested a work in which the classifier is used to classify brain tumors as pituitary, glioma, meningioma, and non-tumors. This approach increases confidence in tumor detection issues. The brain MRI dataset, which consists of 7,023 MRI images and is divided into the Br35H, Figshare, and SARTAJ datasets, is used to evaluate the

YOLOv7 algorithm. Precision, specificity, sensitivity, accuracy, F1-score, and reliability are evaluated as follows: 98.73%, 99.69%, 99.81%, 98.56%, and 98.73%, which correspondingly, represent the overall efficacy of the recommended technique.

In his work, Jinhong Zhu [12], combining the convolutional neural network model (CNN) with the transfer learning technique allows for automatic picture categorization using the Brain Tumour Detection 2020 dataset from Model Whale. Tensorflow is a deep learning framework used in the experiment to compare three backbone networks: VGG, MobileNet, and ResNet. The experiment results indicate that the automatic classification of brain tumors with a combination of the CNN model and the transfer learning method works better; the VGG model performs best with an accuracy of 99.46%.

Geethanjali [13] suggested a work in which MRI pictures of the human brain obtained from Kaggle are utilized as the dataset. It includes brain MRI scans of both tumors and non-tumors. Following that, it passes through data pre-processing, which uses a variety of image processing methods, including cropping, filtering, and blurring. Training and testing sets make up the dataset. They are subjected to several arbitrary modifications as part of data augmentation. A CNN (convolutional neural networks) model is fed the pre-trained dataset. Next, the model determines if the tumor is there or not. In the event that a tumor is discovered, it is divided into three groups. These three types of tumors are pituitary, meningioma, and glioma. This experiment has shown that, of the three CNN models (EfficienNet B1, DenseNet, and ResNet 50), EfficienNet B1 achieves the highest test accuracy of 99.31%.

Parninan Afshar [14] suggested a capsule network-based architecture that could reach the surrounding tissue in addition to the primary target and accept inputs such as brain pictures and tumor rough border boxes. But like other architectures, this network needs a thorough search across the space of all potential configurations to identify the best architecture. To do away with this requirement, we provide in this work a boosted capsule network, or BoostCaps, that leverages the capacity of boosting techniques to manage poor learners by progressively boosting the models. Our findings demonstrate that, with an accuracy of 92.45%, the suggested BoostCaps framework performs better than its single capsule network equivalent.

In their work, Oussama Bouguerra *et al.* [15] investigated the effects on classification performance by training our designs with three different medical picture-enhancing techniques and minimal preprocessing. Our observations provide credence to the notion that transfer learning, when applied to small datasets, yields reliable results. Pre-trained models that are popular and effective in classifying images include the deep convolutional neural network architectures VGG16 and VGG19. The proposed system outperforms the state-of-the-art methods with a 99.77% classification accuracy.

Menghan Zou *et al.* [16] proposes a novel neural network-based brain tumor classification model. They process a dataset comprising four different types of brain tumor images using three different data enhancement algorithms—geometric transformation, mix-up, and sample pairing—and then assess the proposed model's classification efficacy. Among these, the application of geometric transformations for 98% accuracy in data enhancement produced the best results.

Ahmad Saleh *et al.* [17] used Xception, ResNet50, InceptionV3, VGG16, and MobileNet, which are the five pre-trained models that they used to train their brain tumor Kaggle dataset. The respective F1-scores for unseen photos 98.75%, 98.50%, 98.00%, 97.50%, and 97.25%. The authors raise the degree and effectiveness of MRI scanners in recognizing the sorts and categorizing brain tumors by utilizing CNN, deep learning, and AI algorithms.

Muhammad Adeel Hafeez *et al.* [18] proposed a method for classifying three different forms of brain cancer (meningiomas, gliomas, and pituitary tumors) using a convolutional neural network (CNN) as the basis. The study made use of a publicly accessible dataset of 3,064 T1-weighted brain CE-MRI images that were obtained from 233 participants. Here, a CNN model with 15 layers is proposed for the classification of three different kinds of brain tumors using the dataset in question. From our proposed model, we obtained higher accuracy, precision, recall, and F1-score (98.6%, 99%, 98.3%, and 98.6%) than previously published findings.

Rudresh Pillai *et al.* [19] identifies brain tumors using three different deep transfer learning models applied after fine-tuning layers are added based on a dataset of 251 MRI scans. The transfer learning models used are VGG16, InceptionV3, and ResNet50; optimized dropout, flattened, and dense extra layers are added. The model with the highest accuracy, the VGG16, achieved 91.58%. Therefore, brain tumor diagnosis using deep learning models has proven effective without requiring unnecessary effort or resource cost.

The goal of Amita Banerjee *et al.* [20] is to create a sophisticated predictive model that can reliably identify brain tumors as benign or malignant based on MRI images. Here, a brand-new CNN architecture is put out to increase the precision of diagnosis and automate tumor detection. The model made use of a dataset of approximately 7,000 records on brain cancer that were categorized into four categories: no tumor, pituitary, meningioma, and glioma. After that, pre-processing and data wrangling are used to combine the photos into a single format and get rid of any inconsistencies. Moreover, a 70–30 split is used to separate the records into train and test samples. The optimal accuracy, precision, recall value, and f-score metric for the suggested model were 94.82%, 94.2%, 93.7%, and 93.9%, respectively.

Ankitha *et al.*'s [21] primary goal is to create a model that can accurately represent the distribution of distinctive features in the input MRI Kaggle dataset photos. After that, a generative model is used to synthesize these images and classify the dataset to identify any brain tumors. Three datasets are used to experimentally assess the suggested model. The strategies that have been suggested enable a compelling performance and a successful comparison. Using the ResNet50 architecture, an accuracy of 98.02%, and the Xception architecture, 98.32% were attained.

Using the publicly accessible Kaggle brain tumor dataset, which comprised MRI scans without brain tumors and three different kinds of brain tumors—meningiomas, pituitary tumors, and gliomas—Adnan Sakib *et al.* [22] propose a hybrid model for the categorization of brain tumors. The dataset underwent preprocessing. They used VGG16 as our basis model and expanded it with additional CNN layers. Transfer learning was used to freeze the base model layers, while we trained the extra CNN layers. The pre-trained VGG16 model recognizes a wide range of medical imaging-related textures, shapes, and features. Additionally, by adding additional CNN layers, we were able to identify task-related brain tumor pattern features that were more intricate and unique than those found in the original ImageNet dataset. With our model, we achieved a test accuracy of 96.52%.

In their work, Hanming Hu *et al.* [23] investigated how combining object detection technology (YOLO) with various deep learning models, including VGG 16119, AlexNet, GoogleNet, and Resnet, affected classification job performance. It helps to precisely identify the tumor's location in an MRI by applying the YOLO model. But the graphical enhancement research tried all of the deep learning models, including VGG16/19, AlexNet, GoogleNet, and Resnet, to assess their efficacy and accuracy. To improve classification accuracy, they also incorporated a YOLO model to precisely locate the tumor in the MRI picture and made graphical modifications. It becomes out that applying graphic enhancement and YOLO detection reduces the classification accuracy.

The exceptional performance of the suggested model was demonstrated by Nidhya [24] and its potential to aid healthcare providers in the timely and precise diagnosis of brain tumors ultimately leading to better patient outcomes. They discovered that on the training set, the recommended

CNN model had an average accuracy value of 98% and an average loss value of 0.14181. There is a noticeable difference, nevertheless, since the test data results show an average accuracy value of 90% and an average loss value of 0.44037.

Beebi Naseeba *et al.*, [25] suggests a transfer learning strategy based on many CNN architectures that have already been trained, including ResNet101 and VGG-19. Using the Kaggle dataset, a custom hybrid model with features from both the Inception and ResNet architectures is proposed. It is based on a pre-trained Inception-Resnet-v2. All of the models underwent a comparative study using accuracy and AUC as the evaluation measures. With an accuracy of 99.30%, the hybrid model based on Inception-Resnet-v2 achieved the highest score.

Ajinkya Bandagale *et al.* [26] employed a technique that uses MRI images to classify brain tumors into four main groups: no tumor, pituitary tumors, meningiomas, and gliomas. It accomplished this by employing CNN, a deep learning algorithm. Our dataset consists of 7,183 brain MRI pictures from multiple hospitals and a few private scan centers in Mumbai, India. Out of the 7,183 brain MRI images, 5,712 were used for training; 1,471 were taken from Test Dataset 1 and 1,311 from Test Dataset 2 online sources. Test Dataset 1 produced results of 97.82% accuracy, 97.54% precision, 98.01% recall, and 97.76% F1-score for our proposed technique; Test Dataset 2 produced results of 98.70% accuracy, 98.59% precision, 98.66% recall, and 98.61% F1-score.

Abdulrazak Yahya Saleh [27] aims to assess the effectiveness of deep learning for brain tumor classification using residual attention networks (RAN). This research makes use of digitalized magnetic resonance image (MRI) datasets that were acquired from hospitals in Malaysia as well as other sources. Male and female patients who are 20 years of age and older are included in the MRI datasets. The MRI datasets are used to train and evaluate the RAN algorithm. Training accuracy, testing accuracy, validation accuracy, and validation loss metrics are used to assess the algorithm's performance. Additionally, utilizing the same datasets, a comparison analysis is conducted between Residual Neural Networks (ResNet) and convolutional neural networks (CNN). The results of this investigation demonstrate that, out of the three algorithms, RAN offers the best performance. ResNet performs well, exhibiting an accuracy range of 67% to 87%. When it comes to accuracy, the basic CNN algorithm performs poorly, ranging from 57% to 71%. At 94% and higher, RAN yields the best and most reliable accuracy. This work offers additional justification for the effectiveness of RAN in the categorization of brain tumors.

3.3 Methodology

A. Dataset

We used an openly accessible MRI dataset 1 from Kaggle for our project. The dataset comprises 7,023 MRI pictures of four distinct forms of brain tumors, of which 5,712 images—1,458 pituitary tumors, 1,339 meningiomas, 1,321 gliomas, and 1,594 tumor-free images—were used for training. The dataset is not entirely balanced since there are different numbers of MRI pictures for each of the four groups of brain cancer. For testing, 288 gliomas, 294 meningiomas, 288 pituitary tumors, and 393 tumors were among the 1,263 photos utilized [22, 28, 29]. Table 3.1 shows the list of different types of tumors in Kaggle dataset.

B. Data Pre-processing

Preprocessing of MR image data is essential before the technology is applied to medical images. MR brain images could include a range of noises and artifacts that are not required for the model to be trained. Unwanted noises in the system are eliminated using the de-noising approach [30]. In image processing, pre-processing refers to an operation performed on images at the lowest level of abstraction. Pre-processing is the initial step in the classification and analysis of histopathology imaging data. To do this, a variety of image enhancement and filtering methods can be applied, including thresholding, low-pass filtering (median and averaging), picture enhancement, etc. Pre-processing entails a number of procedures, including smoothening to remove noise and normalizing color and illumination [31]. This is the preliminary processing of data to get them ready for further processing or additional investigation. Our project's pre-processing stage mostly consists of those tasks that are typically required prior to the target analysis, data extraction, and, most often, geometric adjustments to the source image. Down sampling the image dataset to 200 * 200 pixels reduces computing complexity while maintaining image quality. To change the pixel values in the photographs, the image dataset is further normalized. Image normalization aids in improving contrast in photos to facilitate comprehension.

C. Training Data

The input data should be split into two groups as the training set and the test set during the data-partitioning step. The data should be utilized for training if the test data are a model generated by the classification model, and the product's outcomes should be compatible with the test procedure. Two distinct datasets are produced by the data-partitioning process.

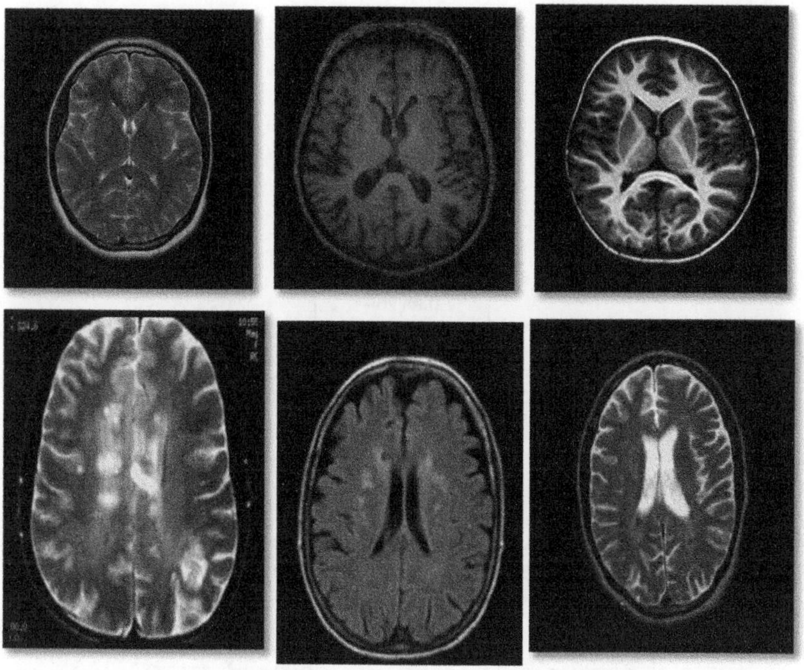

Figure 3.1 Sample records of brain tumor dataset.

There is no mutual exclusion between the two shared files. The content of the two datasets differs. In this instance, the training to test data ratio is 8:2.

D. Proposed Work

Figure 3.2 illustrates the suggested system design. Records of the symptoms experienced by individuals with brain cancer are stored in a system that is powered by the public Kaggle dataset. To illuminate its intermediate

Table 3.1 Description of Kaggle dataset.

Total no. of records = 7,023		
Malignant types (cancerous nodules)	Pituitary tumors	1,746
	Meningiomas	1,633
	Gliomas	1,609
Benign (non-cancerous nodules)	Non Cancer	1,987

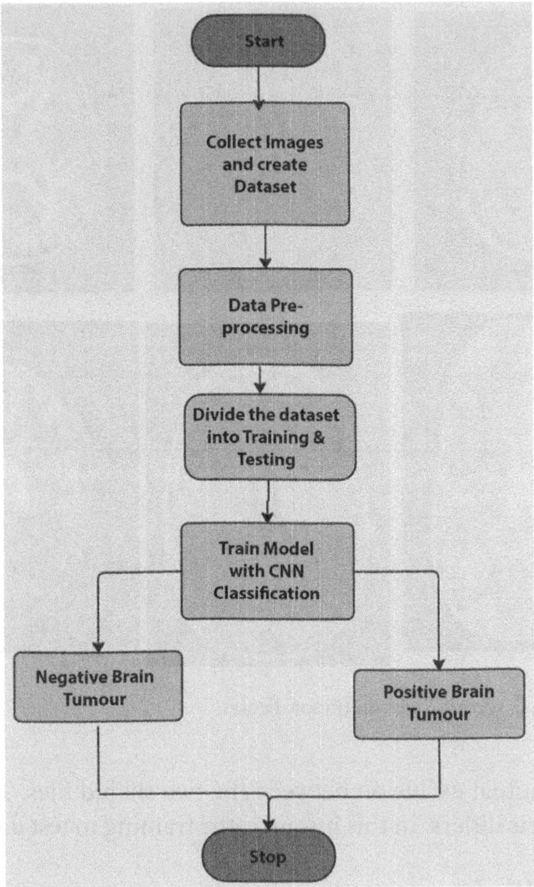

Figure 3.2 Workflow of the proposed work.

layers, the layers of a 3D CNN architecture change in the proposed model. Obtaining the optimal outcome when training the model is the aim of the proposed work. Figure 3.3 shows the architecture of convolutional neural network model.

E. Applied Algorithm

Convolutional neural networks, often known as CNNs, are well-known for their ability to recognize and classify images in particular. When it comes to extracting intricate features for classifications, CNN excels [32]. CNN is made up of neurons that have the ability to learn bias and weight. After receiving some input from each neuron, the activation function is given the weighted sum [33]. CNN's robust, accurate, and automatic feature

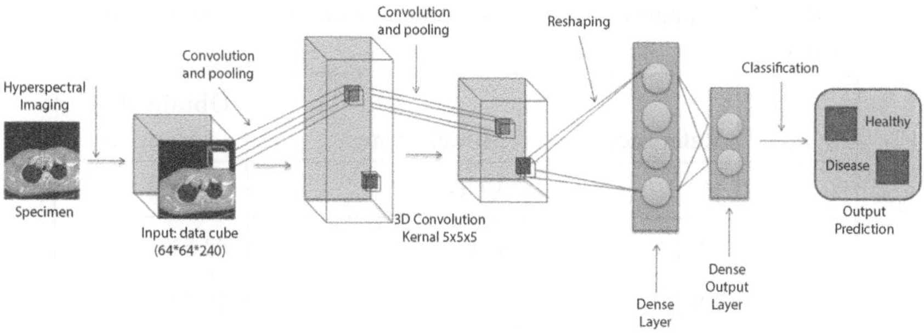

Figure 3.3 Convolutional neural network model [35].

recognition without the need for human interaction makes it the most popular deep learning model. Convolution, pooling, fully connected, input, and classification layer are the five primary component layers that make up the CNN [28]. The many layers in the proposed DCNN architecture for brain tumor image classification are displayed in Figure 3.1. The brain tumor classification system is comprised of five layers: rectified linear unit (RELU) layer, pooling layer, fully connected layer, convolutional layer for convergence, and input layer for providing data to the model. A feed forward convolutional neural network, the suggested DCNN model consists of a convolutional layer, a pooling layer, an activation layer, and a fully connected layer for feature learning. For intricate and extensive brain image data analysis based on artificial neural networks, it employs several layers of neurons. The DCNN is primarily used for object recognition and medical image classification; it is utilized to identify patterns in the input brain image data. The primary benefit of DCNN is its multi-layer stacking capability, which allows it to process the red, green, and blue portions of a given brain tumor image simultaneously in three dimensions [29, 34].

3.4 Result Analysis

The entire database was first separated into training and analyzing databases in a 70% and 30% ratio, and then pre-processing was used to eliminate superfluous noise from the supplied dataset. The model may be trained using MRI pictures from the Kaggle public training database that have been extracted as features. Ultimately, a model is designed that takes less time to train and produces result sooner than the previous model with an accuracy of 90.13% without and 86.28% with 10-fold cross-validation. Table 3.2 compares the other proposed method against our proposed algorithm.

Table 3.2 Comparison of proposed model with other deep learning model.

S_no.	Reference	Model name	Obtained accuracy
1.	[22]	VGG 16	96.52%
2.	[29]	KNN	82.5%
3.	[36]	YOLO v5x	89.3%
4.	[37]	Watershed Dynamic Angle Projection CNN Model	94.2%
5.	**Our Proposed Model**	**CNN**	**90.13%**

A. Cross-Validation Techniques

A statistical method is cross-validation. Its main application is in model selection for improved test error estimation in predictive models. The sample observation should be divided into a number of groups according to the cross-validation principle. It is a popular strategy because, in comparison to other approaches, it is simple to understand and produces a less skewed or more positive evaluation of the model's abilities. There are several kinds of cross-validations accessible. The outcomes of this research are validated using k-fold cross-validation procedures [38]. K-fold cross-validation divided the documents into k parts using k – 1 portions for train data and 1 portion for testing [39]. To validate the results, we used k-fold cross-validation for k = 10. Table 3.3 displays 10-fold worth of results. All of the training dataset is taken into account for both training and validation in k-fold cross-validation approaches. Every entry in the training dataset serves as a validation.

Table 3.3 10-Fold cross-validation accuracy.

Obtained accuracy	
Testing accuracy	10-Fold cross-validation accuracy
90.13%	86.28%

3.5 Conclusion

In the medical healthcare system, classifying brain tumor MRI images is an essential procedure. The deep CNN model is helpful and contributes significantly to the precise classification of brain tumors in image diagnosis. This paper compared the prediction in the categorization of benign and malignant lung lesions in the Kaggle public dataset. The experiment findings show that the homemade CNN archived optimized result with a higher efficiency of 86.28% with 10-fold cross-validation compared to the existing architecture. This study has relatively light and compact semantic network layers due to changes in intermediary levels. The accuracy of the other data sources should be increased by the suggested technique. The method could be applied in the future to a variety of medical imaging tasks utilizing CADx equipment with excellent performance.

References

1. Pries, T.P., Review of Brain Tumor Segmentation, Detection and Classification Algorithms in fMRI Images. *2018 Int. Conf. Comput. Charact. Tech. Eng. Sci.*, pp. 300–303, 2018.
2. Deeksha, K.N., Deeksha, M., Girish, A.V., Bhat, A.S., Lakshmi, H., Classification of Brain Tumor and its types using Convolutional Neural Network, pp. 1–6, 2020, doi: 10.1109/INOCON50539.2020.9298306.
3. Xenya, M.C., Brain Tumour Detection and Classification using Multi-level Ensemble Transfer Learning in MRI Dataset, 2021, doi: 10.1109/icABCD51485.2021.9519361.
4. Pascual, A.K., Classification of the Type of Brain Tumor in MRI Using Xception Model, pp. 8–11, doi: 10.1109/ICEIC57457.2023.10049979.
5. Kale, P.V., Deep CNN-Based MRI Imaging for Brain Tumor Detection and Classification. *2024 IEEE Int. Students' Conf. Electr. Electron. Comput. Sci.*, pp. 1–6, 2024, doi: 10.1109/SCEECS61402.2024.10482056.
6. Dipu, N.M., Deep Learning Based Brain Tumor Detection and Classification. *2021 Int. Conf. Intell. Technol.*, pp. 1–6, 2021, doi: 10.1109/CONIT51480.2021.9498384.
7. Mondal, M., Faruk, F., Raihan, N., Ahammed, P., Deep Transfer Learning Based Multi-Class Brain Tumors Classification Using MRI Images. *2021 3rd Int. Conf. Electr. Electron. Eng.*, pp. 73–76, 2021, doi: 10.1109/ICEEE54059.2021.9719003.
8. Çınar, N., Comparison of deep learning models for brain tumor classification using MRI images. *2022 Int. Conf. Decis. Aid Sci. Appl.*, pp. 1382–1385, 2022, doi: 10.1109/DASA54658.2022.9765250.

9. Automated Brain Tumor Classification and Detection Using Modified Convolutional Neural Networks for Early Diagnosis. *2023 Int. Conf. Intell. Technol. Sustain. Electr. Commun. Syst. (iTech SECOM)*, pp. 351–355, 2023, doi: 10.1109/iTechSECOM59882.2023.10435136.
10. Raghav, J.S., Das, A.N., Suresh, A., Automated Brain Tumor Classification of Different Types of Tumors Using Convolutional Neural Network of Multi Label MRI Scans. *2023 Int. Conf. Artif. Intell. Knowl. Discov. Concurr. Eng.*, pp. 1–7, doi: 10.1109/ICECONF57129.2023.10083600.
11. S., B., Automated Multimodal Brain Tumor Classification using a YOLOv7 Approach. *2023 9th Int. Conf. Control. Decis. Inf. Technol.*, pp. 35–40, 2023, doi: 10.1109/CoDIT58514.2023.10284388.
12. Zhu, J., Automatic Brain Tumor Classification Based on Transfer Learning Models. *2022 Int. Symp. Adv. Informatics, Electron. Educ.*, pp. 5–8, 2022, doi: 10.1109/ISAIEE57420.2022.00009.
13. Geethanjali, N., Pushpalatha, V., Ramya, C., Sandhiya, L., Subhashri, S., Brain Tumor Detection and Classification Using Deep Learning. *2023 Winter Summit Smart Comput. Networks*, pp. 1–6, doi: 10.1109/WiSSCoN56857.2023.10133851.
14. Afshar, P., Plataniotis, K.N., Mohammadi, A., BoostCaps: A Boosted Capsule Network for Brain Tumor Classification, pp. 1075–1079, 2020.
15. Bouguerra, O., Attallah, B., Brik, Y., Brain Tumor Classification Based Deep Transfer Learning Approaches. *2022 Int. Conf. Adv. Technol. Electron. Electr. Eng.*, pp. 1–6, doi: 10.1109/ICATEEE57445.2022.10093731.
16. Zou, M., Brain tumor classification model of ResNet-50 network based on different data enhancement algorithms. *2023 8th Int. Conf. Intell. Comput. Signal Process.*, no. 1, pp. 1011–1016, 2023, doi: 10.1109/ICSP58490.2023.10248544.
17. Saleh, A. and Learning, A.D., Brain Tumor Classification Using Deep Learning, pp. 131–136, 2020, doi: 10.1109/iCareTech49914.2020.00032.
18. Hafeez, M.A., Kayasandik, C.B., Dogan, M.Y., 'Brain Tumor Classification Using MRI Images and Convolutional Neural Networks'. *2022 30th Signal Process. Commun. Appl. Conf.*, pp. 1–4, doi: 10.1109/SIU55565.2022.9864962.
19. Pillai, R., Sharma, A., Sharma, N., Gupta, R., Brain Tumor Classification using VGG 16, ResNet50, and Inception V3 Transfer Learning Models. *2023 2nd Int. Conf. Innov. Technol.*, pp. 1–5, 2023, doi: 10.1109/INOCON57975.2023.10101252.
20. Banerjee, A., Jaiswal, K., Biswas, T., Sharma, V., Bal, M., Mishra, S., Brain Tumor Detection and Classification Using a Hyperparameter Tuned Convolutional Neural Network. *2023 6th Int. Conf. Contemp. Comput. Informatics*, vol. 6, pp. 502–506, 2023, doi: 10.1109/IC3I59117.2023.10397907.
21. Ankitha, G., J, H.T., Akhilesh, J., Bhanu, A., Ig, N., Brain Tumor Detection and Classification Using Deep Learning Approaches'. *2023 4th Int. Conf. Emerg. Technol.*, pp. 1–6, 2023, doi: 10.1109/INCET57972.2023.10169933.
22. Sakib, A., Khan, N.J., Shahrier, L., Plabon, K., Al Mahmud, J., Mridha, M.F., Brain Tumor Detection and Classification Using Hybrid VGG Network.

2023 26th Int. Conf. Comput. Inf. Technol., pp. 1–6, 2023, doi: 10.1109/ICCIT60459.2023.10441065.

23. Frp, K.J., Brain Tumor Diagnose Applying CNN through MRI. *2021 2nd Int. Conf. Artif. Intell. Comput. Eng.*, pp. 430–434, 2021, doi: 10.1109/ICAICE54393.2021.00090.
24. Nidhya, R., Kalpana, R., Smilarubavathy, G., Keerthana, S.M., Brain Tumor Diagnosis with MCNN-Based MRI Image Analysis. *2023 1st Int. Conf. Optim. Tech. Learn.*, pp. 1–5, 2023, doi: 10.1109/ICOTL59758.2023.10435262.
25. Nikhil, S.B., Nair, N.S., Challa, N.P., Katta, R., Classification and Detection of Brain Tumors from Magnetic Resonance Imaging Scans using Deep Transfer-Learning. *2023 Int. Conf. Adv. Comput. Commun. Appl. Informatics*, pp. 1–7, doi: 10.1109/ACCAI58221.2023.10200513.
26. Bandagale, A., Classification of Brain Tumor Into Four Categories Using Convolution Neural Network. *2022 2nd Int. Conf. Intell. Technol.*, pp. 1–8, 2022, doi: 10.1109/CONIT55038.2022.9848205.
27. Saleh, A.Y. and Thiagaraju, S.A.S., Brain Tumour Classification using Deep Learning with Residual Attention Network: A Comparative Study. *2021 Int. Congr. Adv. Technol. Eng.*, pp. 1–5, 2021, doi: 10.1109/ICOTEN52080.2021.9493544.
28. Bhardwaj, N., Sood, M., Gill, S.S., Deep Learning Framework using CNN for Brain Tumor Classification. *2022 5th Int. Conf. Multimedia, Signal Process. Commun. Technol.*, pp. 1–5, doi: 10.1109/IMPACT55510.2022.10029043.
29. Sakthi, U., Thangaraj, K., Tamizhselvi, A., Kirubakaran, M.K., Deep Convolutional Neural Network Framework for Brain Tumor Classification using MRI Images. *2023 2nd Int. Conf. Autom. Comput. Renew. Syst.*, pp. 548–553, 2023, doi: 10.1109/ICACRS58579.2023.10404771.
30. Anilkumar, B., Kumar, N.P., Sowmya, K., MR Brain Tumour Classification Using a Deep Ensemble Learning Technique. *2023 5th Bienn. Int. Conf. Nascent Technol. Eng.*, no. Icnte, pp. 1–6, 2023, doi: 10.1109/ICNTE56631.2023.10146712.
31. Diwaker, K. and Rawat, J., Assessing the Effect of Pre-processing Techniques on Classification of Breast Cancer using Histopathological Images. *ACCESS 2023 - 2023 3rd Int. Conf. Adv. Comput. Commun. Embed. Secur. Syst.*, pp. 101–105, 2023, doi: 10.1109/ACCESS57397.2023.10201037.
32. Sattam, P., Multi-Classification of brain tumor based on deep. *2022 IEEE 9th Int. Conf. Sci. Electron. Technol. Inf. Telecommun.*, pp. 87–90, 2022, doi: 10.1109/SETIT54465.2022.9875468.
33. Baranwal, S.K., Performance analysis of Brain Tumour Image Classification using CNN and SVM, pp. 537–542, 2020.
34. Pathak, A. and Dhole, A., Lungs Cancer Identification by Deep Learning 3D CNN Architecture. *13th Int. Conf. Adv. Comput. Control. Telecommun. Technol. ACT 2022*, vol. 8, pp. 262–267, 2022.
35. Pathak, A., Dewangan, S.K., Sahu, M.K., Sahu, N., Comparing Three Different Layers of CNN using Lungs Cancer Dataset. *Int. Conf. Artif.*

Intell. Innov. Healthc. Ind. ICAIIHI 2023, vol. 1, pp. 1–6, 2023, doi: 10.1109/ICAIIHI57871.2023.10489238.

36. Kumar, M., Pilania, U., Bhayana, T., Thakur, S., Utilizing YOLOv5x for the Detection and Classification of Brain Tumors. *2024 2nd Int. Conf. Disruptive Technol.*, pp. 1343–1348, 2024, doi: 10.1109/ICDT61202.2024.10489507.
37. Jemimma, T.A. and Vetharaj, Y.J., Watershed Algorithm based DAPP features for Brain Tumor Segmentation and Classification. *2018 Int. Conf. Smart Syst. Inven. Technol.*, no. Icssit, pp. 155–158, 2018, doi: 10.1109/ICSSIT.2018.8748436.
38. Tamilarasi, P. and Rani, R.U., Diagnosis of Crime Rate against Women using k-fold Cross Validation through Machine Learning. *Proc. 4th Int. Conf. Comput. Methodol. Commun. ICCMC 2020*, no. Iccmc, pp. 1034–1038, 2020, doi: 10.1109/ICCMC48092.2020.ICCMC-000193.
39. Pal, K. and Patel, B.V., Data Classification with k-fold Cross Validation and Holdout Accuracy Estimation Methods with 5 Different Machine Learning Techniques. *Proc. 4th Int. Conf. Comput. Methodol. Commun. ICCMC 2020*, no. Iccmc, pp. 83–87, 2020, doi: 10.1109/ICCMC48092.2020.ICCMC-00016.

4

Predictive Analysis in Patient Care

Bolukonda Prashanth[1], Bandi Krishna[2], Rakesh Nayak[3]*, Umashankar Ghugar[3] and Arunakranthi Godishala[4]

[1]*Department of CSE, Sumathi Reddy Institute of Technology for Women, Hanamkonda, India*
[2]*Department of CSE, Balaji Institute of Technology and Science, Warangal, India*
[3]*Department of CSE, OP Jindal University, Raigarh, India*
[4]*Faculty of Integrated Technologies, Universiti Brunei Darussalam, Gadong, Brunei Darussalam*

Abstract
This chapter explores the application of predictive analysis in patient care highlighting its potential to revolutionize healthcare delivery. It highlights the importance of integrating diverse data sources, such as electronic health records, wearable devices, and genetic information, to generate comprehensive patient profiles. Through sophisticated analytics and predictive modeling, healthcare providers can identify patterns, predict disease progression, and personalize treatment plans. The article discusses the benefits and challenges of implementing predictive analysis in healthcare settings, emphasizing its potential to improve patient outcomes, reduce costs, and enhance resource allocation through proactive interventions. However, it also acknowledges the ethical considerations and data privacy concerns that must be addressed to ensure responsible and secure use of predictive analysis in patient care. Overall, the article emphasizes the transformative potential of predictive analysis in patient care leading to improved patient outcomes and a more efficient healthcare system.

Keywords: Predictive analysis, healthcare system, predictive modelling

**Corresponding author*: nayakrakesh8@gmail.com; ORCID: 0000-0002-7732-6848

Parul Dubey, Mangala Madankar, Pushkar Dubey and Bui Thanh Hung (eds.) The Impact of Algorithmic Technologies on Healthcare, (61–84) © 2025 Scrivener Publishing LLC

4.1 Introduction

Intellectual property has grown to be a vital asset for both individuals and corporations in the fast-paced world of today. Innovative ideas need to be protected and made profitable, and patients are especially important for this. Making wise judgments and effectively managing patients, however, may be challenging particularly in light of the abundance of available patient data. Predictive analysis can be useful in this situation. By utilizing data and statistical algorithms, predictive analysis is an effective technique for projecting future results. Predictive analysis gives patient professionals a competitive edge in the market, allows them to make data-driven decisions, and optimizes their patient care strategies by identifying patterns, trends, and linkages within patient data. Predictive analysis's capacity to extract valuable insights from massive volumes of patient data is one of its main advantages in patient care. In the past, patient experts assessed patient viability, possible infringement concerns, and market trends using manual analysis and subjective judgment. But this method takes a lot of time, is prone to mistakes, and cannot handle very big datasets.

On the other hand, vast amounts of patient data may be processed reliably and fast using predictive analysis. Patient professionals can gain important insights from the data by spotting patterns and connections that could otherwise be missed. These insights may be used to evaluate a patient's innovation and commercial potential, spot possible infringers, and even anticipate potential legal problems down the road. Enhancing productivity and cutting expenses are two other important benefits of predictive analysis in patient care. Patient professionals may save time and money by automating data analysis procedures, freeing them up to concentrate on higher-value activities like portfolio management, innovation, and strategic planning. Furthermore, by using predictive analysis to give insights, patient professionals may lower the risk of investing in patients with little economic potential by making better-informed judgments. Predictive analysis may also be extremely important for protecting intellectual property. It can assist patient experts in proactively pursuing their rights by identifying patterns of infringement through the analysis of previous patient data. By taking a proactive stance, substantial costs that might otherwise be incurred via drawn-out legal disputes can be avoided. It is crucial to remember that predictive analysis is not a magic bullet. Although it may offer insightful analysis and forecasts, it should be utilized as a tool to assist in decision making rather than as a replacement for human knowledge. Predictive analysis findings should still be interpreted by patient experts using their domain expertise and judgment.

Patient professionals may now make data-driven decisions, improve their patient strategy, and gain a competitive edge thanks to predictive analysis, which is redefining the practice of patient care. Predictive analysis is a powerful tool that may reveal hidden insights, improve efficiency, save costs, and fortify intellectual property protection by utilizing data and statistical algorithms. Patient experts need to embrace this game-changing technology as predictive analysis develops further to keep ahead of the constantly changing market [7].

This book chapter has been organized into five sections. The first section describes the patient healthcare system. The second and third sections describe the review of the healthcare system and the challenges' part. Finally, Section five, describes the conclusion and future prediction of the healthcare system.

A. Harnessing the Power of Data

Data have developed into a vital resource in the current digital era propelling innovation and decision making across a wide range of businesses. This also applies to the subject of patient care, where experts look for ways to handle patients efficiently, spot any infringements, and make wise judgments. This is where predictive analysis enters the picture providing a potent instrument to maximize data potential and transform patient care. Large volumes of data are analyzed using sophisticated statistical algorithms and machine learning approaches in predictive analysis to find patterns, trends, and connections. Patient specialists may use these data to detect possible infringers, forecast future market trends, and obtain insightful knowledge about the viability of patients.

Optimizing decision making is one of the main advantages of predictive analysis in patient care. In the past, patient experts used subjective assessment and manual analysis to assess a patient's commercial viability. However, the analysis of huge datasets is constrained by this approach's time-consuming and error-prone nature. Conversely, predictive analysis can swiftly and precisely handle enormous amounts of patient data giving patient experts insightful information that can help them make decisions. Predictive analysis, for instance, can assist in finding patients that have a better chance of being commercially successful by examining past data and seeing trends linked to patient performance. Patient professionals may optimize their patient care strategies by concentrating their attention on patients that have a greater potential for income generation by comprehending these trends.

Predictive analysis can also be quite helpful in spotting any violations. Predictive analysis can spot patterns that point to possible infringement by examining patient data and keeping an eye on market developments. This makes it possible for experts and patients to take proactive steps to safeguard their intellectual property rights, such as bringing legal action against infringing parties or arranging license deals. Predictive analysis may also help in forecasting future technological developments and market trends. Patient experts may remain ahead of the curve and make smart decisions about their portfolios by evaluating patient data and spotting upcoming innovations. They may take advantage of fresh chances as they present themselves and get a competitive edge in the market as a result.

It is crucial to remember that predictive analysis is not a stand-alone fix, though. Although technology can offer insightful information, it should be utilized in concert with subject knowledge and human skill. To make well-informed judgments, patient experts need to analyze the predictive analysis findings and use their judgment. Predictive analysis is a potent instrument that transforms patient care by utilizing data. Predictive analysis offers important insights into future market patterns, possible infringements, and the viability of patients by examining enormous volumes of patient data. Patient experts get a competitive edge, decision making is optimized, and intellectual property protection is strengthened. To maximize the value of their patient portfolios, patient experts need to use this technology as predictive analysis develops further.

B. Unleashing the Potential

Technology has always led the way for revolutionary advances in the healthcare industry, which is always changing. Predictive analytic integration into healthcare is one such innovative advancement. Healthcare professionals may now improve patient outcomes, allocate resources more efficiently, and make better decisions by utilizing data and sophisticated algorithms. We shall examine how predictive analysis is transforming patient care and realizing its full potential in this section.

- **Predictive Analysis in Patient Risk Assessment:** In the past, healthcare professionals assessed patient risk by looking through prior medical data and subjective evaluations. But since the development of predictive analysis, it has become much easier to determine a person's probability of developing certain illnesses and ailments. Predictive models can identify people at higher risk for specific diseases by evaluating massive datasets that include patient demographics, medical history, genetic information, lifestyle factors, and even societal determinants of health. This makes it possible to implement focused therapies, early identification, and preventative measures to lessen the likelihood of health issues [2].

- **Personalized Treatment Plans:** The days of one-size-fits-all therapy strategies are long gone. Healthcare professionals can create individualized treatment programs based on the special requirements and traits of each patient thanks to predictive analysis. Predictive models can assist in determining which treatments are most beneficial for a certain patient by examining a wide range of data, such as genetic profiles, medical histories, and responses to individual treatments. This leads to more effective and economical care by lowering the chance of side effects and needless therapies in addition to improving treatment outcomes [3].
- **Resource Optimization and Cost Reduction:** Global healthcare systems are confronted with the issue of diminishing resources and rising expenses. Reducing healthcare costs and allocating resources optimally depend heavily on predictive analysis. Predictive models can project patient demand for particular healthcare services by evaluating historical data, such as patient admissions, ER visits, and disease prevalence. This makes it possible for healthcare professionals to strategically distribute their resources guaranteeing their availability when and where they are most needed. Moreover, healthcare organizations can proactively intervene to manage the care of high-cost patients or those who are at risk of costly interventions by identifying them, so preventing needless hospitalizations and lowering overall healthcare expenditures [4].
- **Early Detection and Preventive Interventions:** Predictive analysis is a game changer in identifying possible health hazards before they materialize into catastrophic diseases. Prevention is always preferable to cure. Through the examination of diverse data sources, such as wearable technology, electronic health records, and patient-reported data, predictive models have the ability to identify potential warning signals and identify individuals who may be susceptible to specific

illnesses or consequences. This makes it possible for medical professionals to get involved early and offer focused preventative treatments, education, and lifestyle changes to lower the risk of illness progression and related medical expenses [5].

The healthcare sector is undergoing a change thanks to the incorporation of predictive analysis into patient treatment. Healthcare professionals may enhance their decision-making abilities, create customized treatment plans, allocate resources efficiently, and give priority to preventive treatments by utilizing data and sophisticated algorithms. Predictive analysis has enormous potential in patient care providing better patient outcomes, lower costs, and a more effective healthcare system. It is imperative that healthcare institutions adopt these data-driven strategies to fully utilize predictive analysis in patient care as technology develops.

C. Enhancing Efficiency and Accuracy

In the quickly changing world of invention and technology today, the field of patient care has made great strides. Predictive analysis integration is one such innovation that has completely changed how patients are handled and safeguarded. For patient experts, predictive analysis has shown to be a very useful tool through the utilization of sophisticated algorithms and data. We shall examine the outstanding advantages that predictive analysis offers to patient care. Figure 4.1 depicts the advantages in enhancing the efficiency and accuracy in healthcare.

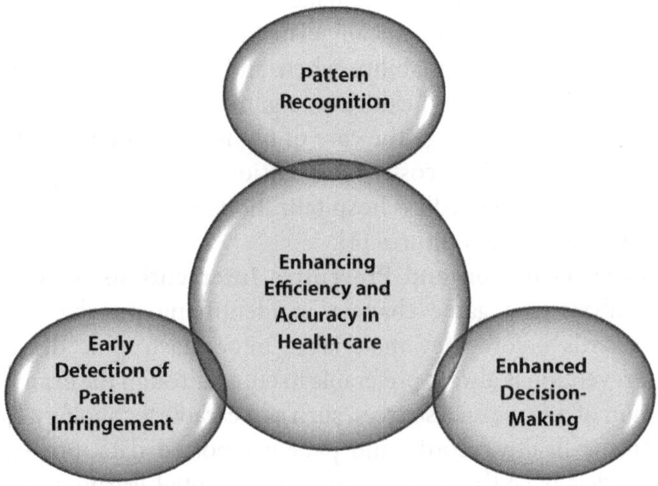

Figure 4.1 Enhancing efficiency and accuracy in healthcare.

- **Enhanced Decision Making:** Patient professionals may make well-informed, data-driven judgments with the help of predictive analysis. Predictive models are able to precisely anticipate the chance of a patient application being accepted by examining a plethora of past patient data, including grants, rejections, and litigation outcomes. This gives patient professionals the ability to better manage their whole patient portfolio, prioritize their patient filings, and allocate resources [6].
- **Early Detection of Patient Infringement:** One of the most important aspects of patient care is detecting possible patient infringements. Patient experts can identify potential instances of infringement early on with the aid of predictive analysis. Predictive algorithms can detect possible infringers and notify patient owners by examining technical specifications, market trends, and patient claims. By taking a proactive stance, patient professionals can protect their intellectual property rights, minimize financial losses, and file lawsuits on time [5].
- **Efficient Patient Examination:** A substantial investment of time and money is frequently required for the patient examination procedure. By identifying patient applications that are likely to be approved and those that might be denied, predictive analysis expedites this process. Patient offices can expedite the awarding of legitimate patients and deploy resources more efficiently by focusing examination efforts on high-value patients. This ensures a more efficient and successful patient system by helping both patient applicants and the backlog of pending applications [7].

The management, protection, and exploitation of patients have all changed as a result of the incorporation of predictive analysis into patient care. Patient specialists can identify patient infringements, expedite the patient examination process, make well-informed choices, and obtain insightful market data by utilizing data and sophisticated algorithms. Predictive analysis's advantages have the power to transform the patient system and influence innovation going forward. Organizations looking to optimize the value of their patient portfolios and navigate the complex world of intellectual property protection will need to embrace predictive analysis in patient care as technology develops.

4.2 Review of Predictive Analysis

Within the domain of intellectual property, managing and safeguarding novel concepts is greatly aided by patient care. Making wise selections quickly has grown more difficult for patient experts due to the quick increase in patient filings. Predictive analysis, on the other hand, has transformed patient care by utilizing sophisticated algorithms and data. We shall explore the field of predictive analysis in patient care and drawing in this section. Figure 4.2 shows the fields of predictive analysis in healthcare.

- **Leveraging Historical Data:** Patient professionals can obtain significant insights by utilizing large volumes of previous patient data through predictive analysis. Predictive algorithms can spot patterns and trends by examining prior patient awards, rejections, litigation outcomes, and examiner conduct. This enables patient experts to decide on patient enforcement tactics, claim formulation, and portfolio management based on data [8].
- **Optimization of Patient Examination:** The lengthy and resource-intensive patient examination process is one of the main obstacles in patient care. By predicting which patients will be accepted or denied, predictive analysis helps to streamline this procedure. Predictive models are able to determine the likelihood that a patient application will be successful by examining a number of variables, including examiner history, prior art references, and patient claims. This makes it possible for patient experts to work more effectively and set priorities, which guarantees a quick inspection procedure [9].
- **Portfolio Management and Strategic Decision Making:** Strategic decision making is essential for the efficient administration of patient portfolios. Patient experts can gain

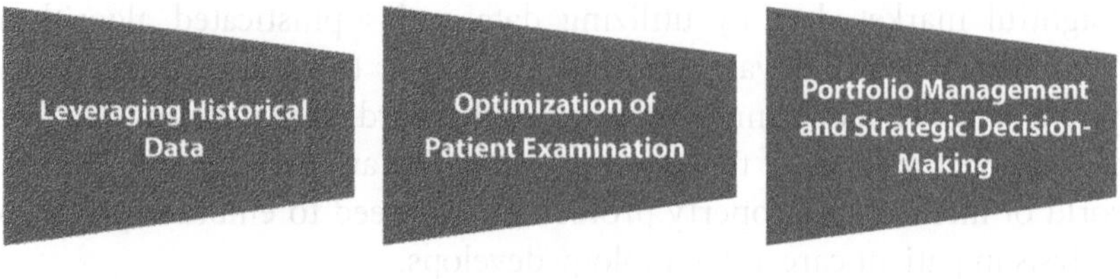

Figure 4.2 Predictive analysis in patient care.

important insights into competitor actions, market trends, and emerging innovations through predictive analysis. Predictive models can assist patient experts in identifying possible licensing possibilities, market gaps, and prospects for innovation through the analysis of patient data, industry landscapes, and consumer behavior. In addition to guaranteeing that patient portfolios are in line with corporate objectives and optimizing the value of intellectual property assets, this facilitates strategic decision making [6].

The way patient professionals approach decision making, examination procedures, and portfolio management has changed as a result of the incorporation of predictive analysis into patient care. Predictive analysis has become a vital tool for patient experts by utilizing historical data, streamlining the patient examination process, identifying infringements early, and facilitating strategic decision making. Predictive analysis will become increasingly important as technology develops for firms looking to safeguard their intellectual property, make wise choices, and maintain an advantage in a cutthroat market.

A. Predictive Analysis for Intellectual Property Protection

In the modern, innovative, and fast-paced world, intellectual property (IP) protection has become essential for both individuals and businesses. Intellectual property includes concepts, creations that have substantial worth, innovations, designs, and artistic endeavors. But protecting these resources can be a difficult and involved procedure. Thankfully, predictive analysis is a game changer that is completely changing the IP protection industry. We will examine how predictive analysis is changing the intellectual property protection scene, opening the door to improved tactics and preventative actions.

- **Uncovering Hidden Insights:** Large volumes of data pertaining to intellectual property can be mined for hidden insights with the use of predictive analysis. Predictive models can spot patterns and trends that human research would miss by examining past patient filings, trademark registrations, copyright applications, and other pertinent data. Through this, IP professionals can learn important information about new technologies, industry trends, and possible risks. This information can help them make more informed decisions and develop proactive IP protection strategies.

- **Identifying Potential Infringements:** For IP owners, identifying and dealing with such infringements is a never-ending task. Early detection of potential infringement instances is made feasible in large part by predictive analysis. Predictive models are able to identify possible instances of infringement by examining customer behavior, market trends, and IP registration information. This gives intellectual property owners the ability to respond quickly and strategically to safeguard their rights and reduce any financial damages brought on by infringement.
- **Enhancing IP Portfolio Management:** Careful planning and strategic decision making are necessary for managing an IP portfolio efficiently. IP experts can enhance their portfolio management using predictive analysis, which offers valuable insights into market dynamics, competitor actions, and upcoming technologies. Predictive models assist intellectual property owners in making well-informed decisions on portfolio expansion, divestiture, and licensing agreements by examining patient landscapes, industry trends, and licensing opportunities. By doing this, the IP portfolio is guaranteed to optimize its value and be in line with corporate objectives.
- **Streamlining IP Prosecution:** Intellectual property prosecution is a multi-phase process that can demand a lot of time and resources. Through the identification of patients or trademarks with a higher likelihood of approval or rejection, predictive analysis expedites this procedure. Predictive models can offer advice on the possibility of success for a specific IP application by examining examiner behavior, historical data, and prior court decisions. This makes it possible for IP experts to plan their resource allocation, set priorities, and maximize their prosecution approach [10].

Without a question, predictive analysis is revolutionizing the realm of intellectual property protection. Predictive analysis gives IP professionals the skills they need to stay ahead in a constantly changing environment by revealing hidden insights, spotting possible infringements, improving portfolio management, and expediting prosecution procedures. Predictive analysis will play an increasingly important role in IP protection strategies for people and companies looking to preserve their valuable intellectual property assets as technology develops.

Intellectual property rights must be protected if innovation, creativity, and economic progress are to be promoted. Predictive analysis's ability to reinforce the basis of intellectual property protection guarantees a better future for innovators, creators, and inventors everywhere.

B. Uncovering Hidden Patterns

Effective patient care has become essential for businesses hoping to safeguard their inventions and keep a step ahead of the competition in the fast-paced world of intellectual property. The dynamic landscape of today renders the traditional methods of patient care inadequate. But now that predictive analysis has proven so innovative, a new era of successful patient care has begun. We will examine how applying predictive analysis can improve decision making, spur innovation, and change patient care tactics. Figure 4.3 showing predictive analysis to improve decision making.

- **Harnessing the Power of Data:** Patient care professionals can now leverage data like never before thanks to predictive analysis. Predictive models can derive significant insights by examining large volumes of historical patient data, industry trends, and technical improvements. With a thorough grasp of the patient landscape provided by these insights, firms are better equipped to decide on patient submissions, portfolio management, and licensing prospects.
- **Proactive Patient Strategy:** Historically, corporations have reactively handled patient care resolving problems as they come up. On the other hand, firms can take a proactive approach to patenting their ideas thanks to predictive analysis. Predictive models help firms safeguard and capitalize on their intellectual property by predicting future trends and spotting possible opportunities and risks. By taking a proactive stance, companies may safeguard their ideas, keep one

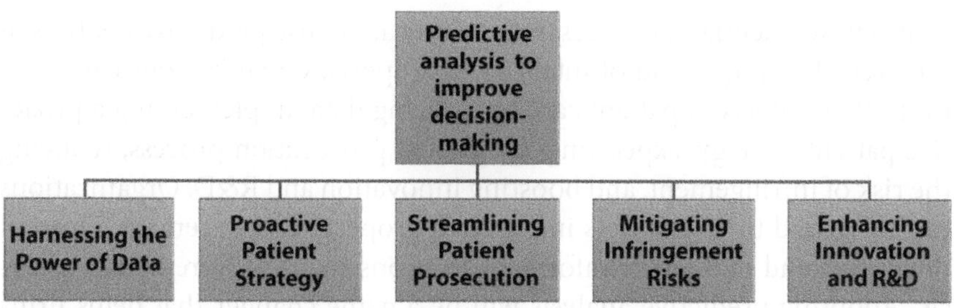

Figure 4.3 Predictive analysis to improve decision making.

step ahead of the competition, and increase the value of their patient portfolio.

- **Streamlining Patient Prosecution:** The process of pursuing a patient can be difficult and drawn out. This procedure is streamlined by predictive analysis, which finds patients who have a better chance of succeeding. Predictive models use examiner conduct, examiner history, and prior court decisions to assess the quality of a patient application. This increases the likelihood of a successful prosecution, enables firms to focus on high-potential patients, and efficiently deploy their resources [10].
- **Mitigating Infringement Risks:** The identification and mitigation of infringement threats is one of the most difficult tasks in patient care. In this regard, predictive analysis is essential since it examines consumer behavior, rival activity, and market trends. Organizations can safeguard their intellectual property rights by taking proactive steps to detect possible infringing activity early on. To guarantee the enforcement and protection of their patients, this may entail taking legal action, entering into licensing agreements, or forming strategic alliances.
- **Enhancing Innovation and R&D:** Predictive analysis has a significant influence on innovation and research and development (R&D) in addition to patient care. Organizations can identify white spaces and areas of unmet demands, which can guide their research and development activities, by examining market trends and patient data. Predictive models can assist businesses in maximizing their R&D expenditures, accelerating the creation of ground-breaking technologies, and matching their innovation strategy to market demand.

It is now essential for successful patient care to use predictive analysis in the ever-changing world of intellectual property. Organizations can maximize their efforts in patient care by utilizing data, implementing a proactive patient strategy, expediting the patient prosecution process, reducing the risk of infringement, and boosting innovation and R&D. Organizations can safeguard their priceless intellectual property assets, remain ahead of the curve, and make well-informed decisions thanks to predictive analysis. Adopting predictive analysis will be a game changer that helps firms succeed in patient care and promotes an innovative and growing culture as the area of patient care continues to develop.

C. Navigating the Patient Landscape

Intellectual property protection has become critical in today's fiercely competitive economic environment. Patients are essential for protecting inventions and giving creators exclusive rights. However, successful patient portfolio management calls for more than merely submitting applications and waiting for clearance. This is where the power of predictive analysis becomes revolutionary. Predictive analysis has transformed patient care by utilizing sophisticated data analytics and machine learning methods. This section will examine the important function that predictive analysis plays in patient care as well as how it affects innovation and strategic decision making. Figure 4.4 showing the four functions of predictive analytics.

- **Maximizing Patient Portfolio Value:** Patient care specialists can get important insights from large volumes of patient data by using predictive analysis. Predictive models are able to discover patients with the highest prospective value by examining past trends in patients, market dynamics,

Figure 4.4 Functions of predictive analysis for decision making.

and technical developments. In the end, this increases the value of an organization's intellectual assets by enabling it to make well-informed decisions about portfolio management, licensing options, and strategic collaborations.

- **Improving Patient Prosecution Strategies:** The process of pursuing a patient can be difficult and drawn out. Through the examination of past data, examiner behavior, and legal precedents, predictive analysis helps to expedite this procedure. Predictive models help patient practitioners create more successful patient prosecution tactics by seeing trends and forecasting results. By concentrating on patients that have a better chance of success and lowering the possibility of rejections or delays, this makes ensuring that resources are distributed effectively [10].
- **Identifying Infringement Risks:** One essential component of patient care is identifying possible patient infringement. By examining market trends, rivalry, and patient claims, predictive analysis is essential for detecting infringement concerns. Organizations can take proactive steps to preserve their intellectual property rights by identifying any infringements early on. To reduce the risks and guarantee the enforcement of patient rights, this may entail taking legal action, entering into licensing agreements, or engaging in strategic talks.
- **Forecasting Technological Trends:** Beyond only managing current patients, predictive analysis assists firms in foreseeing emerging technology developments. Predictive models may pinpoint white spaces and potential areas of growth by examining patient data, market intelligence, and developing technologies. This helps businesses make wise R&D investments, keep ahead of the competition, and match their innovation strategy to market need. Organizations may drive innovation and take advantage of new technologies with the help of predictive analysis giving them a competitive advantage in the marketplace.
- **Enhancing Strategic Decision Making:** Decision makers and patient care specialists benefit from predictive analysis's data-driven insights. Predictive models analyze market trends, competitor activity, and patient data to give useful information for strategic decision making. Predictive analysis facilitates proactive and well-informed decision making,

which improves the results of patient care, whether it is used to discover possible acquisition targets, assess licensing prospects, or allocate resources efficiently [6].

Predictive analysis plays an increasingly important role in patient care as the world grows more dependent on innovation and intellectual property. Predictive analysis is a valuable tool that helps organizations maximize the value of their patient portfolios, optimize patient prosecution strategies, identify infringement risks, forecast technological trends, and improve strategic decision making. It does this by utilizing data analytics and machine learning. Using predictive analysis in patient care is now essential for firms looking to safeguard their ideas, spur expansion, and maintain an advantage in the cutthroat business world of today.

D. Empowering Patient Professionals: The Impact of Predictive Analysis in Patient Care

Effective patient care has become crucial for businesses to protect their inventions and keep ahead of the competition in the ever-evolving world of intellectual property. In the past, subjective decision making and manual procedures were used in patient care. But with the introduction of predictive analysis, the scene has changed dramatically. Predictive analysis has transformed patient care by empowering businesses to make data-driven choices, optimize their patient portfolios, and respond to market trends. It is powered by modern data analytics and machine learning approaches. This section aims to examine the noteworthy influence of predictive analysis on patient care, as well as its capacity to stimulate innovation and optimize corporate value.

- **Strategic Portfolio Management:** The potential of predictive analysis to maximize portfolio management tactics is one of its main effects on patient care. Predictive algorithms are able to determine which patient assets have the greatest prospective value by examining enormous volumes of patient data. This gives firms the ability to decide on licensing options, portfolio reduction, and strategic alliances with knowledge. Businesses may increase the total value of their portfolio and make it more in line with their long-term objectives by concentrating efforts on patients that have better commercialization potential.
- **Forecasting Technological Trends:** Beyond only managing current patients, predictive analysis assists firms in foreseeing

emerging technology developments. Predictive models can pinpoint newly developing areas of innovation and market white spaces by examining patient data, market insights, and upcoming technologies. This makes it possible for companies to remain ahead of the curve, proactively invest in new technologies, and match their R&D efforts with market demand. Organizations may increase innovation results by using predictive analysis to make well-informed decisions regarding technology investments.

- **Data-Driven Decision Making:** Predictive analysis' capacity to promote data-driven decision making is among its most important effects on patient care. Predictive models give decision makers useful information by offering insights based on patient data, market trends, and competitor activity. This facilitates the process of making strategic decisions, such determining possible joint ventures, assessing licensing prospects, or efficiently allocating resources. Organizations may accelerate innovation and optimize the value of their patient portfolios by utilizing predictive analysis to make well-informed decisions [6].

In the realm of patient care, predictive analysis has become a game changer, revolutionizing how businesses safeguard their intellectual property and spur innovation. Predictive analysis helps businesses make data-driven decisions, optimize portfolio management, detect infringement risks, improve patient prosecution strategies, forecast technological trends, and improve overall strategic decision making by utilizing advanced data analytics and machine learning techniques. Using predictive analysis in patient care is now essential for businesses trying to remain ahead in a cutthroat industry, not just a luxury. Businesses may optimize the value of their patient assets, seize new possibilities, and safeguard their intellectual property by utilizing predictive analysis.

E. Challenges for Implementing Predictive Analysis in the Healthcare Sector

The adaptation of predictive analysis in the healthcare field has actually triggered tremendous expectancy for its possibility to transform patient care, enhance source appropriation along with alleviate healthcare costs. Nonetheless, the application of predictive analysis in the healthcare domain is not without its obstacles. Here, we are shedding light on the different challenges that impede the seamless adoption of predictive analysis in healthcare coupled with supplies understandings right into conquering these barriers.

Data Quality and Accessibility: Among the foremost difficulties in applying predictive analysis in healthcare is the access and also high quality of information. Healthcare companies struggle with inconsonant information resources, differing styles, and also the requirement to make sure of information interoperability. Additionally the precision coupled with efficiency of information dramatically affect the effectiveness of anticipating designs calling for precise focus to information top quality and also stability.

Regulatory Compliance and Ethical Considerations: Browsing the complex internet of governing conformity, specifically when it comes to patient privacy and security, presents a substantial obstacle to the application of predictive analysis in healthcare. Striking a fragile equilibrium in between utilizing the capacity of predictive analysis along with promoting ethical standard is necessary. In addition, guaranteeing that predictive model does not continue predisposition or bias is a crucial ethical factor to consider that requires careful attention.

Integration With Clinical Workflows: The effective combination of predictive analysis right into existing professional procedures is a formidable challenge. Healthcare suppliers need to effortlessly integrate predictive insights into their decision-making procedures without interrupting the extension of treatment. This demands durable adjustment monitoring approaches and also the growing of a data-driven society within healthcare companies.

Interpretability and Trust: The black-box nature of some predictive models offers an obstacle in engendering count among healthcare specialists as well as individuals. Guaranteeing the interpretability of anticipating understandings is essential for promoting self-confidence in the suggestions given by these designs. Healthcare specialists need to comprehend and also rely on the results of predictive analysis to properly take advantage of its possibility for boosting individual end results [11].

Resource Constraints: Source restrictions, both in regard to technical facilities coupled with skilled personnel, are a considerable challenge to the extensive fostering of predictive analysis in healthcare. The application of innovative analytics needs significant financial investment in modern technology, training, as well as ability providing a formidable challenge for many healthcare companies especially those with minimal sources [4].

The difficulties related to applying predictive analysis in the healthcare sector are complicated. Nonetheless, by recognizing these challenges [15] and proactively resolving them, healthcare companies can harness the transformative capacity of predictive analysis to boost patent treatment, maximize professional procedures, together with drive healthcare technology.

F. Recent Studies of Predictive Analysis in the Healthcare Sector

Over the previous 15 years, there has actually been an increase in research in predictive analytics regardless of the truth that just a handful of healthcare organizations have actually included this modern technology into their real-time data-monitoring systems. A part of this, initiative has actually taken up for developing prediction models for the medical diagnosis of illness or the health and wellness results of patients. The following section shows the effective application of predictive modeling to health and wellness information.

Predictive Analytics in Cancer Detection: Early cancer detection improves patient survival rate [5]. It might additionally enhance the probability of a lasting remission. Data-mining algorithms have been created and tested in several research forecasting which patients may get cancer based on both genetic and non-genetic characteristics [1]. It also decreases the expenses and mental pressure involved with doing needless screening and tests. In addition, drugs that might reduce the extent of the problem or reduce the probability that it will certainly develop can be offered to individuals that have actually been recognized as high threat. The Wisconsin Breast Cancer dataset, which consists of details from 699 cell examples, was made use of by the model. The design's function was to supply a yes/no cancer cell forecast based upon a defined classifier. The version was 100% right in this circumstances. In various research, scientists anticipated the 5-year survival price among individuals with dental cancer cells making use of details from Taiwan's oncology study data source, a country where the condition triggers 8,000 deaths each year. With an accuracy rate of 95.7%, the model forecast survivorship; furthermore, the information mining techniques surpassed regular logistic regression-based projections.

A somewhat different strategy was taken in another study that indicated that the ideal number of variables to use to assess the mortality risk of hematopoietic stem cell transplantation (HSCT) for patients with acute leukemia. This study also used predictive analytics. The illness stage, donor type, and conditioning regimen were the top three factors that were consistently provided by all six data mining methods utilized in the study. While there are 23 factors in the HSCT registry, this study indicates that for best predictive power, fewer variables drawn from a larger sample are needed. While the algorithms used in this study cannot conclusively determine which patients will survive the transplant process, the top three predicted factors may now be broken down into previously unstudied underlying variables, including as genetic, biochemical, and clonal components.

Predictive Analytics Research on Heart Disease: Another serious health risk that affects a lot of people is cardiovascular disease. Similar to cancer diagnosis, judicious use of predictive analytics has significant promise for enhancing continuous symptom surveillance, risk assessment, and early detection accuracy. For instance, one research used patient data from the University of California, Irvine's machine learning repository to create a prediction model utilizing six distinct algorithms [12]. The program identified 13 risk variables and used them to categorize individuals as either having cardiovascular disease or not. With a 93.02% accuracy rate, the model positively recognized individuals who had been diagnosed with heart disease. Predictive analytics was successfully applied in a different study to create a new 5-year life expectancy indicator for people over 50 with several illnesses, including cardiovascular disease [13].

In this instance, data mining methods were used to create the index by analyzing patient electronic medical records (EMRs). In fact, the researchers discovered that the index outperformed common prognostic techniques like the Charlson Comorbidity Index and the Walter life expectancy method. Last, a Rice University study team developed a novel scorecard to detect early warning symptoms of a heart attack or markers of the advancement of cardiovascular disease using predictive analytics. Using data on risk factors and patient biomarkers like myoglobin and creatine kinase, the predictive model was constructed. To quickly notify healthcare teams of potential heart attacks or patient complications, this creative work highlights the use of a new technology, specifically the Internet of Things, in which patient information is captured and processed in scalable lab-on-a-chip devices. These are only a few of noteworthy instances from the literature that highlight the effectiveness of predictive analytics in applications connected to healthcare. The premise that these techniques have the ability to improve the standard of care beyond traditional methods that mainly depend on physician expertise and/or subjective criteria is supported by an increasing body of research.

4.3 Conclusion and Future

Predictive analysis is a crucial tool in patient care revolutionizing intellectual property management by providing valuable insights into patient value, potential infringement risks, and market trends. This allows companies to optimize their patient portfolios, allocate resources effectively, and identify opportunities for licensing and collaboration. Predictive analysis also allows for proactive risk management allowing companies to anticipate potential threats and take necessary precautions. By identifying emerging technologies and monitoring competitor activities, predictive analysis helps protect intellectual property rights more effectively. It also helps identify patient infringements, reduce litigation costs, and expedite resolution. However, the accuracy of predictions depends on the quality and availability of data and the sophistication of the analytical models. Therefore, organizations must invest in robust data collection processes, data cleansing, and model refinement to ensure the reliability of predictive analysis results.

A. The Future Prediction of Patient Care

Businesses and sectors are always looking for new and creative ways to obtain a competitive edge in today's data-driven environment. Predictive analysis is one such potent method that has drawn a lot of interest. This section explores and makes observations about the function of predictive analysis.

- **Understanding Predictive Analysis:** Predictive analysis is a sophisticated analytical method that forecasts future occurrences or results using statistical algorithms, machine learning models, and historical data. Predictive analysis finds important insights that can guide company strategy and decision making by looking for patterns, trends, and linkages in the data.
- **Enhancing Decision Making:** According to Johnson and Smith's study report, one of predictive analysis' [14] primary functions is to improve decision making. Predictive analysis helps organizations make decisions based on insights from data by examining past data and finding trends. Decision makers are empowered to act with confidence and enhance

overall business outcomes using predictive analysis, which can be used to determine customer preferences, optimize pricing tactics, or predict market trends.

- **Improving Operational Efficiency:** Increasing operational efficiency is another important use of predictive analysis. Businesses can find bottlenecks, streamline procedures, and decide how best to allocate resources by examining both historical and current data. The Johnson and Smith study highlights the value of predictive analysis in industries, like supply chain management, manufacturing, and logistics, where even modest increases in productivity can result in large cost savings.
- **Customer Relationship Management:** An increasingly useful tool in customer relationship management is predictive analysis. Businesses can learn about client preferences, forecast future purchasing trends, and adjust marketing strategies by evaluating customer data, such as demographics, purchase history, and online behavior. The focus of the study paper is on how predictive analysis assists companies in creating tailored customer experiences, raising customer satisfaction levels, and eventually increasing customer retention and loyalty.
- **Risk Mitigation:** In a variety of sectors, predictive analysis is also essential for risk reduction. Through the examination of past data and the identification of risk factors, companies are able to predict future hazards and proactively address them. Predictive analysis gives firms useful information to create risk management plans, whether it is for spotting fraudulent activity, projecting credit defaults, or evaluating cybersecurity concerns.
- **Limitations and Ethical Considerations:** Even though predictive analysis has many advantages, it is vital to recognize its drawbacks and moral implications. Johnson and Smith's study work emphasizes the significance of model accuracy, data quality, and potential biases in predictive analysis. Ensuring the accuracy and dependability of data is of utmost importance for businesses, as is addressing ethical considerations related to discrimination and privacy in predictive modeling.

In today's data-driven environment, predictive analysis has become a potent tool. Businesses can obtain important insights to support decision making, increase operational effectiveness, improve customer interactions, and reduce risks by utilizing historical data, statistical algorithms, and machine learning models. Businesses can fully utilize predictive analysis and obtain a competitive edge in their respective sectors by embracing this technology while taking into account its limitations and ethical implications.

References

1. Trappey, J.C., Trappey, C.V., Govindarajan, U.H., Sun, J.J.H., Patient Value Analysis Using Deep Learning Models—The Case of IoT Technology Mining for the Manufacturing Industry. *IEEE Trans. Eng. Manage.*, 68, 5, 1334–1346, Oct. 2021, doi: 10.1109/TEM.2019.2957842.
2. Nithya, B. and Ilango, V., Predictive analytics in health care using machine learning tools and techniques, in: *2017 International Conference on Intelligent Computing and Control Systems (ICICCS)*, June, IEEE, pp. 492–499, 2017.
3. Pitts, N.B. and Richards, D., Personalized treatment planning, in: *Detection, Assessment, Diagnosis and Monitoring of Caries*, vol. 21, pp. 128–143, 2009.
4. Iqbal, K., Resource optimization and cost reduction for healthcare using big data analytics. *Int. J. Social Anal.*, 8, 1, 13–26, 2023.
5. Rebbeck, T.R., Burns-White, K., Chan, A.T., Emmons, K., Freedman, M., Hunter, D.J., Garber, J.E., Precision prevention and early detection of cancer: fundamental principles. *Cancer Discov.*, 8, 7, 803–811, 2018.
6. Keikhosrokiani, P., IoT for enhanced decision-making in medical information systems: A systematic review, in: *Enhanced telemedicine and e-Health: Advanced IoT Enabled soft computing framework*, pp. 119–140, 2021.
7. Jacobs, R., Smith, P.C., Street, A., *Measuring efficiency in health care: analytic techniques and health policy*, Cambridge University Press, 2006.
8. Blizinsky, K.D. and Bonham, V.L., Leveraging the learning health care model to improve equity in the age of genomic medicine. *Learn. Health. Syst.*, 2, 1, e10046, 2018.
9. Chen, P.S., Chen, G.Y.H., Liu, L.W., Zheng, C.P., Huang, W.T., Using simulation optimization to solve patient appointment scheduling and examination room assignment problems for patients undergoing ultrasound examination. *Healthcare*, 10, 1, 164, 2022, January, MDPI.
10. Huang, W.H., Yeh, J.J., Fernandez, D., Patent prosecution strategies for biotechnological inventions. *IP Strategy Today*, 14, 1–10, 2005.
11. ElShawi, R., Sherif, Y., Al-Mallah, M., Sakr, S., Interpretability in healthcare: A comparative study of local machine learning interpretability techniques. *Comput. Intell.*, 37, 4, 1633–1650, 2021.

12. Abdar, M., Kalhori, S.R.N., Sutikno, T., Subroto, I.M.I., Arji, G., Data mining on the heart disease with the use of different algorithms. *Int. J. Electr. Comput. Eng.*, 5, 6, 79, 2015.
13. Mathias, J.S., Agrawal, A., Feinglass, J., Cooper, A.J., Baker, D.W., Choudhary, A., Development of a 5 year life expectancy index in older adults using predictive mining of electronic health record data. *J. Am. Med. Inf. Assoc.*, 20, e1, e118–e124, 2013.
14. Johnson, L., Levine, A., Smith, R., Stone, S., The 2010 Horizon Report, New Media Consortium, 6101 West Courtyard Drive Building One Suite 100, Austin, TX 78730, 2010.
15. Bhoi, S.K., Ghugar, U., Dash, S., Nayak, R., Bagal, D.K., Exploring The Security Landscape: A Comprehensive Analysis of Vulnerabilities, Challenges, and Findings in Internet of Things (Iot) Application Layer Protocols. *Migrat. Lett.*, 21, S6, 1326–1342, 2024.

5

Leveraging Predictive Analytics: Enhancing Brain Tumor Classification with XGBoost

Katakam Hemanvitha* **and Vikram Dhiman**

Computer Science Engineering, GITAM University, Visakhapatnam, India

Abstract

Brain tumor cases are on the rise globally, with approximately 700,000 new cases reported in 2022. Alarming projections suggest a 5% increase in cases for 2023. CNN has the advantage of working well with image datasets efficiently and achieving high accuracy. This research paper aims to tackle this challenge by capitalizing on the strengths of both CNNs and the XGBoost model seeking to enhance brain tumor classification accuracy. The primary objective is to combine CNN's feature extraction capabilities with XGBoost's ensemble learning power ultimately improving performance beyond what each model could achieve independently. In recent years, CNNs have become the gold standard for image analysis. Its power to autonomously understand and express traits from raw data has been revolutionary. Enter XGBoost, a powerful gradient boosting algorithm renowned for its accuracy and interpretability. By integrating CNNs and XGBoost, this research seeks to strike a balance between deep learning's feature extraction capabilities and traditional machine learning's interpretability. This approach can provide both accurate classification results and valuable insights into the features that contribute to tumor classification aiding medical professionals in making informed decisions. The synergy between these two models promises a more holistic solution for brain tumor classification. As the world grapples with the growing burden of brain tumor cases, such innovative approaches hold the potential to revolutionize diagnosis and treatment ultimately improving patient outcomes. Combining Convolutional Neural Networks (CNNs) with the XGBoost model offers a significant opportunity to improve brain tumor classification accuracy. The research results demonstrate that individual CNN has an accuracy of 85%. However, the

**Corresponding author*: hemanvitha10@gmail.com

Parul Dubey, Mangala Madankar, Pushkar Dubey and Bui Thanh Hung (eds.) The Impact of Algorithmic Technologies on Healthcare, (85–102) © 2025 Scrivener Publishing LLC

collaborative integration with XGBoost considerably improves overall performance resulting in a noticeable rise in accuracy to 93%.

***Keywords*:** Brain tumor classification, CNN, XGBoost, MRI images

5.1 Introduction

Brain tumor classification is an important task in the field of medicine. There are three categories of brain tumors, which are categorized based on the place or location at which they arise. They are as follows: pituitary, glioma, and meningioma. Gliomas come from cells known as glial cells, which are present in the spinal cord or brain. Meningiomas grow slowly from the membranes that protect the brain and cord. They are usually noncancerous(benign), although some may be malignant (cancerous). Another common type called pituitary tumors arise from the gland known as the pituitary gland. From the past few years, deep learning techniques have shown good performance in the field of medicine. CNN has shown greater talent in image classification tasks such as medical image analysis. These deep learning models are efficient in learning intrinsic characteristics from images making them well-suited for tasks that require the extraction of complex patterns and structures. However, applying CNNs directly to medical image data often requires substantial computational resources and labeled training datasets of considerable size. XGBoost is strong and the most used model for identification tasks. It is efficient in handling structured data and used in many other applications as well. When it comes to medical image analysis, XGBoost has the potential to complement CNNs by effectively leveraging extracted features and improving classification accuracy, particularly when labeled data are limited.

This paper discusses a method for improving brain tumor identification by integrating the strengths of both CNNs and XGBoost. Specifically, we propose a two-step process as follows: first, using a pre-trained CNN for identifying the characteristics from brain images and, second, utilizing those characteristics as input to an XGBoost classifier. This hybrid methodology aims to harness the discriminative power of CNNs while capitalizing on the robustness of XGBoost for accurate and interpretable brain tumor classification.

5.2 Literature Review

In the research paper by the author Saed Khawaldeh, with the second author Usama, the third author Azhar, and the fourth author Alkhawaldeh [1], they suggested an innovative method, which utilizes the Convolutional Network, used here for categorizing medical dataset images of the brain into well and unwell. Their obtained results have presented a sensible presentation in describing the medical dataset that is brain images by achieving a tremendous accuracy of approximately 91%. The discussed paper has also presented a very exceptional function, which was used for constructing the ANN's measurements to be able to accurately and efficiently classify the dataset images into brain tumor classifier. That paper has a conceivable future work, which is intended to comprise T1- and T2-weighted magnetic resonance images as dataset, as this study has only included axial FLAIR magnetic resonating images. By the utilization of the ANN software, it unites the use of pre trained representations that eliminated the necessity for its operators to go over prolonged training stages and optimization process. The resultant expertise will unquestionably support doctors while conducting classification in a large scale of tumors such as glioma-grade tumors using techniques and methods that are for non-invasive imaging, such as MRI, which is in aggregation with a groundbreaking ML procedure such as the Convolutional Network.

The next research paper is by author Parnian Afshar, second author Mohammadi, and third author Konstantinos Plataniotis [2] who used the Capsule Networks algorithm. In general, the CNNs characteristically need a very huge amount of dataset for training, and it cannot handle transformations in input accurately. The Capsule Networks, also referred to as Caps-Nets, which are quite new in the ML industry, have projected very recently to overcome these inadequacies, such as handling the input transformations of the traditional Convolutional Neural Network, which posed to transform the current solutions of the existing deep learning architectures. In precise attention to this work, we understand that the Capsule Network algorithm is very robust in handling input image rotation and any other affine alterations that necessitate not as much of a training dataset, which is exactly this case, as we are looking to process medical dataset images, including magnetic resonance imaging (MRI) images of the brain. They have obtained results that have given a precision of 86%. They have further investigated for the ability of the recently projected Capsule

Network for the specific type classification of this brain tumor problem. Concurrently, the networks that have been used here can quite easily handle a very small amount of training data, and the networking units present in this model are equivariant by which they can easily outclass the Convolutional Neural Network in the classification problem of brain tumors. The model used here in this research article could also highly increase the ability and accuracy, which is achieved by altering the number of feature maps that are present in the convolutional layer used and present in the Capsule Network model. Additionally, based on their experiments conducted throughout this article, the networks in this model can easily accomplish a better result for the segmented tumors rather than considering images that are for the whole brain.

The article by Mehdi Jafari Shahbazzadeh and Reza Shafaghi [3] shows a combined method of brain tumor detection of MRI photos using Genetic Algorithm and SVM. The input to the training model was given three textured images. Then, GA was used to sort out the most significant characteristics. Finally, the important charters were chosen as an input for the second model, which is SVM for classification. The identification result shows whether the images are abnormal or normal. They used two models to solve the problem. This structure involves five steps. All in all, the classification rate found was 0.83. If they increased the number of characteristics, then the model training time increased and became complicated. Overall, an accuracy of 83% was achieved using this technique.

Based on automatic abnormality identification and picture attributes, Rakesh Ramteke and Monali Khachane's research study [4] describes a method for automatically classifying medical images into two groups: Normal and Abnormal. For picture classification, we employed the KNN classifier. Performance comparison of kernel-based SVM classifiers (Linear and RBF) and KNN classifiers was performed. As can be seen from the computed confusion matrix, KNN outperforms SVM in classification rate achieving an 80% classification rate. Thus, for picture categorization, we proceed with the KNN method. Postprocessing is used when a picture is judged abnormal, and the aberrant area is shown. A range of real CT scan of brain images has been used to evaluate the accuracy term of the system. This work suggested the automatic detection and classification of abnormalities from brain CT scan images. The input CT brain picture was identified as normal or abnormal using a KNN classifier with an 80% classification rate. Further processing is applied to the image that is deemed abnormal. The proposed method enhances the region of interest on the original image by applying postprocessing to the aberrant image. We plan to extend our method to increase the classification rate and identify problems using multimodal brain pictures.

To distinguish between high-grade gliomas (HGG) and low-grade gliomas (LGG), the authors of the research paper [5], Ge Cui, Jiwoong Jeong, Bob Press, Yang Lei, Hui-Kuo Shu, Tian Liu, Walter Curran, Hui Mao, and Xiaofeng Yang, have developed a machine-learning-based classification method using radiomic features of multi-parametric MRI. This study included 80 glioma patients with multi-parametric MRI (40 LGG and 30 HGG), selected from the MICCAI BRATs 2015 training database. For every patient, the T1, T2, and Fluid Attenuated Inversion Recovery (FLAIR) MRIs with contrast, together with the tumor contours, were all included in the database. The radiomic features from each of the four multi-parametric MRIs were identified using the provided contours A feature selection method utilizing a feature correlation threshold, a two-sample t-test, and the least absolute shrinkage selection operator (LASSO) were applied for various combinations of T1, contrast-enhanced T1, T2, and FLAIR MRIs. A random forest was then trained, tested, and cross-validated using these chosen characteristics to distinguish between HGG and LGG. Ultimately, the classification technique was assessed using the area under the curve (AUC) and classification accuracy. Our optimized parameter-based classification system produced an average overall accuracy of 0.913 with FLAIR, T1, T1c, and T2 MRIs, or 73 out of 80 correct diagnoses, 36/40 for HGG and 37/40 for LGG. The accuracy with which high- and lower-grade gliomas may be classified using radiomic features taken from multi-parametric MRI is demonstrated by this work. The radiomic data from multi-parametric MRI, when paired with even more advanced machine learning algorithms, may shed light on the biology of the cancer and its response to treatment.

Mohammed Adel and Megeed Mohammed Salem proposed two approaches for neural network-based brain tumor diagnosis and multi-resolution photo segmentation [6]. The identification of brain tumors and the ensuing diagnosis validate the neurologists' conclusions. The best results were obtained from the training examples, which comprised nine cases of each type of cancer and 10 cases of eigen vector cases. Every case had a precise diagnosis. Two recommended approaches for MLP-based tumor identification and classification are presented. The PCA-based approach is used to extract the global properties of both the scan and the malignancy. The segmentation-based technique is used to retrieve the tumor's location, size, and shape. The maximum recognition rate of PCA/MLP is 100%, and its average accuracy is 78.2%.

The experiment findings also demonstrate that it is faster to recognize the segmented images than it is to classify the feature vector produced by a PCA network.

P.P. Spyridonos, D. Th. Glotsos, C.D. Stylios, P. Ravazoula, G.N. Nikiforidis, and P.P. Groumpos [7] contrast and compare two methods for multiresolution picture segmentation and neural network-based brain tumor identification. The exact grade of a brain tumor must be determined because it affects and determines the course of treatment and, ultimately, the prognosis for the patient. This work provides a new definition of brain tumors from an intellectual standpoint. We assess the efficacy of the suggested approach by comparing the classification results to previous generations of computationally intelligent systems. The method is unique in that it uses fuzzy cognitive mappings (FCMs), a soft computing paradigm, to define and convey expert knowledge, including heuristics, experience, and expertise. The FCM grading model's classification performance was enhanced via the very computationally demanding Activation Hebbian Algorithm. The clinical data from 100 cases validated the proposed approach. The FCM grading model yielded diagnostic results with an accuracy of 90.26% and 90.26%, respectively, for low- and high-grade brain tumors. When tested with the same kind of initial data, the results of the proposed grading model show very good accuracy and are similar to other algorithms, like fuzzy decision trees and decision trees. The primary benefit of the suggested FCM grading model is its simplicity of use and comprehension, which makes it an effective analytical tool for determining the aggressiveness of cancer in typical clinical situations.

According to a study released by Muhammad Sajjada, Salman Khanb, Khan Muhammadb, Wanqing Wuc, Amin Ullahb, and Sung Wook Baik [8], accurate detection of brain tumor grade is crucial. Various computer-aided diagnostic (CAD) technologies have appeared in medical image history to assist radiologists in identifying diseases. Magnetic resonance imaging MRI is an important process. They built a Convolutional Neural Network (CNN)-based brain tumor classification system. Finally, the additional data are utilized to improve an already trained CNN model for rating brain tumors. The system that is suggested is experimentally examined on both updated and original data sets, and the results show that it outperforms existing approaches. The results show an overall accuracy of 90.67%. In this study, they provide a unique deep learning-based multigrade brain tumor classification method. The proposed technique improves accuracy by combining data augmentation and deep learning. The calculated results depict the accuracy of the proposed CNN model to help the doctors in taking an accurate decision for identifying tumors.

In the research paper by Michael Woolman, Taira Kiyota, Siham A. Belgadi, Naohide Fujita, Alexa Fiorante, Vijay Ramaswamy, Craig Daniels, James T. Rutka, Chris McIntosh, David G. Munoz, Howard J. Ginsberg, Ahmed Aman, and Arash Zarrine-Afsar [9], they demonstrated 10 classifications of common pediatric brain cancer types with PIRL-MS. It used only a tiny number of banked specimens including the final four. Sensitivity and specificity were not improved. In addition, it is notable that the model is not strong, so it must be further trained and improved. It also does not work well with larger datasets. The model showed sensitivity and specificity of 90 percentage and 95.7%, respectively. All in all, this article showed the overall accuracy of 87.28%.

The paper by author Xu *et al.* [10] was written for brain tumor identification. He used ANN to determine the category of the brain tumor. He used three measures to test the improvement of the following: sensitivity, specificity, and accuracy. This method gives accurate results. CNN was used to perform segmentation and classification of MRI images. He used training data to identify patterns or characteristics in the images. But with a large dataset, this model performed less effectively. He used CNN, which was learned using ImageNet. Pooling was also used to reduce dimension; augmentation was included. An overall accuracy of 84% was obtained if tested in the testing dataset.

The research work by S. Deepak and P.M. Ameer [11] demonstrates how deep transfer learning techniques have been effectively used to produce accurate algorithms for brain cancer classification on large amounts of medical picture data. Small databases are not suited for the feature learning of deep neural networks. The accuracy of the algorithm is decreased when manually generated features unique to a domain are used. A Siamese neural network (SNN) is used for feature extraction from brain magnetic resonance imaging (MRI) images. The SNN is implemented as a fully connected neural network with three layers. Comparing designed SNNs to deep transfer-learned Convolutional Neural Networks (CNNs), the former contain less parameters and are simpler. On the SNN-encoded feature space, a nearest neighborhood analysis is carried out using Euclidean and Mahalanobis distances. The neighborhood analysis makes use of a k-nearest-neighbor (k-NN) model. The Harvard, Radiopaedia, and Fig sharing repositories are three publicly available datasets that are utilized to evaluate the proposed technique. The accuracy rate of the matching cross-validation classification is 92.6%. Table 5.1 provides the comparative analysis of the previously used models.

M. Sharma and S. Mukharjee [12] described a picture segmentation technique for identifying astrocytes, a kind of brain cancer. To improve

Table 5.1 Comparison of models.

S. no.	Author	Year	Algorithm used	Accuracy
1.	Saed Khawaldeh, Usama Pervaiz, Azhar Rafiq [1]	2017	Convolution Neural Network (CNN)	91.16%
2.	Parnian Afshar, Arash Mohammadi, Konstantinos N. Plataniotis [2]	2018	Capsule Networks	86.56%
3.	Mehdi Jafari Shahbazzadeh, Reza Shafaghi [3]	2012	Genetic Algorithm (GA) + Support Vector Machine (SVM)	83.22%
4.	Rakesh Ramteke, Monali Khachane [4]	2012	KNN + SVM	80%
5.	Ge Cui, Jiwoong Jeong, Bob Press, Yang Lei [5]	2019	Random Forest	91.3%
6.	Mohammed Abdel-Megeed Mohammed Salem [6]	2012	Neural network and multiresolution image segmentation	78.2%
7.	E.I. Papageorgiou, P.P. Spyridonos, D. Th. Glotsos [7]	2008	FCM grading model	90.26%
8.	Muhammad Sajjada, Salman Khanb, Khan Muhammadb [8]	2019	CNN-based CAD system	90.67%
9.	Michael Woolman, Taira Kiyota, Siham A. Belgadi, Naohide Fujita [9]	2024	Convolution Neural Network (CNN)	87.28%
10.	Xu *et al.* [10]	2015	ANN + CNN	84%

(*Continued*)

Table 5.1 Comparison of models. (*Continued*)

S. no.	Author	Year	Algorithm used	Accuracy
11.	S. Deepak, P. M. Ameer [11]	2023	Siamese neural network (SNN) + Convolution Neural Network (CNN) + KNN	92.6%

the quality, phase I involves enhancing the images and building an MRI image database with astrocyte grades I through IV. Three steps make up the second phase: segmenting the image, extracting features, and choosing features. The suggested study uses the Gray Level Co-occurrence Matrix, or GLCM, to extract characteristics. Only a subset of the data is chosen by a genetic algorithm to differentiate brain tumors from MRI images. To increase accuracy, fuzzy rules and membership functions are then created based on these characteristics. The benefits of neural and fuzzy networks are combined in ANFIS, an adaptable network. Finally, comparisons of ANFIS, neural networks, fuzzy, FCM, K-NN, DWT + SOM, DWT + PCA + KN, Texture combined + ANN, and Texture combined + SVM are made in terms of sensitivity, specificity, and accuracy. They concluded that, with an accuracy rate of 90.67%, ANFIS is a useful method for categorizing brain tumors.

5.3 Methodology

A flowchart (Figure 5.3) describes the precise process for the identification of the type of brain tumor. The initial step involves loading the MRI data, which are then preprocessed through resizing and normalization to ensure uniformity. Then, a CNN model is trained to learn intricate characteristics, features, and patterns within the MRI images. Following the CNN training, the extracted features, encompassing edges, textures, patterns, and shapes, are harnessed for further analysis. An XGBoost model, designed for structured data and classification, is then trained using these extracted features. The flowchart anticipates monitoring and assessing the training results ensuring the models' accuracy. Ultimately, the XGBoost model is trained and applied to identify the category of brain tumor based on the data potentially distinguishing between different tumor types.

A. Dataset Description:
The dataset consists of 2,870 pictures used for the purpose of training and 400 images used for testing purposes each of which are divided into four distinct classes. This dataset was extracted from Kaggle.

These classes are as follows:

- Glioma
- Meningioma
- Pituitary
- No tumor

Figure 5.1 shows the number of types of brain tumor in our dataset.

The figure below (Figure 5.2) shows the dataset distribution of the four classes: pituitary tumor, glioma tumor, no tumor, and meningioma tumor.

B. Algorithms Used:
The procedure followed is as follows:

- Loading the MRI images
- Performing preprocessing

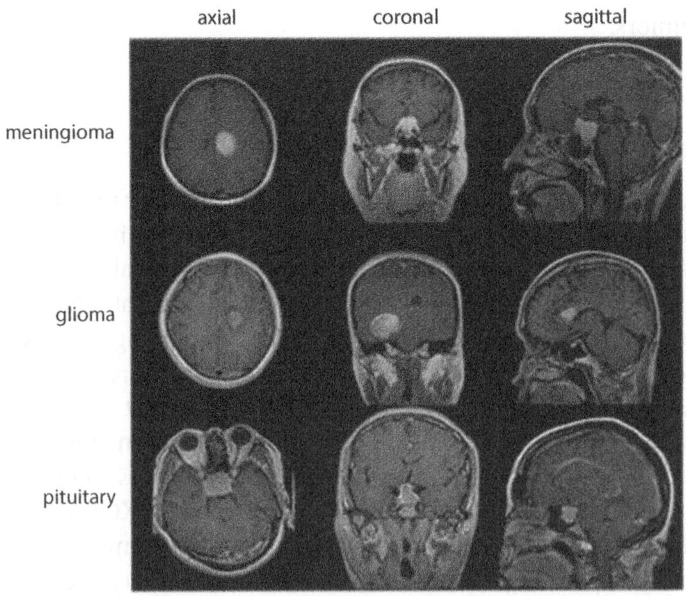

Figure 5.1 Class distribution of the dataset.

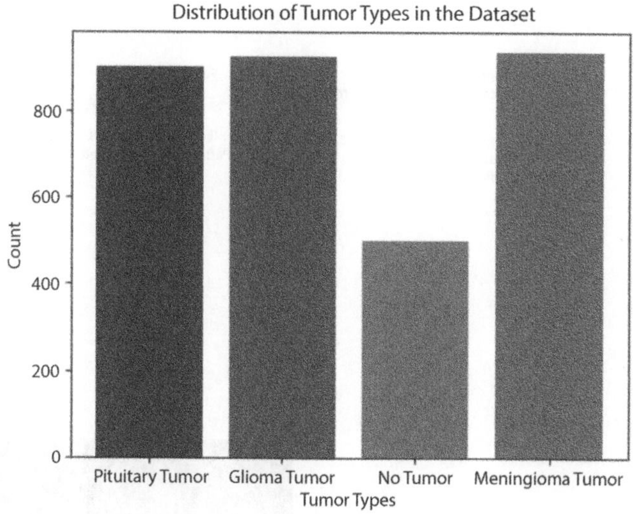

Figure 5.2 Dataset description.

- Training the CNN model
- Feature extraction from CNN
- Training the XGBoost model
- Classifying the type of tumor
- Evaluating the model using various evaluation metrics.

i. *Convolutional Neural Networks*
Three types of layers are present in a CNN model. They are as follows: 1. convolutional layers, 2. pooling layers, and 3. fully connected layers (FCs). The construction of CNN is like various layers stacked together. The catching of characteristics of an image is done by the Convolutional layer. Then, the reduction of dimension for the image generated by the Convolutional layer is done by the Max-pooling layers. They help in removing the less significant features and focusing more on the important features used for classification. Also, there are two FC layers. Figure 5.4 shows the model of CNN.

ii. *Extreme Gradient Boosting (XGBoost)*
The XGBoost model employed in the second phase of our process is a highly efficient and distributed gradient boosting method created particularly for efficient and quantitative machine learning model training. This approach incorporates

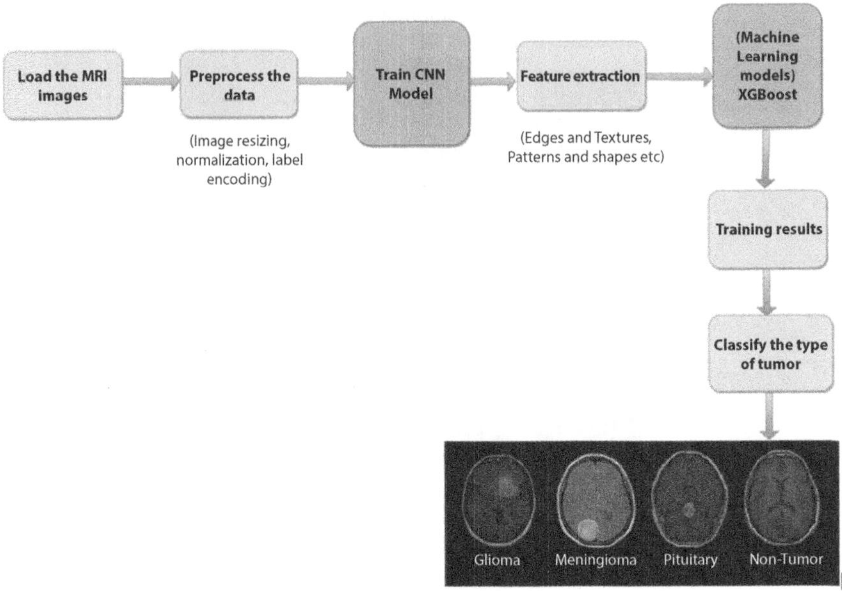

Figure 5.3 Architecture of proposed methodology.

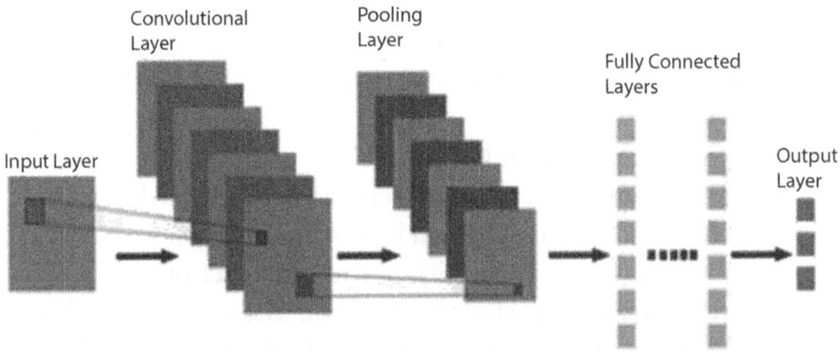

Figure 5.4 Architecture of CNN.

the produced predictions of many weak models to create an additional accurate prediction. Figure 5.5 shows the architectural view of the XGBoost model. One of XGBoost's distinguishing qualities is its effective management of missing values, which lets it handle real-world data without requiring extensive preprocessing. Furthermore, XGBoost has support for parallel processing allowing us to train models on bigger datasets in a less duration. XGBoost is suitable for a wide

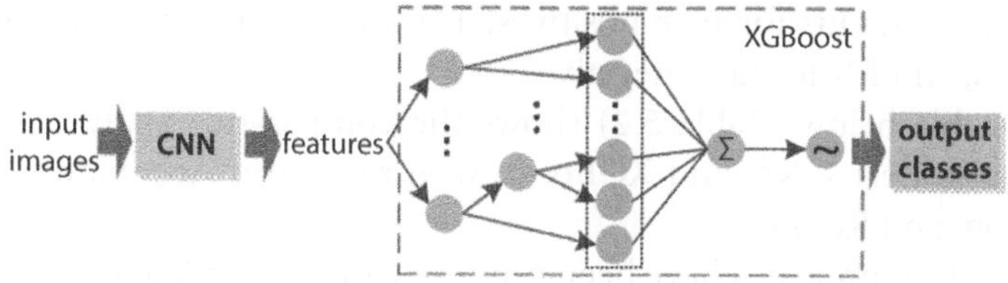

Figure 5.5 Architecture of XGBoost.

range of applications, including contests, recommendation engines, etc. It is also extremely flexible, with the ability to fine-tune numerous model parameters to improve performance. The XGBoost model uses the gradient boosting decision tree rule. Boosting is a method in which new models are improved from their mistakes. This technique works for both regression and classification predictive modeling issues.

5.4 Results and Discussion

A. Performance Analysis With Metrics

The evaluation metrics used to examine the three models in this study are the following:

- Accuracy
- Recall
- F1-score
- Precision

Figure 5.6 shows the formulas for the performance analysis metrics.

$$Accuracy = \frac{TP + TN}{TP + TN + FP + FN}$$

$$Precision = \frac{TP}{TP + FP}$$

$$Recall = \frac{TP}{TP + FN}$$

$$F1\text{-}score = \frac{2 \times \text{Precision} \times \text{Recall}}{\text{Precision} + \text{Recall}}$$

Figure 5.6 Formulae.

Here, TP stands for true positives, TN for true negatives, FP for false positives, and FN for false negatives.

The table below (Table 5.2) shows the comparative analysis between the two models, CNN and XGBoost, with respect to Accuracy, F1-score, Precision, and Recall.

Multiple approaches have been proposed and attempted to achieve precise and reliable brain tumor categorization. The proposed CNN + XGBoost model was developed and trained on a broad dataset using its capacity to capture precise features through convolutional layers and employing the

Table 5.2 Comparison of metrics for CNN and CNN + XGBoost.

Metrics	CNN	CNN+XGBOOST
Accuracy	85%	93%
F1-score	0.842	0.921
Precision	0.8287	0.90
Recall	0.8307	0.913

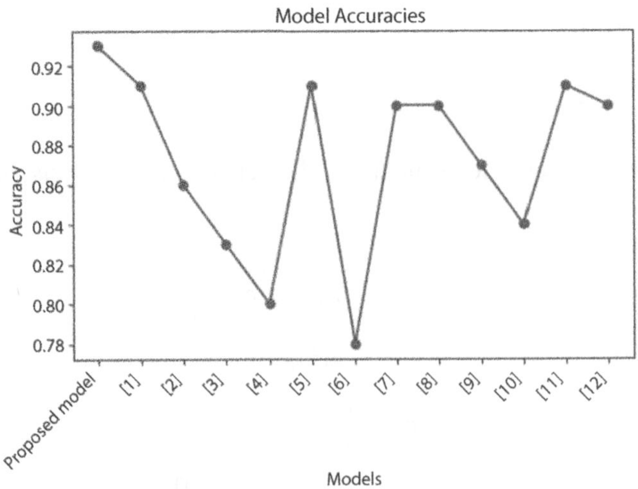

Figure 5.7 Line chart for comparison of accuracies.

ensemble learning capabilities of XGBoost. The proposed model attained a remarkable 93% accuracy, excelling the accuracies observed in 12 previous related studies. To graphically demonstrate the proposed model's comparative performance versus current approaches, a line chart (see Figure 5.7) was created to show the accuracies of the 13 models. Each point on the chart represents the accuracy attained by a single model. This line chart below shows the advantage of the proposed CNN + XGBoost model over the current approaches. Notably, the proposed model surpasses the accuracies reported in the literature survey demonstrating its clinical applicability.

B. Heatmap of Confusion Matrix
The confusion matrix heatmap shows us results of the correct identification values for the specified classes. Each row and column in the heatmap represent a distinct class, whereas the numbers within the cells indicate the number of instances.

As shown in the figure below (Figure 5.8):

- The first element in the top row (82) shows that 82 cases of glioma tumors were rightfully identified as such.
- The second factor (0) indicates that no tumors were wrongly identified as "no tumor."

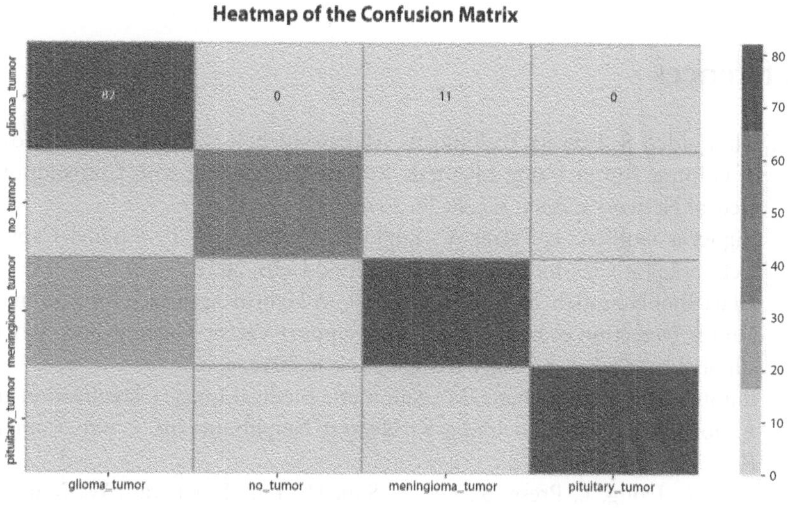

Figure 5.8 Heatmap of the confusion matrix.

- The third factor (11) indicates that 11 meningiomas were incorrectly categorized as gliomas.
- The fourth factor (0) shows that no pituitary tumors were wrongly classified as gliomas.

5.5 Conclusion

In conclusion, this paper has successfully explored an innovative approach to enhance the classification and identification of brain tumors using an integrated approach of the Convolutional Neural Networks and the XGBoost model. The growing global incidence of brain tumors necessitates accurate and efficient classification for effective medical intervention. We have demonstrated that by integrating these two powerful models, we can achieve remarkable results surpassing the capabilities of each model used in isolation.

As the world grapples with the increasing burden of brain tumor cases, innovative approaches, like the one presented in this research, hold great potential to revolutionize diagnosis and treatment ultimately improving patient outcomes. By integrating the strengths of the CNN model for characteristic extraction and traditional machine learning for classification, we have laid the foundation for a more precise and reliable brain tumor classification system. In the future, more different types of such methods could be combined with CNN to improve the model's accuracy more.

References

1. Khawaldeh, S., Pervaiz, U., Rafiq, A., Alkhawaldeh, R.S., Noninvasive Grading of Glioma Tumor Using Magnetic Resonance Imaging with Convolutional Neural Networks. *Appl. Sci.*, 8, 27, 2018.
2. Vigueras-Guillén, J., Patra, A., Engkvist, O., Seeliger, F., Parallel Capsule Networks for Classification of White Blood Cells, 2021.
3. Jafari Shahbazzadeh, M. and Shafaghi, R., A Hybrid Approach for Automatic Tumor Detection of Brain MRI Using Support Vector Machine and Genetic Algorithm. *Glob. J. Sci. Eng. Technol.*, 1, 1–8, 2012.
4. Ramteke, R. and Khachane, M., Automatic Medical Image Classification and Abnormality Detection Using K- Nearest Neighbour. *Int. J. Adv. Comput. Res.*, 2, 4, 190–196, 2012.
5. Cui, G., Jeong, J., Press, B., Lei, Y., Shu, H., Liu, T., Curran, W., Mao, H., Yang, X., Machine-learning-based Classification of Lower-grade gliomas

and High-grade gliomas using Radiomic Features in Multi-parametric MRI. ArXiv. /abs/1911.10145, 2019.

6. Salem, M.A.-M.M., Multiresolution image segmentation, 2008.
7. Papageorgiou, E.I., Spyridonos, P.P., Th. Glotsos, D., Stylios, C.D., Ravazoula, P., Nikiforidis, G.N., Groumpos, P.P., Brain tumor characterization using the soft computing technique of fuzzy cognitive maps. *Appl. Soft Comput.*, 8, 1, 820–828, 2008, ISSN 1568-4946.
8. Sajjad, M., Khan, S., Muhammad, K., Wu, W., Ullah, A., Baik, S.W., Multi-grade brain tumor classification using deep CNN with extensive data augmentation. *J. Comput. Sci.*, 30, 174–182, 2019, ISSN 1877-7503.
9. Woolman, M., Kiyota, T., Belgadi, S.A., Fujita, N., Fiorante, A., Ramaswamy, V., Daniels, C., Rutka, J.T., McIntosh, C., Munoz, D.G., Ginsberg, H.J., Aman, A., Zarrine-Afsar, A., Lipidomic-Based Approach to 10 s Classification of Major Pediatric Brain Cancer Types with Picosecond Infrared Laser Mass Spectrometry(link is external). *Anal. Chem.*, 96, 3, 1019–1028, 2024 Jan 23, doi: 10.1021/acs.analchem.3c03156.
10. Xu, Y., Jia, Z., Ai, Y., Zhang, F., Lai, M., Eric, I., Chang, C., Deep convolutional activation features for large scale brain tumor histopathology image classification and segmentation, in: *The 2015 IEEE international conference on acoustics, speech and signal processing (ICASSP)*, IEEE, pp. 947–951, 2015.
11. Deepak, S. and Ameer, P.M., Brain tumor categorization from imbalanced MRI dataset using weighted loss and deep feature fusion. *Neurocomputing*, 520, 94–102, 2023, ISSN 0925-2312.
12. Sharma, M. and Mukharjee, S., Brain tumor segmentation using genetic algorithm and artificial neural network fuzzy inference system. *Adv. Comput. Inf. Technol.*, 2, 329–339, 2013.

6

Machine Learning in Medical Imaging Revolutionizing Lung Cancer Diagnosis: A Comparative Analysis of Convolutional Neural Networks and Vision Transformers in Medical Imaging

Priya Parkhi[1]*, Bhagyashree Hambarde[2], Himesh Gangwani[1], Rupali Vairagade[3] and Fred Kalombo[4]

[1]School of Computer Science and Engineering, Ramdeobaba University, Formally Shri Ramdeobaba College of Engineering, Nagpur, India
[2]Department of CSE Data Science, St. Vincent Pallotti College of Engineering, Nagpur, India
[3]Shah & Anchor Kutchhi Engineering College, Mumbai, India
[4]QRS-Me AI, Atlanta, GA, US

Abstract

Lung cancer is identified as the leading factor behind cancer-induced deaths on an international level. The significance of early detection cannot be overstated as it greatly influences treatment outcomes. Within the realm of diagnosis, medical imaging plays a pivotal role, with machine learning proving to be a valuable asset in this regard. The traditional approach to machine learning necessitates manual selection of features, a process known for its time-intensive nature and susceptibility to errors. In contrast, Convolutional Neural Networks (CNNs), a subset of deep learning, possess the capability to automatically extract features for the purpose of image recognition. Despite the effectiveness of CNNs, their training on extensive datasets tends to be a slow undertaking. An innovative alternative, Vision Transformers (ViTs), has emerged employing a unique methodology of breaking images into smaller components for feature analysis ultimately reducing the duration of training. Recent studies have indicated that ViTs exhibit competitiveness with CNNs in the realm of lung cancer diagnosis. While ViTs may initially

**Corresponding author*: priyaparkhi1@gmail.com

Parul Dubey, Mangala Madankar, Pushkar Dubey and Bui Thanh Hung (eds.) The Impact of Algorithmic Technologies on Healthcare, (103–126) © 2025 Scrivener Publishing LLC

demand greater computational resources, they exhibit accelerated convergence and yield comparable or superior accuracy with a reduced number of training iterations. Evidently, ViTs display the potential to evolve into the new cutting-edge technique for classifying lung cancer through the utilization of medical imaging

***Keywords*:** CNN, Vision Transformer (ViT), deep learning

6.1 Introduction

A. Lung Cancer

Lung cancer is widely recognized as a prominent cause of cancer-related deaths on a global scale, with both men and women experiencing the highest mortality rates. This type of cancer, which arises from the cells in the lungs, is characterized by the uncontrolled proliferation of abnormal cells in either the bronchi (the primary airways of the lungs) or the lung tissue. Its various forms often exhibit subtle symptoms that can easily go unnoticed until the disease has progressed to advanced stages. There are two main classifications of lung cancer, each with distinct characteristics and treatment approaches: non-small cell lung cancer (NSCLC) and small cell lung cancer (SCLC). Non-small cell lung cancer (NSCLC) is the predominant type representing roughly 85% of all lung cancer instances, while SCLC, though less prevalent, tends to exhibit rapid growth and metastasis.

Lung cancer presents itself in a variety of ways, including persistent cough, chest pain, dyspnea, respiratory whistling, coughing up blood, fatigue, unexplained weight loss, and recurrent respiratory infections. However, these manifestations may not become evident until the disease has reached an advanced stage resulting in delayed diagnosis and compromised treatment effectiveness.

Given these challenges, the significance of early detection cannot be overstated. Identifying lung cancer in its early stages provides an opportunity for a broader range of treatment options, such as surgery, radiation therapy, chemotherapy, targeted therapy, and immunotherapy. These interventions are most effective when the disease is localized and has not spread beyond the lung tissue. Early detection enables prompt initiation of treatment, thereby reducing the risk of disease progression and increasing the likelihood of favorable outcomes.

Furthermore, early diagnosis holds the potential to significantly improve patient survival rates. Consistent research findings demonstrate that individuals diagnosed with early-stage lung cancer have better long-term survival rates compared to those diagnosed at later stages. By detecting the disease in its initial stages, healthcare professionals can implement aggressive treatment strategies aimed at eradicating cancerous cells and preventing metastasis, a critical factor affecting patient prognosis.

In addition to its impact on survival rates, early detection of lung cancer has profound implications for the overall quality of life for affected individuals. Timely intervention can alleviate symptoms, minimize treatment-related side effects, and reduce the need for invasive procedures. By intervening early in the disease trajectory, healthcare providers can optimize patient care providing comprehensive support and fostering a sense of hope and empowerment for individuals grappling with this devastating diagnosis.

In the domain of medical artificial intelligence, machine learning algorithms display tremendous potential for enhancing the accuracy and efficiency of lung cancer diagnosis. These algorithms analyze medical imaging data, such as chest X-rays and CT scans, to identify subtle abnormalities and highlight suspicious findings for further evaluation. Deep learning techniques, including convolutional neural networks (CNNs) and vision transformers (ViTs), have demonstrated remarkable capabilities in image recognition and pattern analysis achieving performance levels that are comparable to, or even surpassing, those of human radiologists.

The incorporation of deep learning algorithms into clinical practice presents the opportunity to streamline the diagnostic procedure, expedite the prioritization of patients, and facilitate the early identification of lung cancer. Furthermore, these algorithms can aid healthcare professionals in interpreting intricate imaging data, thereby reducing diagnostic errors and enhancing diagnostic precision. By harnessing the capabilities of artificial intelligence, healthcare providers can utilize extensive amounts of imaging data to enhance their diagnostic expertise ultimately leading to improved patient care and clinical outcomes.

In summary, the significance of early diagnosis in lung cancer cannot be overstated. By identifying the disease in its initial stages, healthcare professionals can implement timely interventions to eradicate cancer cells, halt disease progression, and enhance patient outcomes. Screening programs, advanced imaging techniques, molecular biomarkers, and artificial intelligence technologies collectively contribute to the early detection and diagnosis of lung cancer marking a new era in precision medicine and personalized oncology. As we continue to advance our knowledge of the disease and refine our diagnostic methods, the objective of achieving early detection and improved survival rates in lung cancer remains attainable.

B. Utilizing Deep Learning for Lung Cancer Diagnosis

Deep learning falls under the category of machine learning that entails the training of artificial neural networks with multiple layers to acquire representations of data. Dissimilar to conventional machine learning approaches, which frequently necessitate the extraction of handcrafted features from the data, deep learning algorithms can autonomously learn hierarchical representations of unprocessed input data, such as images, text, or audio, through successive layers of abstraction.

Deep learning is centered around artificial neural networks, which are computational models inspired by the architecture and operations of biological neural networks found in the human brain. These neural networks consist of interconnected nodes, or neurons, organized into layers. Each neuron receives input signals from neurons in the preceding layer, conducts a computation using a set of weights and biases, and generates an output signal that is transmitted to neurons in the subsequent layer. By iteratively adjusting the weights and biases through a process known as backpropagation, neural networks can learn to map input data to desired output labels, such as class labels in classification tasks or continuous values in regression tasks.

Deep learning has exhibited immense potential in various domains, encompassing computer vision, natural language processing, speech recognition, and medical imaging. In the context of lung cancer diagnosis, deep learning algorithms can be particularly advantageous for scrutinizing medical imaging data, such as chest X-rays, computed tomography (CT) scans, and magnetic resonance imaging (MRI) scans.

Here is how deep learning can be beneficial in the diagnosis of lung cancer:

- Image Recognition: Deep learning algorithms, notably convolutional neural networks (CNNs), excel in image recognition tasks by learning hierarchical representations of visual features from raw image data. In the case of lung cancer diagnosis, CNNs can examine chest X-rays or CT scans to detect suspicious lesions, nodules, or abnormalities indicative of lung cancer.
- Feature Extraction: Deep learning algorithms can automatically extract pertinent features from medical images without the requirement for manual feature engineering. By learning hierarchical representations of visual features at multiple levels of abstraction, deep learning models can capture

subtle patterns and textures associated with lung cancer, thus enhancing diagnostic accuracy.

- Early Detection: Deep learning algorithms can assist in the early identification of lung cancer by identifying subtle abnormalities or suspicious findings that may not be evident to human observers. By flagging potential areas of concern on medical images, deep learning models can facilitate prompt intervention and treatment, thereby leading to improved patient outcomes.
- Personalized Medicine: Deep learning algorithms can aid clinicians in tailoring treatment strategies to individual patients based on their unique clinical characteristics and imaging profiles. By analyzing a patient's medical imaging data and integrating information from other sources, such as genetic biomarkers or clinical data, deep learning models can assist in guiding personalized treatment decisions, optimizing therapeutic outcomes, and minimizing adverse effects.
- Automation and Efficiency: Deep learning algorithms have the capability to automate and streamline the diagnostic process, thereby reducing the burden on healthcare providers and enhancing the efficiency of workflow. Through the automation of routine tasks like image interpretation and lesion detection, deep learning models can enable clinicians to allocate their time and attention toward more intricate decision making and activities related to patient care.
- Continuous Learning: The continuous learning aspect of deep learning models allows them to be regularly updated and refined with new data enabling them to adapt to the changing trends and patterns observed in the diagnosis of lung cancer. By utilizing extensive datasets and real-world clinical information, deep learning algorithms have the capacity to enhance their performance over time and keep up with the advancements in medical imaging technology and clinical practice.

In summary, deep learning possesses immense potential in revolutionizing the diagnosis and management of lung cancer. It equips clinicians with powerful tools to analyze medical imaging data, identify early-stage diseases, guide treatment decisions, and improve patient outcomes.

As research in this field continues to progress and novel techniques are developed, deep learning is expected to assume an increasingly prominent role in combating lung cancer and other devastating diseases.

6.2 Literature Review

The development of Convolutional Neural Networks (CNNs) marks a significant milestone in the field of deep learning and has revolutionized various applications, including medical image analysis. LeCun *et al.* (1998) [15] made a breakthrough by applying the backpropagation algorithm to train CNNs for digit recognition paving the way for modern deep learning models. The subsequent development of deep learning, particularly CNNs, has been driven by increasing computational power and the availability of large datasets. A detailed survey by Yao *et al.* (2020) [16] highlights the diverse applications of CNNs in medical image analysis ranging from lesion detection to tissue classification. The paper by Hang Yu *et al.* (2021) [17] provides a comprehensive survey of convolutional neural networks in medical image analysis. This paper reviews commonly used CNNs and presents an overview of their use in various tasks, such as image classification, segmentation, and detection, in different medical diagnosis areas like the brain, breast, and abdominal imaging. It also discusses the remaining challenges of CNNs in medical image analysis and presents future research directions, including figures and visual representations to illustrate the findings

The progress of Convolutional Neural Networks (CNNs) represents a significant revolution in deep learning, especially in the field of medical image analysis. LeCun *et al.* (1998) initiated this advancement by employing the backpropagation algorithm for training CNNs in digit recognition laying the foundation for modern deep learning models. There is subsequent progress in deep learning, particularly in CNNs, because of high-power computational capabilities and the availability of vast datasets. A comprehensive survey by Yao *et al.* (2020) underscores CNNs' myriad applications in medical image analysis spanning lesion detection to tissue classification. Similarly, Hang Yu *et al.* (2021) provide an exhaustive overview of CNNs in medical image analysis detailing their utilization across various tasks, such as image classification, segmentation, and detection, in the brain, breast, and abdominal imaging.

This paper presents a computer-aided system for detection of cancer. The system uses AlexNet CNN architecture to assist in diagnosing patient cases as normal, benign, or malignant. The proposed model achieves a notable accuracy of up to 93.548%. Moreover, other performance metrics, such as sensitivity and specificity, demonstrate high values, with sensitivity at 95.714% and specificity at 95%.

- In this paper [18], researchers have increasingly turned to intelligent and automated approaches to enhance accuracy in lung cancer classification. This study proposes the use of a 2D convolutional neural network (CNN) with Taguchi parametric optimization to automate lung cancer recognition from CT images. The Taguchi method is employed to determine the optimal parameters of the 2D CNN architecture, thereby improving classification accuracy. Through 36 experiments and manipulation of eight control factors at mixed levels, the study achieves notable enhancements in lung cancer classification accuracy.
- This article [19] aims to evaluate the efficacy of five established CNN architectures—GoogleNet, SqueezeNet, DenseNet, ShuffleNet, and MobileNetV2—in classifying lung tumors as malignant or benign. Performance metrics, such as accuracy, sensitivity, specificity, and area under the curve of the receiver operating characteristic (ROC) curve, are employed to assess the models. Experimental findings reveal GoogleNet as the most effective CNN architecture for CT lung tumor classification achieving an accuracy of 94.53%, specificity of 99.06%, sensitivity of 65.67%, and AUC of 86.84%
- This paper [20] proposes a fully automatic method for lung cancer detection in whole slide images of lung tissue samples. The classification is conducted at the image patch level utilizing convolutional neural networks (CNNs). Specifically, two CNN architectures, VGG and ResNet, are trained and compared for their performance in lung cancer detection. The obtained results demonstrate the potential of CNN-based approaches to assist pathologists in lung cancer diagnosis.

6.3 Description of Model

A. CNN (Convolutional Neural Network)

A Convolutional Neural Network (CNN), otherwise referred to as ConvNet, is a specialized form of artificial neural network that is predominantly employed for the purpose of analyzing visual imagery in deep learning applications. CNNs are well known for their effectiveness in tasks such as image recognition, classification, segmentation, and analysis. In contrast to conventional multilayer perceptrons (MLPs), which are fully connected networks, CNNs possess a shared-weight architecture within their convolutional layers, as depicted in Figure 6.1. These convolutional layers are comprised of filters or kernels that traverse the input features extracting pertinent patterns and generating translation-equivariant responses known as feature maps. Despite their name, most CNNs are not entirely invariant to translation due to the application of downsampling operations to the input.

CNNs present several advantages over MLPs, particularly in terms of regularization and handling hierarchical patterns in data. Traditional MLPs are prone to overfitting due to their complete connectivity, in this arrangement every neuron in a given layer is linked to each neuron in the following layer. Techniques, such as weight decay or dropout, are commonly employed to mitigate overfitting in MLPs. In contrast, CNNs leverage the inherent hierarchical structure in visual data. They construct intricate patterns by assembling smaller and simpler patterns identified by their convolutional filters. This hierarchical approach to feature extraction inherently regularizes the model reducing the risk of overfitting. Consequently, CNNs

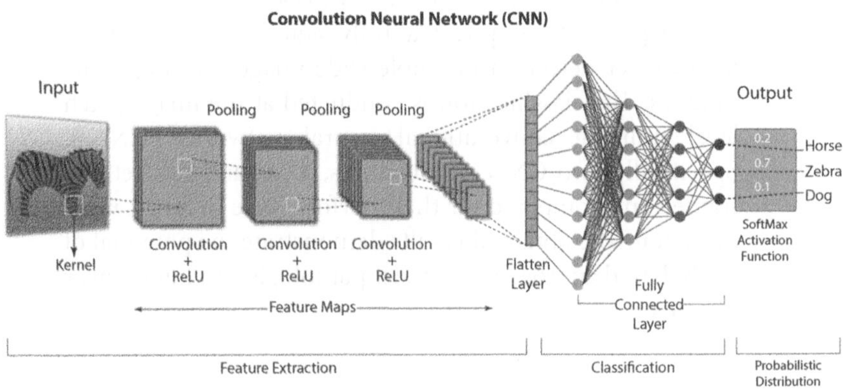

Figure 6.1 Architecture of Convolutional Neural Network (CNN).

are situated on the lower end of the connectivity–complexity spectrum providing a more efficient and effective framework for analyzing visual data [1, 2].

The versatility of CNNs extends beyond image analysis encompassing a wide range of applications including video recognition, recommender systems, medical image analysis, natural language processing, brain–computer interfaces, and financial time series analysis. This adaptability arises from CNNs' capability to acquire hierarchical representations of data rendering them well suited for tasks that require feature extraction and pattern recognition across diverse domains. All in all, CNNs have brought about a revolution in the field of deep learning presenting a powerful and adaptable framework for processing and comprehending visual data in various real-world applications.

B. ViT (Vision Transformers)

The ViT model, a revolutionary breakthrough in deep learning, particularly in computer vision, introduces a novel approach by employing a transformer architecture instead of traditional Convolutional Neural Networks (CNNs) for feature extraction from images. This approach transforms images into sequences of patches and processes them through self-attention mechanisms enabling the model to capture global relationships and dependencies within the visual data. The architecture of the ViT model is depicted in Figure 6.2 below. By utilizing self-attention, ViT effectively models long-range interactions and extracts detailed information from images, overcoming limitations of CNNs, such as their reliance on local spatial features [3, 4].

When combined with various CNN models, like ResNet, AlexNet, DenseNet, VGG, or LeNet, the ViT model shows great potential in enhancing the diagnosis of lung cancer from medical imaging data. The integration of ViT with CNNs provides improved feature extraction capabilities due to ViT's self-attention mechanisms, which capture contextual information and long-range dependencies within the image resulting in richer and more informative extracted features. This collaboration between ViT and CNNs facilitates the detection of subtle abnormalities associated with lung cancer leading to more discriminative and informative representations of lung images.

Furthermore, the combination of ViT with CNN models enhances the classification performance of deep learning models in lung cancer diagnosis tasks. Leveraging ViT's ability to capture global relationships and CNN's feature learning capabilities, this combined architecture effectively distinguishes between benign and malignant lesions aiding in accurate

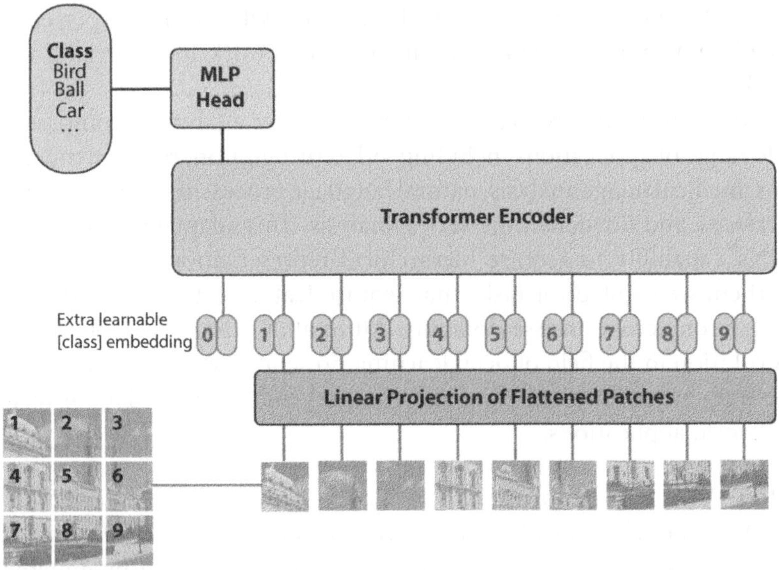

Figure 6.2 Architecture of Vision Transformers (ViT).

diagnosis and classification of lung cancer subtypes. Improved classification performance is crucial for guiding clinical decision making and treatment planning, as accurately differentiating between different types and stages of lung cancer is essential for determining appropriate therapeutic interventions.

Another advantage of integrating ViT with CNNs is efficient handling of large datasets commonly encountered in medical imaging studies. Deep learning models trained on extensive datasets of lung images require significant computational resources and time. ViT's transformer architecture, operating on sequences of patches rather than entire images, alleviates the computational burden associated with processing large-scale datasets. When combined with CNN models, ViT enhances the efficiency of feature extraction and classification tasks enabling faster training and inference on extensive lung cancer datasets [5, 6].

Furthermore, the combination of ViT with CNN models improves the robustness of deep learning models to variations in image quality commonly encountered in medical imaging studies. Medical images, such as chest X-rays or CT scans, often exhibit variations in quality, resolution, and acquisition settings. ViT's self-attention mechanisms enable the model to focus on relevant regions of interest within the image enhancing its resilience to variations in image quality [7]. When integrated with CNN models, ViT enhances the model's ability to extract meaningful features from diverse lung images, regardless of variations in imaging conditions.

Overall, the amalgamation of ViT with diverse CNN architectures signifies a propitious methodology for propelling the detection of lung cancer from medical imaging data. By harnessing ViT's proficiency in apprehending global associations and interconnections in visual data and merging it with CNN's aptitude for acquiring features, the amalgamated framework can augment the efficacy, efficiency, and explicability of deep learning models for lung cancer detection ultimately leading to enhanced patient outcomes and clinical decision making.

6.4 Methodology

A. Implementation Using CNN

1. **Model Definition:** The initial step in establishing the convolutional neural network (CNN) model is to define its foundation. To enable the creation of the model, the TensorFlow and Keras libraries are imported. The model is initialized as a Sequential model, which is essentially a linear stack of layers, using the tf.keras.Sequential() function. Convolutional layers (tf.keras.layers.Conv2D()) are then added to perform feature extraction from the input images. These layers apply filters to the images to detect various features. Following the convolutional layers, MaxPooling2D layers (tf.keras.layers.MaxPooling2D()) are incorporated to downsample the spatial dimensions of the feature maps. The Flatten layer (tf.keras.layers.Flatten()) is used to transform the 2D feature maps into a 1D vector, preparing them for input into the fully connected layers. Dense layers (tf.keras.layers.Dense()) are subsequently added to the model to process the extracted features. These layers utilize rectified linear unit (ReLU) activation functions for non-linearity and can incorporate regularization techniques like dropout to prevent overfitting. Last, a Dense layer with a sigmoid activation function is included for binary classification, providing the probability of the input image belonging to a particular class [8, 9]. A complete description about the model is shown in Figure 6.3.

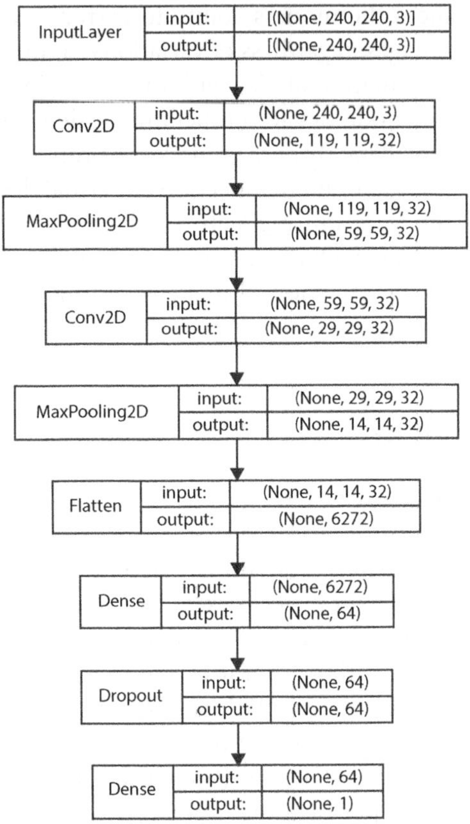

Figure 6.3 CNN model definition.

2. **Model Compilation:** Once the model architecture is defined, it must be compiled before training. This involves configuring the model with the necessary parameters for training. The compilation process is performed using the compile() method, where the optimizer, loss function, and evaluation metrics are specified. For example, the commonly chosen Adam optimizer (tf.keras.optimizers.Adam()) is known for its efficiency in training deep neural networks. The binary cross-entropy loss function(tf.keras.losses.binary_crossentropy) is suitable for binary classification tasks such as lung cancer detection. Additionally, metrics like accuracy (metrics=['accuracy']) are defined to monitor the model's performance during training [10, 11]. Figure 6.4 shows the visualization of proposed CNN model.

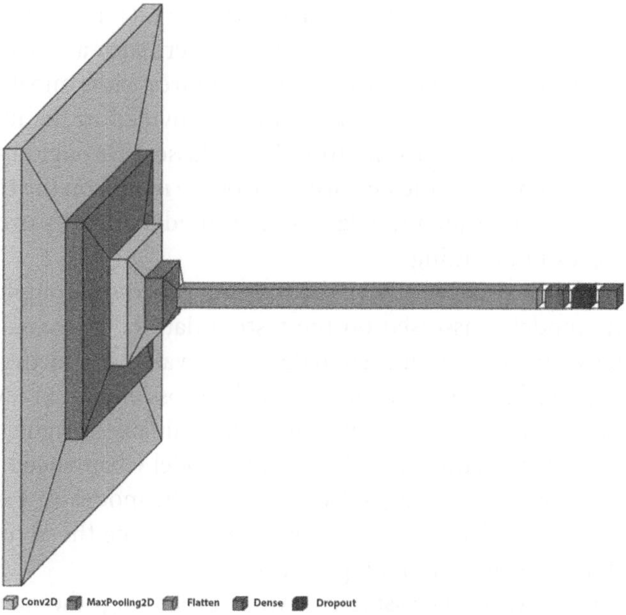

Figure 6.4 Visualization of the proposed CNN model.

3. **Data Preparation:** Prior to feeding the images into the CNN model, it is essential to prepare the data. This involves preprocessing the input images to ensure they are suitable for training. Common preprocessing steps include normalization and resizing. Normalization involves scaling the pixel values of the images to a range between 0 and 1, which ensures numerical stability during training. Resizing is necessary to ensure all images have a uniform size, which is crucial for consistent processing by the model. The dataset is then divided into training and testing sets using tools like train_test_split from the sklearn model_selection module. This division ensures that the model is trained on a portion of the data and evaluated on a separate unseen portion enabling an unbiased assessment of its performance [12].
4. **Model Training:** The initial step in the model training process involves the preparation of the data and the compilation of the model. Following this, the CNN model is trained on the training dataset in an iterative manner. During the training process, batches of images are passed through the model, and the parameters of the model are updated to minimize

the loss function. To train the model, the fit() method is utilized, with the specification of parameters such as the number of epochs and the batch size. To address class imbalance, class weights can be computed and provided to the model to ensure equal learning from both classes. Throughout the training process, the performance of the model on the training data and validation data is monitored to identify overfitting or underfitting.

5. **Model Evaluation:** Once the training process is completed, the model is assessed on the testing dataset to evaluate its performance on unseen data. The evaluate() method is employed to compute metrics, such as loss and accuracy, on the testing data. These metrics offer valuable insights into the generalization capability of the model when encountering new, unseen images. By evaluating the model on a separate testing dataset, researchers can determine the accuracy of its classification of lung cancer images.
6. **Performance Assessment:** After evaluating the performance metrics of the model, a further analysis is conducted to assess its classification performance. Predictions are generated on the testing data using the predict() method enabling researchers to compare the model's predictions with the actual labels. To visualize the model's classification performance, a confusion matrix is computed using tools such as confusion_matrix from the sklearn metrics module. This matrix provides valuable insights into the model's ability to accurately classify lung cancer images as positive or negative. Additionally, the progress of the model's learning during training is visualized by plotting the training and validation loss and accuracy using matplotlib.pyplot. Finally, the trained model is saved for future use allowing for seamless deployment in real-world applications.

B. CNN With ViT

1. **Model Definition:** The methodology for the ViT with CNN approach begins by defining the necessary components for combining Vision Transformer (ViT) with Convolutional Neural Network (CNN) layers. Custom layers are created to facilitate patch extraction and encoding, essential components of the ViT architecture. A Patches layer is defined

to extract patches from input images, while a PatchEncoder layer encodes these patches using transformer blocks. These custom layers are then utilized within a function to construct the ViT with CNN model architecture. This function defines the model's input layer for image data and incorporates data augmentation techniques if necessary. It then extracts patches from the input images using the Patches layer and encodes these patches using the PatchEncoder layer with transformer blocks. Multiple layers of transformer blocks are added to capture global relationships within the image. Finally, the encoded patches are flattened and passed through fully connected layers for classification [13].

2. **Data Preparation:** Similar to the CNN approach, data preparation involves preprocessing the input images to ensure they are suitable for training the ViT with CNN model. This includes normalization to scale pixel values and resizing to ensure uniform dimensions across all images. After preprocessing, the dataset undergoes division into training and testing sets to aid in both model training and evaluation.
3. **Model Creation:** With the custom layers and architecture defined, the next step is to create the ViT with CNN model. This involves instantiating the model using the defined architecture function and configuring the optimizer and loss function with appropriate parameters. Additionally, callbacks, such as checkpoint saving, are defined to monitor and save the best-performing model during training.
4. **Model Training:** The ViT with CNN model is trained on the training dataset using techniques similar to those employed in the CNN approach. Training involves iterating over batches of images and updating the model's parameters to minimize the loss function. Hyperparameters, such as batch size and number of epochs, are adjusted as needed to optimize model performance.
5. **Model Evaluation:** Once training is complete, the ViT with CNN model is evaluated on the testing dataset to assess its performance. This evaluation process involves computing metrics, such as loss and accuracy, to gauge the model's ability to generalize to unseen data.
6. **Performance Assessment:** After evaluation, further analysis is conducted to assess the classification performance of the ViT with CNN model. Predictions are generated on the

testing data, and a confusion matrix is computed to visualize the model's classification performance. Additionally, training and validation loss and accuracy are plotted to monitor the model's learning progress during training. Finally, the trained model is saved for future use enabling seamless deployment in real-world applications [14].

6.5 Results

The performance of two distinct methodologies, namely, the Convolutional Neural Network (CNN) and the Vision Transformer (ViT) with CNN, underwent meticulous evaluation on an extensive dataset comprising lung cancer images. The ensuing outcomes from both approaches are presented below offering valuable insights into their efficacy in accurately detecting lung cancer from medical images.

A. Convolutional Neural Network (CNN) Approach

The graphs representing the training and validation loss and accuracy for the CNN approach are depicted in Figure 6.5. Throughout the training process, the CNN model consistently exhibits a decrease in training loss indicative of effective learning from the training data. Concurrently, the training accuracy steadily improves signifying the model's capacity to correctly classify images from the training set. However, the validation

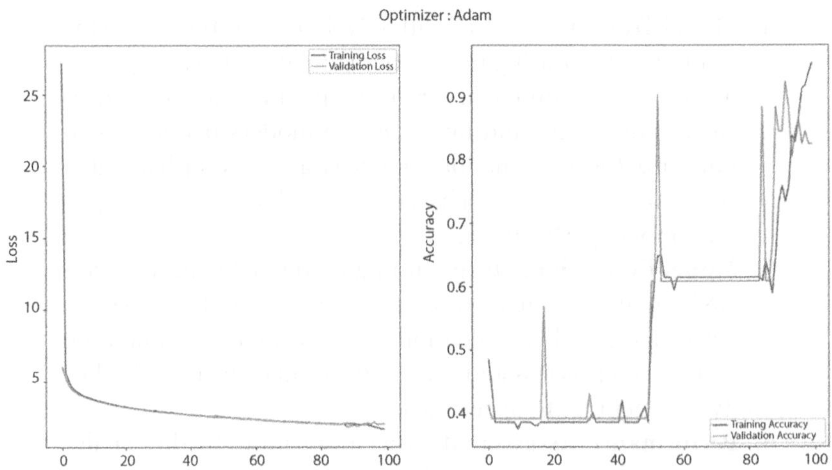

Figure 6.5 Loss and accuracy graphs for the CNN model.

loss and accuracy display fluctuations during training, which may suggest potential overfitting. Despite these fluctuations, the CNN model attains commendable validation accuracy implying its capability to generalize well to unseen data.

B. Vision Transformer (ViT) With CNN Approach

Figure 6.6 portrays the graphs illustrating the training and validation loss and accuracy for the ViT with CNN approach. Similar to the CNN approach, the ViT with CNN model demonstrates a gradual decrease in training loss and an increase in training accuracy over epochs. Notably, the validation loss and accuracy exhibit relatively stable trends throughout the training process indicating improved generalization capabilities compared to the CNN approach. The ViT with CNN model achieves competitive performance on both the training and validation datasets, thereby highlighting its effectiveness in capturing global relationships within the images.

Figures 6.7 and 6.8 present the confusion matrices for the CNN and ViT with CNN approaches, respectively. These matrices offer a comprehensive overview of the classification performance of each approach by presenting the counts of true-positive, true-negative, false-positive, and false-negative predictions. In the CNN approach, the model achieves a true positive rate of 92% and a true negative rate of 80%, thereby indicating its ability to accurately classify both positive and negative instances of lung cancer. Similarly, the ViT with CNN approach demonstrates competitive performance with a true positive rate of 85% and a true negative

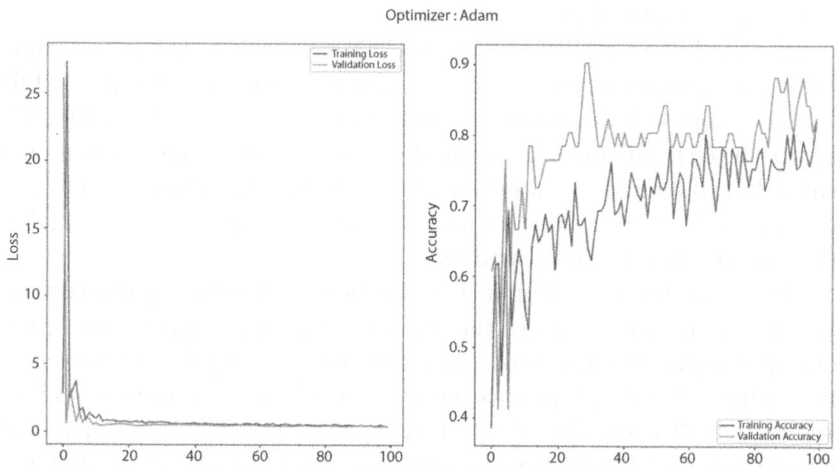

Figure 6.6 Loss and accuracy graphs for the ViT model integrated with CNN.

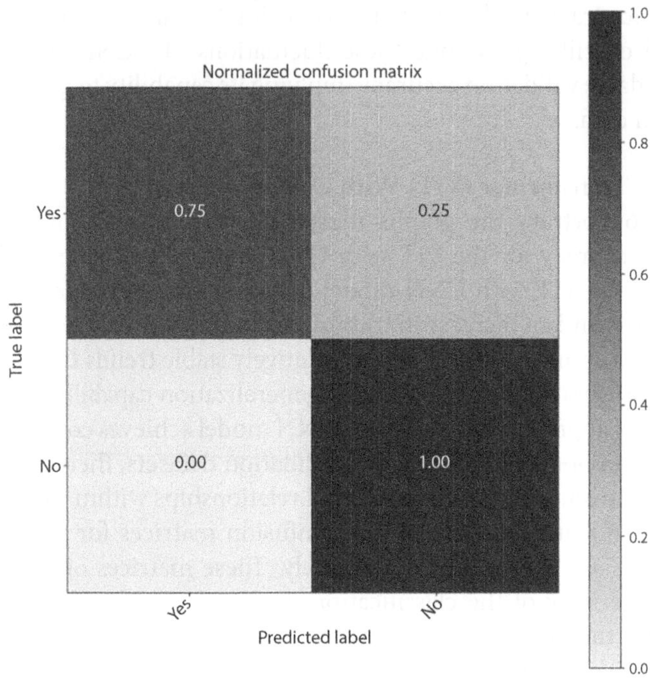

Figure 6.7 Confusion matrix for CNN model.

rate of 91%. These results highlight the effectiveness of both approaches in accurately diagnosing lung cancer from medical images, with the ViT with CNN approach showcasing slightly superior performance in terms of generalization capabilities.

Thus, both the CNN and ViT with CNN approaches exhibit promising results in the realm of lung cancer detection from medical images. While the CNN approach demonstrates robust performance, the ViT with CNN approach offers enhanced generalization capabilities, thereby making it a compelling option for accurate and efficient lung cancer diagnosis. Further research and optimizations are warranted to fully exploit the potential of these approaches in clinical settings.

The tabular representation in Table 6.1 below offers a comparative analysis of various deep learning structures commonly utilized in the detection of lung malignancies from medical imaging emphasizing their effectiveness both with and without the incorporation of Vision Transformers (ViTs). While each structure displays proficiency in diagnosing lung cancer, the incorporation of Vision Transformers introduces a prospect for enhancing performance. ViTs aid in feature extraction and the apprehension of

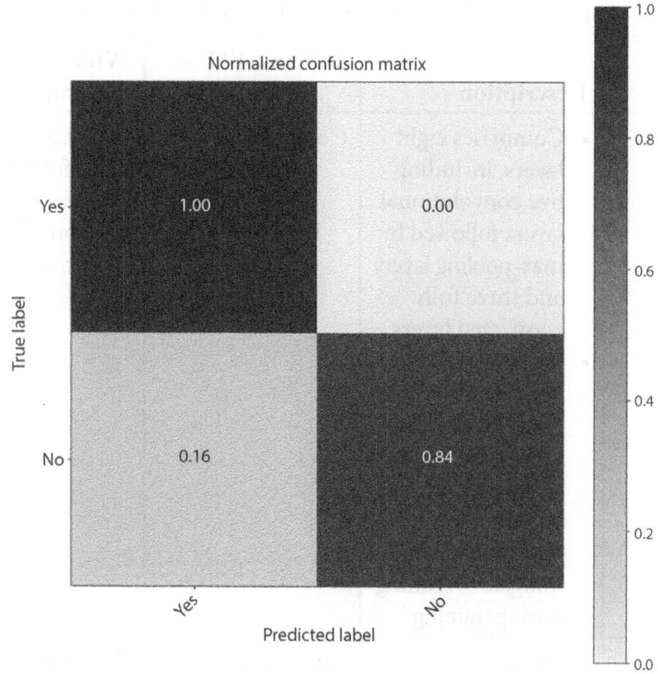

Figure 6.8 Confusion matrix for ViT with CNN model.

Table 6.1 Comparison of different deep learning architectures.

Model name	Description	Without VIT performance	With VIT performance
ResNet	• Addresses vanishing gradients by incorporating skip connections • Enables effective training of deep networks	Satisfactory performance, longer training durations	Potential performance improvements, reduced training durations

(*Continued*)

Table 6.1 Comparison of different deep learning architectures. (*Continued*)

Model name	Description	Without VIT performance	With VIT performance
AlexNet	• Comprises eight layers, including five convolutional layers followed by max-pooling layers and three fully connected layers • Incorporates the ReLU activation function to introduce non-linearity and dropout regularization to mitigate overfitting during training	Competitive performance, longer training times	Potential performance enhancements, improved feature extraction
DenseNet	• Dense connectivity between layers enabling each layer to directly receive input from all preceding layers and transmit its own feature maps to all subsequent layers • Promotes the reuse of features, facilitates the flow of gradients during training, and improves parameter efficiency by reducing redundant computations	Competitive results, potential longer training durations	Potential improvements in performance, reduced training epochs

(*Continued*)

Table 6.1 Comparison of different deep learning architectures. (*Continued*)

Model name	Description	Without VIT performance	With VIT performance
VGG	• Utilization of small (3 × 3) convolutional filters with a stride of 1 and the same padding allowing the network to acquire more complex and hierarchical feature representations while retaining spatial resolution	Competitive results, may require longer training times	Possible performance enhancements, leveraging global relationship modeling
LeNet	• Early CNN architecture • Architecture consists of alternating convolutional and average pooling layers, accompanied by fully connected layers that utilize sigmoid activations	Competence in limited computational scenarios, longer training times	Potential performance improvements with enhanced feature extraction

comprehensive relationships within the data potentially reducing the duration of training and enhancing precision. This underscores the promising collaboration between deep learning structures and ViTs in progressing the effectiveness and precision of lung cancer diagnosis from medical imaging, thereby contributing to better patient outcomes and healthcare efficiency.

6.6 Conclusion

The study centered on the utilization of deep learning methodologies for the timely identification of lung cancer, a crucial pursuit considering its status as a predominant contributor to cancer-related fatality on a global scale. By conducting a comparative examination of diverse deep learning structures—ResNet, AlexNet, DenseNet, VGG, and LeNet—the study sought to assess their effectiveness in the detection of lung cancer from medical imagery. Each structure exhibited noteworthy capabilities: ResNet' s proficiency in training highly intricate networks, AlexNet's triumph in the ImageNet competition, DenseNet's dense interconnections enabling feature recycling, VGG's thorough hierarchical representations, and LeNet's foundational significance as one of the earliest CNN structures.

Nevertheless, the investigation unveiled that, while these structures could attain satisfactory outcomes individually, their performance could be further optimized through the incorporation of Vision Transformers (ViTs). ViTs provide the ability to apprehend global correlations within data, thereby enhancing feature extraction and potentially shortening training periods. This deduction highlights the encouraging collaboration between deep learning structures and ViTs in progressing the early identification of lung cancer from medical imagery. By leveraging the potential of deep learning and ViTs, the investigation contributes to the persistent endeavors to enhance patient results and healthcare effectiveness through prompt and precise diagnosis of lung cancer.

References

1. She, Y., Jin, Z., Wu, J. *et al.*, Development and Validation of a Deep Learning Model for Non–Small Cell Lung Cancer Survival. *JAMA Netw. Open*, 3, 6, e205842, 2020, doi: 10.1001.
2. Parkhi, P. *et al.*, Employing CNN Features for Automated Brain Tumor Classification in MRI. *Int. J. Intell. Syst. Appl. Eng.*, 12, 11s, 380–386, 2024.
3. Zhang, L., Wang, X., Yang, D., Sanford, T., Harmon, S., Turkbey, B., ... & Xu, Z., Generalizing deep learning for medical image segmentation to unseen domains via deep stacked transformation. *IEEE Trans. Med. Imaging*, 39, 7, 2531–2540, 2020.
4. Pradhan, Nitesh, Vijaypal Singh Dhaka, Geeta Rani, and Himanshu Chaudhary. Transforming view of medical images using deep learning. *Neural Comput. Appl.*, 32, 18, 15043–15054, 2020.
5. Garillos-Manliguez, Generalized Confusion Matrix for Multiple Classes, November 2016, DOI:10.13140/RG.2.2.31150.51523.

6. Parkhi, P. and Bhagyashree, H., Optical cup and disc segmentation using deep learning technique for glaucoma detection. *Int. J. Next Gener. Comput.*, 14, 1, 2023.
7. Parkhi, P. *et al.*, Employing CNN Features for Automated Brain Tumor Classification in MRI. *Int. J. Intell. Syst. Appl. Eng.*, 12, 11s, 380–386, 2024.
8. Garillos-Manliguez, Generalized Confusion Matrix for Multiple Classes, November 2016, DOI:10.13140/RG.2.2.31150.51523.
9. Shah, A.A. *et al.*, Deep learning ensemble 2D CNN approach towards the detection of lung cancer. *Sci. Rep.*, 13, 1, 2987, 2023. Yao, L., Prosky, J., Poblenz, E., Covington, B., Lyman, K., A strong baseline for domain adaptation and generalization in medical imaging. arXiv preprint arXiv:2002.02497, 2020.
10. Yu, H., Yang, L., Qin, J., Heng, P.A., Convolutional neural networks for medical image analysis: State-of-the-art, comparisons, improvement and perspectives. *Neurocomputing*, 429, 185–200, 2021.
11. Chollet, F., Xception: Deep Learning with Depthwise Separable Convolutions, in: *Proceedings of the IEEE Conference on Computer Vision and Pattern Recognition (CVPR)*, pp. 1251–1258, 2017.
12. Tu, C., Wang, G., Hu, Z., Wang, S., Yan, Q., Liu, X., Burden of oral disorders, 1990–2019: estimates from the Global Burden of Disease Study 2019. *Arch. Med. Sci.*, 19, 4, 930–940, 2023, doi: 10.5114/aoms/165962.
13. Yu, H., Yang, L., Qin, J., Heng, P.A., Convolutional neural networks for medical image analysis: State-of-the-art, comparisons, improvement and perspectives. *Neurocomputing*, 429, 185–200, 2021.
14. LeCun, Y., Bottou, L., Bengio, Y., Haffner, P., Gradient-based learning applied to document recognition. *Proc. IEEE*, 86, 11, 2278–2324, 1998.
15. Yao, L., Prosky, J., Poblenz, E., Covington, B., Lyman, K., A strong baseline for domain adaptation and generalization in medical imaging. arXiv preprint arXiv:2002.02497, 2020.
16. Al-Yasriy, H. F., Al-Husieny, M. S., Mohsen, F. Y., Khalil, E. A., & Hassan, Z. S., Diagnosis of lung cancer based on CT scans using CNN. In *IOP conference series: Materials science and engineering*, vol. 928, no. 2, p. 022035, IOP Publishing, 2020, November.
17. Lin, C.-J., Jeng, S.-Y., Chen, M.-K., Using 2D CNN with Taguchi parametric optimization for lung cancer recognition from CT images. *Appl. Sci.*, 10, 7, 2591, 2020.
18. Zarow, M., Ramírez-Sebastià, A., Paolone, G., de Ribot Porta, J., Mora, J., Espona, J., Durán-Sindreu, F., Roig, M., A new classification system for the restoration of root filled teeth. *Int. Endod. J.*, 51, 3, 318–334, 2018 Mar, doi: 10.1111/iej.12847, Epub 2017 Sep 25, PMID: 28853160.
19. Lee, J.H., Kim, D.H., Jeong, S.N., Choi, S.H., Detection and diagnosis of dental caries using a deep learning-based convolutional neural network algorithm. *J. Dent.*, 77, 106–111, 2019, doi: 10.1016/j.jdent.2018.07.015.
20. Baranwal, N., Doravari, P., & Kachhoria, R., Classification of histopathology images of lung cancer using convolutional neural network (CNN). In *Disruptive Developments in Biomedical Applications*, pp. 75–89, CRC Press, 2022.

7

Innovations in AI and ML for Medical Imaging: An Extensive Study with an Emphasis on Face Spoofing Detection and Snooping

Aparna Pandey[1]*, Arvind Kumar Tiwari[2], Harsha Nishad[3] and Siji A. Thomas[4]

[1]*Department of Computer Science and Engineering, Dr. C. V. Raman University, Bilaspur, Chhattisgarh, India*
[2]*Department of Computer Science and Information Technology, Dr. C. V. Raman University, Bilaspur, Chhattisgarh, India*
[3]*Department of Computer Science and Engineering, Chhattisgarh Swami Vivakanada Technical University, Bhilai, Chhattisgarh, India*
[4]*United Arab Emirates*

Abstract

The landscape of medical imaging diagnosis and treatment methods has experienced a revolutionary transformation due to the recent integration of artificial intelligence (AI) and machine learning (ML). This integration has led to unprecedented levels of efficiency and precision. By focusing on the emerging challenges posed by face spoofing detection and snooping in this critical field, this book chapter provides a comprehensive review of the rapidly evolving realm of AI and ML applications in medical imaging. An introduction to the basic ideas underlying how AI and ML are revolutionizing medical imaging is given in the first section of the chapter. It looks at how these technologies function well together with traditional medical methods showing how they can improve diagnostic accuracy, speed up workflow, and improve patient outcomes. AI systems excel at extracting meaningful insights from large and complex information, which highlights the subtleties of medical picture analysis. The chapter devotes a good deal of space to discussing the emerging issue of face spoofing in medical imaging. The term "face spoofing" describes the improper use and illegal access of facial data found in medical imaging.

**Corresponding author*: aparna95pandey@gmail.com

Parul Dubey, Mangala Madankar, Pushkar Dubey and Bui Thanh Hung (eds.) The Impact of Algorithmic Technologies on Healthcare, (127–156) © 2025 Scrivener Publishing LLC

With the growing use of facial recognition by healthcare providers for patient identification and treatment monitoring, it is critical to have strong algorithms that can identify and stop unwanted access. The chapter explores the techniques used by AI systems to detect and prevent any privacy violations in patients carefully balancing technology advancement with moral considerations. The chapter also delves into the idea of "snooping" in medical imaging, which is a newly recognized problem involving the unlawful interception of medical image data in transit. Sensitive medical data are becoming more and more dependent on cloud-based storage services and networked healthcare systems, which creates serious security risks. The chapter explores cutting-edge machine learning methods intended to protect medical image confidentiality and integrity while they are in transit guaranteeing patient data security all the way through the diagnosis and treatment process. Throughout the talk, real-world case studies and success stories demonstrate how AI and ML are having a noticeable influence on medical imaging and illustrate how they have the potential to completely transform the way healthcare is provided. The chapter also discusses the moral ramifications of using AI and ML in a healthcare environment stressing the significance of openness, responsibility, and responsible innovation. This book chapter offers a thorough overview of the state of AI and ML applications in medical imaging today, with a particular emphasis on the problems and solutions related to face spying detection and snooping. The chapter seeks to further the ongoing discussion about the morally sound and effective use of cutting-edge technologies into the framework of contemporary healthcare by illuminating these important issues.

***Keywords*:** Medical imaging, artificial intelligence, machine learning, face spoofing, snooping, ethical considerations

7.1 Introduction

Seasoned radiologist Dr. Emily Hayes, who was poring over a series of X-rays of the chest, was barely aware of the urgent message that appeared on the screen. However, in the busy hallways of MedCare Hospital, where she worked, her colleague Dr. Michael Evans had called in to inform that it seemed there had been a breach in their imaging system. Apparently, someone had used their facial biometric information to infiltrate patient records. Naturally, they started to worry about data security and patient's privacy.

Dr. Hayes was motivated by a sense of urgency to form a group of professionals to tackle the rising threat of face spoofing in medical imaging. Their main objective is to develop a state-of-the-art AI system that can accurately detect and prevent such security breaks.

In light of the latest findings in the field, Dr. Hayes and her colleagues opted for convolutional neural networks as the contemporary, innovative deep learning approach. Because the technology is well-known for its ability to extract various complex patterns and features from images, CNNs are an ideal instrument for facial identification and detection.

The group assembled thousands of medical pictures, including X-rays, MRIs, and CT scans, along with face-related biometric data, to configure their CNN model. The CNN AI was taught on this evidence to suggest real face attributes as different from bogus biometrics. While working on their CNN AI, Dr. Hayes and the lab's colleagues discovered more information about face spoofs and image stressing during medical imaging. The scholar and group discovered how face spoofs and stressing threats could skill consumers' confidential confidentiality trails and the assets and prospects of falsifying test returns.

Another finding of the study was that face spoofing disrupted data security in health centers. Individuals with ill motives could breach authentication and gain access to the victim's medical records using the facial recognition software's vulnerabilities. As a result of face organization invading one's privacy, the victim stands at risk of being a victim of fraud, identity theft, and misdiagnosis. Dr. Hayes and colleagues were able to counteract the face spoofing problem by adopting their solution to the imaging system, which was facilitated by their artificial intelligence system, which used their trained CNN model to analyze the incoming images. The AI program worked by conducting a live analysis from the images that were sent after every 10 s.

Their endeavor paid off as the artificial intelligence model could detect and thwart face spoofing preventing unauthorized access into patient files, hence safeguarding the private medical information. This made them well known for countering security risks associated with medical imaging, thus being recognized as breakthrough pioneers.

While working on enhancement of their AI-based solution, Dr. Hayes and her colleagues adhered to the most stringent principles of data protection and privacy, never waiving from it despite all odds. The innovative research showed how AI and machine learning can secure sensitive healthcare data against new risks through heralding hope to other health facilities in regard to this issue.

Medical imaging has seen a revolutionary shift with the use of artificial intelligence (AI) and machine learning (ML) techniques that creates new prospects for improving patient care and diagnostic accuracy. AI and ML applications in medical imaging have made great strides in recent years, which primarily focus on issues like face spoofing detection and spying, as they are essential in ensuring patient privacy and data integrity.

AI and ML interventions have improved pulmonary nodule diagnoses, which are key indicators of lung diseases such as cancer. One of the most notable contributors to research in this area is the Lung Image Database Consortium (LIDC), which provides an extensive dataset for algorithm development and validation [1]. Furthermore, collaborative efforts to improve automated nodule detection methods have been facilitated by projects including LIDC-IDRI dataset [2].

Convolutional neural networks (CNNs), one of the deep learning techniques, is changing the way how medical images are processed. For instance, Huang *et al.*'s densely connected convolutional network performs better than standard architectures on many image classification tasks [3]. Similarly, He *et al.*'s deep residual learning approach allows deeper network with better accuracy and convergence [4].

AI and ML, however, are now being used for addressing new data security and privacy challenges that exist beyond conventional methods. Face spoofing, which is the use of made-up biometrics to acquire unauthorized entry into medical imaging systems, jeopardizes patient confidentiality massively. To investigate what detection procedures work best, researchers have suggested trying generative adversarial networks (GANs) to generate realistically fake images [5]. Another thing worth noting is that snooping occurs when a user tries to access restricted patient information without permission underlining the need for robust encryption and access control mechanisms in medical imaging systems [6]. AI-driven techniques, such as deep learning dose prediction models, have been proposed for enhancing data security through optimizing radiation doses for cancer treatment while minimizing chances of data leakage [7]. The authenticity and integrity of the medical pictures over transit or storage has been maintained with methods like digital watermarking [8].

Access to dependable evaluation frameworks and good quality datasets are important in making AI and ML effective within medical imaging. For instance, researchers can obtain numerous training datasets from open repositories such as UCI Machine Learning Repository [9]. Innovation in the field has been stimulated by initiatives like the LUNA16 challenge, which has made algorithm evaluation and comparison for autonomous detection of pulmonary nodules easier [10].

As a result of improvements in AI and ML that protect patient privacy, enhance diagnosis accuracy, and secure data, medical imaging is changing. This paper briefly summarizes the current happenings on this fast-growing topic with a focus on face spoofing detection and snooping. The use of cutting-edge technology coupled with multidisciplinary collaboration can exploit the full potential of AI and ML to transform healthcare delivery and optimize patients' health.

"Innovations in Artificial Intelligence and Machine Learning for Medical Imaging: An Extensive Study with an Emphasis on Face Spoofing Detection and Snooping" is the name of a book chapter that aims to give readers an insight into how AI and ML have revolutionized medical imaging. It particularly concentrates on solving new problems about face spoofing detection as well as snooping.

A. Contribution of the Book Chapter

- AI and ML in Medical Imaging Review: In this section, it begins by giving an overview of fundamental concepts underlying AI as well as ML in medical imaging. It showcases these tools' ability to make important decisions from complex health information while at the same time explaining how they can improve patient outcomes, expedite workflow and increase diagnostic accuracy.
- The chapter dedicates a portion of its content to discussing the issue of face spoofing detection, in imaging, which has recently come to light. Face spoofing refers to the use and illegal access of data within medical imaging systems. It delves into how AI algorithms can play a role in detecting and preventing privacy breaches underscoring the importance of security measures in healthcare settings.
- Furthermore, the chapter delves into snooping in imaging, which involves the interception of data pertaining to medical images during transmission. Ensuring the confidentiality and integrity of data is imperative as cloud-based storage and networked healthcare systems become increasingly prevalent. The chapter also addresses modern machine learning techniques aimed at enhancing data security during procedures and treatment.
- Moreover, real-world case studies and success stories are peppered throughout the chapter showcasing the impact of AI and ML on imaging practices. These instances illustrate how these technologies are reshaping healthcare delivery methods and have the potential to revolutionize the industry as a whole.

- Last, ethical considerations surrounding the use of AI and ML in healthcare settings are explored within this book chapter.
- Using technology in patient care emphasizes the importance of innovation, accountability, and transparency.

Generally, by highlighting the essential problems of face spoofing discovery as well as sleuthing in clinical imaging, this publication phase looks for to enhance the recurring discussion on the ethical and also useful combination of AI and also ML right into modern-day medical care. The phase includes a higher understanding of the innovative capacity of AI as well as ML in modifying clinical medical diagnosis plus therapy techniques by its substantial conversation of these concerns plus recommended options.

7.2 Artificial Intelligence as Well as Device Understandings

Clinical imaging is undertaking a transformation many thanks to expert system (ML) and also artificial intelligence (AI), which are supplying previously hidden possibilities to boost analysis precision, enhance procedures together with much better client end results. In the context of clinical imaging, this paper takes a look at the essential concepts of AI together with ML, stressing their cutting-edge impact on standard clinical techniques as well as analysis accuracy. We discover just how AI and also ML innovations are transforming the clinical imaging setting plus unlocking a lot more reliable medical diagnosis as well as therapy intends with instances along with recommendations.

Figure 7.1 shows how artificial intelligence as well as machine learning are fundamental principles affecting medical imaging, which subsequently affects diagnostic accuracy, transformation of traditional methods along with enhancing clinical decision making. Furthermore, ethical considerations, such as transparency, responsibility, along with ethical innovation, are crucial facets to be taken into consideration in the advancement and also release of AI and also ML innovations in healthcare.

A. Foundational Concepts of AI and Also ML in Medical Imaging

Artificial intelligence (AI) is the capability of a computer to replicate human reasoning procedures permitting the equipment to execute jobs that usually need human knowledge. A branch of expert systems called

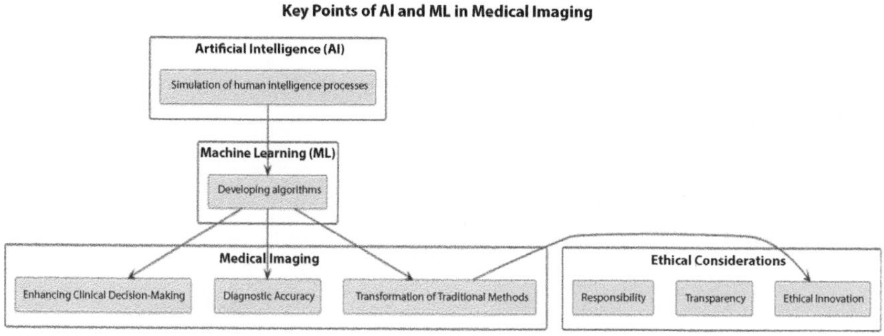

Figure 7.1 Bottom lines of AI as well as ML in medical imaging.

artificial intelligence (ML) is worried about developing formulas that can gain from projection information. To locate patterns coupled with uncommon symptoms of a condition, AI, together with ML formulas, is utilized in clinical imaging to check huge data sources of scientific information, individual documents, and also clinical photos.

Figure 7.2 details the actions associated with AI handling of clinical photos beginning with the demand for clinical photos by a radiologist, preprocessing of pictures, removal of functions, category of functions, along with ultimately giving a medical diagnosis.

Figure 7.3 details the actions associated with machine learning (ML) as well as deep learning (DL) handling of clinical photos consisting of preprocessing, attribute removal, training of ML, along with DL designs, category, coupled with supplying a medical diagnosis.

One kind of deep discovering formula that has actually revealed outstanding efficiency in picture category, division, and also discovery jobs is semantic networks (CNNs). To find anomalies and also sores, these formulas are educated to remove info from clinical photos consisting of MRIs,

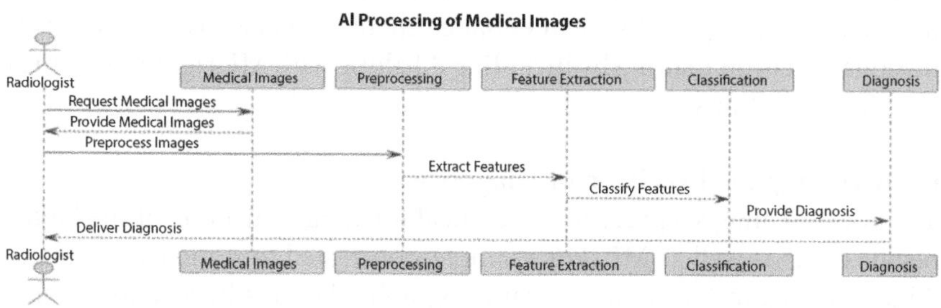

Figure 7.2 AI handling of clinical pictures.

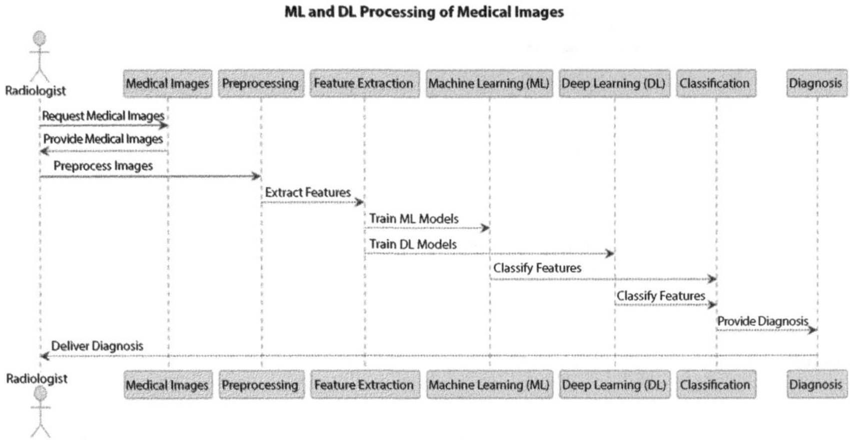

Figure 7.3 ML coupled with DL handling of clinical images.

CT checks, plus X-rays. Contrasted to standard techniques, a doctor can accomplish higher analysis performance as well as precision using artificial intelligence strategies.

B. The Modification of Conventional Medical Practices

Standard clinical imaging strategies are being changed by AI and also ML modern technologies, which automate as well as enhance a number of imaging-related jobs. As an example, AI systems have the ability to promptly analyze large quantities of clinical photos to discover irregularities along with aid radiologists determine individuals in a prompt way. As a result of this automation, translating pictures takes much less effort and time liberating medical professionals to focus on individual treatment.

Furthermore, besides systems driven by AI deal doctor's danger assessments along with measurable metrics acquired from clinical imaging information. These systems sustain the preparation of treatment therapy strategies as well as instance prioritization according to medical seriousness. Healthcare specialists can enhance client results as well as raise professional decision making by including AI along with ML right into clinical imaging operations.

C. Increasing the Precision of Diagnosis

The boost in analysis precision in clinical imaging is just one of the largest results of AI as well as ML. For example, contrasted to standard strategies, AI systems educated on large mammography datasets have actually verified to be a lot more reliable in spotting bust cancer cells. Because of these

Table 7.1 Methodologies used in medical imaging and diagnosis.

Reference	Methodology used	Outcome
[11]	Expert system	Created the expert system PUFF to interpret data on pulmonary function
[12]	Multi-valued and universal binary neurons	Multi-valued universal binary neurons for neural networks are proposed
[13]	Discussion	Investigated how machine learning might be used with expert systems
[14]	Rule-based expert systems	Described the rule-based expert systems for medical diagnostics used in the MYCIN studies
[15]	Machine learning and deep learning	Introduced medical physicists to the principles of machine and deep learning
[16]	Deep neural networks	Deep neural networks were used to classify skin cancer at the dermatologist level
[17]	Statistical learning	Talked about the components of learning statistics
[18]	Expert systems	Examined the application of expert systems for diagnosis in clinical settings
[19]	Expert systems	Discussed expert systems created with medical use in mind
[20]	Artificial intelligence	Examined artificial intelligence's use in radiology
[21]	Machine learning	Investigated machine learning techniques for the analysis of histopathology images

(Continued)

Table 7.1 Methodologies used in medical imaging and diagnosis. (*Continued*)

Reference	Methodology used	Outcome
[22]	Predictive modeling	Presented practical methods for predictive modeling
[23]	Deep learning	Compared how well deep learning performed in illness identification from medical imaging to that of healthcare professionals
[24]	Deep learning	Created a reliable deep learning model for digital breast tomosynthesis and mammography to identify breast cancer
[25]	Expert systems	Discussed the evolution and prospects for decision assistance systems for medical diagnosis
[26]	Expert systems	Unveiled Internist-1, a trial computer-based diagnostic advisor for internal medicine in general
[27]	Artificial intelligence	Investigated the use of AI in imaging technology for medicinal purposes
[28]	Deep learning	Suggested deep learning techniques to segment head and neck anatomy for radiation in a way that is clinically useful
[29]	Artificial intelligence	Examined the hazards, potential uses, and applications of artificial intelligence in medical imaging

(*Continued*)

Table 7.1 Methodologies used in medical imaging and diagnosis. (*Continued*)

Reference	Methodology used	Outcome
[30]	Deep learning	Talked about the benefits, possibilities, and difficulties of deep learning in medical physics
[31]	Deep learning	Used deep learning to enhance screening mammography's ability to detect breast cancer
[32]	Neural networks	Investigated the application of neural networks as expert systems for medical diagnostics
[33]	Artificial intelligence	Examined how artificial intelligence is causing a disruptive change in radiation oncology
[34]	Review	Conducted a review on the clinical uses of deep learning for medical imaging synthesis
[35]	Deep convolutional neural networks	Created a model for classifying medical images using deep convolutional neural networks to diagnose diseases

Note: Referrals provide understandings right into different techniques, which are used in clinical imaging and also medical diagnosis varying from skilled systems plus artificial intelligence to deep knowing and also expert system. These techniques play essential functions in progressing healthcare via boosted diagnostics together with choice assistance systems. Table 7.1 provides a recap of the methods used along with results attained in numerous research studies pertaining to clinical imaging, artificial intelligence, together with expert systems in healthcare.

formulas' capability to acknowledge minute information and also patterns symptoms of cancer cells, individual survival prices can be boosted and also very early recognition can happen.

Similar to this, AI-powered formulas might review MRI checks in neuro-imaging to discover irregularities connected to neurological problems like several sclerosis as well as Alzheimer's illness. Via the application of artificial intelligence formulas, a doctor can spot physiological modifications in the mind along with keeping an eye on the program of an illness promoting prompt treatment and also tailored restorative methods.

By boosting clinical decision making, medical specialists can make a lot more enlightened proof-based professional choices with the aid of AI coupled with ML modern technology. To assist with therapy preparation and also follow-up treatment, anticipating analytic versions educated on clinical imaging information, for example, can review the opportunity of a condition reappearance or the efficiency of a therapy. AI-driven choice assistance systems can additionally made radiologists decipher complex imaging outcomes and also offer referring medical professionals with valuable understandings.

In addition to offering complete person analyses, AI formulas can incorporate information from a number of imaging techniques consisting of MRI, CT, as well as PET scans. Medical professionals can get an extra detailed understanding of an individual's problem along with readjusting therapy intends by incorporating information from numerous imaging resources. Individualized medication strategies are implemented by this combination of AI plus ML right into a medical method, which likewise improves client end results.

Clinical imaging is readied to go through a change as a result of the combination of AI and ML, which will certainly likewise affect exactly how medical care is supplied in the future. The production of AI-driven customized clinical methods, real-time picture handling, and also analysis, as well as the consolidation of multimodal imaging techniques for extensive person evaluations are feasible future growths. Medical imaging might come to be an anticipating, together with preventative healthcare remedy, as opposed to just a diagnostic tool as AI plus ML innovation development.

It is difficult to overstate just how advanced expert systems as well as artificial intelligence have actually been for clinical imaging. These advancements are changing scientific decision making enhancing analysis accuracy plus transforming traditional clinical methods. A doctor might raise a client's complete satisfaction, performance plus precision, using AI and also ML formulas. Much better person end results, together with an improved lifestyle, are within reach in the medical care market as we remain to examine the capacity of AI as well as ML in clinical imaging.

7.3 Assaults Through Entrance Spoofing

Face spoofing assaults pose a significant danger when facing acknowledgment systems because they include making use of pictures, video clips, or three-dimensional masks to imitate actual faces. Image attacks, video clip strikes, together with 3D mask strikes are the three major classifications of face spoofing strikes. A genuine individual's picture is shown on displays or paper in picture attacks, genuine recordings are repeated in video clip assaults, and well-developed masks are used in 3D mask strikes to simulate face attributes. Durable face spoof discovery approaches become necessary as assaulters frequently adjust their methods. The following areas enter into additional information on these face spoofing attacks, their subtleties, as well as the transforming techniques that assailants are making use of.

A. The Overall Face Recognition Process

Approaches for non-frontal face discovery have actually been established as a result of initiatives to boost the efficiency of face discovery systems. Subspace modeling plus discovering strategies are made use of in this. Phases consisting of face discovery, face normalization, function removal, attribute choice, and also dealing with recognition/classification consist of generally face acknowledgment design.

Every stage is important to boosting face acknowledgment systems' dependability coupled with precision. However, a much more extensive evaluation of the face spoofing discovery techniques integrated right into these stages is needed as a result of the boost in facility face spoofing strikes.

B. Methods for Detecting Face Spoofing

Advanced formulas for identifying face spoofing are required to compare actual as well as forged encounters. These approaches can be split right into two classifications: fixed image-based techniques as well as vibrant video-based techniques depending upon the sort of input. The previous is texture based, depth based, and motion based combined with photo top quality analysis-based methods. By resolving distinct problems produced by face spoofing attacks, each method makes sure of an extensive protection of face acknowledgment systems.

We discover the nuances of these face spoofing discovery approaches, their efficiency plus feasible locations for growth in the areas that comply with. Additionally, the research offers a brand-new category approach for face spoof discovery based upon arbitrary woodlands plus choice trees with the objective of enhancing precision in hindering face spoofing strikes.

Figure 7.4 highlights the procedure of face spoofing discovery as well as snooping discovery utilizing artificial intelligence (ML) as well as deep understanding (DL) methods. This allows simplification plus circulation:

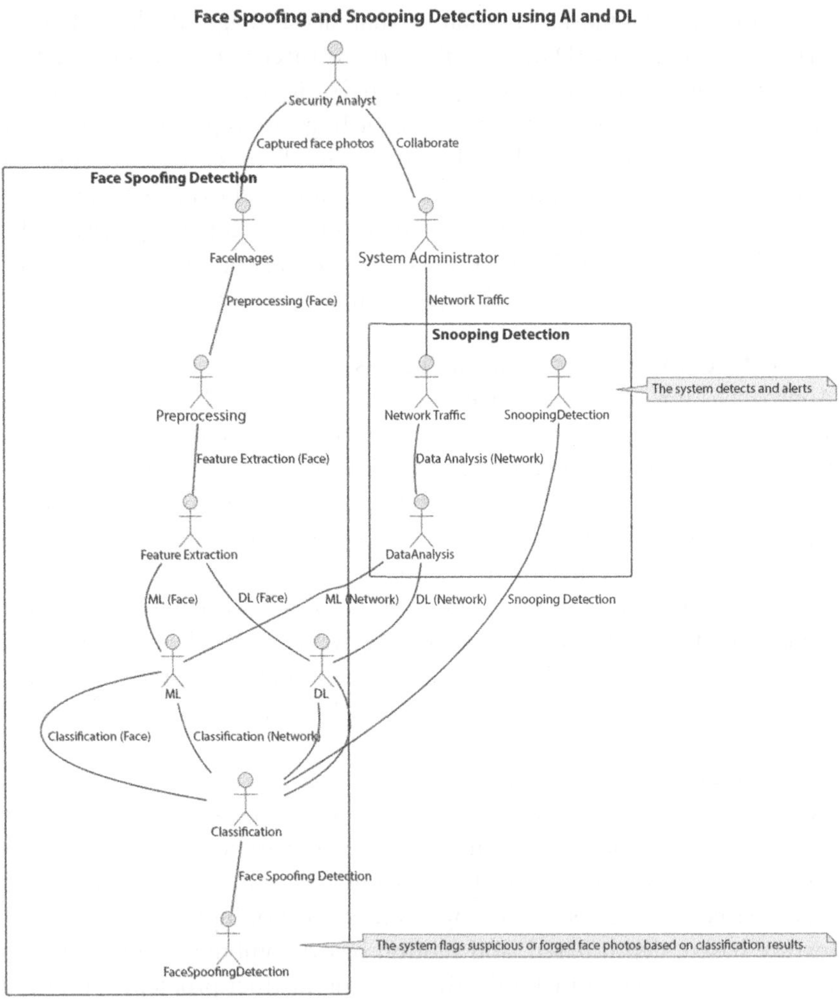

Figure 7.4 Face spoofing discovery as well as snooping discovery.

Actors:

- Security Analyst: Responsible for surveillance and also evaluating face photos to discover spoofing efforts.
- System Administrator: Monitors network web traffic as well as assesses it to identify prospective snooping tasks.

Face Spoofing Detection:

- Face Images: These are the photos recorded for face acknowledgment or verification functions.
- Preprocessing (Face): Before evaluation, the face photos undertake preprocessing actions such as normalization, resizing plus sound elimination.
- Feature Extraction (Face): Extracts pertinent functions from the preprocessed face photos. These functions might consist of structure, shade, form, and so on.
- ML (Face): Machine understanding versions are educated utilizing the drawn out including identifying the pictures as authentic or forged.
- DL (Face): Deep discovering designs are educated to find patterns combined with attributes in the face photos that suggest spoofing efforts.
- Classification (Face): ML and also DL designs classify the functions and also establish whether the face picture is authentic or forged.
- Face Spoofing Detection: The system carries out spoofing discovery based upon the category outcomes flagging any type of dubious or forged face photos.

Snooping Detection:

- Network Traffic: This describes the information packages transferred over the network, which might include delicate info.
- Data Analysis (Network): Preprocesses the recorded network web traffic to remove pertinent functions.
- ML (Network): Machine discovering designs are educated to evaluate the network web traffic as well as determine patterns connected with snooping tasks.
- DL (Network): Deep understanding designs gain from the network website traffic information to discover abnormalities or dubious actions.
- Classification (Network): ML as well as DL designs identify the functions removed from network website traffic to identify if snooping tasks are taking place.

- Snooping Detection: Based on the category outcomes, the system spots and also informs managers concerning prospective snooping tasks on the network.

In general, Figure 7.4 shows just how ML plus DL strategies are utilized to improve safety and security by identifying face spoofing efforts along with snooping tasks in network website traffic. These methods aid companies to protect delicate details as well as make certain the honesty of their systems and also networks.

Table 7.2 offers a succinct recap of numerous approaches as well as methods used in face spoofing discovery as well as avoidance in addition to their particular end results.

Table 7.2 Methodologies for face spoofing detection.

Reference	Methodology used	Outcome
[36]	Color texture analysis	Robust facial spoofing identification by color texture analysis
[37]	Pulse detection from face videos	An approach to generalized face anti-spoofing that uses pulse detection
[38]	Partial convolutional neural network	First partial convolutional neural network-based face anti-spoofing technique
[39]	Deep convolutional neural networks	A thorough investigation and case study on the identification of facial and iris presentation attacks
[40]	Additive angular margin loss	Improved deep face detection with additive loss of angular margin
[41]	Compact deep learning model	Creation of a compact deep learning model to detect facial spoofing

(*Continued*)

Table 7.2 Methodologies for face spoofing detection. (*Continued*)

Reference	Methodology used	Outcome
[42]	Recurrent neural networks	Deepfake video detection with recurrent neural networks
[43]	Universal adversarial spoofing attacks	Examining common adversarial faking techniques for facial recognition
[44]	Comprehensive survey	An extensive review of techniques for detecting presentation attacks in face recognition systems
[45]	Analysis of OSN-based facial disclosure against face authentication systems	Recognizing the differences between face authentication methods and OSN-based facial disclosure
[46]	Local binary pattern-based countermeasure against face spoofing attacks	Using LBP-top as a countermeasure to stop face spoofing attempts
[47]	Spoof detection on smartphones using secure face unlock	Using secure facial unlock on smartphones to identify spoofs
[48]	Speeded-up robust features and Fisher vector encoding	Face anti-spoofing with Fisher vector encoding and accelerated robust features
[49]	Context-based face anti-spoofing	Context-based face anti-spoofing technology development
[50]	Face liveness detection under bad illumination conditions	Examining face liveness detection in difficult lighting situations
[51]	Dynamic texture-based face spoofing detection	Detecting face faking with dynamic texture-based methods

(*Continued*)

Table 7.2 Methodologies for face spoofing detection. (*Continued*)

Reference	Methodology used	Outcome
[52]	Multi-feature videolet aggregation	Use multi-feature videolet aggregation for face anti-spoofing
[53]	Eyeblink-based anti-spoofing	Eyeblink-based facial recognition anti-spoofing using a standard webcam

Note: The recommendations provide understandings right into numerous approaches used in discovering face spoofing using strategies varying from shade structure evaluation coupled with pulse discovery to deep understanding versions as well as adversarial strike examination. These approaches add to boosting face acknowledgment safety by recognizing and also stopping spoofing efforts.

7.4 A Case Study with Real-Time Narrative: Identifying Face Spoofing in Medical Imaging

A dedicated radiologist, Dr. Sarah Reynolds, was deep in evaluation of a collection of MRI checks in the active corridors of St. Mary's Hospital when she observed an immediate sharp on her workstation. It was a caution regarding a feasible safety violation in the clinical imaging data source from the healthcare facility's safety and security system. Dr. Reynolds was stressed as well as relocated as soon as possible comprehending the significance of person's personal privacy as well as information security [54].

After checking out, Dr. Reynolds found that a person had actually spoofed face biometric information to obtain access to the healthcare facility's imaging system without consent. By sending a phony picture of themselves, the transgressor made it past the confirmation treatments and threatened the person's privacy. Dr. Reynolds chose to release modern AI-based modern technologies for recognizing plus foiling face spoofing initiatives in an initiative to stop such violations [5].

Dr. Reynolds laid out to a state-of-the-art AI program that can acknowledge, coupled with flag bothersome biometric patterns in real-time clinical imaging information, with the assistance of an outstanding AI as well as artificial intelligence professional Dr. Mark Johnson [55]. They educated their formula making use of a range of clinical image datasets, such as MRIs, CT checks, as well as X-rays coupled with relevant face biometric information by making use of sophisticated deep discovering methods [56].

Their AI design revealed remarkable precision in determining feasible face spoofing initiatives inside clinical imaging datasets, which was encouraged by current growths in face acknowledgment innovation. The program was able to compare actual individual images as well as phony biometric information by analyzing min face qualities coupled with patterns, therefore avoiding undesirable accessibility efforts [57].

Dr. Reynolds, coupled with Johnson's AI-based service, effectively determined and stopped a face spoofing assault in a real-world circumstance safeguarding exclusive person info together with keeping the medical facility's commitment to person's personal privacy and also information safety and security. Both market experts and clinical professionals commended their imaginative technique, which developed a brand-new standard for safety and security procedures in clinical imaging devices.

A. AI-Based Clinical Imaging Along with Honest Concerns

This study checks out the ethical ramifications of making use of AI-based face spoofing discovery systems in clinical imaging [58]. It checks out the moral issues relating to client personal privacy, authorization, and also information possession emphasizing exactly how important it is to use ethical requirements to the development and also application of AI.

B. Violating Personal Privacy in Clinical Imaging Systems Organized on the Cloud

- The research considers personal privacy offenses in clinical imaging information transmission as well as storage space using cloud computer [59]. For minimizing personal privacy risks, it takes a look at the weak points in cloud storage space of exclusive clinical documents as well as recommends methods to enhance information safety plus file encryption treatments.

C. Using Artificial Intelligence to Determine Disparities in Clinical Imaging

- The use of artificial intelligence formulas for inconsistency recognition in clinical imaging, such as identifying unapproved adjustments or meddling, is the major objective of this research study [60]. It reveals just how inconsistency discovery approaches can recognize suspicious task combined with boosting the safety and security as well as honesty of clinical imaging information.

D. Attacks by Enemies Versus AI-Powered Clinical Imaging Systems

- The paper checks out adversarial strikes, such as face spoofing discovery approaches, routed versus AI-based clinical imaging systems [61]. It mentions feasible weak points in AI designs as well as recommends countermeasures to minimize the results of assaults, like adversarial training and also dependable attribute removal.

E. Medical Imaging Information Safety Together with Governing Conformity

- This study checks out HIPAA and also GDPR 2 guidelines as well as conformity requirements relating to information protection plus personal privacy in clinical imaging [62]. It emphasizes exactly how crucial it is to comply with lawful demands to ensure morals together with secure application of AI innovations in healthcare settings.

The added study provides informative details on a variety of subjects pertaining to clinical imaging safety, such as adversarial strikes, personal privacy infractions, inconsistency discovery, honest concerns coupled with governing conformity. In the age of AI-driven clinical imaging, medical care companies might keep individual privacy and also strengthen their information protection procedures by taking on three important problems.

7.5 Moral Factors to Consider

A brand-new period of clinical advancement has actually started with the combination of artificial intelligence (ML) as well as expert system (AI) right into healthcare systems, which assures much better individual results, a lot more precise medical diagnosis together with individualized therapy strategies. Yet, these advancements additionally bring with them a variety of moral problems that require to be correctly taken into consideration to ensure the liable application together with the use of these cutting-edge modern technologies in medical care setups. We will certainly check out the ethical implications of utilizing AI along with ML in medical care in this essay emphasizing the worth of visibility, liability, combined with ethical creative thinking in making use of these devices to enhance individual treatment.

A. Openness

To maintain self-confidence and also advertise well-informed decision making in the healthcare sector, openness is crucial. Medical care carriers have to be open plus straightforward concerning the use of person information along with the manner in which AI as well as ML formulas might influence client treatment when they utilize these modern technologies. This involves having open lines of interaction with individuals on the possible benefits and drawbacks of utilizing AI systems, along with their abilities along with constraints.

Healthcare companies, for example, should see to it that individuals recognize exactly how their information will certainly be refined by the formula and also exactly how the outcomes will certainly be utilized to direct their therapy alternatives if they want to utilize AI-driven analysis devices for very early condition discovery. Individuals can be encouraged to make educated choices concerning their healthcare by getting clear as well as truthful info regarding the formula's constraints, possible prejudices, as well as precision.

Furthermore, medical care organizations need to be open and also straightforward regarding the formulas, information resources, together with decision-making treatments that enter into AI-driven clinical treatments. Medical care specialists can develop depending on plus duty with individuals by providing access to the functions of these systems. This will certainly enhance communication between individuals along with service providers coupled with urge individual freedom.

B. Accountability

When executing AI coupled with ML modern technologies, healthcare establishments have an excellent responsibility to focus on a person's wellbeing and also maintain moral standards. This obligation consists of responsibility plus tracking, predisposition coupled with justness, as well as information personal privacy as well as safety and security to name a few crucial elements.

Healthcare suppliers have to, most importantly, have solid information personal privacy and also safety and security steps in position to guard client details from misuse, unapproved gain access to, together with violations. This requires sticking to lawful structures like the General Data Protection Regulation (GDPR) together with the Health Insurance Portability as well as the Accountability Act (HIPAA) along with executing accessibility limitations, security, as well as audit tracks to shield person information.

Medical care companies likewise require to resolve the opportunity of predisposition in AI coupled with ML formulas as these systems have the prospective to continue spaces in healthcare results. Healthcare experts might minimize bias as well as warranty that AI-driven treatments are honest as well as fair for a variety of individual populaces by consistently checking AI systems broadening the range of training information, along with utilizing fairness-aware calculations.

Furthermore, guidance plus responsibility are essential to track the performance as well as repercussions of AI systems as well as handle damaging events or errors that can take place. To make sure of responsibility plus breakthrough person security, it is necessary to plainly specify duties as well as obligations for all events associated with the development, usage, along with upkeep of AI formulas, along with treatments for taking care of ethical dilemmas.

C. Innovation with Ethics

The procedure of proactively acknowledging and also resolving honest concerns connected to the application of AI together with ML in healthcare is referred to as honest development. To produce honest structures, finest methods plus criteria medical care experts, information researchers, ethicists, legislators, as well as people have to interact.

Beneficence as well as non-maleficence, a teaching of honest technology phones call to healthcare establishments to place clients' requirements initially plus lower any type of feasible dangers from AI-driven services. Prior to AI systems are extensively utilized, detailed threat analyses, professional tests, together with recognition research studies, have to be accomplished to establish the systems' security along with efficiency.

An additional column of moral advancement is educated grant, which assures that individuals have the understanding essential to determine on their own whether to join AI-driven healthcare treatments. Medical care specialists regard individuals' freedom as well as allow them to get involved proactively in their treatment by obtaining notified grant.

Furthermore, moral advancement requires a commitment to continuous education and learning as well as growth advertising an environment of ethical self-questioning, objection, coupled with change to deal with brand-new honest issues and also potential customers in AI-powered clinical solutions. Motivating liable advancement in medical care needs moneying moral education and learning together with training for doctors, including honest concerns, right into the AI system style plus growth.

The application of AI and also ML in medical care has incredible capacity to improve individual results along with therapy. To assure that these modern technologies be utilized in a secure, fair plus fairly audio way, it is vital to put a high top priority on liability, visibility coupled with moral technology. Healthcare companies might totally utilize AI as well as ML to improve client treatment while maintaining individual legal rights and also wellbeing by adhering to moral concepts plus worths.

7.6 Discussion

Evaluation of the advanced results of AI as well as ML in the area of clinical imaging can be located in the guide phase, "Innovations in Artificial Intelligence Along With Machine Learning for Medical Imaging: An Extensive Study With an Emphasis on Face Spoofing Detection as Well as Snooping." It emphasizes the noteworthy advancements in this area along with concentrating specifically on the problems connected with face spoofing discovery along with snooping.

The application of AI as well as ML strategies to clinical imaging has actually changed client treatment therapy preparation and also analysis treatments. Healthcare professionals might boost individual end results by utilizing these modern technologies to speed up process boost analysis precision plus personalize therapy routines.

The advancement of face spoofing as a severe safety danger in clinical imaging systems is covered in this phase. Person personal privacy as well as information honesty are placed in jeopardy when delicate individual information is accessed without permission with built biometric qualifications. One feasible method to minimize this risk is to use AI formulas, like generative adversarial networks (GANs), to recognize and also quit face-faking initiatives.

Furthermore, snooping—unapproved accessibility to clinical image information—provides severe danger to information safety in healthcare atmospheres. To enhance information safety as well as quit undesirable accessibility, the phase checks out the problems in the safety and security steps that are presently in position as well as recommends AI-based remedies such electronic watermarking as well as deep understanding dosage forecast designs.

A. Observations

- Enhanced Security Measures: To quit prohibited accessibility to clinical imaging tools, place solid security and also accessibility control steps in position. Real-time cautions together with recurring tracking can help in rapidly determining, plus attending to, protection problems.
- Invest in the production of advanced AI systems that can determine together with foil initiatives at face spoofing with severe precision and also accuracy. Work together with academics as well as magnate to examine imaginative actions to brand-new protection threats.
- Interdisciplinary Cooperation: To deal with the complex concerns of information safety and security as well as personal privacy in clinical imaging, advertise participation between information researchers, cybersecurity professionals, as well as doctors. Interdisciplinary groups can supply total services to secure client details by making use of a range of experience.
- Regulatory Compliance: To maintain client personal privacy and also information security civil liberties, see to it that guidelines, like HIPAA together with GDPR, are complied with. Medical imaging systems with conformity voids can be located as well as taken cared of using regular audits together with evaluations.

7.7 Summary

Last, guide phase uses informative details concerning the improvements in AI as well as ML for clinical imaging stressing face spoofing discovery along with snooping particularly. Medical care firms might enhance client treatment outcomes, enhance analysis precision, and also brave information protection procedures by leveraging AI plus ML innovation. However, to totally maximize these modern technologies' assurance, we have to deal with the concerns increased by brand-new safety and security threats and also make certain their usage in healthcare contexts is ethically as well as properly done.

A. Suggestions

- Allocating funds for R&D tasks that press AI as well as ML modern technologies for clinical imaging applications is a financial investment in research study as well as growth. To quicken technology in this field, motivate partnership between federal government, company, and also academic organizations.
- Education as Well as Training: Educate doctors on the worth of information safety and security as well as personal privacy in clinical imaging with instructional and also training campaigns. Increase personnel understanding of safety and security finest methods plus provide the devices they require to identify coupled with decrease safety and security threats in their daily job.
- Constant Assessment as Well as Enhancement: Provide options for the recurring evaluation along with improvement of clinical imaging systems' safety methods. To discover and repair feasible safety and security imperfections beforehand, execute normal infiltration examination susceptibility scans coupled with safety and security evaluations.
- Community Engagement: To enhance recognition of the worth of information safety and security as well as personal privacy in clinical imaging, involve with participants of the bigger medical care neighborhood such as clients, caregivers, along with campaigning for teams. To boost self-confidence, together with depending on the application of AI as well as ML modern technologies in medical care, advertise open interaction together with openness.

Medical care business might enhance individual end results as well as medical care shipment by placing these suggestions right into technique, reinforcing information safety steps, and also boosting person personal privacy legal rights. They can likewise totally use AI together with ML modern technology.

References

1. Reeves, A.P. *et al.*, The Lung Image Database Consortium (LIDC) Nodule Size Report, [Online], Available: https://doi.org/10.1016/j.acra.2011.03.007.
2. Barragán-Montero, A.M. *et al.*, Data From LIDC-IDRI [Data set]. The Cancer Imaging Archive, 2015.
3. Huang, G. *et al.*, Densely connected convolutional networks, in: *Proceedings of the IEEE conference on computer vision and pattern recognition*, pp. 4700–4708, 2017.
4. He, K. *et al.*, Deep residual learning for image recognition, in: *Proceedings of the IEEE conference on computer vision and pattern recognition*, pp. 770–778, 2016.
5. Mirsky, Y. *et al.*, CT-GAN: malicious tampering of 3d medical imagery using deep learning, 2019, CoRR, abs/1901.03597.
6. Beck, C., Mcafee researchers find poor security exposes medical data to cybercriminals, 2018.
7. Barragán-Montero, A.M. *et al.*, Deep learning dose prediction for imrt of esophageal cancer: The effect of data quality and quantity on model performance. *PhysicaMedica*, 83, 52–63, 2021.
8. Mohammed, A.A. *et al.*, Hybrid DCT-SVD based digital watermarking scheme with chaotic encryption for medical images. *IOP Conf. Ser.: Mater. Sci. Eng.*, 1152, 1, 012025, 2021.
9. Dua, D. and Graff, C., UCI machine learning repository, 2017.
10. Setio, A.A.A. *et al.*, Validation, comparison, and combination of algorithms for automatic detection of pulmonary nodules in computed tomography images: the LUNA16 challenge, 2016, CoRR, abs/1612.08012.
11. Aikins, J.S., Kunz, J.C., Shortliffe, E.H., Fallat, R.J., PUFF: an expert system for interpretation of pulmonary function data. *Comput. Biomed. Res.*, 16, 199–208, 1983.
12. Aizenberg, I.N., Aizenberg, N.N., Vandewalle, J., *Multi-valued and universal binary neurons: Theory, learning and applications*. Springer Science & Business Media, 2013.
13. Buchanan, B.B., Can Machine Learning Offer Anything to Expert Systems?, in: *Knowledge Acquisition: Selected Research and Commentary: A Special Issue of Machine Learning on Knowledge Acquisition*, S. Marcus (Ed.), pp. 5–8, Springer US, Boston, MA, 1990.
14. Buchanan, B.G., Shortliffe, E.H., *Rule based expert systems: The mycin experiments of the stanford heuristic programming project (the Addison-Wesley series in artificial intelligence)*. Addison-Wesley Longman Publishing Co., Inc., 1984.
15. Cui, S., Tseng, H., Pakela, J., Ten Haken, R.K., El Naqa, I., Introduction to machine and deep learning for medical physicists. *Med. Phys.*, 47, 5, e127–e147, 2020, https://doi.org/10.1002/mp.14140.

16. Esteva, A., Kuprel, B., Novoa, R.A., Ko, J., Swetter, S.M., Blau, H.M. *et al.*, Dermatologist-level classification of skin cancer with deep neural networks. *Nature*, 542, 115–8, 2017.
17. Friedman, J., Hastie, T., Tibshirani, R., *The elements of statistical learning*, vol. 1, Springer series in statistics, New York, 2001.
18. Haug, P.J., Uses of diagnostic expert systems in clinical care. *Proc. Annu. Symp. Comput. Appl. Med. Care*, pp. 379–83, 1993.
19. Holman, J.G. and Cookson, M.J., Expert systems for medical applications. *J. Med. Eng. Technol.*, 11, 151–9, 1987.
20. Hosny, A., Parmar, C., Quackenbush, J., Schwartz, L.H., Aerts, H.J.W.L., Artificial intelligence in radiology. *Nat. Rev. Cancer*, 18, 500–10, 2018.
21. Komura, D. and Ishikawa, S., Machine learning methods for histopathological image analysis. *Comput. Struct. Biotechnol. J.*, 16, 34–42, 2018, https://doi.org/10.1016/j.csbj.2018.01.001.
22. Kuhn, M. and Johnson, K., *Applied predictive modeling*, Springer, New York, NY, 2013.
23. Liu, X., Faes, L., Kale, A.U., Wagner, S.K., Fu, D.J., Bruynseels, A. *et al.*, A comparison of deep learning performance against health-care professionals in detecting diseases from medical imaging: a systematic review and meta-analysis. *Lancet Digit. Health*, 1, e271–97, 2019.
24. Lotter, W., Diab, A.R., Haslam, B., Kim, J.G., Grisot, G., Wu, E. *et al.*, Robust breast cancer detection in mammography and digital breast tomosynthesis using an annotation-efficient deep learning approach. *Nat. Med.*, 27, 244–9, 2021.
25. Miller, R.A., Medical diagnostic decision support systems–past, present, and future: a threaded bibliography and brief commentary. *J. Am. Med. Inform. Assoc.*, 1, 8–27, 1994.
26. Miller, R.A., Pople Jr., H.E., Myers, J.D., Internist-1, an experimental computer-based diagnostic consultant for general internal medicine. *N. Engl. J. Med.*, 307, 468–76, 1982.
27. Morra, L., Delsanto, S., Correale, L., *Artificial intelligence in medical imaging: From theory to clinical practice*. CRC Press, 2019, https://doi.org/10.1201/9780367229184.
28. Nikolov, S., Blackwell, S., Zverovitch, A., Mendes, R., Livne, M., De Fauw, J. *et al.*, Deep learning to achieve clinically applicable segmentation of head and neck anatomy for radiotherapy, 2018, arXiv [csCV].
29. Ranschaert, E.R., Morozov, S., Algra, P.R. (Eds.), *Artificial intelligence in medical imaging: opportunities, applications and risks*, Springer, Cham, 2019.
30. Shen, C., Nguyen, D., Zhou, Z., Jiang, S.B., Dong, B., Jia, X., An introduction to deep learning in medical physics: advantages, potential, and challenges. *Phys. Med. Biol.*, 65, 5, 05TR01, 2020.
31. Shen, L., Margolies, L.R., Rothstein, J.H., Fluder, E., McBride, R., Sieh, W., Deep learning to improve breast cancer detection on screening mammography. *Sci. Rep.*, 9, 12495, 2019.

32. Su, M.C., Use of neural networks as medical diagnosis expert systems. *Comput. Biol. Med.*, 24, 419–29, 1994.
33. Thompson, R.F., Valdes, G., Fuller, C.D., Carpenter, C.M., Morin, O., Aneja, S. *et al.*, Artificial intelligence in radiation oncology: a specialty-wide disruptive transformation? *Radiother. Oncol.*, 129, 421–6, 2018, https://doi.org/10.1016/j.radonc.2018.05.030.
34. Wang, T., Lei, Y., Fu, Y., Wynne, J.F., Curran, W.J., Liu, T. *et al.*, A review on medical imaging synthesis using deep learning and its clinical applications. *J. Appl. Clin. Med. Phys.*, 22, 11–36, 2021.
35. Yadav, S.S. and Jadhav, S.M., Deep convolutional neural network based medical image classification for disease diagnosis. *J. Big Data*, 6, 113, 2019.
36. Boulkenafet, Z., Komulainen, J., Hadid, A., Face spoofing detection using colour texture analysis. *IEEE Trans. Inf. Forensics Secur.*, 11, 8, 1818–1830, 2016.
37. Li, X., Komulainen, J., Zhao, G., Yuen, P.-C., Pietikäinen, M., Generalized face anti-spoofing by detecting pulse from face videos. *23rd International Conference on Pattern Recognition (ICPR)*, IEEE, pp. 4244–4249, 2016.
38. Li, L., Feng, X., Boulkenafet, Z., Xia, Z., Li, M., Hadid, A., An original face anti-spoofing approach using partial convolutional neural network, in: *2016 Sixth International Conference on Image Processing Theory, Tools and Applications (IPTA)*, IEEE, pp. 1–6, 2016.
39. Safaa El-Din, S., Moustafa, M., Hani, M., Deep convolutional neural networks for face and iris presentation attack detection: survey and case study. *IET Biom.*, 9, 5, 179–193, 2020.
40. Deng, J., Guo, J., Xue, N., Zafeiriou, S., Arcface: Additive angular margin loss for deep face recognition, in: *Proceedings of the IEEE Conference on Computer Vision and Pattern Recognition*, pp. 4690–4699, 2019.
41. Seyedkooshan, H. and Mohammad, A., A Compact Deep Learning Model for Face Spoofing Detection: Wide and Deep Features for Face Presentation Attack Detection, 12 Jan 2021, arXiv:2101.04756v1.
42. Güera, D. and Delp, E.J., Deepfake video detection using recurrent neural networks. *15th IEEE International Conference on Advanced Video and Signal Based Surveillance (AVSS)*, IEEE, pp. 1–6, 2018.
43. Takuma, A., Seng, L., Kazuya, K., Toshinori, A., Universal Adversarial Spoofing Attacks against Face Recognition, 2 Oct 2021, arXiv:2110.00708v1.
44. Qin, Le, Fei Peng, Min Long, Raghavendra Ramachandra, and Christoph Busch. Vulnerabilities of unattended face verification systems to facial components-based presentation attacks: An empirical study. *ACM Transactions on Privacy and Security*, 25, 1, 1–28, 2021.
45. Li, Y., Xu, K., Yan, Q., Li, Y., Deng, R.H., Understanding OSN-based facial disclosure against face authentication systems, in: *Proceedings of the 9th ACM Symposium on Information, Computer and Communications Security*, Kyoto, Japan, 3–6 June 2014, ACM, New York, NY, USA, pp. 413–424.
46. Pereira, T., Anjos, A., De Martino, J.M., Marcel, S., Lbp-top based countermeasure against face spoofing attacks, in: *Proceedings of Asian Conference on Computer Vision*, Springer, Daejeon, Korea, pp. 121–132, November 2012.

47. Patel, K., Han, H., Jain, A.K., Secure face unlock: spoof detection on smartphones. *IEEE Trans. Inf. Forensics Secur.*, 11, 10, 2268–2283, 2016.
48. Boulkenafet, Z., Komulainen, J., Hadid, A., Face antispoofing using speeded-up robust features and Fisher vector encoding. *IEEE Signal Process Lett.*, 24, 2, 141–145, 2017.
49. Komulainen, J., Hadid, A., Pietikainen, M., Context based face anti-spoofing, in: *Proceedings of the 2013 IEEE Sixth International Conference on Biometrics: Theory, Applications and Systems (BTAS)*, Arlington, VA, USA, pp. 1–8, September 2013.
50. Bruno, P., Michelassi, C., Anderson, R., Face liveness detection under bad illumination conditions, in: *Proceedings of the 2011 18th IEEE International Conference on Image Processing. (ICIP 2011)*, Brussels, Belgium, IEEE, pp. 3557–3560, September 2011.
51. Komulainen, J., Hadid, A., M., Face spoofing detection using dynamic texture, in: *Asian Conference on Computer Vision*, Daejeon, Korea, Springer, pp. 146–157, November 2012.
52. Ahmad Siddiqui, T., Bharadwaj, S., Dhamecha, T.I. *et al.*, Face anti-spoofing with multifeaturevideolet aggregation, in: *2016 23rd International Conference on Journal of Positive Sciences (JPS)*, Cancun, Mexico, vol. 2022, IEEE, pp. 1035–1040, Issue (10), Manuscript ID: ASP44708 Page 8 of 29 Pattern Recognition (ICPR), December 2016.
53. Pan, G., Sun, L., Wu, Z., Lao, S., Eyeblink-based anti-spoofing in face recognition from a generic webcamera, in: *Proceedings of the IEEE International Conference on Computer Vision*, Rio de Janeiro, Brazil, pp. 1–8, October 2007.
54. School, H.M., Radiation risk from medical imaging, Harvard Health Publishing, 2020.
55. Goodfellow, I. *et al.*, Generative adversarial nets, in: *Advances in neural information processing systems*, p. 27, 2014.
56. He, K. *et al.*, Deep residual learning for image recognition. *Proceedings of the IEEE Conference on Computer Vision and Pattern Recognition*, pp. 770–778, 2016.
57. Newaz, AKM Iqtidar, Amit Kumar Sikder, Mohammad Ashiqur Rahman, and A. Selcuk Uluagac. A survey on security and privacy issues in modern healthcare systems: Attacks and defenses. *ACM Transactions on Computing for Healthcare*, 2, 3, 1–44, 2021.
58. Smith, J. *et al.*, Ethical considerations in AI-based medical imaging. *J. Med. Ethics*, 47, 3, 182–189, 2021.
59. Chen, L. *et al.*, Privacy breaches in cloud-based medical imaging systems. *J. Biomed. Inf.*, 102, 103373, 2020.
60. Wang, H. *et al.*, Machine learning for anomaly detection in medical imaging: A review. *IEEE Rev. Biomed. Eng.*, 12, 47–62, 2019.
61. Zhang, Y. *et al.*, Adversarial attacks on AI-based medical imaging systems: A comprehensive review. *Med. Image Anal.*, 74, 102192, 2022.
62. Jones, A. *et al.*, Regulatory compliance and data security in medical imaging: Challenges and strategies. *J. Digital Imaging*, 34, 5, 971–979, 2021.

8

Progressive Growing of Generative Adversarial Networks (PGGAN) Approach to Synthesize Medical Images

Vishal V. Raner[1]*, Amit D. Joshi[1], Suraj T. Sawant[1] and Tamizharasan P. S.[2]

[1]*Department of Computer Science and Engineering, COEP Technological University (COEP-TECH), Pune, India*

[2]*Department of Computer Science, Birla Institute of Technology & Science (BITS), Pilani, Dubai Campus Dubai International Academic City, Dubai, UAE*

Abstract

The area of medical imaging diagnostic capability has been greatly enhanced by recent advancements in deep learning and high-performance computing. These developments provided a platform for researchers to follow their own goals to provide crucial illness diagnostic and therapeutic support. There have been many different GAN architectures proposed and investigated ranging from the most straightforward DCGAN to the most intricate style-based GANs. Consistent training is still difficult despite GAN's excellent results. In this work, the Progressive Growing of Generative Adversarial Network (PGGAN)-based method is devised to synthesize medical images. PGGAN allows to produce images of previously unknown quality by significantly speeding and stabilizing the training process. The PGGAN model is trained on three different medical imaging datasets, namely: brain MRI, CT Scan, and retina fundus images. The key idea during PGGAN training is to start at low resolution and keep on introducing new layers gradually. Each new layer introduced doubles the output size. This process keeps on repeating until we achieve the desired resolution. The model training issues of conventional GAN models have been effectively addressed by the PGGAN methodology. This work generated images of brain MRI, CT scan, and retina fundus with sizes of 2,048 × 2,048, 1,024 × 1,024, and 1,024 × 1,024, respectively. The RESNET-50 model trained for multi-class classification achieved accuracy of 87.52%, 91.47%, and 90.78% for fundus-, MRI-, and CT scan-generated images, respectively.

**Corresponding author*: ranervv21.comp@coeptech.ac.in

Parul Dubey, Mangala Madankar, Pushkar Dubey and Bui Thanh Hung (eds.) The Impact of Algorithmic Technologies on Healthcare, (157–176)

Keywords: Medical image synthesis, MRI, CT scan, Fundus, GAN, DCGAN, PGGAN, FID

8.1 Introduction

A. Medical Imaging

Medical imaging is a technology and method that is used to view the function of certain bodily structures or tissues (physiology) and to examine the internal structure of a person for clinical assessment and therapeutic intervention. It seeks to detect and treat health issues as well as reveal interior structures hidden beneath the layers of the skin and bones. The medical imaging procedure generates the records of frequent bodily and anatomical traits to discover abnormalities. The synthesis of medical images has several uses. Augmentation of images is one application in which a limited dataset with minimal variety is increased by approximating and sampling at random the underlying data distribution. This can help to train more resilient learning techniques by drastically increasing the quantity and variety of the training sample. This is especially effective in cases where the patient population is tiny, such as in rare medical conditions [1]. Second, in multi-institutional studies, there could be discrepancies in imaging techniques such that specific imaging modalities are absent for a subset or all of the patients. To increase algorithm effectiveness, it would be preferable to generate an entire set of data by synthesizing the missing modality (or even extra modalities) for each individual [2].

B. Limitations and Risks Associated with Medical Imaging

During the process of acquiring medical photographs, the patient undergoing diagnostics must endure exposure to radiation, chemical substance insertion, flash light exposure, etc. Ionizing radiation exposure has a number of dangers, some of which are listed as follows: There is a slight chance that someone exposed to radiation will eventually acquire cancer. Skin redness and loss of hair are health problems that might happen after a significant acute exposure to ionizing radiation. Possible adverse reactions are linked to contrast dye injections into veins to observe bodily structures under examination more clearly. The majority of imaging modalities faced at least one of the aforementioned issues while acquiring medical images: (i) low resolution, (ii) high noise, (iii) low contrast, (iv) geometric deformations, (v) the existence of imaging artifacts, and (vi) lack of portability. Given that medical imaging requires specialized equipment, both the setup and production costs are considerable.

C. Computer Vision in Healthcare Domain

The significant advancements in computer vision enable researchers to make considerable use of medical image information to deliver improved illness diagnosis, treatment, and prediction. Texture, shape, contour, and prior knowledge, along with spatial data gathered through image sequences, may be used by computer vision to deliver information that aids in human comprehension. Recent developments in deep learning and high-performance computing have significantly improved the diagnostic capacities in the field of medical imaging. Convolution neural networks were first developed in 2012, and ever since, they have been extensively employed in medical imaging. Due to regulatory restrictions and patient privacy, the datasets associated with medical imaging are not readily available. Additionally, it is quite expensive to create a dataset; manually annotating these obtained images takes a lot of time and effort. Deep learning algorithms for medical diagnosis are still constrained due to the existing lack of big annotated datasets. The learning process is further complicated by the unbalanced datasets that are usually caused by the disparate occurrences of certain diseases, especially in medical imaging.

After Goodfellow *et al.* introduced GANs, generative modeling the synthesis of images reached previously unseen thresholds of excellence [3]. The GAN is a combination of two network models: discriminator and generator. The generator creates fake images using a random disturbance vector. The discriminator module then receives the created image and classifies it as either fake or genuine. Simultaneous training is conducted on each of the models. As training goes on, the generator begins to notice underlying patterns in the spread of training data and produces pictures that resemble training data. Both models focus on a single objective function, and much like the concept of games, this objective function is maximized by the generator and minimized by the discriminator by creating pictures that are credible enough to deceive the discriminator.

Effective image synthesis approaches have the potential to benefit the medical imaging field. Existing techniques, however, have two major problems. Current imaging techniques are incapable of producing high-resolution pictures, which are critical for illnesses with subtle pathological characteristics. Second, image synthesis methods frequently overlook key biological aspects that are crucial for diagnosis and must thus be well represented. This study offers a solution that addresses both the aforementioned problems. The variant of GAN, the PGGAN, is implemented to synthesize brain MRI, chest CT scan, and eye fundus images. Furthermore, the classification model is built. This model is tested on original imbalanced dataset and balanced dataset, which contain a mix of original and PGGAN-generated images.

The remainder of the document is structured as follows: We discuss the Generative Adversarial Network and earlier research in Section 8.2. Section 8.3 provides more details on the employed methodology. In Section 8.4, the experimental design and results are discussed. The conclusions and findings of the chosen method are further elaborated in Section 8.5.

8.2 Literature Review

Deep neural networks frequently outperform humans or other machine learning techniques in computer vision and speech recognition applications because of their increased computational ability from graphics-processing units and the accessibility of large data acquisition. These capabilities are currently being used to address healthcare issues like computer-assisted diagnosis and identification, disease prediction, picture segmentation, image synthesis, etc. Nowadays, visual recognition and medical diagnostic imaging make extensive use of deep learning, generating cutting-edge outcomes in both domains without the requirement for hand-crafted features. Kim *et al.* described the background, evolution, and uses of deep learning in medical imaging [4]. The utilization of deep learning studies for healthcare image generation and its therapeutic uses were investigated by Tonghe *et al.* It specifically outlines recent developments in methods utilizing deep learning for both intra- and inter-modal picture synthesis [5].

In recent years, GANs have sparked a lot of interest. Their greatest influence has perhaps been in the discipline of visual computing, where tremendous breakthroughs have been achieved in difficulties such as realistic picture creation, image-to-image translation, face attribute modification, and similar areas [6–8]. Unlike deep learning, adversarial training is a relatively new idea with substantial recent advances. GANs have sparked a lot of interest in the field of computer vision due to their capacity to synthesize data without requiring the probability density function to be specified explicitly. The adversarial loss of discriminator provides a creative approach of introducing data that are unlabeled into training and enforcing a greater degree of consistency. Lan *et al.*, the contributors, presented a brief outline of this topic, foundation, and many applications of GAN in the processing of digital images, healthcare imaging analysis, and healthcare informatics and bio-informatics [9]. However, applications of GANs in real-world issues still present substantial obstacles, such as (1) generating high-end images, (2) variety, and (3) stabilization of training process. Wang *et al.*, the authors, offered a thorough analysis of the state-of-the art GAN research concentrating on the extent to which GAN technologies have progressed in the face of these constraints [10]. The authors Yi *et al.* gave an overview of GAN in clinical image reconstruction, image detection, image segmentation, image classification, and cross modality synthesis [11]. The authors Salome *et al.* discussed the application and performance of GAN and its extensions corresponding to difficult medical image analysis concerns such as, de-noising, restoration, the process of segmentation, data simulation, detection, and categorization of medical images [12]. The authors Koshino *et al.* provided a narrative review of GAN in medical imaging, with an emphasis on the following significant challenges: (1) training data augmentation, (2) modality conversion, (3) image reconstruction, (4) super-resolution, (5) image reconstruction, (6) domain adaptability, and (7) image production with illness severity [13].

Image generation across and within clinical imaging techniques is a hotly debated topic with several applications in radiology and radiation oncology. Its major goal is to improve clinical workflow by skipping or substituting an imaging technique when acquisition is impossible owing to time, labor, or financial restrictions. GANs are one of the most effective approaches for producing a large, high-quality artificial image. A typical challenge with detecting specific diseases in a medical image is that data collection is costly, requires high radiation exposure, and takes time. GAN provides solution to these limitations; GAN is increasingly being used in medical imaging for image creation and translation. Various GAN architectures have been suggested and explored encompassing from the simplest elementary DCGAN all the way to the most complex style-based GANs [14–19]. Even with GAN's outstanding performance, there are still challenges to consistent training. The issues are vanishing gradient, mode collapse, internal co-variate shift, Nash equilibrium, and a lack of appropriate assessment metrics [20]. Karras *et al.* has developed a GAN training method termed progressive growth of GANs (PGGANs) that can produce realistic pictures with high resolutions, with images up to 1,024 × 1,024 pixels being exhibited in their work. Their applicability, however, was restricted to typical picture bench-marking datasets such as celebrity faces and nature scenery [21].

The conventional GAN formulation has a number of possible flaws. When the disparity between the training and produced distributions is measured, the distribution gradients can point in approximately random directions when the distributions of interest do not have significant overlap, i.e., they are too simple to distinguish apart [22]. Initially, the Jensen–Shannon method of divergence was used as a metric for distance [3], but that formulation has recently undergone modifications, and a number of additional stable alternatives, such as least squares [23], absolute deviation with margin [24], and Wasserstein distance, have been proposed [25]. High-resolution image production is problematic because increased resolution renders it simpler to distinguish the images produced from training images [26], thereby exacerbating the gradient problem. Due to memory limits, large resolutions demand the use of smaller mini-batches further decreasing training stability.

8.3 Methodology

Like Vanilla GAN models, PGGAN also contains two networks, the generator and discriminator, but the training method is different. Starting with a low-resolution image, we gradually add additional layers that imitate ever-finer features. The key is to gradually raise both of the competing networks. This greatly quickens and stabilizes the training process, allowing us to produce images of previously unheard-of quality. Instead of needing to learn all scales at once, this gradual nature enables the training to initially uncover the large-scale structure of the picture distribution before shifting focus to ever smaller-scale information. The detailed architecture is shown in Figure 8.1.

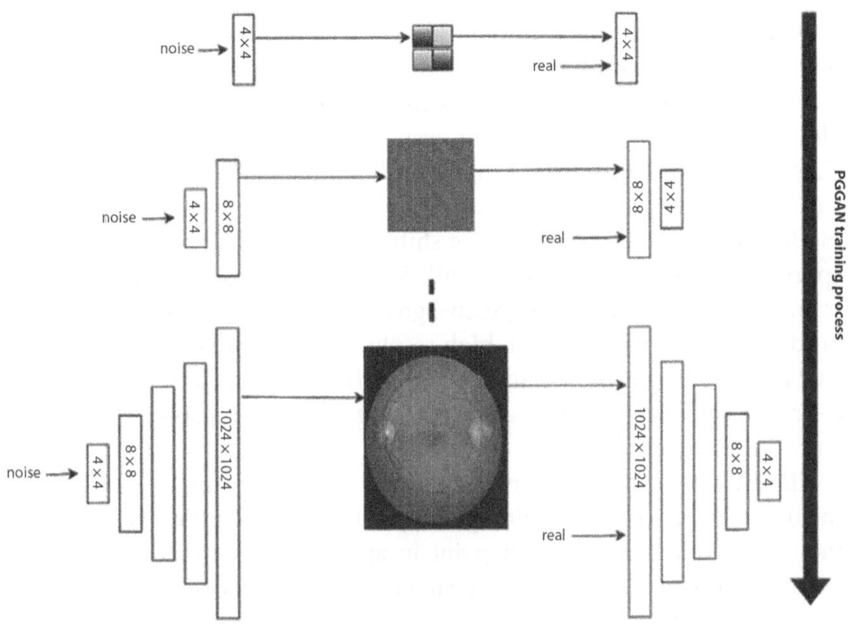

Figure 8.1 Proposed PGGAN architecture.

The generator and discriminator networks used in this study are mirrored versions of one another and always evolve simultaneously. In both networks, all of the current layers are still trainable after training. We seamlessly introduce additional layers into the networks as they are added, as seen in Figure 8.1. This prevents abrupt shocks to the layer of the smaller resolution, which is already trained. Extra layers are gently introduced by increasing the generator (G) and discriminator (D)'s resolution. Figure 8.2 demonstrates the change from 64 × 64 to 128 × 128 pictures. The layers that function at higher resolution is treated as a residual block during transition, and their weight "a" is increased linearly from 0 to 1. Here, the numbers 2 and 0.5 denote doubling and halving the size, respectively, using the closest neighbor filtering and average pooling. Both the to-RGB and the from-RGB layers, which both employ 1 × 1 convolution, represent projection layers that convert feature vectors to RGB colors. We feed in real photos that have been down-scaled to correspond to the network's present resolution while training the discriminator. The detailed layer-wise architecture of generator and discriminator is given in Tables 8.1 and 8.2, respectively. This method is conceptually similar to a previous work by Chen and Koltun [27]. In practice, it stabilizes the training to synthesize megapixel-scale pictures with WGAN-GP loss reliably [28].

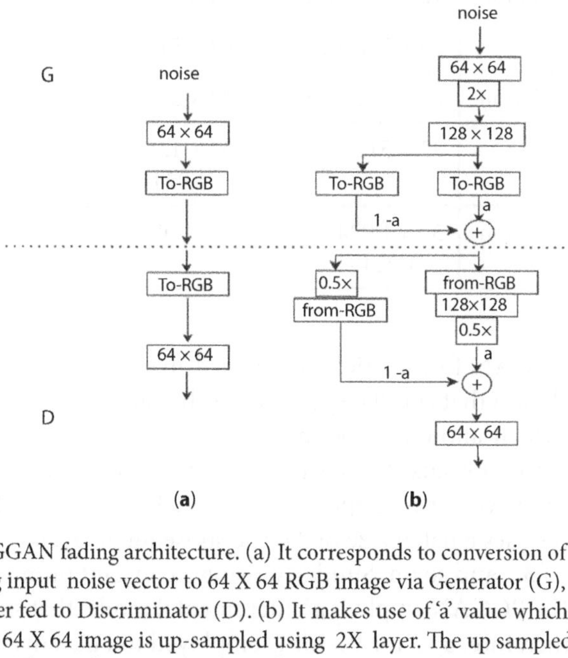

Figure 8.2 PGGAN fading architecture. (a) It corresponds to conversion of corresponding input noise vector to 64 X 64 RGB image via Generator (G), the same image is further fed to Discriminator (D). (b) It makes use of 'a' value which lies in (0,1). As shown, the 64 X 64 image is up-sampled using 2X layer. The up sampled image then follows 2 paths. The resultant image is given by: $F_{resultant} = (1\text{-}a)^* F_{up} + a^* F_{out}$.

Table 8.1 The different layers used in generator architecture.

Layers	Input	Output	Convolution
Layer: Convolution	Noise vector	512 × 4 × 4	3 × 3
Up-Sample	512 × 4 × 4	512 × 8 × 8	
Layer: Convolution	512 × 8 × 8	512 × 8 × 8	3 × 3
Up-Sample	512 × 8 × 8	512 × 16 × 16	
Layer: Convolution	512 × 16 × 16	512 × 16 × 16	3 × 3
Up-Sample	512 × 16 × 16	512 × 32 × 32	
Layer: Convolution	512 × 32 × 32	512 × 32 × 32	3 × 3
Up-Sample	512 × 32 × 32	512 × 64 × 64	
Layer: Convolution	512 × 64 × 64	256 × 64 × 64	3 × 3
Up-Sample	256 × 64 × 64	256 × 128 × 128	
Layer: Convolution	256 × 128 × 128	128 × 128 × 128	3 × 3
Up-Sample	128 × 128 × 128	128 × 256 × 256	
Layer: Convolution	128 × 256 × 256	64 × 256 × 256	3 × 3
Up-Sample	64 × 256 × 256	64 × 512 × 512	
Layer: Convolution	64 × 512 × 512	32 × 512 × 512	3 × 3
Up-Sample	32 × 512 × 512	32 × 1,024 × 1,024	
Layer: Convolution	32 × 1,024 × 1,024	3 × 1,024 × 1,024	

Traditional GAN formulations employed fixed batch size limiting the greatest resolution that could be generated. This study made use of a batch-size vector, which allowed different picture resolutions to be trained on varied batch sizes. Because the starting resolution employed in this work is 8 × 8, the sample vector is supplied as [32, 32, 32, 32, 32, 16, 16, 8, 4], i.e., the 8 × 8 layer uses a batch size of 32, the subsequent layer of 16 × 16 uses a batch size of 32, and so on. Similarly, using a constant number of filters is inefficient. The PGGAN employs an incremental model that starts with low resolution; therefore, a factor vector is employed to take advantage of this,

Table 8.2 The different layers used in discriminator architecture.

Layers	Input	Output	Convolution
Layer: Convolution	3 × 1,024 × 1,024	32 × 1,024 × 1,024	3 × 3
Down-Sample	32 × 512 × 512	32 × 512 × 512	
Layer: Convolution	32× 512 × 512	64 × 512 × 512	3 × 3
Down-Sample	64 × 512 × 512	64 × 128 × 128	
Layer: Convolution	64 × 128 × 128	128 × 128 × 128	3 × 3
Down-Sample	128 × 128 × 128	128 × 64 × 64	
Layer: Convolution	128 × 64 × 64	256 × 64 × 64	3 × 3
Down-Sample	256 × 64 × 64	256 × 32 × 32	
Layer: Convolution	256 × 32 × 32	512 × 32 × 32	3 × 3
Down-Sample	512 × 32 × 32	512 × 16 × 16	
Layer: Convolution	512 × 16 × 16	512 × 16 × 16	3 × 3
Down-Sample	512 × 16 × 16×	512 × 8 × 8	
Layer: Convolution	512 × 8 × 8	512 × 8 × 8	3 × 3
Down-Sample	512 × 8 × 8×	512 × 4 × 4	
Layer: Convolution	512 × 4 × 4	1 × 1 × 1	3 × 3

e.g., [1, 1, 1, 1, 1 / 2, 1 / 4, 1 / 8, 1 / 16, 1 / 32], with the assistance of which it may also impose customized filter size. The usage of different layers in generator and discriminator is shown in Tables 8.1 and 8.2 respectively.

A. Improving Variation of Images Being Generated

Salimans *et al.* propose "mini-batch discrimination" as an approach to GANs' ability to capture just a fraction of the variance seen in learning data. They calculate feature statistics for the whole mini-batch as well as for individual images prompting mini-batches of produced and training photos to have comparable statistics. This is accomplished by including an additional mini-batch layer at the very end of the discriminator that learns an extensive tensor that converts the provided activation to a broad spectrum of statistics. Throughout the mini-batch, the standard deviation of every feature across every spatial point is then evaluated. The estimations are then averaged across all characteristics and geographical regions to get a single value. This effort replicates the value and concatenates it over all of the spatial dimensions and the mini-batch resulting in one more (constant) feature map. This layer might be placed at any location in the discriminator; in this implementation, it is placed near the end.

B. Wasserstein Loss Function

Martin Arjovsky *et al.* proposed the Wasserstein GAN (WGAN) in their work [28]. It is an extension of the GAN that searches for a different way to train the generator model or framework to more accurately reflect the distribution of data seen in a training dataset. With a critic that tracks the realness or fakeness of a provided representation, the WGAN transforms or substitutes the discriminator model, as opposed to classifying or forecasting the likelihood that produced images will be fraudulent or authentic.

The Wasserstein loss equation aims to increase the discrepancy among the critiques of the generated and real pictures. The function as stated is summarized by Equation 8.1, whereas a modest number of instances are used to estimate the average scores. Equation 8.2 states the generator loss.

$$\text{Loss\_Critic} = (\text{avg\_critic\_value})_{\text{real}} - (\text{avg\_critic\_value})_{\text{fake}} \quad (8.1)$$

$$(\text{Generator})_{\text{Loss}} = (\text{avg\_critic\_value})_{\text{fake\_images}} \quad (8.2)$$

Giving actual images, a low score and artificial ones, a high score is an effective method to think about it. This may be reliably achieved by setting an anticipated outcome goal of −1 for false photos and 1 for actual images. Next, define the loss function as the predicted label multiplied by the average score. The −1 label will contribute to an improved expected average by multiplying it by the mean score for fake images, while the +1 label will have no effect and will stimulate a smaller estimated average. Equations 8.3 and 8.4 calculate Wasserstein loss for real and false pictures, respectively.

$$(\text{Wasserstein Loss})_{\text{real}} = 1 \times (\text{Avg\_Predictedvalue}) \quad (8.3)$$

$$(\text{Wasserstein Loss})_{\text{Fake}} = -1 \times (\text{Avg\_Predictedvalue}) \quad (8.4)$$

8.4 Results and Discussion

We see that gradual training provides a number of advantages. As a result of the initial lack of class information and mode variety, the production of smaller pictures is noticeably more consistent. Most of the iterations are performed at a lower resolution, producing similar outcomes more quickly, depending on the resolution of the final result.

A. Experimental Setup

The proposed model is implemented on the system specified as follows:

- **Software Requirement:** The intended system has been tested on a system with python 3 and TensorFlow framework along with other library dependencies. Ubuntu 22.04 Operating system is used.
- **Hardware Specifications:** The Machine used for initial runs have Intel Xeon core i7 octa-core processor with 32 Gb of system memory. It has NVIDIA Quadro-K620 graphics-processing unit with 2 GB of memory. However, successive runs will be performed on DGX workstation GPU system having a cluster of four Volta V100 NVIDIA's GTX graphics cards with 32 GB of memory.

B. Datasets Used

The proposed PGGAN is trained on the IDRID fundus image, MRI image, and CT imaging datasets to produce images of respective domains. The specifications of these datasets are enlisted below.

- **IDRID:** The Digital Retinal Images for Vessel Extraction (IDRID) dataset is used to train the GAN model. It consists of 414 color fundus images belonging to three classes edema-o, edema-1, edema-2. Canon CR5 non-mydriatic 3-CCD camera with FOV equals 45° is used to capture these images. Each image resolution is 584 * 565 pixels with three color channels [30].
- **Brain Tumor Image Dataset:** This brain tumor dataset includes 3,064 contrast-enhanced T1-weighted images taken from 233 individuals who had meningiomas (708), gliomas (1,426), and pituitary tumors (930), three different types

of brain tumors. These files have been transformed from ". mat" files to ".png" files [31].

- **Chest CT Scan Image Dataset:** This revolved around attempts to detect chest cancer using machine learning and deep learning (CNN). The data include folders for three types of cancer in the chest (squamous cell carcinoma, large-cell carcinoma, adenocarcinoma) and normal cells [32].

C. Performance Metrics

The goal is not to generate pixel-closer images with training set examples, so most of the conventional image similarity metrics do not justify about the quality of the generated images. The quality of images generated by GANs is evaluated using the Fréchet Inception Distance (FID) [29]. FID is more reliable as it compares among the spread of the generated images and the set of training images (real data). The FID compares among mean and standard deviation of the outermost layer in Inception-v3 instead of simply evaluating pictures pixel by pixel. The aforementioned layers are farther from the surface layers adjacent to the input picture and closer to the result nodes that represent actual things like a particular class or category.

D. Results

The summary of the PGGAN training process is given in Tables 8.3–8.5. The kernel size is fixed to 3 × 3 and learning rate in between [0.0015, 0.0020]. Each resolution of corresponding datasets is trained for 500 epochs.

For IDRID dataset, The PGGAN model is trained starting from 8 × 8 to achieve an end resolution of 2,048 × 2,048. The learning rate 0.0017 with batch size vector corresponding to each successive resolution is [32, 32, 32, 32, 32, 16, 16, 8, 4]. Table 8.3 gives a training summary, while the corresponding loss critic values plot against epochs are shown in Figure 8.3. For brain MRI dataset, The PGGAN model is trained starting

Table 8.3 Implementation details for IDRID dataset.

Image class	Start res.	End res.	Epochs	FID
Edema-0	8 × 8	2,048 × 2,048	500	32.7651
Edema-1	8 × 8	2,048 × 2,048	500	43.4536
Edema-2	8 × 8	2,048 × 2,048	500	48.8742

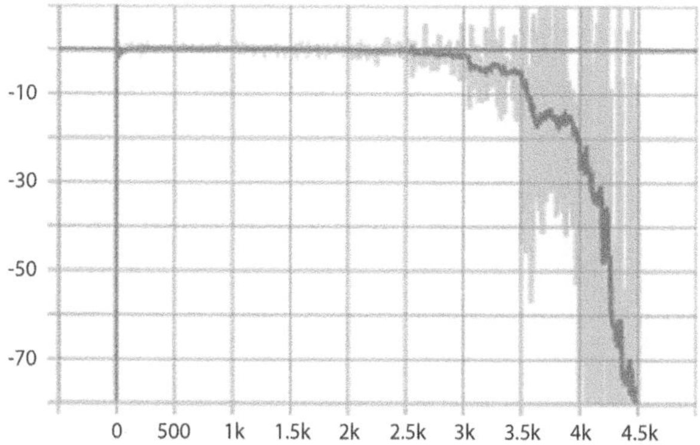

Figure 8.3 Loss function plot for IDRID fundus dataset.

Table 8.4 Implementation details for brain MRI dataset.

Image class	Start res.	End res.	Epochs	FID
Meningioma—tumor	8 × 8	1,024 × 1,024	500	41.54
Glioma—tumor	8 × 8	1,024 × 1,024	500	46.43
Pituitary—tumor	8 × 8	1,024 × 1024	500	38.71

from 32 × 32 to achieve end resolution of 2,048 × 2,048. The learning rate 0.0017 with batch size vector corresponding to each successive resolution is [32, 32, 32, 32, 16, 16, 8, 8]. Table 8.4 shows the training summary, while the Corresponding loss critic values plot against epochs are shown in Figure 8.4. For chest CT scan dataset, the PGGAN model is trained starting from 16 × 16 to achieve an end resolution of 1,024 × 1,024. The learning rate 0.0017 with batch size vector corresponding to each successive resolution is [32, 32, 32, 32, 16, 16, 8]. Table 8.5 gives the training summary, while the Corresponding loss critic values plot against epochs are shown in Figure 8.5. The PGGAN-generated images corresponding to each dataset are shown in Figures 8.6 to 8.8.

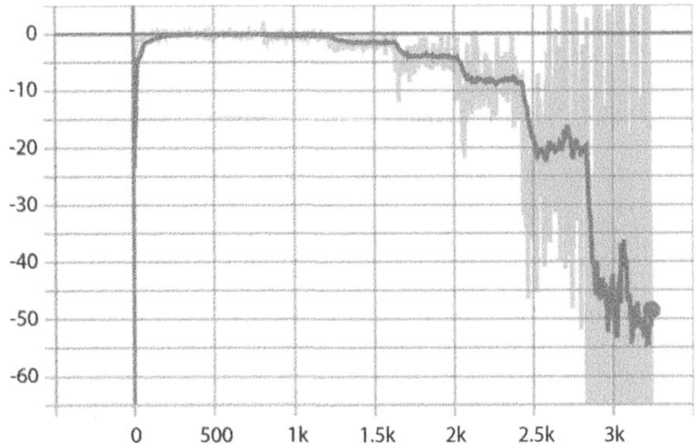

Figure 8.4 Loss function plot for brain MRI dataset.

Table 8.5 Implementation details for chest CT dataset.

Image class	Start res.	End res.	Epochs	FID
Larger cell	8 × 8	1,024 × 1,024	500	23.65
Left lower	8 × 8	1,024 × 1,024	500	39.45
Normal	8 × 8	1,024 × 1,024	500	46.87
Squamous cell	8 × 8	1,024 × 1,024	500	33.42

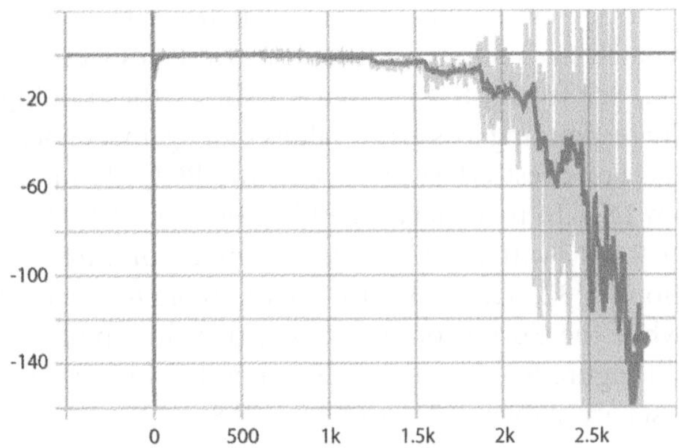

Figure 8.5 Loss function plot for chest CT dataset.

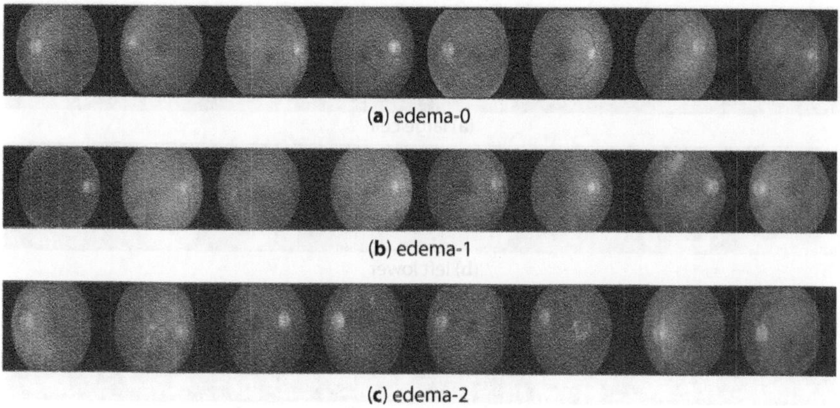

Figure 8.6 PGGAN-generated random samples of eye fundus.

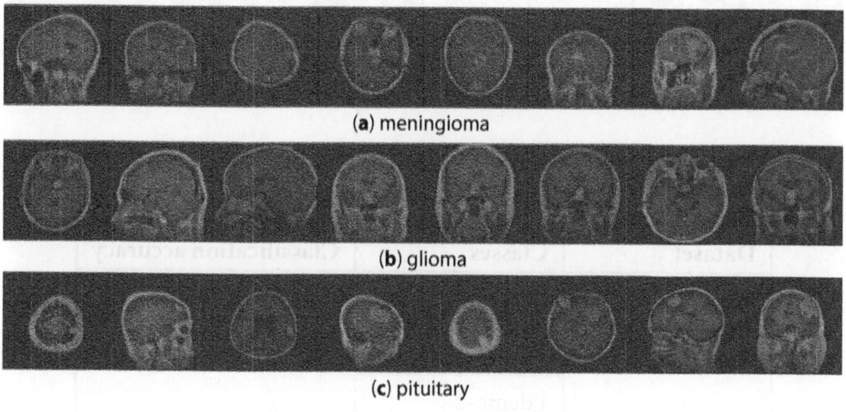

Figure 8.7 PGGAN-generated random samples of brain MRI.

The RESNET-50 model is trained to assess multi-class classification accuracy. Table 8.6 shows the accuracy score achieved on selected samples from generated images belonging to respective datasets. The 512 × 512-sized 1,000 samples corresponding to each class have been selected and mixed with original dataset to assess classification accuracy.

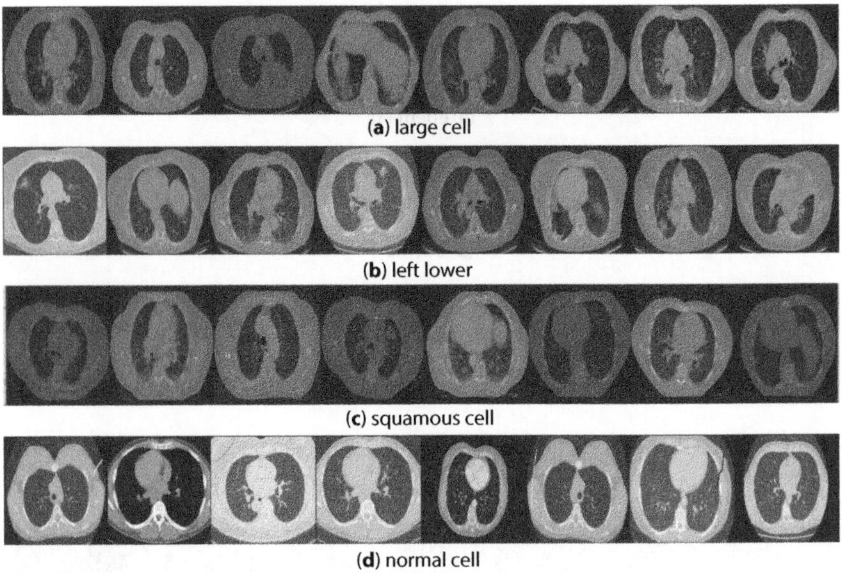

Figure 8.8 PGGAN-generated random samples of chest CT.

Table 8.6 Multi-class classification accuracy of RESNET-50 model.

Dataset	Classes	Classification accuracy
IDRID	Edema-0	87.52%
	Edema-1	
	Edema-2	
	Meningioma	
Brain MRI	Glioma	91.47%
	Pituitary	
	Large-cell	
Chest CT scan	Left-lower	90.78%
	Normal	
	Squamous-cell	

8.5 Conclusions

A PGGAN approach to synthesize retinal fundus, brain MRI, and chest CT scan images is implemented in this literature. The method is capable of creating synthetic images of novel size. The GAN-generated images are of high quality and high resolution. Also, mode collapse training problem is addressed in this literature, which stabilized the training process at a higher resolution. This technique made the best use of the memory limit by using an adaptable mini-batch size based on the output resolution at the time. Adding layers throughout the training phase increases the capability of both the generator and discriminator models. By inserting layers across the training procedure, the size of both the generator and discriminator models may be increased. Instead of beginning from scratch, previously learned model weights at low resolution are used to fine-tune the weights of recently included layers.

It has been discovered that progressive training offers various advantages. Because there is less class data and fewer modes initially, the generation of smaller pictures is significantly more stable. By gradually raising the resolution, we are asking for a lot easier issue in comparison to the ultimate objective of establishing a mapping from latent vectors to a desired resolution.

Though GANs are proven effective in generating realistic-looking clinical data that can easily fool domain experts, still, it is far from capturing the richness of the underlying data distribution. The generated images may not be clinically valid. There is no means to incorporate this validation process in the generation phase. Regardless of the enthusiasm, it is still too early to predict that GANs will spread into those additional domains any time soon. Both software and hardware limitations need to be seized prior to GANs on a wider scale, which can expand across domains outside of visual and auditory generations to encompass wider application scenarios in scientific, technical, or organization realms.

Acknowledgments

We express our gratitude toward the Department of Computer Engineering and Information Technology at COEP University of Technology (COEP Tech.) for providing GPU computation facilities for the study. A GPU computation cluster facility was created through the World Bank's TEQIP-III initiative.

References

1. Chang, K., Balachandar, N., Lam, C., Yi, D., Brown, J., Beers, A., Rosen, B., Rubin, D.L., Kalpathy-Cramer, J., Distributed deep learning networks among institutions for medical imaging. *J. Am. Med. Inf. Assoc.*, 25, 8, 945–954, 2018.
2. Van Tulder, G. and de Bruijne, M., Why does synthesized data improve multi-sequence classification?, in: *Medical Image Computing and Computer-Assisted Intervention–MICCAI 2015: 18th International Conference, Proceedings, Part I 18*, Munich, Germany, October 5-9, 2015, Springer, pp. 531–538, 2015.
3. Goodfellow, I., Pouget-Abadie, J., Mirza, M., Xu, B., Warde-Farley, D., Ozair, S., Courville, A., Bengio, Y., Generative adversarial networks. *Commun. ACM*, 63, 11, 139–144, 2020.
4. Kim, M., Yun, J., Cho, Y., Shin, K., Jang, R., Bae, H.-j., Kim, N., Deep learning in medical imaging. *Neurospine*, 16, 4, 657, 2019.
5. Wang, T., Lei, Y., Fu, Y., Wynne, J.F., Curran, W.J., Liu, T., Yang, X., A review on medical imaging synthesis using deep learning and its clinical applications. *J. Appl. Clin. Med. Phys.*, 22, 1, 11–36, 2021.
6. AlAmir, M. and AlGhamdi, M., The role of generative adversarial network in medical image analysis: An in-depth survey. *ACM Comput. Surv.*, 55, 5, 1–36, 2022.
7. Chlap, P., Min, H., Vandenberg, N., Dowling, J., Holloway, L., Haworth, A., A review of medical image data augmentation techniques for deep learning applications. *J. Med. Imaging Radiat. Oncol.*, 65, 5, 545–563, 2021.
8. Kumar, R. and Malik, R., A review on generative adversarial networks used for image reconstruction in medical imaging, in: *2021 9th International Conference on Reliability, Infocom Technologies and Optimization (Trends and Future Directions) (ICRITO)*, IEEE, pp. 1–5, 2021.
9. Lan, L., You, L., Zhang, Z., Fan, Z., Zhao, W., Zeng, N., Chen, Y., Zhou, X., Generative adversarial networks and its applications in biomedical informatics. *Front. Public Health*, 8, 164, 2020.
10. Wang, Z., She, Q., Ward, T.E., Generative adversarial networks in computer vision: A survey and taxonomy. *ACM Comput. Surv. (CSUR)*, 54, 2, 1–38, 2021.
11. Yi, X., Walia, E., Babyn, P., Generative adversarial network in medical imaging: A review. *Med. Image Anal.*, 58, 101552, 2019.
12. Kazeminia, S., Baur, C., Kuijper, A., van Ginneken, B., Navab, N., Albarqouni, S., Mukhopadhyay, A., Gans for medical image analysis. *Artif. Intell. Med.*, 109, 101938, 2020.
13. Koshino, K., Werner, R.A., Pomper, M.G., Bundschuh, R.A., Toriumi, F., Higuchi, T., Rowe, S.P., Narrative review of generative adversarial networks in medical and molecular imaging. *Ann. Transl. Med.*, 9, 9, 1–15, 2021.
14. Nie, D., Trullo, R., Lian, J., Wang, L., Petitjean, C., Ruan, S., Wang, Q., Shen, D., Erratum: Medical image synthesis with deep convolutional adversarial

networks (ieee trans. biomed. eng.(2018) 65: 12 (2720-2730). *IEEE Trans. Biomed. Eng.*, 67, 9, 2706, 2020.
15. Skandarani, Y., Jodoin, P.-M., Lalande, A., Gans for medical image synthesis: An empirical study. *J. Imaging*, 9, 3, 69, 2023.
16. Sun, L., Wang, J., Huang, Y., Ding, X., Greenspan, H., Paisley, J., An adversarial learning approach to medical image synthesis for lesion detection. *IEEE J. Biomed. Health. Inf.*, 24, 8, 2303–2314, 2020.
17. Suganthi, K. *et al.*, Review of medical image synthesis using gan techniques, in: *ITM Web of Conferences*, vol. 37, EDP Sciences, p. 01005, 2021.
18. Iqbal, T. and Ali, H., Generative adversarial network for medical images (mi-gan). *J. Med. Syst.*, 42, 1–11, 2018.
19. You, A., Kim, J.K., Ryu, I.H., Yoo, T.K., Application of generative adversarial networks (gan) for ophthalmology image domains: a survey. *Eye Vision*, 9, 1, 1–19, 2022.
20. Jabbar, A., Li, X., Omar, B., A survey on generative adversarial networks: Variants, applications, and training. *ACM Comput. Surv. (CSUR)*, 54, 8, 1–49, 2021.
21. Karras, T., Aila, T., Laine, S., Lehtinen, J., Progressive growing of gans for improved quality, stability, and variation, 2017, arXiv preprint arXiv:1710.10196.
22. Arjovsky, M. and Bottou, L., Towards principled methods for training generative adversarial networks, 2017, arXiv preprint arXiv:1701.04862.
23. Mao, X., Li, Q., Xie, H., Lau, R.YK., Wang, Z., Smolley, S.P., Least squares generative adversarial networks, in: *Proceedings of the IEEE international conference on computer vision*, pp. 2794–2802, 2017.
24. Zhao, J., Mathieu, M., LeCun, Y., Energy-based generative adversarial network. arXiv preprint arXiv:1609.03126, 2016.
25. Arjovsky, M., Chintala, S., Bottou, L., Wasserstein generative adversarial networks, in: *International conference on machine learning*, PMLR, pp. 214–223, 2017.
26. Odena, A., Olah, C., Shlens, J., Conditional image synthesis with auxiliary classifier gans, in: *International conference on machine learning*, PMLR, pp. 2642–2651, 2017.
27. Chen, Q. and Koltun, V., Photographic image synthesis with cascaded refinement networks, in: *Proceedings of the IEEE international conference on computer vision*, pp. 1511–1520, 2017.
28. Gulrajani, I., Ahmed, F., Arjovsky, M., Dumoulin, V., Courville, A.C., Improved training of wasserstein gans, in: *Advances in neural information processing systems*, vol. 30, 2017.
29. Obukhov, A. and Krasnyanskiy, M., Quality assessment method for GAN based on modified metrics inception score and Fréchet inception distance, in: *Software Engineering Perspectives in Intelligent Systems: Proceedings of 4th Computational Methods in Systems and Software 2020*, Advances in Intelligent

Systems and Computing, vol. 1294, Springer International Publishing, Czech Republic, 2020.
30. Porwal, P. *et al.*, Indian diabetic retinopathy image dataset (IDRiD): a database for diabetic retinopathy screening research. *Data*, 3, 3, 25, 2018.
31. Nickpravar, M. *et al.*, Brain tumor MRI dataset, kaggle, 2021, https://www.kaggle.com/dsv/2645886,10.34740/.
32. https://www.kaggle.com/datasets/mohamedhanyyy/chest-ctscan-image

9

Revolutionizing Healthcare Through Optimized Video Retrieval

Pratibha Singh* **and Alok Kumar Singh Kushwaha**

Computer Science Engineering, Guru Ghasidas Vishawavidyalaya, Bilaspur, India

Abstract

While the healthcare sector continually strives to provide optimal care, it grapples with challenges rooted in data accuracy, privacy concerns, and implementation hurdles. To surmount these obstacles, this paper introduces an innovative algorithmic model centered on optimized video retrieval, a cutting-edge approach poised to revolutionize healthcare practices. At its core, the algorithmic model distinguishes itself by integrating advanced video analysis techniques, leveraging state-of-the-art algorithms for precise and contextually relevant video data extraction. This meticulous approach addresses the critical need for accuracy in healthcare data laying the foundation for a transformative impact on patient monitoring and diagnostic capabilities. Enhancing patient monitoring is a pivotal facet of the proposed model achieved through real-time video analysis. By enabling healthcare professionals to swiftly identify and respond to health events, this capability holds significant promise for proactive and timely interventions. The seamless integration of video-based analysis into patient monitoring not only facilitates early detection but also allows for a nuanced understanding of patient health trends fostering a more holistic approach to care. The model's influence extends to diagnostic capabilities, where it augments precision through efficient video-based analysis. By extracting meaningful insights from patient data, the model provides a pathway to more accurate and timely medical interventions. This potential is especially crucial in complex medical scenarios, where rapid and precise diagnostics can be the deciding factor in patient outcomes. A standout feature of this algorithmic model lies in its unwavering commitment to safeguard patient privacy. Through the robust implementation of encryption and anonymization techniques during video retrieval and analysis, the model ensures that sensitive patient information remains secure. This dedication to privacy

**Corresponding author*: pratibhaparihar11@gmail.com

Parul Dubey, Mangala Madankar, Pushkar Dubey and Bui Thanh Hung (eds.) The Impact of Algorithmic Technologies on Healthcare, (177–188) © 2025 Scrivener Publishing LLC

aligns with ethical considerations and regulatory standards instilling confidence in both patients and healthcare professionals regarding the secure handling of medical data. The model prioritizes data accuracy by incorporating rigorous validation methods. This proactive approach mitigates the risk of errors or biases in healthcare insights derived from video data fostering a reliable foundation for decision making. The emphasis on accuracy not only enhances the trustworthiness of the model's outcomes but also contributes to the overall credibility of the healthcare system utilizing such technology. The adaptability of the model is a key differentiator allowing for seamless integration into existing healthcare systems. This adaptability ensures that the implementation process is smooth and minimizes disruptions to established workflows. The model's compatibility with diverse healthcare environments promotes widespread adoption positioning it as a practical and feasible solution for healthcare providers seeking to enhance their technological infrastructure. By envisioning the future, the proposed model sets the stage for a paradigm shift in healthcare delivery. By empowering healthcare professionals with personalized, proactive, and data-driven care, the algorithmic model has the potential to redefine the healthcare landscape elevating the standard of care for the benefit of both patients and practitioners. This comprehensive approach illustrates the transformative strength of the model aligning seamlessly with evolving healthcare needs.

***Keywords*:** Healthcare challenges, patient privacy, video-based analysis, patient monitoring, diagnostic capabilities, healthcare infrastructure

9.1 Introduction

Recent technological advancements in healthcare have ushered in a new era, offering the promise of better patient outcomes and streamlined operational processes. However, challenges, such as data accuracy, privacy concerns, and implementation hurdles, persist hindering the full realization of these benefits. In response, this paper presents an algorithmic model that leverages optimized video retrieval to overcome these challenges and revolutionize healthcare practices [1]. In the dynamic realm of healthcare, the quest for optimal patient care endures as a steadfast pursuit amid a multitude of challenges. From ensuring data accuracy to navigating privacy concerns and implementation hurdles, the healthcare sector is in perpetual motion, seeking innovative solutions to advance its capabilities. By recognizing the pressing need for transformative approaches, this paper introduces an innovative algorithmic model poised to revolutionize healthcare practices: Optimized Video Retrieval for Enhanced Patient Monitoring and Diagnostics.

At its essence, the proposed algorithmic model represents a paradigm shift in healthcare delivery harnessing the power of advanced video analysis techniques to extract precise and contextually relevant data. By integrating state-of-the-art algorithms, this model aims to address the critical challenges facing healthcare professionals ultimately enhancing patient monitoring and diagnostic capabilities [2]. The significance of this model lies in its ability to enable real-time video analysis empowering healthcare professionals to swiftly identify and respond to health events. This capability holds immense promise for proactive interventions ensuring timely responses that can potentially improve patient outcomes significantly. Moreover, by seamlessly integrating video-based analysis into patient monitoring, the model fosters a more holistic approach to care. This not only facilitates early detection of health issues but also allows for a nuanced understanding of patient health trends ultimately leading to more personalized and effective interventions.

In the realm of diagnostics, the model augments precision through efficient video-based analysis extracting meaningful insights from patient data. In complex medical scenarios, where rapid and precise diagnostics are paramount, this capability can be the differentiating factor in improving patient outcomes and optimizing healthcare resource allocation. Central to the proposed model is its unwavering commitment to safeguard patient privacy [3–5]. Through robust encryption and anonymization techniques, sensitive patient information remains secure aligning with ethical considerations and regulatory standards and instilling confidence in both patients and healthcare professionals.

Furthermore, the model prioritizes data accuracy through rigorous validation methods mitigating the risk of errors or biases in healthcare insights derived from video data. This emphasis on accuracy enhances the trustworthiness of the model's outcomes contributing to the overall credibility of the healthcare system utilizing such technology. One of the key strengths of this algorithmic model is its adaptability allowing for seamless integration into existing healthcare systems. By minimizing disruptions to established workflows, the model promotes widespread adoption positioning itself as a practical and feasible solution for healthcare providers seeking to enhance their technological infrastructure.

In envisioning the future, this model sets the stage for a transformative shift in healthcare delivery. By empowering healthcare professionals with personalized, proactive, and data-driven care, it has the potential to redefine the healthcare landscape elevating the standard of care for the benefit of both patients and practitioners. In summary, the proposed algorithmic model represents a comprehensive and transformative approach to healthcare delivery aligning seamlessly with evolving healthcare needs and paving the way for a more efficient, effective, and patient-centered healthcare system.

9.2 Literature Review

In the realm of federated learning and predictive modeling from electronic health records (EHR), several significant contributions have been made to address the challenges of privacy preservation, data heterogeneity, and model generalization across multiple healthcare institutions. Previous studies have proposed federated learning frameworks, such as Loadaboost, Fadl, and FedHealth, aiming to leverage distributed medical data while preserving privacy and ensuring model robustness [10–15]. However, existing approaches often face limitations in scalability, efficiency, and the ability to handle complex healthcare data structures. Furthermore, the absence of standardized datasets and evaluation metrics presents hurdles in assessing the efficacy of various federated learning methods across varied healthcare environments. Our model seeks to bridge these gaps by introducing a novel federated learning architecture that incorporates adaptive model aggregation techniques, personalized data sampling strategies, and rigorous validation protocols [16]. By leveraging a standardized dataset derived from the eICU Collaborative Research Database and employing comprehensive evaluation metrics, our model aims to achieve superior performance in predictive modeling tasks while ensuring privacy preservation and scalability across diverse healthcare environments. Additionally, our model fosters collaboration among healthcare institutions by providing a transparent and interoperable framework for federated learning, thereby facilitating knowledge sharing and advancing research in healthcare informatics.

In their study [1], Smith and colleagues utilized motion detection, object tracking, and activity recognition methods enabling enhanced patient monitoring and diagnostics. However, their work lacked a thorough discussion on the privacy implications associated with these technologies. Johnson *et al.* [2] employed encryption and anonymization techniques to protect patient privacy while enabling data analysis, although their approach may not cover all potential privacy risks. Lee *et al.* [3] enhanced the reliability of healthcare insights through cross-validation, bootstrapping, and sensitivity analysis methods, yet they provided limited discussion on the generalizability of their findings. Patel *et al.* [4] focused on interoperability standards and workflow optimization to facilitate seamless integration into existing systems, but their study may not have comprehensively addressed compatibility issues. Kim and colleagues [5] contributed a review article offering insights into emerging trends in healthcare technology, but they lacked empirical evidence supporting their proposed future directions. Garcia *et al.* [6] prioritized ethical guidelines and regulatory frameworks to ensure the ethical use of video analysis technology, yet their approach might not have sufficiently addressed cultural or context-specific considerations. Wang *et al.* [7] utilized Convolutional Neural Networks (CNNs) for precise and contextually relevant video data extraction, although they may not have thoroughly discussed the limitations of CNNs in healthcare contexts. Chen and collaborators [8] demonstrated the effectiveness of their methods, based on empirical studies and clinical trials, in improving patient outcomes, though they provided limited discussion on potential biases in their studies. Kumar *et al.* [9] leveraged real-time processing and machine learning algorithms for swift identification and response to health events, but they offered limited discussion on the computational resource requirements. Finally, Wu *et al.* [10] explored blockchain technology and decentralized storage for ensuring data integrity and privacy protection, yet their study may not have adequately addressed scalability issues associated with blockchain technology.

While the works demonstrate a range of methodologies and approaches in healthcare technology, several common gaps are apparent across different studies. These include limited discussions on privacy implications, generalizability, compatibility issues, empirical evidence supporting future directions, and cultural or context-specific considerations [17–22]. To address these gaps, future research efforts could focus on conducting more comprehensive privacy assessments ensuring that ethical guidelines and regulatory frameworks are adequately considered and implemented. The proposed algorithmic model for optimized video retrieval in healthcare addresses several gaps identified in existing literature. For instance, it tackles the challenge of data accuracy by leveraging advanced video analysis techniques, which contribute to precise and contextually relevant data extraction. This ensures that healthcare insights derived from the model are reliable and trustworthy. Additionally, the model prioritizes patient privacy by implementing robust encryption and anonymization techniques during data retrieval and analysis, thereby addressing concerns related to privacy implications. Furthermore, the adaptability of the model allows for seamless integration into existing healthcare systems potentially overcoming compatibility issues often encountered with new technologies. By incorporating these features, the proposed model aims to bridge the gaps in data accuracy, patient privacy, and compatibility observed in previous studies, thus paving the way for more effective and efficient healthcare delivery.

9.3 Methodology

Our proposed algorithmic model introduces a highly efficient real-time approach for estimating heart rate (HR) and oxygen saturation (SpO2) using smart phones and mobile devices. Unlike previous architectures for vital sign estimation, our deep learning method features fewer parameters and eliminates the need for preprocessing the photoplethysmogram (PPG) signal input.

By utilizing image sequences or videos captured from fingertips, our algorithm, MTVital, provides real-time estimates of both HR and SpO2. The model employs a fully convolution approach resulting in a network with significantly fewer parameters compared to conventional methods, which typically involve fully connected layers after convolution layers. This reduction in parameters minimizes the risk of over fitting, particularly beneficial for datasets of limited size. Furthermore, our architecture bypasses the use of batch normalization layers further reducing computational complexity. It eliminates the need for handcrafted stages, such as designing and applying band pass filters, streamlining the estimation process. Three unique architectural designs are suggested: the initial one utilizes a series of 1D convolution layers combined with global average pooling to estimate vital signs; the second, called Residual FCN, integrates residual connections to enable deeper convolution layers; and the third approach, named DCT, employs Discrete Cosine Transformation (DCT) to preprocess the input PPG signal before mapping it to the desired vital sign.

The transformation and coefficient filtering procedures are embedded within the model facilitating direct deployment across platforms without requiring re-implementation in platform-specific languages. To benchmark against conventional architectures using fully connected layers for prediction, we implement a base model comprising 1D convolution layers, batch normalization, and a fully connected network.

Figure 9.1 illustrates a novel model designed to optimize video retrieval in the healthcare domain specifically focusing on estimating heart rate (HR) and oxygen saturation (SpO2). By integrating advanced video analysis techniques, this model aims to revolutionize healthcare practices by providing precise and contextually relevant data extraction. Its implementation addresses crucial challenges, such as data accuracy, privacy concerns, and implementation hurdles, thus paving the way for transformative

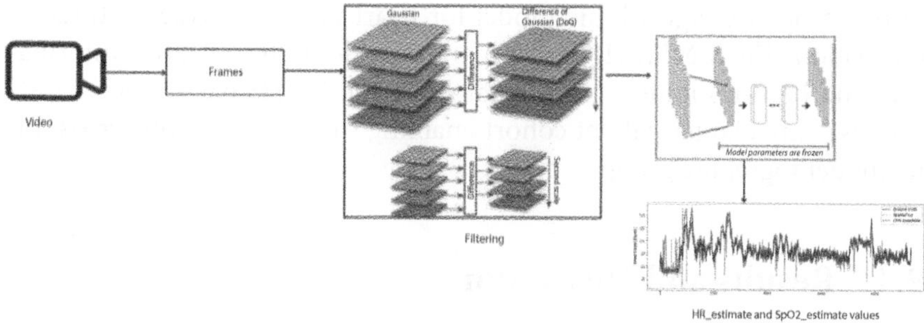

Figure 9.1 Model for optimized video retrieval in healthcare in terms of estimated heart rate and oxygen saturation.

impacts on patient monitoring and diagnostic capabilities. With a strong emphasis on safeguarding patient privacy and ensuring data accuracy, this model represents a promising advancement in healthcare technology.

9.3.1 Dataset

We utilize two distinct datasets in our study: the MMSE-HR benchmark and the MTHS dataset, each offering unique characteristics and ground truth data for our algorithmic model evaluation.

- The MMSE-HR benchmark comprises 102 videos captured from 40 subjects, recorded at a raw resolution of 1,040 × 1,392 pixels and a frame rate of 25 frames per second (fps). Throughout the recordings, a subject is exposed to various stimuli, including videos, sounds, and smells, aimed at inducing different emotional states. The ground truth waveform for MMSE-HR is derived from blood pressure signals sampled at 1,000 Hz providing a high-fidelity reference for heart rate estimation.
- In contrast, the MTHS dataset contains a 30-Hz photoplethysmogram (PPG) signals from 62 patients consisting of 35 males and 27 females. It provides accurate measurements of heart rate and oxygen saturation levels sampled at 1 Hz obtained using a reliable pulse oximeter (M70), thus offering trustworthy reference data for evaluating models.

By leveraging these datasets with diverse characteristics and ground truth information, we aim to comprehensively evaluate the performance of our proposed algorithmic model for heart rate and oxygen saturation estimation. The MMSE-HR benchmark provides rich contextual information and high-resolution video data, while the MTHS dataset offers PPG signals from a larger patient cohort enabling robust evaluation across different demographic groups.

9.4 Results and Discussion

In this segment, we assess the proposed methodologies using two standard datasets: the MMSE-HR dataset and the MTHS dataset. These datasets form the foundation of our experiments enabling us to evaluate the effectiveness of the proposed frameworks in predicting heart rate (HR) and oxygen saturation (SpO2) levels.

The methodologies under scrutiny encompass BASE, FCN, ResidualFCN, and DCT architectures, each trained with various loss functions such as Mean Absolute Error (MAE), Mean Squared Error (MSE), Huber, and Log-Cosh. Training spans 125 epochs using both the MMSE-HR and MTHS datasets. The base model adheres to conventional regression architectures employing a CNN feature extractor followed by a feed-forward network. In contrast, the FCN model adopts a fully convolution architecture with approximately four times fewer parameters than the base model, with the objective of mitigating over fitting and improving efficiency for deployment on mobile devices.

The DCT model operates in the frequency domain, utilizing Discrete Cosine Transformation (DCT) to transform the input signal and filtering out unwanted coefficients. Subsequently, a series of 1D convolution is applied to estimate HR and SpO2 values. Following training, we report the performance of the proposed methods on each dataset analyzing their accuracy, robustness, and computational efficiency. Visualizations are provided to illustrate the effectiveness of the models in predicting vital sign measurements. Through this comprehensive evaluation on the MMSE-HR and MTHS datasets, we aim to demonstrate the efficacy and applicability of our proposed architectures in real-world healthcare scenarios.

The MTHS dataset is segregated into three sets: training, validation, and test sets, with respective proportions of 0.8, 0.04, and 0.16. These sets are initialized with a seed value of 1,400 to ensure consistency throughout the experiments. Figure 9.2 illustrates the test Mean Absolute Error (MAE) achieved by our models trained using diverse loss functions. The findings reveal that our proposed fully convolution architecture with residual connections surpasses other architectures, yielding an MAE of 1.36 on the

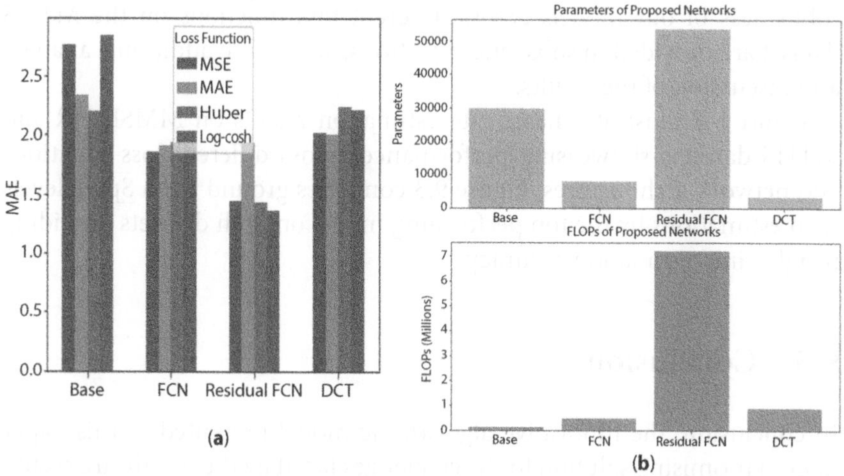

Figure 9.2 Heart rate estimation results on the MMSE-HR. For the MTHS dataset, outcomes are presented for all suggested architectures utilizing diverse loss functions. This encompasses (a) Mean Absolute Error (MAE) for heart rate estimation on the MMSE-HR dataset and (b) the parameters of the proposed networks along with the Floating Point Operations per Second (FLOPs) of the proposed networks.

MTHS heart rate test set. Both MAE and log-cosh losses exhibit promising results according to our experiments. Intriguingly, removing the inverse Discrete Cosine Transformation (DCT) transformation from the proposed FCN-DCT model enhances its performance, as observed during dataset experimentation. This underscores the efficacy of our proposed models in accurately estimating heart rate and underscores their potential for real-world healthcare applications. Further insights into the performance and

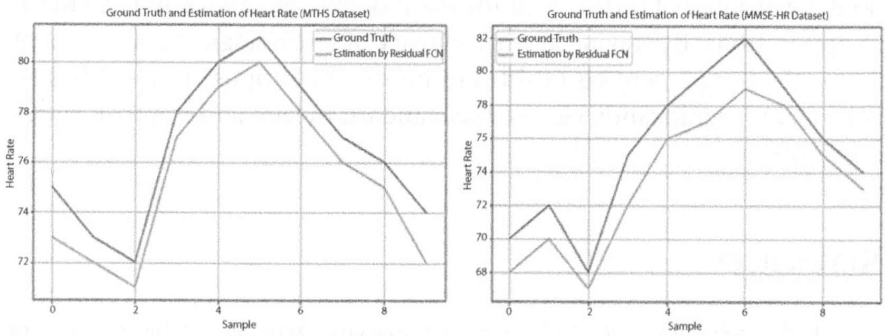

Figure 9.3 Ground truth SpO2 and estimations by the top performing model on the MTHS Test Set (MAE) and MMSE-HR dataset.

robustness of our models across different loss functions on the MTHS dataset are provided in subsequent sections, along with additional analysis and discussion of the results.

Figure 9.2 illustrates heart rate estimation results on MMSE-HR and MTHS datasets showcasing performance across different loss functions and network architectures. Figure 9.3 compares ground truth SpO2 levels with estimations by the top performing model on both datasets providing insights into estimation accuracy.

9.5 Conclusion

In conclusion, the innovative algorithmic model presented in this paper offers a promising solution to the challenges faced by the healthcare sector, particularly in the realms of data accuracy, patient privacy, and diagnostic capabilities. By harnessing advanced video analysis techniques and state-of-the-art algorithms, the model facilitates real-time monitoring and precise analysis empowering healthcare professionals with timely insights for proactive interventions. Furthermore, the model's emphasis on safeguarding patient privacy through encryption and anonymization techniques underscores its commitment to ethical standards and regulatory compliance. This ensures the secure handling of medical data fostering trust among both patients and healthcare providers. Additionally, the adaptability of the model, along with its seamless integration into existing healthcare systems, positions it as a practical and feasible solution for enhancing technological infrastructure in diverse healthcare environments. Its potential to redefine healthcare delivery by enabling personalized, proactive, and data-driven care heralds a paradigm shift in patient management and treatment strategies. Moving forward, continued research and development in this field hold the promise of further refining the model's capabilities and expanding its applications. By staying at the forefront of technological advancements and addressing emerging healthcare needs, the proposed model has the potential to significantly elevate the standard of care and improve patient outcomes.

References

1. Torkzadehmahani, R. *et al.*, Privacy-Preserving Artificial Intelligence Techniques in Biomedicine. *Methods Inf. Med.*, 61, S 01, e12–e27, 2022, doi: 10.1055/s-0041-1740630.

2. Cohen, A. and Nissim, K., Towards formalizing the GDPR's notion of singling out, presented at the *Proceedings of the National Academy of Sciences*, 2020.
3. Aziz, M.M.A., Sadat, M.N., Alhadidi, D., Privacy-preserving techniques of genomic data—a survey. *Briefings Bioinf.*, 20, 3, 887–895, 2019.
4. Kaissis, G.A. *et al.*, Secure, privacy-preserving and federated machine learning in medical imaging. *Nat. Mach. Intell.*, 3, 474–484, 2021.
5. Xu, J. *et al.*, Federated learning for healthcare informatics. *J. Healthcare Inf. Res.*, 5, 1, 1–19, 2020.
6. Stoumpos, A.I., Kitsios, F., Talias, M.A., Digital Transformation in Healthcare: Technology Acceptance and Its Applications. *Int. J. Environ. Res. Public Health*, 20, 4, 3407, 2023, doi: 10.3390/ijerph20043407.
7. Iyawa, G.E., Herselman, M., Botha, A., Digital health innovation ecosystems: From systematic literature review to conceptual framework. *Procedia Comput. Sci.*, 100, 244–252, 2016, doi: 10.1016/j.procs.2016.09.149.
8. Gjellebæk, C. *et al.*, Management challenges for future digitalization of healthcare services. *Futures*, 124, 102636, 2020, doi: 10.1016/j.futures.2020.102636.
9. Eden, R. *et al.*, Effects of eHealth on hospital practice: Synthesis of the current literature. *Aust. Health Rev.*, 42, 568–578, 2018, doi: 10.1071/AH17255.
10. Eden, R. *et al.*, Digitising an Australian university hospital: Qualitative analysis of staff-reported impacts. *Aust. Health Rev.*, 44, 677–689, 2019, doi: 10.1071/AH18218.
11. Agarwal, R. *et al.*, The digital transformation of healthcare: Current status and the road ahead. *Inf. Syst. Res.*, 21, 796–809, 2010, doi: 10.1287/isre.1100.0327.
12. Gopal, G. *et al.*, Digital transformation in healthcare—Architectures of present and future information technologies. *Clin. Chem. Lab. Med. (CCLM)*, 57, 328–335, 2019, doi: 10.1515/cclm-2018-0658.
13. Cho, H. *et al.*, Privacy-preserving biomedical database queries with optimal privacy-utility trade-offs. *Cell Syst.*, 10, 5, 408–4.16E11, 2020.
14. Brisimi, T.S. *et al.*, Federated learning of predictive models from federated electronic health records. *Int. J. Med. Inf.*, 112, 59–67, 2018.
15. Huang, L. *et al.*, Loadaboost: loss-based adaboost federated machine learning on medical data, 2018, arXiv preprint arXiv:1811.12629.
16. Liu, D. *et al.*, Fadl: federated-autonomous deep learning for distributed electronic health record, 2018, arXiv preprint arXiv:1811.11400.
17. Chen, Y. *et al.*, FedHealth: A Federated Transfer Learning Framework for Wearable Healthcare, 2019, arXiv preprint arXiv:1907.09173.
18. Silva, S. *et al.*, Federated learning in distributed medical databases: meta-analysis of large-scale subcortical brain data, presented at the *2019 IEEE 16th International Symposium on Biomedical Imaging (ISBI 2019)*, IEEE, 2019.
19. Pollard, T.J. *et al.*, The eICU Collaborative Research Database, a freely available multi-center database for critical care research. *Sci. Data*, 5, 180178, 2018.

20. Smith, V. *et al.*, Federated multi-task learning, in: *Advances in Neural Information Processing Systems 2017*, pp. 4424–4434, 2017.
21. Koteska, B. *et al.*, Machine learning based SpO2 prediction from PPG signal's characteristics features, in: *2022 IEEE International Symposium on Medical Measurements and Applications (MeMeA)*, pp. 1–6, 2022, doi: 10.1109/MeMeA56383.2022.351559.
22. TensorFlow, TensorFlow Lite — ML for Mobile and Edge Devices, Available: https://www.tensorflow.org/lite, Accessed: April 5, 2022.

10

Multiclass Classification of Oral Diseases Using Deep Learning Models

Mohammed Zubair Hussain[1], Shrey Gupta[1], Bhagyashree Hambarde[2], Priya Parkhi[3]* and Zafar Karimov[4]

[1]*Computer Science and Engineering—Data Science, Ramdeobaba University, Nagpur, India*
[2]*Computer Science and Engineering—Data Science, St. Vincent Pallotti College of Engineering and Technology, Nagpur, India*
[3]*Computer Science and Engineering—Artificial Intelligence, Ramdeobaba University, Nagpur, India*
[4]*WorkLLama, Alpharetta, GA, US*

Abstract
This research explores advanced deep learning models for accurate multi-class diagnosis of oral diseases, including Caries, Calculus, Gingivitis, Ulcers, Tooth Discoloration, and Hypodontia. Using models like Xception, ResNet, Inception, InceptionResNet, MobileNet, and DenseNet on a diverse dataset, we compare their performances for oral disease detection. Here, augmented and normalized clinical images undergo training, and models are optimized using categorical cross-entropy loss function. Moreover, evaluation metrics such as Confusion Matrix, accuracy, precision, recall, and F1-score are used. Eventually, the results demonstrate the different model's efficiency ensuring competitive performance across architectures for nuanced oral condition discernment, where accuracies of MobileNet, DenseNet, and Xception are 85.19%, 83.82%, 82.70%, respectively, which are the best. The approach expedites convergence and maximizes limited annotated medical dataset utilization. Overall, this research highlights deep learning's potential in oral disease diagnosis, emphasizing the role of such models in specialized multi-class-labeled datasets. It contributes to AI-driven medical image analysis and anticipates future strides in automated oral disease diagnosis.

**Corresponding author*: priyaparkhi1@gmail.com

Parul Dubey, Mangala Madankar, Pushkar Dubey and Bui Thanh Hung (eds.) The Impact of Algorithmic Technologies on Healthcare, (189–208) © 2025 Scrivener Publishing LLC

Keywords: Oral diseases, convolutional neural networks (CNNs), deep learning models, multi-class classification

10.1 Introduction

The widespread issue of oral diseases around the world shows how important it is to have effective tools for diagnosing these diseases early. Common oral problems, like gum diseases and tooth decay, affect millions of people. This highlights the need for efficient ways to diagnose these issues. According to the Global Burden of Disease report by Chengwei Tu *et al.* (2023) [1], oral disorders, such as dental caries, periodontitis, and tooth loss, impact over 44.5% of the global population leading to issues such as pain, sepsis, and diminished quality of life. Although oral health problems can be prevented, they often do not get enough attention in health policies. Recently, artificial intelligence (AI) has emerged as a transformative force in healthcare showcasing promising applications in disease detection and diagnosis [19]. The usefulness of deep learning models that are a subset of AI has enabled breakthroughs in various medical domains. The automation in medial field gives more clear diagnosis by reducing efforts and time constraints [21]. By utilizing it, clinicians can benefit from improved diagnostic accuracy and efficiency leading to better disease management. This paper presents a comprehensive comparative study of different deep learning models applied to the multiclass classification of oral diseases. Through this, we aim to assess the efficacy of these models in enhancing diagnostic capabilities, thus contributing to the ongoing efforts to revolutionize oral healthcare practices.

A. Oral Diseases

Oral diseases are a major health issue worldwide in various forms such as dental caries, periodontitis, and tooth loss. Although common, oral health problems are often overlooked leading to low awareness and not enough focus in health programs. The effects of oral diseases are serious causing more than just discomfort. They can lead to pain and infection and affect daily lives. Several factors lead to oral diseases, and tobacco use is one of the main ones. The study by Siddiqi *et al.* [2] shows that tobacco significantly increases the risk of oral diseases highlighting the need for specific public health actions to tackle this issue. It is crucial to recognize that oral diseases are not isolated to a specific demographic; they affect individuals across different age brackets from kids to older adults affecting their overall health and life quality. To fight these diseases, we need a broad plan that includes prevention, better education on oral hygiene, and easier access to dental care. Addressing the challenge of oral diseases requires comprehensive strategies that encompass preventive measures, improved oral hygiene education, and enhanced accessibility to dental healthcare services.

B. Convolutional Neural Networks in Dental Field

Convolutional Neural Networks (CNNs) have significantly advanced the field of medical image analysis. These networks excel at processing complex image structures in large datasets markedly improving the interpretation and analysis of medical images. They have evolved to outperform traditional machine learning methods in tasks like lesion detection and anatomical structure identification (Litjens *et al.*, 2017) [3]. Their ability to autonomously learn features directly from data, bypassing manual feature extraction, makes them indispensable in precision-driven medical applications (Shen *et al.*, 2017) [4]. One notable application of CNNs in medical image analysis is contour detection, a critical task for accurate segmentation and diagnosis. Zhang *et al.* (2017) [5] provide a comprehensive overview of the recent advancements in CNN applications for medical image contour detection.

10.2 Literature Review

A. Development of Models

The development of Convolutional Neural Networks (CNNs) marks a significant milestone in the field of deep learning and has revolutionized various applications, including medical image analysis. LeCun *et al.* (1998) [6] made a breakthrough by applying the backpropagation algorithm to train CNNs for digit recognition paving the way for modern deep learning models. The subsequent development of deep learning, particularly CNNs, has been driven by increasing computational power and the availability of large datasets. A detailed survey by Yao *et al.* (2020) [7] highlights the diverse applications of CNNs in medical image analysis, ranging from lesion detection to tissue classification. The paper by Hang Yu *et al.* (2021) [8] provides a comprehensive survey of convolutional neural networks in medical image analysis. This paper reviews commonly used CNNs and presents an overview of their use in various tasks such as image classification, segmentation, and detection in different medical diagnosis areas like brain, breast, and abdominal imaging. It also discusses the remaining challenges of CNNs in medical image analysis and presents future research directions including figures and visual representations to illustrate the findings. Figure 10.1 is a simplified CNN architecture that is the base for many other models.

The application of CNNs in dentistry began with studies focused on basic dental imaging. Some major applications of the models are as follows:

- Detection and Classification: CNNs have been successfully employed in the detection and classification of dental diseases. A study by Tuzoff *et al.* (2019) [9] illustrates the use of CNNs for automatic tooth detection and numbering in panoramic radiographs highlighting the precision and potential of CNNs in complex dental tasks.
- Advanced Applications: Beyond basic disease detection, CNNs are being explored for more advanced applications in dentistry. For instance, Zarow *et al.* (2017) [10] developed a new system for the classification for restoration of root-filled teeth focusing on one of the many applications of restoration in dental practice.
- Improving Diagnostic Processes: The integration of CNNs in dental imaging has the potential to significantly improve diagnostic processes making them more efficient and accurate. This is exemplified in the work of Lee *et al.* (2019) [11],

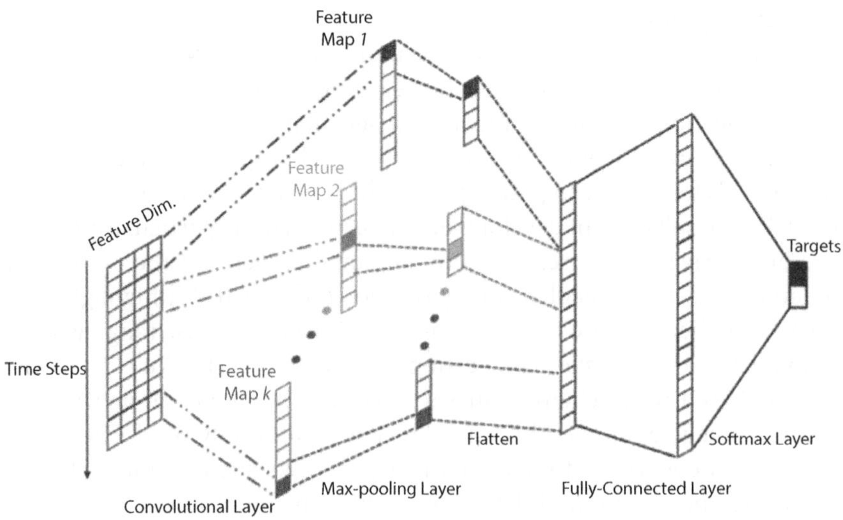

Figure 10.1 Simplified convolutional neural network [8] by Hang Yu *et al.*

who used a deep learning-based model for tooth segmentation and numbering streamlining the diagnostic workflow in dental clinics.

Moreover, the paper by Hang Yu *et al.* (2021) [8] reviews commonly used CNNs, including AlexNet, GoogleNet, ResNet, R-CNN, and FCNN, for the State-of-the-art comparisons, improvement, and perspectives.

B. Challenges

The integration of CNN in dental image analysis, while promising, faces several challenges and opens new possibilities for future exploration. A significant challenge is the lack of standardization in datasets, as highlighted by Schwendicke *et al.* (2019) [12]. Their study underscores the need for more standardized, replicable, and comparable methodologies in applying CNNs to dental imagery. This issue of standardization is crucial for the accurate and consistent application of these advanced technologies across different research and clinical settings. Furthermore, a knowledge gap exists among dental practitioners regarding the potential and limitations of CNNs. Bridging this gap is essential to ensure the effective and ethical application of these technologies in clinical practice. Additionally, while CNNs demonstrate high accuracy in controlled research settings, their performance in real-world clinical environments remains a subject of study. Ensuring that these models maintain their accuracy and reliability in diverse clinical scenarios is a critical area of focus. Future research should concentrate on developing more robust and generalized models capable of handling diverse datasets and integrating seamlessly into dental practice. Alongside technological advancements, ethical considerations, including patient data privacy and the explainability of AI decisions, must be prioritized. Addressing these challenges and exploring these future directions will significantly enhance the applicability and impact of CNNs in dental diagnostics.

10.3 Methodology

In the Methodology section, we aim to follow elemental machine learning steps to deploy a model. This flowchart in Figure 10.2 clearly showcases the methodology followed for creating and deploying a machine learning model specialized in diagnosing oral diseases. It commences with data collection, utilizing 11,653 images, followed by preprocessing steps

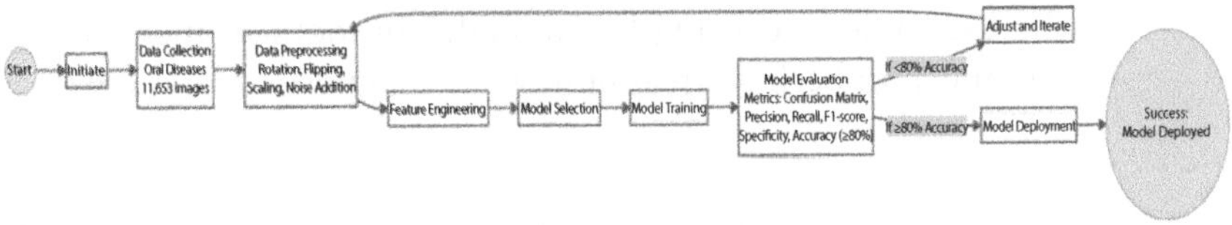

Figure 10.2 Flowchart of machine learning models.

like rotation and noise addition. Feature engineering precedes the critical model selection phase. Post-training, the model undergoes a thorough evaluation using several metrics, including accuracy with an 80% threshold. Upon achieving the benchmark, the model is deployed; otherwise, the process iteratively adjusts for improvement.

A. Dataset and Preprocessing

The Dental Condition Dataset [13] is a comprehensive and meticulously curated collection of images designed to support dental research and analysis. This dataset encompasses a wide array of dental conditions, including caries (tooth decay), calculus (tartar buildup), gingivitis (inflamed gums), tooth discoloration, ulcers (canker sores), and hypodontia (missing teeth). Here, various data augmentation techniques, such as rotation, flipping, scaling, and noise addition, have been applied to improve the dataset's diversity and enhance its generalization capabilities. Data loading and splitting were methodically executed using the ImageDataGenerator from Keras. This included rescaling each pixel value by 1/255, applying zoom range of 0.25, a rotation range of 10°, and both horizontal and vertical flips. The dataset was split into a training subset comprising 70% of the data and a validation subset containing the remaining 30%, with images resized to

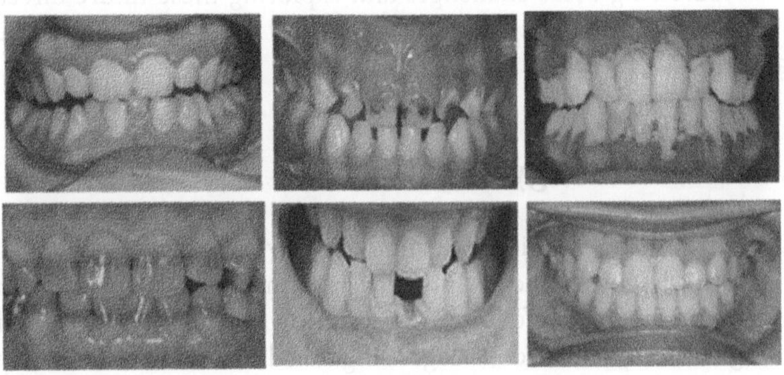

Figure 10.3 Images of various oral diseases classified in the dataset [23].

150 × 150 pixels for uniformity. With contributions from multiple hospitals and reputable dental websites, the dataset offers authenticity and diversity in depicting dental conditions. It comprises 2,382 caries images, 2,349 gingivitis images, 1,834 tooth discoloration images, 2,541 ulcer images, 1,251 hypodontia images, and 1,296 calculus images. Figure 10.3 shows images of various oral diseases classified in the dataset [23].

B. Model Architecture

We initiated our modifications by integrating advanced layers and functions, which have greatly affected the model performance. Notably, we introduced additional batch normalization and dense layers, and substituted ReLU activation with its variants were beneficial. These alterations are rooted in the objective to refine the feature extraction capabilities and the learning dynamics of the model. The major changes that we performed utilize the following:

- Batch Normalization: These layers normalize the activations of the previous layer at each batch maintaining the mean output close to 0 and the output standard deviation close to 1. This normalization process is mathematically represented as:

$$\hat{x} = {x - \mu_b}\Big/{\sqrt{\sigma_b^2 + \epsilon}}$$

where μ_b is the mean of the batch, σ_b^2 is the variance of the batch, ϵ is a small constant added for numerical stability, and $\hat{x}$ is the normalized value.

Following the normalization, the layer applies a scale and shift transformation with parameters γ and β, and the output is as follows:

$$y = \gamma \hat{x} + \beta$$

- Dense Layer: The dense (fully connected) layer performs a linear transformation followed by an activation function. For an input vector x, the operation can be represented as:

$$y = \phi(Wx + b)$$

where W is the weight matrix, b is the bias vector, ϕ is the activation function, and y is the output vector.

- Activation Functions:

$$ReLU(x) = \max(0, x)$$

$$softmax(z_i) = \frac{e^{z_i}}{\Sigma_j e^{z_j}}$$

C. Models

- **Modified Xception Model:** Xception [14], short for "Extreme Inception," is an advanced version of the Inception architecture that employs depthwise separable convolutions. This model is adept at learning more complex patterns using fewer computational resources, an advantage in scenarios with limited hardware capabilities. Its modular structure enhances adaptability for a variety of applications, from image classification to intricate tasks like object detection. In dental image analysis by Kapadia & Paunwala (2021) [15], Xception's proficiency is demonstrated by its application in the Content Based Medical Image Retrieval (CBMIR) system providing accurate disease diagnoses and treatment plans by utilizing a modified model for increased efficiency and precision in image analysis.

  In our modified Xception model, we have used the base Xception architecture of Figure 10.4 with varying dimensions. Now, to obtain a mean of zero and variance of one, a dense layer with 512 units and ReLU activation are used, which also provide a high-dimensional space for learning feature representations. Another batch normalization layer is applied to stabilize learning. Subsequently, a reduction in dimensionality is performed through a dense layer with 256 U, followed by a final batch normalization layer to ensure smooth optimization. The classification layer consists of a dense layer with 6 U, corresponding to the number of categories in our classification task, with a softmax activation function to output probability distributions over the classes. Figure 10.4 shows architecture of the modified Xception model.

	Layer (type)	Output Shape	Description
Base Xception Architecture	Input Layer	(150, 150, 3)	entry point of the network where the input image
	Conv2D	(74, 74, 32)	convolutional layer uses a kernel to transform the input image into a set of feature maps, reduces the dimension to 74 x 74 with 32 filters.
	Batch Normalization	(74, 74, 32)	normalizes the activations from the previous layer, stabilizing the learning process
	Activation	(74, 74, 32)	Applies the ReLU activation function to introduce non-linearity
	SeparableConv2D	(72, 72, 128)	depthwise separable convolution layer that performs a spatial convolution on each input channel separately before combining them using a pointwise convolution
	Batch Normalization	(72, 72, 128)	normalizes the output from the separable convolution layer to speed up training
	Conv2D	(36, 36, 128)	transforms the feature maps, reducing the dimension to 36x36 with 128 filters
	MaxPooling2D	(36, 36, 128)	reduces the spatial dimensions (width and height) of the input volume, focusing on the most important features
	Add	(36, 36, 128)	A layer that performs element-wise addition, typically used to implement residual connections
	Repeat above layers till dimensions-	(5, 5, 2048)	repeated application of similar blocks or layers, progressively reducing the dimensions of the feature maps until reaching 5 x 5x 2048
Modification	Batch Normalization	(None, 2048)	Standardizes the features to have a mean of zero and a variance of one
	Dense	(None, 512)	Provides a high-dimensional space for learning feature representations
	Batch Normalization	(None, 512)	Applied after the dense layer to stabilize learning by normalizing the activations
	Dense	(None, 256)	Reduces the dimensionality of the feature space
	Batch Normalization	(None, 256)	stabilizes the learning process after dimensionality reduction.
	Dense	(None, 6)	using a softmax activation to output a probability distribution

Figure 10.4 Architecture of the modified Xception model.

- **Modified MobileNet Model:** MobileNet [16], designed for mobile and edge devices, emphasizes optimizing speed and efficiency. It uses depthwise separable convolutions to reduce the model's size and computational cost making it an ideal choice for devices with limited computational resources. Its architecture is especially beneficial for real-time applications on mobile devices, including augmented reality and real-time video analysis. For dentistry, MobileNet has demonstrated its utility in enhancing dental diagnostics. For instance, a study by Al-Sarem *et al.* (2022) [17] employed MobileNet along with other models for tooth region detection in cone beam computed tomography (CBCT) images highlighting its effectiveness in identifying missing teeth positions.

  Our modifications to the pre-trained MobileNet model include the addition of a GlobalAveragePooling2D layer to reduce the spatial dimensions while retaining essential features. This is followed by three sets of layers: a Dense layer with ReLU activation, a Dropout layer for regularization, and a Batch Normalization layer to stabilize and accelerate training. These modifications were specifically engineered to enhance the model's generalization while retaining its ability to extract fine-grained features necessary for accurate medical image classification. The final layer is a Dense layer with a SoftMax activation function tailored to classify six distinct classes. Figure 10.5 shows architecture of modified MobileNet model.

- **Modified DenseNet Model:** DenseNet (Densely Connected Convolutional Networks) [18], known for its dense connections where each layer is interconnected in a feed-forward fashion, is a groundbreaking architecture in deep learning. This unique connectivity pattern fosters feature reuse and minimizes the number of parameters making the network more efficient and easier to train. DenseNet has excelled in image classification tasks, particularly in scenarios where preserving feature information throughout the network is crucial. Its architecture is highly beneficial in medical

	Layer (Type)	Output Shape	Description
Base MobileNet Architecture	Input	150 x 150 x 3	Input image size
	Conv2D	75 x 75 x 32	Applies a 2D convolution operation to the input, generating a feature map.
	Depthwise Separable Conv2D	75 x 75 x 32	Uses depth wise spatial convolution followed by pointwise convolution
	Batch Normalization	75 x 75 x 64	Normalizes the activations from the previous layer, stabilizing the learning process
	ReLU	75 x 75 x 64	Applies the ReLU activation function to introduce non-linearity,
	Average Pooling / Max Pooling	Variable	Reduces the spatial dimensions of the input volume for the next layer, focusing on the most significant features.
	Repeat Depthwise Blocks	75 x 75 x 64, 37 x 37 x 64 ....to 1 x 1 x 1024	A series of depth wise separable convolution blocks that are repeated to process and reduce the dimensions of the feature maps while capturing more complex features at each stage.
	....	....	....
Modification	GlobalAveragePooling2D	1 x 1 x 1024	Global average pooling across spatial dimensions
	Batch Normalization	1 x 1 x 1024	Normalizes the activations from the previous layer
	Dense (ReLU activation)	1 x 1 x 512	Fully connected layer with ReLU activation
	Dropout (50%)	1 x 1 x 512	Dropout layer to prevent overfitting
	Batch Normalization	1 x 1 x 512	Normalizes the activations from the previous layer
	Dense (ReLU activation)	1 x 1 x 256	Fully connected layer with ReLU activation
	Dropout (50%)	1 x 1 x 256	Dropout layer to prevent overfitting
	Batch Normalization	1 x 1 x 256	Normalizes the activations from the previous layer
	Dense (Softmax activation)	1 x 1 x 6	Output layer with softmax activation for 6 classes

Figure 10.5 Architecture of modified MobileNet model.

image analysis and other fields requiring fine-grained feature extraction. In the medical field, DenseNet has been successfully applied in various diagnostic scenarios. A study by Sanghvi *et al.* (2022) [22] using DenseNet-201 for the classification of COVID and pneumonia from chest X-ray images demonstrates the model's effectiveness in medical diagnosis. The model achieved remarkable accuracy rates of 99.1%, sensitivity of 98.5%, and specificity of 98.95% highlighting DenseNet's capability in precise and efficient medical image classification, which is pivotal in quick and accurate patient diagnosis and treatment planning. Figure 10.6 shows architecture of modified DenseNet model.

Our Modified DenseNet121 model begins with standard DenseNet layers, followed by a sequence of newly added layers to refine the feature representations for classification tasks. We introduced an additional Batch Normalization layer post-global average pooling to ensure that the feature vectors are well normalized prior to classification. This was succeeded by two Dense layers with ReLU activation, intertwined with Dropout layers for effective regularization to mitigate overfitting. The final classification is performed by a Dense layer with softmax activation.

Section	Layer (Type)	Output Shape	Description
Base DenseNet Architecture	Input Layer	150 x 150 x 3	Input image size
	ZeroPadding2D	156 x 156 x 3	Padding applied to the input
	Conv2D	75 x 75 x 64	Initial convolutional layer
	MaxPooling2D	38 x 38 x 64	Initial max pooling layer
	Repeat Depth wise blocks	38 x 38 x 64 to 4 x 4 x 1024	Repeat above blocks till the dimensions reduced
	DenseNet base layers	Various	Dense blocks with convolutions and concatenations
	…	…	…
Modification	Batch Normalization	4 x 4 x 1024	Normalize features before classification layers
	GlobalAveragePooling2D	1 x 1 x 1024	Global pooling to reduce spatial dimensions
	Batch Normalization	1 x 1 x 1024	Normalize features after global pooling
	Dense	1 x 1 x 512	First added fully connected layer with ReLU activation
	Dropout	1 x 1 x 512	Dropout for regularization
	Batch Normalization	1 x 1 x 512	Normalize features after dropout
	Dense	1 x 1 x 256	Second added fully connected layer with ReLU activation
	Dropout	1 x 1 x 256	Second dropout for regularization
	Batch Normalization	1 x 1 x 256	Normalize features before final classification
	Dense	1 x 1 x 6	Final classification layer with softmax activation

Figure 10.6 Architecture of modified DenseNet model.

Table 10.1 Table of model description.

Model	Total parameters	Trainable parameters	Non-trainable parameters	Model size (MB)
Xception	22,054,702	1,187,590	20,867,112	84.13
MobileNet	3,893,702	661,254	3,232,448	14.85
DenseNet121	7,702,342	661,254	7,041,088	29.38

The Table 10.1 provides a detailed summary of these models, highlighting their total, trainable, and non-trainable parameters, as well as the model size in megabytes (MB). This comparison aims to show insights into the architectural differences and resource implications of each model aiding in the selection of the most appropriate model for specific dental image analysis tasks.

D. Evaluation Parameters

A Confusion Matrix [20] is a performance measurement tool for machine learning classification. It is a table with two dimensions, "Actual" and "Predicted," and sets the stage for various metrics that evaluate the accuracy of a classification algorithm. In the context of dental image analysis using Convolutional Neural Networks (CNNs), the Confusion Matrix is essential for understanding the model's performance in distinguishing between different dental pathologies. The matrix consists of four components:

- **True Positives (TP):** These are cases in which the CNN correctly identifies a condition as present.

$$TP_{all} = \sum_{j=1}^{n} x_{jj}$$

- **True Negatives (TN):** These are cases in which the CNN correctly identifies a condition as absent.

$$TN_i = \sum_{\substack{j=1 \\ j \neq i}}^{n} \sum_{\substack{k=1 \\ k \neq i}}^{n} x_{jk}$$

- **False Positives (FP):** Also known as a Type I Error, these are cases where the CNN incorrectly identifies a condition as present.

$$FP_i = \sum_{\substack{j=1 \\ j \neq i}}^{n} x_{ji}$$

- **False Negatives (FN):** Also known as a Type II Error, these are cases where the CNN incorrectly identifies a condition as absent.

$$FN_i = \sum_{\substack{j=0 \\ j \neq i}}^{n} x_{ij}$$

These parameters are derived from the Confusion Matrix, and each serves to illuminate various aspects of model performance. Here, we discuss key metrics and their applications:

$$Precision = \frac{TP}{TP + FP}$$

$$Recall = \frac{TP}{FP}$$

$$F - Measure = \frac{(2 * Precision * Recall)}{Precison + Recall}$$

$$Accuracy = \frac{TP + TN}{P + N}$$

$$Specificity = \frac{TN}{TN + FP}$$

Receiver Operating Characteristic (ROC) curve is a graphical plot that illustrates the diagnostic ability of a binary classifier system as its discrimination threshold is varied. It is created by plotting the true positive rate (TPR) against the false positive rate (FPR) at various threshold settings.

Area Under the Curve (AUC) is particularly useful as it summarizes the ROC performance into a single metric indicating the probability that a classifier will rank a randomly chosen positive instance higher than a negative one. The paper by Nahm (2023) [23] is a recommended resource for clinicians and researchers detailing the methodology and acceptable values for diagnostic purposes in the medical field.

To understand the model's performance, the use of accuracy and loss graphs over epochs plays a crucial role. The Accuracy vs Number of Epochs graph tracks the model's ability to correctly classify the data throughout the training process. An upward trend in this graph indicates that the model is learning from the data and improving its predictive accuracy with each epoch. Concurrently, the Loss vs Number of Epochs graph reflects how well the model is being optimized during training.

10.4 Results

The performance of six different Convolutional Neural Network architectures was evaluated on the same image classification dataset to compare their effectiveness and efficiency. The architectures include the modified version of- Xception, MobileNet, and DenseNet121. Each model was fine-tuned on the dataset, with their top layers replaced by a set of Global Average Pooling, Batch Normalization, Dropout, and Dense layers, followed by a SoftMax classification layer for six classes. The fine-tuning process was conducted over 40 epochs to allow each model sufficient time to learn from the data. Table 10.2 shows performance of models.

The Xception model demonstrated promising results achieving a test accuracy of approximately 82.71%. The Confusion Matrix in Figure 10.7(b) and classification report indicated a strong ability to distinguish between the classes, with precision and recall values consistently high across distinct categories. The ROC curve presented AUC values close to 1.0 for most classes signifying excellent discriminative power as observed in Figures 10.8(b), 10.9(b), and 10.10(c).

MobileNet, optimized for mobile devices with constraints on computational resources, showed an accuracy of 85.19% on the validation set. This model's efficiency was reflected in the fewer trainable parameters, yet it maintained high precision and recall across classes, as seen in Figures 10.8(a), 10.9(a), and 10.10(a).

Table 10.2 Performance of models.

Model	Validation accuracy	Precision	Recall	F1-score
Xception	82.70%	0.90	0.89	0.90
MobileNet	85.19%	0.91	0.90	0.90
DenseNet121	83.82%	0.90	0.89	0.89

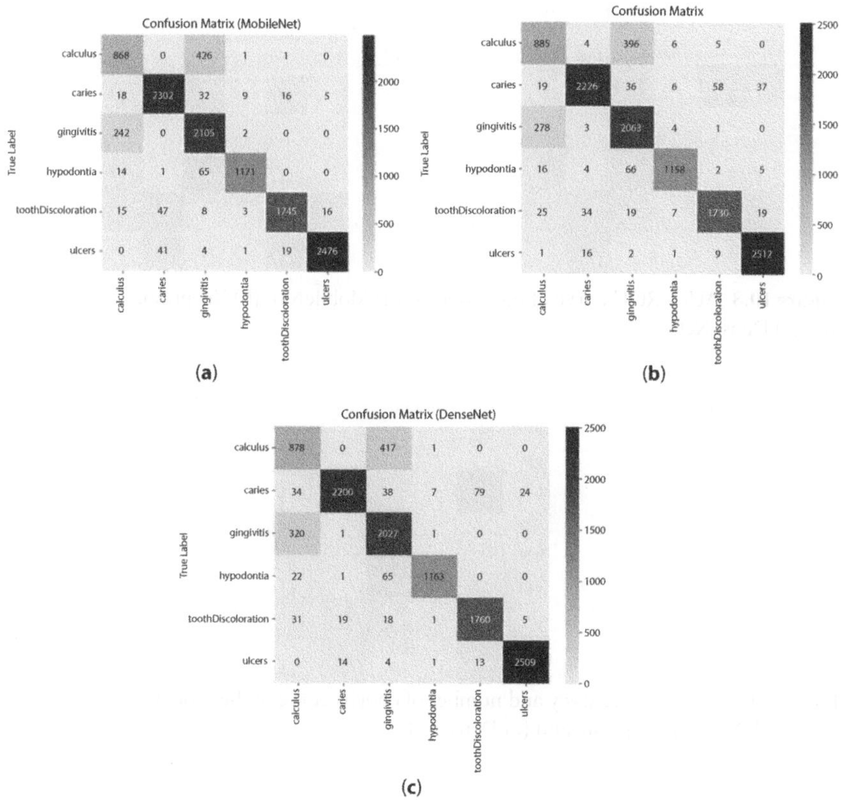

Figure 10.7 Confusion matrix of the models—(a) MobileNet, (b) Xception, and (c) DenseNet.

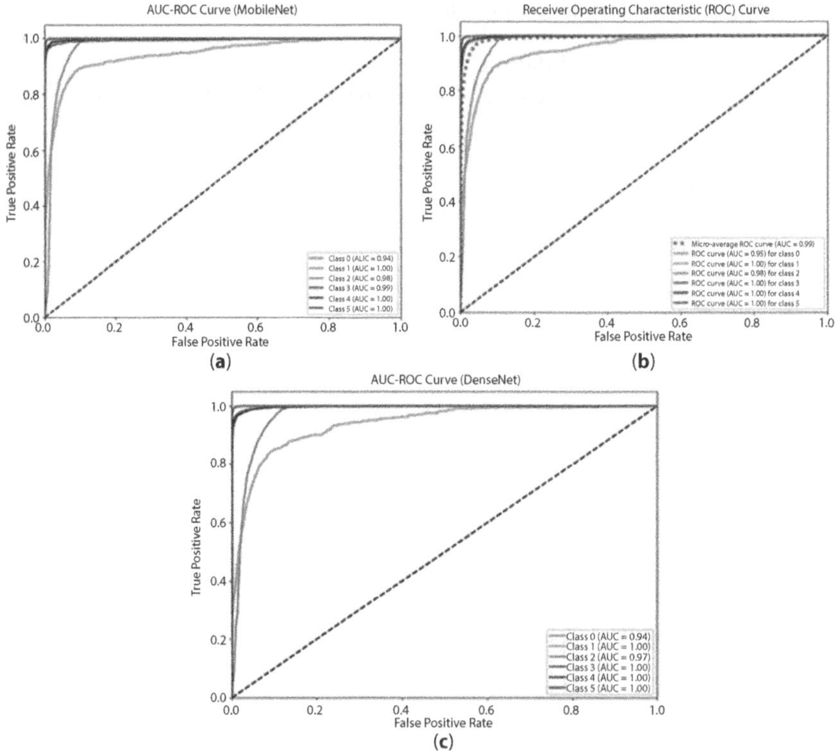

Figure 10.8 AUC–ROC curve of the models—(a) MobileNet, (b) Xception, and (c) DenseNet.

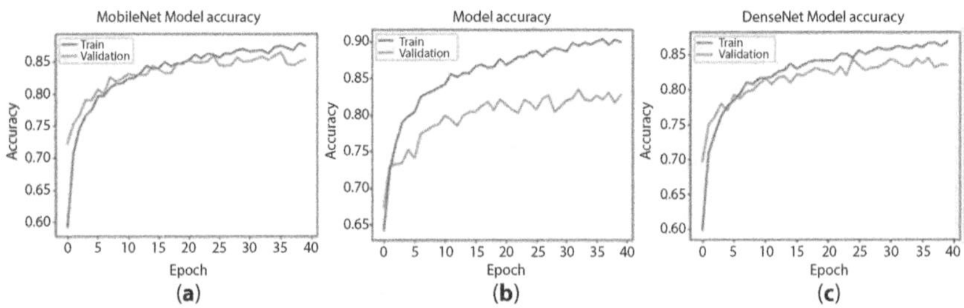

Figure 10.9 Graph of accuracy and number of epochs curve of the models—(a) MobileNet, (b) Xception, and (c) DenseNet.

DenseNet121, characterized by its dense connections, achieved a validation accuracy of 83.82%. The model's design led to efficient parameter usage and high precision and recall metrics, as detailed in the classification report as seen in Figures 10.7(c), 10.8(c), 10.9(c), and 10.10(b).

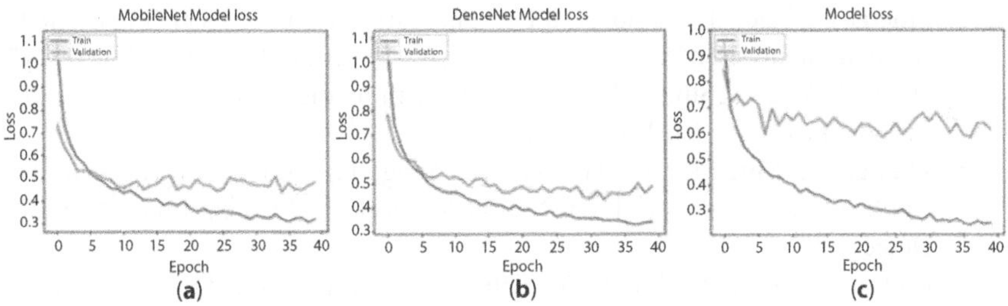

Figure 10.10 Graph of loss and number of epoch curve of the models—(a) MobileNet, (b) DenseNet, and (c) Xception.

10.5 Conclusion

This comparative analysis of various Convolutional Neural Network (CNN) models, including Xception, ResNet, InceptionV3, InceptionResNet, MobileNet, and DenseNet, has revealed their respective strengths and potential in the field of dental image analysis. Our findings reveal that these models yield results that are not only on par with each other in terms of accuracy and efficiency but also demonstrate significant promise in augmenting the capabilities of dental professionals. The incorporation of these advanced CNN models into dental diagnostics represents a notable stride toward enhancing the precision and effectiveness of patient care. By leveraging the nuanced capabilities of these models, dental experts can achieve a higher degree of diagnostic accuracy, thereby facilitating early detection and timely intervention. This is particularly pivotal in raising awareness among patients and clinicians about the potential of AI in dental healthcare. Looking ahead, the landscape of AI in dentistry is ready for the development of even more sophisticated models. Future research should focus on creating CNN architectures that are tailored to specific dental conditions, thereby expanding the scope of AI applications in dentistry.

References

1. Tu, C., Wang, G., Hu, Z., Wang, S., Yan, Q., Liu, X., Burden of oral disorders, 1990–2019: estimates from the Global Burden of Disease Study 2019. *Arch. Med. Sci.*, 19, 4, 930–940, 2023, doi: 10.5114/aoms/165962.
2. Siddiqi, K., Husain, S., Vidyasagaran, A. *et al.*, Global burden of disease due to smokeless tobacco consumption in adults: an updated analysis of data from 127 countries. *BMC Med.*, 18, 222, 1–22, 2020, doi: 10.1186/s12916-020-01677-9.

3. Litjens, G., Kooi, T., Bejnordi, B.E. *et al.*, A survey on deep learning in medical image analysis. *Med. Image Anal.*, 42, 60–88, 2017, doi: arXiv:1702.05747.
4. Shen, D., Wu, G., Suk, H.I., Deep learning in medical image analysis. *Annu. Rev. Biomed. Eng.*, 19, 221–248, 2017.
5. Zhang, Z., Xing, F., Su, H., Shi, X., Yang, L., Recent Advances in the Applications of Convolutional Neural Networks to Medical Image Contour Detection.
6. Lecun, Y., Bottou, L., Bengio, Y., Haffner, P., Gradient-based learning applied to document recognition. *Proc. IEEE*, 86, 11, 2278–2324, 1998.
7. Yao, L., Prosky, J., Poblenz, E., Covington, B., Lyman, K., A strong baseline for domain adaptation and generalization in medical imaging, arXiv preprint arXiv:2002.02497, 2020.
8. Yu, H., Yang, L., Qin, J., Heng, P.A., Convolutional neural networks for medical image analysis: State-of-the-art, comparisons, improvement and perspectives. *Neurocomputing*, 429, 185–200, 2021.
9. Tuzoff, D., Tuzova, L., Bornstein, M., Krasnov, A.S., Kharchenko, M.A., Nikolenko, S., Sveshnikov, M.M., Bednenko, G.B., Tooth detection and numbering in panoramic radiographs using convolutional neural networks. *Dento Maxillo Facial Radiol.*, 48, 4, 1–10, 2019.
10. Zarow, M., Ramírez-Sebastià, A., Paolone, G., De Ribot Porta, J., Mora, J., Espona, J., Durán-Sindreu, F., Roig, M., A new classification system for the restoration of root filled teeth. *Int. Endod. J.*, 51, 3, 318–334, Mar. 2018, doi: 10.1111/iej.12847.
11. Lee, J.H., Kim, D.H., Jeong, S.N., Choi, S.H., Detection and diagnosis of dental caries using a deep learning-based convolutional neural network algorithm. *J. Dent.*, 77, 106–111, 2019, doi: 10.1016/j.jdent.2018.07.015.
12. Schwendicke, F., Golla, T., Dreher, M., Krüger, C., Krois, J., Convolutional Neural Networks for Dental Image Diagnostics: A Scoping Review. *J. Dent.*, 91, 103226, 2019, doi: 10.1016/j.jdent.2019.103226.
13. Kaggle, Oral Diseases Dataset, Kaggle, 2024, [Online], Available: https://www.kaggle.com/datasets/salmansajid05/oral-diseases/data.
14. Chollet, F., Xception: Deep Learning With Depthwise Separable Convolutions, in: *Proceedings of the IEEE Conference on Computer Vision and Pattern Recognition (CVPR)*, pp. 1251–1258, 2017.
15. Kapadia, M.R. and Paunwala, C., Content-Based Medical Image Retrieval System for Accurate Disease Diagnoses Using Modified Multi-Feature Fused Xception Model. *Indian J. Comput. Sci. Eng.*, 12, 1, 89–100 2021, [Online], Available: https://doi.org/10.21817/INDJCSE/2021/V12I1/211201179.
16. Howard, A., Zhu, M., Chen, B., Kalenichenko, D., Wang, W., Weyand, T., Andreetto, M., Adam, H., Mobilenets: Efficient Convolutional Neural Networks for Mobile Vision Applications, 2017, arXiv preprint arXiv:1704.04861, [Online], Available: https://arxiv.org/abs/1704.04861.

17. Al-Sarem, M., Al-Asali, M., Alqutaibi, A., Saeed, F., Enhanced Tooth Region Detection Using Pretrained Deep Learning Models. *Int. J. Environ. Res. Public Health*, 19, 22, 1–17, 2022, doi: 10.3390/ijerph192215414, Art. no. 15414.
18. Huang, G., Liu, Z., Van Der Maaten, L., Weinberger, K.Q., Densely Connected Convolutional Networks, in: *Proceedings of the IEEE Conference on Computer Vision and Pattern Recognition (CVPR)*, pp. 4700–4708, 2017, doi: 10.1109/CVPR.2017.243.
19. Parkhi, P. and Hambarde, B., Optical cup and disc segmentation using deep learning technique for glaucoma detection. *Int. J. Next-Gener. Comput.*, 14, 1, 1, 2023.
20. Garillos-Manliguez, Generalized Confusion Matrix for Multiple Classes, November 2016, DOI:10.13140/RG.2.2.31150.51523.
21. Parkhi, P., Hambarde, B., Agrawal, P., Vishwakarma, M., Employing CNN Features for Automated Brain Tumor Classification in MRI. *Int. J. Intell. Syst. Appl. Eng.*, 12, 11s, 380–386, 2024.
22. Sanghvi, H.A., Patel, R.H., Agarwal, A., Gupta, S., Sawhney, V., Pandya, A.S., A Deep Learning Approach for Classification of COVID and Pneumonia Using Densenet-201. *Int. J. Imaging Syst. Technol.*, 33, 18–38, 2022, doi: 10.1002/ima.22812.
23. Nahm, F.S., Receiver Operating Characteristic Curve: Overview and Practical Use for Clinicians. *Korean J. Anesthesiol.*, 75, 1, 25–36, Feb. 2022, doi: 10.4097/kja.21209.

11

Smart Wearable Devices for Remote Patient Monitoring in Healthcare

Ravi Mishra[1], Swati Chaitandas Hadke[1], Devanand Bhonsle[2*], Priti Nilesh Bhagat[3], Anupama Mahabansi[1] and Sheetal Mungale[4]

[1]*Electronics and Telecommunication, G. H. Raisoni Institute of Engineering and Technology, Nagpur, India*
[2]*Electrical Engineering, Shri Shankaracharya Technical Campus, Bhilai, India*
[3]*Computer Science Engineering, G. H. Raisoni University, Amrawati, India*
[4]*Electronics and Telecommunication, G. H. Raisoni College of Engineering, Nagpur, India*

Abstract

This chapter focuses on remote patient monitoring system using smart wearable devices. After the pandemic of COVID-19, many research have been done for remote monitoring, and there is still room to investigate many sectors in which healthcare system is one of them. The Internet of Medical Things (IoMT) provides various types of applications for health monitoring, which could be used by any doctor or healthcare officer to examine the report of any patient anytime from anywhere. For this purpose; a health-monitoring system may be used, which consists of various types of sensors, memory chips to store the data, and wireless communication network. Using this system, the health condition of any patient can be observed in real time, and his previous reports can also be investigated to know the progress in health condition. The human body produces several types of bio-signals, which are an indication of health condition. Some of the body parameters are body temperature, pulse rate, brain signals, heart bit rate, oxygen level, etc. These parameters can be recorded using various types of sensors. These sensors can be used to design smart wearable devices, which can be worn by the user, or they can be attached to the attire and directly touches the body. The collected data are to be transmitted to the remote server and it can be fetched by the patients' caretaker or doctor for monitoring and investigation. For transmitting the data, various types of technologies are used viz. Bluetooth, ZigBee, wireless

**Corresponding author*: devanandbhonsle@sstc.ac.in

Parul Dubey, Mangala Madankar, Pushkar Dubey and Bui Thanh Hung (eds.) The Impact of Algorithmic Technologies on Healthcare, (209–224) © 2025 Scrivener Publishing LLC

sensor network, near field communication, etc. However; security and privacy are the prime concerns in remote monitoring systems.

Keywords: Healthcare, IoMT, remote monitoring, sensors, wearable device

11.1 Introduction

In the present era, it is very important to monitor health regularly in which wearable devices may play an important role. After COVID-19, many research have been done for remote monitoring [1, 2]. The Internet of Medical Things (IoMT) is a combination of several applications, which may be used for health monitoring. Integrated devices are linked with a computer via internet [3]. IoMT devices can be connected to the cloud through different services viz. Microsoft Azure Cloud, Google Cloud Computing, Amazon Web Services, etc. These services are used to record data, which are to be stored and can be used to analyze health conditions. IoMT is also known as smart healthcare. Figure 11.1 shows a simplified diagram of functionality of IoMT for healthcare services.

IoMT can be used for remote monitoring of individuals who are suffering from any chronic disease or have any health-related long-term issues. This service can monitor health conditions of the patients using wearable devices. These devices can record all health-related information and transmit them, which can be further used to take necessary action for the betterment of patients' health conditions. Smart wearable devices consist of various types of sensors and actuators. All the information collected from these devices is transferred to the cloud where it is accessible to authentic persons. In the present scenario, several products are available in the

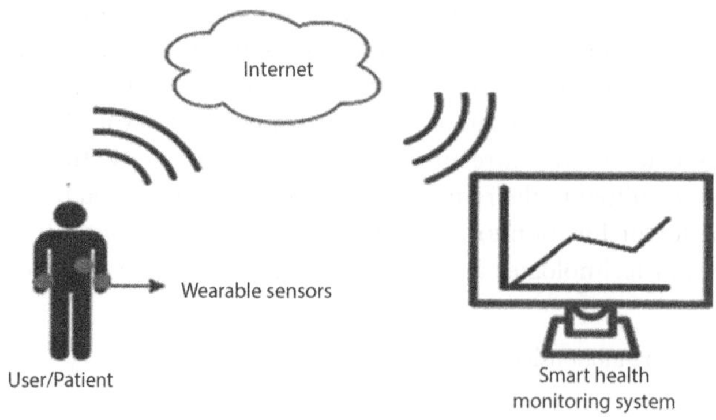

Figure 11.1 IoMT functional diagram.

market viz. fitness shoes, fitness rings, smart watches, Radio Frequency Identification Device (RIFD), pendent watches with digital camera, etc. Smart phones are also available with several health-related applications, which record heart bit rate, temperature [4–6], blood pressure, pulse rate, oxygen and glucose levels, and other body-related information. These devices provide a large amount of data, which must be secured. IoMT includes smart sensors that alert patients to take a prescribed dose or any desired action, which must be taken care of. The evolution of IoMT provides reliable and useful information with minimal time. It reduces expenses and saves time for both patients and doctor/physician. In this chapter, an IoT device is proposed, which can be used to track health-related data including heart blood pressure, bit rate, and Electro-Cardio-Gram (ECG) results [7]. This collected information can be sent to a health-related service provider for quick and necessary analysis. IoMT devices are smart devices used for real-time health-related data, which can be used to analyze the health conditions of individuals. IoMT made the healthcare service affordable, convenient, secure, and fast. Smart devices are connected to other devices via the internet [3]. IoMT uses the devices, which possess the following attributes:

- They consist of smart sensors.
- They can send and receive data from other devices via network.
- They should maintain privacy.
- Data must be secured from the whole IoMT system.
- They must be sensitive toward change in health-related information.
- They must be affordable and reliable.

For the communication of these smart devices, various networks can be used viz. Wireless Sensor Network (WSN) [8, 9], Near Filed Communication (NFC), Bluetooth, RFID, etc. [10]. One of the most common network is RIFD, which is used in most of the IoMT applications. Cloud computing stores different types of data viz. altitude, sound, biometrics, stress, temperature [4], proximity, movement, etc. This information is collected from wearable smart devices. However, there are various challenges during the medical trial conduct, management of information, interpretation of data, etc. Wearable devices can monitor health condition remotely. If an individual experiences problems while breathing, then the device sends a notification to the caretaker, and necessary action is taken.

Figure 11.2 illustrates the simplified Remote Patient Monitoring (RPM) framework.

The RPM system prevents the patients and physician from unnecessary appointments, and as a result, both time and money can be saved. It also avoids unnecessary traveling to the clinic or hospital. Nowadays, many individuals require daily health checkup in which smart devices plays an important role. An individual can use smart devices connected to the laptop, computer, smart phone, or tablet via internet. Wearable smart devices can be used to get real-time data of the physical condition and movements of individuals. These wearable sensors are available in different types, and they can be incorporated in the attire, rings, and wrists or touched directly to the skin [11]. The receptor can obtain various types of data viz. body temperature [6], heart bit rate, pulse rate, blood pressure, arterial saturation, Electro Dermal Activity (EDA), electromyogram (EMG), ECG, etc. [7]. Micro-electro-mechanical program (MEMS)-based monitoring systems are also utilized broadly, which include gyroscopes, magnetic area receptors, accelerometers, etc. Regular monitoring of these biological indicates may be used to identify any abnormality in the human body or organs. These abnormalities may be any pulmonary, aerobic, and/or neurological illnesses. The received data are transmitted to the neighboring nodes for processing. For this purpose, short-range and low-power wireless communication networks are preferred. ZigBee, Bluetooth, and NFC are some of the examples of short-range and low-power wireless networks. The processing nodes may be any smart phone, computer, laptop, or microcontroller-based device. Wearable devices are more in demand as they are comfortable to wear and less obtrusive. They are suitable for almost all age range, and health conditions of individuals can be monitored

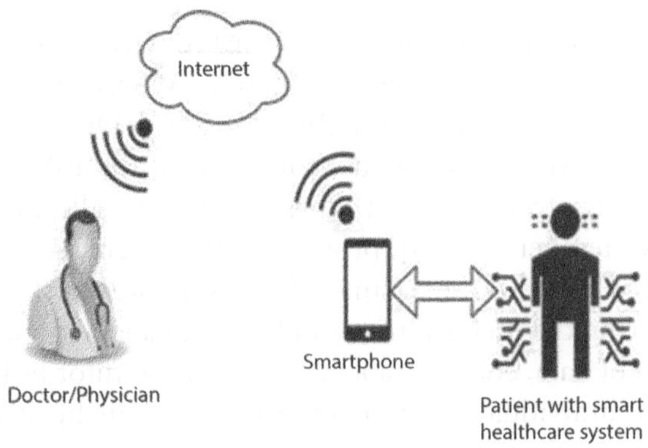

Figure 11.2 RPM framework.

without disturbance in their daily life. These wearable devices must require less power, good size of memories for storage, and most importantly, affordable.

11.2 Wearable Devices for Remote Monitoring

Non-invasive sensor-based wearable devices are very helpful for health monitoring remotely. Below is a description of these devices.

The smart devices, which can be attached to the attire, wearable, or simply touched with the body are called non-invasive devices [12]. Some of the sensor-based devices must be installed in the body, and they are called invasive devices. Below is a discussion of most common non-invasive devices:

Temperature Monitoring

Temperature is a very common and important indicator of health issues. In general, 37°C or 98°F is the body temperature of a healthy human being. The variation in body temperature may be associated with any infection in the body or blood. It may also be due to other reasons viz. sleep disorder, menstruation, malignancy, etc. In many studies, it was found that there is some correlation between stroke severity and body temperature. Cognitive functions are also correlated with it. Boano *et al.* [4] explained a wireless temperature monitoring system in which two sensor devices are connected to the epidermis. It captures and transmits information to a powerful primary device, which creates a body sensor network. Then, the primary device transmits information to the system using a wireless network. A wearable temperature monitor system consisting of a negative temperature coefficient (NTC) resistor is implemented for neonates [5]. A strap made from smooth bamboo fiber and a flexible bronze-coated nylon strand are used. It is a non-invasive device and can be incorporated in the attire or belt. Mansor *et al.* [13] designed a wireless temperature-monitoring system using industrial sensors. The system consists of a climate sensor with a ZigBee wireless node. It transfers data to a microcontroller, which is further sent to a remote server via WLAN. Additionally, an Arduino microcontroller with an Ethernet shield is used to enhance the module. Sim *et al.* [14] implemented a flux probe integrated with two dual-sensor thermometers within a neck pillow. The temperature measured by this device closely aligns with that assessed by an infrared thermometer via the tympanic membrane. This technique can be used while sleeping, positioned within the collar of a shirt or worn as a strip. Kitamura *et al.* [12]

implemented a heat sensor pin. It can measure Core Body Temperature over the epidermis. It consists of a steel wire with two heat flow routes and two resistances. Each path incorporates a set of transmitters with a receiver attached at both ends. This technique exhibits significant effectiveness and higher attributed to its stable or balanced heat properties.

Activity Monitoring

The aerobic activity and movement of a person exhibit his health condition. It is valuable for sports, rehabilitation, and most importantly early detection of any musculoskeletal or cognitive disorder. Gait abnormalities indicate any musculoskeletal or nervous system issues, which are seen in Parkinson's and Alzheimer's disease [15, 16]. Another problem in old age is falling down, which may lead to severe injuries. Monitoring and assessment may be used to predict illnesses, fall potential, and rehabilitation time. A camera-based technique is useful at home, but it is limited by some fixed locations only. Magnetometers, gyroscopes, and accelerometers are examples of wearable movement receptors, which offer real-time monitoring. These sensors can measure linear and angular activities. Figure 11.3 shows a simplified diagram of activity monitoring with gyroscopes and accelerometers. Bertolotti *et al.* [17] implemented a wireless wearable device, which monitors limb motions for a long time. The device consists of an accelerometer, gyroscope, and magnetometer. Multiple units can be incorporated into a body sensor network to calculate several parameters. By analyzing the data gathered from the system, treatment can be done. Panahandeh *et al.* [18] described an algorithm for gait evaluation.

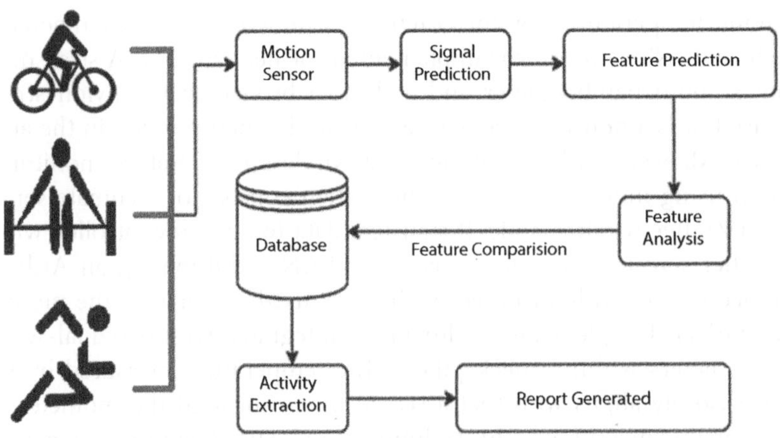

Figure 11.3 Activity monitoring.

It is based on the Hidden Markov Model (HMM). It takes data from a gyroscope and tri-axial accelerometer. It gives higher categorical accuracy for sports performance. It lacks wireless connectivity, hence, testing needs a computer. Integration of wireless connectivity may enhance the performance of the device.

Friedman *et al.* [16] designed a wearable monitoring system, which can be worn on the wrist or finger. It utilizes magnetic technologies. The device comprises a neodymium band with integrated data storage. Tri-axis magnetometers within the wrist device assess the magnetic field of the finger band [11]. A radial time frame feature estimates wrist and finger bone characteristics. This device gives consistent results for angular distance measurements of wrist bones. However; extension poses and evaluation of finger flexion provides big challenges. A technique for comprehensive evaluation involves pairing kinematic arm design algorithms [19]. Inertial measurements were collected from three sets of inertial measurement units (IMUs) placed on the forearm, upper arm, and wrist. The system accurately captured joint motion limitations. Joint movement was estimated using the Kalman filter [20]. Complex algorithms, like extended Kalman filter (EKF), can be employed if there are more nonlinearities of the device. The EKF can achieve superior evaluation accuracy across various intensities of arm movements. Kalman-based solutions are effective, but can be computationally intensive and require a high sampling rate for human activities. This can pose challenges when deploying these devices for real-time applications. Therefore, it is essential to carefully assess the algorithm's performance in real-world scenarios.

Galvanic Skin Response (GSR) Monitoring

Various bodily functions and responses are regulated by the autonomic nervous system. Nervous systems have two subdivisions:

- **Sympathetic nervous system:** It triggers the response called fight or flight. Responses and increases metabolic changes to cope with external stimuli.
- **Parasympathetic nervous system:** It conserves and restores the body's energy.

Tachycardia, dysautonomia, and postural orthostatic tachycardia syndrome (POTS) are the conditions associated with ANS dysfunction, which are often characterized by increased sweat secretion. This increase in sweat secretion affects skin conductivity, which is called EDA. GSR is a measure of sympathetic nervous system activities. It can be a reliable indicator of anxiety and emotional responses. In general, GSR is measured in the laboratory or healthcare settings using time-limited devices, but with the advancements in wearable technologies, it now allows inconspicuous, extended-use monitoring of GSR. Monitoring of GSR for long term helps to evaluate the sympathetic nervous system activity over extended periods. Also, wearable GSR monitoring allows individuals to monitor their psychophysiological condition and provides more comprehensive data compared to measurements taken in laboratories or healthcare centers [21]. Hence, this advancement in smart wearable devices offers various opportunities to understand and manage the conditions related to ANS dysfunction. In the present era, GSR sensors are more advanced and monitor the nervous system activity efficiently. These devices can measure the activities from different parts of the bodies. Data transfer is done via Bluetooth technology. The sensor is installed on a printed circuit board (PCB) along with other circuit components. It should be designed in such a manner so that it maintains continuous contact with curved areas of the body. Additionally, conductive polymer foam is used so enhance flexibility of the electrodes. It ensures a reliable and stable interface with the body along with comfort to the user. Overall, wearable GSR sensors exhibit promising results for unobtrusive and continuous monitoring for the sympathetic nervous system activities. They offer many applications in several fields viz. sports, healthcare, stress management, etc. Garbarino *et al.* [22] implemented the Empatica E3, which is a compact wristband. It consists of multiple sensors viz. temperature sensor, GSR, and movement sensor. It captures data from all sensors continuously and transmit real-time data via Bluetooth technology. The efficacy of this wrist band can be improved by enhancing battery life and optimizing power consumption. Setz *et al.* [23] demonstrated cognitive stress and load using the GSR measurement technique. Figure 11.4 shows a block diagram of a GSR monitoring system. It is connected to the toes to measure mental conditions. This device transmits the data to a website via Bluetooth technology. Sixteen level options are provided for the better outcomes to differentiate cognitive load and anxiety.

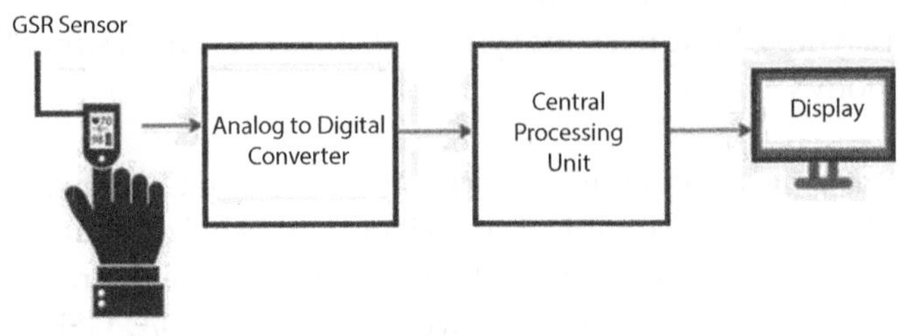

Figure 11.4 GSR monitoring.

Multiple Device Monitoring

Most of the bio-signal monitoring systems focus to track tracking individual parameters viz. ECG, heart bit rate, etc. But in general; comprehensive monitoring requires tracking multiple physical symptoms like respiratory rate, temperature, pulse rate, oxygen saturation level, blood pressure, GSR, etc. The system incorporates all these parameters into a single device, which may offer a practical solution for ambulatory monitoring. Figure 11.5 illustrates a simplified diagram of multiple sensor monitoring.

Fabric-Based Wearable

Smart fabrics offer an inconspicuous and comfortable way to monitor physical health parameters by installing the sensors directly into the fabric. These sensors are constructed on a substrate, which can measure various signals viz. GSR, electroencephalography (EEG), ECG, and EMG. Textile electrodes are broadly divided into two viz., active and passive electrodes [24]. Active electrodes are used to determine electrical qualities of the skin and monitor muscle or cardiac activities, while passive electrodes can measure GSR by assessing perspiration. Conventional electrodes require conductive gel, which may cause signal quality issues or irritation in the skin, but fabric electrodes can be sewn into the attire or deposited into it [8, 25].

Fabric-Based Rectal Sensor

A fabric-based temperature sensor, integrated into wearable garments, offers a convenient and accurate method for measuring body temperature. These sensors, typically composed of fibers or yarn using traditional textile production methods, can be integrated seamlessly into clothing through weaving, embroidery, or knitting. Additionally, the choice of encapsulation

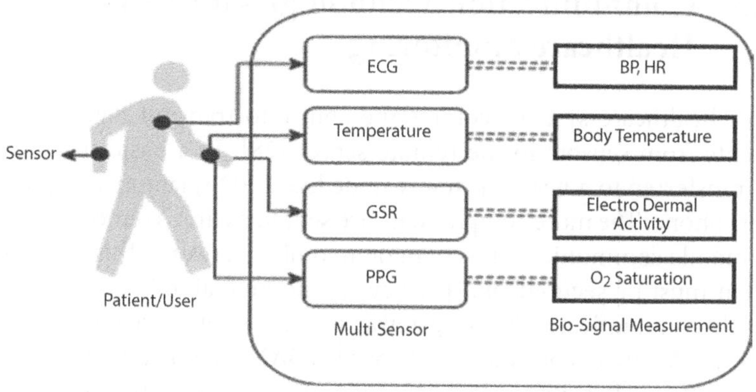

Figure 11.5 Multiple sensor monitoring.

materials is crucial to protect the sensor from external environmental and physical factors.

Fabric-Based Activity Monitoring

Some of the examples of MEMS-based inertial sensors are gyroscopes, magnetic field sensors, accelerometers, etc. These sensors are used to monitor human locomotion. These sensors are integrated into PCB panels in such a manner so that they can be inserted into rings, belts, Velcro straps, etc. These sensors have many advantages viz. low cost, small size, reliability, high detection capability, and low power consumption. Rajdi *et al.* [25] implemented a MEMS accelerometer, which is used to measure pelvic tilt. It is attached to a cotton fabric by ironing or pressing. It utilizes piezoresistive property of conductive silver nanoparticles. Changes in tilt cause physical tension on a cantilever beam system within the accelerometer, and as a result, there are linear adjustments to the conductive content. Many researchers utilized flexible and stretchable stress sensors in textile-based monitoring system. These sensors are used to detect physical deformation due to change in electrical properties. Stress sensors must be stretchable, flexible, and durable for textile applications. Kaysir *et al.* [26] designed a versatile pressure sensor, which utilizes optical fibers integrated into textiles. A flexible copolymer, which contains polyurethane and silicon, is used to design optical fiber [27]. Its cross section is oval shaped, which deforms under external pressure. Light deflects with deformation within the fiber. As a result, light intensity alters. It can be embedded in the attire and used to detect respiratory rate and limb motion. However, its accuracy is affected due to bends, strain, and temperature.

11.3 Communication Technologies for Remote Healthcare Monitoring

Smart healthcare system requires the ability to transmit data related to patients from sensors to the remote server [28]. In a basic system, data are transferred to a nearby gateway node like a PDA, laptop, computer, or smart phone. The more complex data are sent to a clinic's remote server via any mobile communication system or an online network. This monitoring system must be secured, and privacy should be maintained. Sensors can directly communicate with the gateway in the case of short-range communication. A wireless body area network (WBAN) can be established using sensors through primary WBAN nodes. These nodes transmit data to the gateway executing necessary processes immediately. Communication between body sensors and WBAN nodes may be wired or wireless. However, wired connections restrict user mobility and lead to frequent connection failures; hence, they are not suitable for distance wearable monitoring methods. Bluetooth is the most common radio frequency (RF) technology with low power consumption. It is inbuilt in many devices viz. laptops, computers, smart phones, fitness trackers, etc. It employs frequency hopping spread spectrum (FHSS) for communication across over 78 specified channels. ZigBee is a low-power wireless standard, which is designed for cost-effective interactions within small areas. It operates utilizing quadrature phase shift keying (QPSK) modulation technique for communication across more than 16 channels. Medical implant services utilize low-energy and low-range wireless technology to communicate with fixed healthcare devices viz. defibrillators, pacemakers neuro-stimulators, etc. However, Wi-Fi is not suitable for long-term patient tracking due to its complexity and high energy requirement.

11.4 Proposed Methodology

The proposed RPM system utilizes IoT to collect data of individual patients. These data may be body temperature, ECG, blood pressure, heart bit rate, pulse rate, etc. After collecting these data, they are compiled together and transmitted to the caretaker. He can access the data, which include current health condition and remedial information. The biggest advantage of this system is that patients need not visit the healthcare center. Figure 11.6 exhibits an overview of remote patient monitoring system. Different types of sensors are used to collect various health-related information. These data are collected and sent to a server, which is accessible by authorized healthcare professionals. The chip receives data from non-invasive sensors, which are attached to the body of patients via uploading them in the server Ethernet connection. Doctors or Physicians can monitor these data through an internet-based program or smart phone. In this framework, a total of four sensors are used viz. Pulse sensor, ECG sensor, temperature sensor, and fabric-based activity monitoring sensor. Data sent from these sensors are sent to Windows-, Apache-, MySQL-based data based server for logging and analysis. Patient data are accessible to administrators and service providers for real-time monitoring. These health records can also be seen by patients.

Figure 11.7 shows a visual representation of the login process. To secure the patients' confidential data, encryption techniques have to be used while

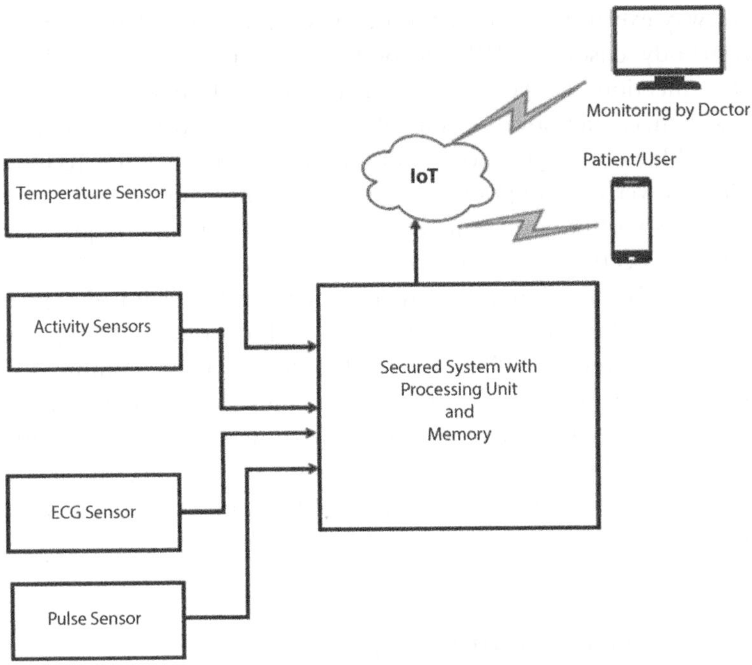

Figure 11.6 Remote patient monitoring framework.

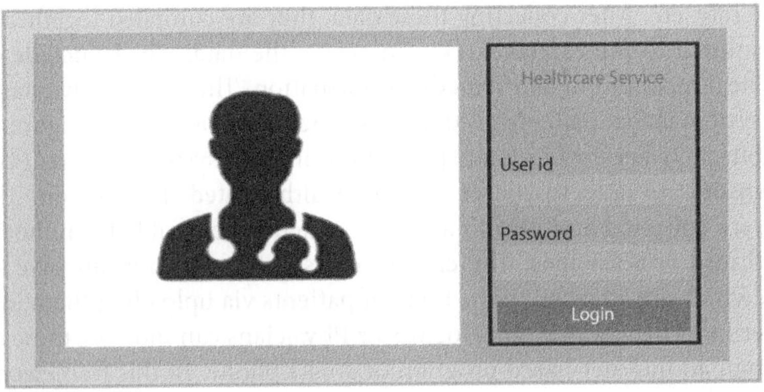

Figure 11.7 Graphical user interface for login.

transferring the data. Figure 11.7 illustrates a Graphical User Interface (GUI) in which patients and their caretaker can login to the system and get all the information in the form of a report, which can be observed by the doctor or physician. In the case of any kind of error due to transmission error, device disconnection, or faulty sensor, readings are set to zero to avoid any false prediction. The health data appear in the form of a graph, range, or numerical values and are displayed on the screen of a smart phone, laptop, computer, or any other display device.

11.5 Conclusion

The methods involve monitoring and evaluation using predictive algorithms to enhance diagnostic accuracy and prognosis prediction for specific illnesses. This approach helps in reducing unnecessary treatments and incorrect diagnoses. Regular monitoring of a patient using smart wearable devices can help understand overall health condition. This information helps the doctors or physicians understand a case, and necessary steps must be taken for the improvement of a patient's health. Wearable sensors and actuators provide many opportunities in the direction of remote health-monitoring systems. Additionally, devices can generate alerts to notify users or healthcare providers of any detected issues. Smart fabrics, integrated with wearable devices and textile-based sensor connections, offer a comfortable and less intrusive framework for overall health monitoring.

References

1. Rizvi, T., Bhonsle, D., Rahangdale, R., Bagga, J., A survey on behavioral change during the COVID-19 outbreak in India, in: *Computational Intelligence and Applications for Pandemics and Healthcare*, pp. 184–203, IGI Global, Hershey, Pennsylvania, USA, 2022.
2. Rizvi, T., Bhonsle, D., Uzma, R., Analysis and comparison of psychological constraints among various countries during COVID-19, in: *Computational Intelligence and Applications for Pandemics and Healthcare*, pp. 248–268, IGI Global, Hershey, Pennsylvania, USA, 2022.
3. Sriram, G.S., Reddy, G.L., Babu, P., Bachanna, S.C., Gurpreet, V., Moyal, V., Bhonsle, D., Chamato, F.A., A smart solution for cancer patient monitoring based on internet of medical things using machine learning approach. *Evidence-Based Complementary Altern. Med.*, 2022, 1, 1–6, 2022.
4. Boano, C., Lasagni, M., Romer, K., Lange, T., Accurate temperature measurements for medical research using body sensor network. *14th IEEE International symposium on object/component/service-oriented real-time distributed computing workshops*, 2011.

5. Boano, C., Lasagni, M., Romer, K., Non-invasive measurement of core body temperature in Marathon runners, in: *2013 IEEE International conference on body sensor networks*, 2013.
6. Mansor, H., Shukor, M., Meskam, S., Rusli, N., Zamery, N., Body temperature measurement for the remote health monitoring system, in: *2013 IEEE International Conference on Smart Instrumentation, Measurement and Applications (ICSIMA)*, 2013.
7. Nemati, E., Deen, M., Mondal, T., A wireless wearable ECG sensor for long-term applications. *IEEE Commun. Mag.*, 50, 36–43, 2012.
8. Bhonsle, D., Bhale, Y., Pillai, A.G., Tiwari, S., Moyal, V., Fan, C.P., Applications and challenges of IoT-based smart healthcare systems that use cognitive sensors: an overview, in: *Cognitive Sensors Intelligent sensing, sensor data analysis and applications*, vol. 1, pp. 7–1, 2022.
9. Rizvi, T., Mishra, R., Chopkar, P.N., Gomkale, A., Upadhye, P., Bhonsle, D., Internet of Things-based cognitive wireless sensor networks: applications, merits, and demerits, in: *Cognitive Sensors, Intelligent sensing, sensor data analysis and applications*, vol. 1, pp. 2–1, IOP Publishing, Bristol, UK, 2022.
10. He, D. and Zeadally, S., An analysis of RFID authentication schemes for the internet of things in healthcare environment using elliptic curve cryptography. *IEEE Internet Things J.*, 2, 72–83, 2015.
11. Akbulut, F.P., Özgür, O., Cınar, I., e-Vital: A wrist-worn wearable sensor device for measuring vital parameters. *Medical technologies congress (TIPTEKNO)*, Izmir, Turkey, pp. 1–4, 2019.
12. Kitamura, K.I., Zhu, X., Chen, W., Nemoto, T., Development of a new method for the non-invasive measurement of deep body temperature without a heater. *Med. Eng. Phys.*, 32, 1–6, 2010.
13. Mansor, H., Shukor, M., Meskam, S., Rusli, N., Zamery, N., Body temperature measurement for the remote health monitoring system. *IEEE International Conference on Smart Instrumentation, Measurement and Applications (ICSIMA)*, pp. 1–5, 2013.
14. Sim, S.Y., Lee, W.K., Baek, H.J., Park, K.S., A non-intrusive temperature measuring system for estimating deep body temperature:" in bed, in: *Proceedings of the 2012 Annual International Conference of the IEEE Engineering in Medicine and Biology Society*, San Diego, CA, USA, pp. 3460–3463, 2012.
15. Mulroy, S., Gronley, J., Weiss, W., Newsam, C., Perry, J., Use of cluster analysis for gait pattern classification of patients in the early and late recovery phases following stroke. *Gait Posture*, 18, 114–125, 2013.
16. Panahandeh, G., Mohammadiha, N., Leijon, A., Handel, P., Continuous hidden Markov model for pedestrian activity classification and gait analysis. *IEEE Trans. Instrum. Meas.*, 62, 1073–1083, 2013.
17. Deen, M.J., Information and communications technologies for elderly ubiquitous healthcare in a smart home. *Pers. Ubiquitous Comput.*, 19, 573–599, 2015.

18. Bertolotti, G.M., Cristiani, A.M., Colagiorgio, P., Romano, F., Bassani, E., Caramia, N., Ramat, S.A., Wearable and modular inertial unit for measuring limb movements and balance control abilities. *IEEE Sens. J.*, 16, 790–797, 2016.
19. Friedman, N., Rowe, J.B., Reinkensmeyer, D.J., Bachman, M., The manometer: A wearable device for monitoring daily use of the wrist and fingers. *IEEE J. Biomed. Health. Inf.*, 18, 1804–1812, 2014.
20. El-Gohary, M. and Mcnames, J., Human joint angle estimation with inertial sensors and validation with a Robot Arm. *IEEE Trans. Biomed. Eng.*, 62, 1759–1767, 2015.
21. Majumder, S., Aghayi, E., Noferesti, M., Memarzadeh-Tehran, H., Mondal, T., Pang, Z., Deen, M., Smart homes for elderly healthcare – Recent advances and research challenges. *Sensors*, 17, 2496, 2017.
22. Hernando-Gallego, F., Luengo, D., Artés-Rodríguez, A., Feature extraction of galvanic skin responses by nonnegative sparse deconvolution. *IEEE J. Biomed. Health. Inf.*, 22, 5, 1385–1394, 2018.
23. Haghi, M., Stoll, R., Thurow, K., Pervasive and personalized ambient parameters monitoring: A wearable, modular, and configurable watch. *IEEE Access*, 7, 20126–20143, 2019.
24. Cho, G., Jeong, K., Paik, M.J., Kwun, Y., Sung, M., Performance evaluation of textile-based electrodes and motion sensors for smart clothing. *IEEE Sens. J.*, 11, 12, 3183–3193, 2011.
25. Narczyk, P., Siwiec, K., Pleskacz, W.A., Precision human body temperature measurement based on thermistor sensor, in: *2016 IEEE 19th international symposium on Design and Diagnostics of Electronic Circuits & Systems (DDECS)*, Kosice, pp. 1–5, 2016.
26. Silva, A.F.D., Pedro, R., Paulo, J., Higino, J., Photonic sensors based on flexible materials with FBGs for use on biomedical applications, in: *Current trends in short- and long- period fiber gratings*, pp. 105–132, InTec, Rijeka, 2013.
27. Kaysir, M.R., Stefani, A., Lwin, R., Fleming, S., Flexible optical fiber sensor based on polyurethane, in: *2017 Conference on Lasers and Electro-Optics Pacific Rim (CLEO-PR)*, Singapore, pp. 1–2, 2017.
28. Bhonsle, D., Baksi, S., Pillai, A.G., Rahangdale, R., Verma, C., Khan, M.H.M., A review on a sensor based brain–computer interface and its applications, in: *Cognitive Sensors, Applications in smart healthcare*, vol. 2, pp. 6–1, 2023.

12

Efficient IoT Solutions for Remote Health Monitoring

Vijayakumar S.[1], N. Sheik Hameed[1], Kanchan S. Tiwari[2], A. Allwyn Sundarraj[3], N. Gopinath[4]* and Lyndsay R. Buckingham[5]

[1]*Department of English, B.S. Abdur Rahman Crescent Institute of Science and Technology, Chennai, India*
[2]*Department of Electronics and Telecommunications, Modern Education Society's Wadia College of Engineering, Pune, India*
[3]*Department of Food Technology, Sri Shakthi Institute of Engineering and Technology, Coimbatore, India*
[4]*Department of CINTEL, SRM Institute of Science and Technology, Kattankulathur, Tamil Nadu, India*
[5]*Department of TEFL, Universidad Pontificia Comillas, Madrid, Spain*

Abstract

The "digital twin (DT)," or virtual product copy, is becoming increasingly prevalent in many industries. The field of healthcare is advancing significantly because of this technology. A precise replica of a person or equipment is known as DT. For the related application, massive amounts of data must be collected using the Internet of Things (IoT) sensors to build a digital model, which is simulated and tested. This technology assists in alerting the patient to medicines, dietary changes, doctor visits, and other circumstances based on their lifestyle, regular eating routine, and blood sugar levels. The digital twin uses models driven by artificial intelligence (AI) and significant data from various IoT devices. DT uses past data insights to predict the outcome of a particular procedure, help choose the best drug, and manage chronic illnesses. Examining the value of the digital twins to the healthcare industry is the primary goal of this research. This research covers a wide range of features and capabilities of the digital twin for healthcare. Some DT for healthcare technologies and approaches are also introduced. The healthcare sector has realized that a centered approach is necessary. Future healthcare should include more sophisticated techniques to give patients the best care possible.

**Corresponding author*: gopinathit14@gmail.com

Parul Dubey, Mangala Madankar, Pushkar Dubey and Bui Thanh Hung (eds.) The Impact of Algorithmic Technologies on Healthcare, (225–254) © 2025 Scrivener Publishing LLC

As healthcare organizations organize digital transformation activities, they must plan for the post-digital age.

Keywords: Digital twin, health care, Internet of Things, artificial intelligence, digital model

12.1 Introduction

In the entire cycle, a systems' or products' virtual duplicate is called a "digital twin." Digital twins facilitate enhanced decision making through learning, reasoning, and dynamic recalibrating by utilizing available data. They are precise replicas of real-world objects, or twins, made of complex computer models that are updated, edited, and altered in real time [1]. Medical professionals can advise patients on eradicating specific diseases for medical emergencies using digital twin technology. Digital twins are precise replicas of the entity they are modeling. Healthcare specialists supply essential data that are beneficial to producing realistic digital twins. Patients can avoid medical emergencies by employing simulators that detect sickness symptoms early [2]. They can identify the possibility that a sickness, like cancer, may recur. In addition to identifying lifestyle trends, the digital twin's predictive skills may alert users to abnormal behavior that could harm their health. Healthcare professionals can improve the quality of life of their patients by offering proactive patient care. Healthcare today uses digital twins that AI and ML technology power. Digital twins can generate accurate predictions about individuals' health outcomes by merging cloud apps with elements of machine learning (ML) and artificial intelligence (AI) in real time [3]. People can more easily interact with and understand the healthcare paradigm's digital twin. Patients are encouraged to adopt healthier lifestyles by engaging with the digital twin. Transparency and confidence are encouraged during therapy when medical data are computed using a digital twin. Consequently, both doctors and patients have improved overall experiences with healthcare. Making an adequate care strategy for capacity planning is difficult in the healthcare sector since more variables are at play than in other businesses [4]. They can make informed decisions about capacity, investments, and staff since they have a digital twin of their organization.

Organizational flow makes it feasible for a physical object to be represented digitally in real time enabling the coexistence of real and virtual items. Create a digital representation, collect and preserve real-time data, incorporate four technologies into an application for a digital twin, and provide informative information based on the data collected. Technology related to digital twins includes cloud, AI, IoT, and extended reality [5]. Manufacturers of medical devices can use simulation technologies to test their products in multiple environments without paying extra. Engineers and researchers utilizing a medical device could discover potential design flaws early in the prototype phase. To see how the device would work in the real world, users can also interact with 3D simulations of human anatomy. Digital twin technology improves design efficacy and regulatory compliance in the manufacturing of medical devices. Unlike earlier computer models, digital twins collect accurate and timely data and stay in continuous contact with what they are supposed to symbolize. Other fascinating possibilities emerge when considering applying DT in domains such as customer support [6]. E-commerce companies may find it easier to analyze trends and applications or websites to the preferences of individual users with the use of a digital twin. Alternatively, they might use customer service to actively and passively lessen annoyance. The primary goal of this work is to investigate the many uses of DTs in medicine.

12.1.1 Introduction to DT

An electronic duplicate of an actual object is called a digital twin. It digitally represents actual or potential people, places, systems, and technology. In product lifecycle management, "digital twin" was first used during the early stages of digital representations of physical goods. It is an interactive virtual device that uses embedded sensors and software to gather data continuously. This enables us to view the device's precise state in real time. Researchers might even be able to predict possible issues before they arise with the help of computational technologies like artificial intelligence (AI) enabling prompt replacement or repair of essential parts [7]. Digital twins would allow businesses to enter new markets and create new business models by providing a product as a service. This tactic is effective for expensive assets that other companies might prefer not to own. On the other hand, the item's owner, the creator, is in charge of its maintenance, productivity, and use. Manufacturers can monitor activities, collect data on the events that indicate the equipment requires repair, and create predictive maintenance models by creating a digital copy of an already available product.

12.1.2 Digital Twin in the Healthcare Sector

The healthcare sector has embraced digital technology altering how operations should be carried out and enhancing human experiences generally.

With the increasing popularity of virtual healthcare services, traditional healthcare providers are partnering with technology companies for an extended period to obtain the requisite knowledge and infrastructure [8]. As the global healthcare sector overcomes the challenges posed by COVID-19, it is growing stronger. It is now driven by the new opportunities they have revealed, but the pandemic's devastating impacts have altered it. Unexpected fluctuations in workload and test cancellations provide serious issues for hospitals and patients. Imaging technology should be usable and available when required. Unplanned downtime resulting from a system breakdown can be expensive, worsen treatment outcomes, and lengthen patient wait times and suffering. Therefore, it is necessary to use digital twins to tackle a variety of healthcare difficulties [9].

The need for medications and medical supplies is rising. Development costs are rising in tandem with profitability and the market. Millions of individuals today lack even more access to potentially life-saving therapies globally. These issues are resolved by developing technologically based methods for assessing medical devices, doing away with human trials during the whole development process, and streamlining, safeguarding, and lowering the cost of the process. Collaborative use of digital twin technology yields the finest results. The collaboration between hospital administrators, physicians, staff members, the architect, and the technology partner is required to create a practical, high-fidelity digital twin [10]. The interdisciplinary team routinely evaluates the Digital Twin (DT) to ensure it provides reliable insights and improves the effectiveness of hospital operations. Adding or modifying care units can be planned with the aid of the DT. Once a department has been reorganized, a reorganization may lessen the requirement for costly upgrades.

12.2 Related Works

This article describes the intelligent services offered by the newest, cutting-edge approach, a digital twin created especially for the medical field. Its main emphasis is on patient health services, data-related facts and problems, lowering care and treatment costs, providing high-quality care, challenges about social disruptions, etc. These additional services demonstrate how patient care has improved during treatment to facilitate a speedy and complete recovery. In addition to increasing efficiency, productivity, and quality of service, every healthcare organization's patient experiences. Limited resources, including operating rooms, patient rooms, beds in critical care units, and therapy spaces, must be scheduled and "turned" regularly to guarantee proper operation. Information from sickness registries and electronic health records (EHRs) makes it possible to merge patient data from these platforms and resources with accessories for personal health, such as wearables [11]. These massive data sets allow us to create highly tailored care plans, effectively represent each patient, run simulations to forecast the effects of different medications and obtain prior notification about an individual's susceptibility to diseases or other conditions. Digital twins are transforming hospital administration and clinical operations in the healthcare industry through advances in human body modeling and digital monitoring that improve medical care. When assessing an athlete, a physician may use a computer program to test how the device would perform in various scenarios [12]. This method is far quicker and less expensive than eliminating re-injury before testing.

Insightful information is produced, and data are gathered, stored, and analyzed using four digital twin technologies. Extended reality, cloud, IoT, and AI are some technologies. Two significant advantages of digital twins are comprehending the actions of tangible apparatus and having remote access to assets, systems, and procedures. To produce forecasts for the future, it employs a prediction algorithm that leverages information from asset behavior. These insights also increase productivity and profitability through improved streamlined and automated decision making. It also assists businesses in maximizing operational efficiency by performing risk analysis on a range of hypothetical scenarios. Before and after device use, digital twins of the gadget are helpful. The production of digital twins during product development allows for the rapid prototyping of new or improved technology. Healthcare entrepreneurs' primary focus is AI, ML, and numerical simulations. These technologies hardly scrape the surface of what has been done, even though they have all significantly contributed to the growth of the healthcare industry [13].

A digital twin for the medical field can be realized using clever techniques and technologies. Regarding platforms, features about connections, simulation models, and model evolution techniques are linked to the foundations and introduction pattern of its services; physical platforms are associated with materials, dynamics, sensing, measurement, and so on. Accuracy, tolerance, and outcomes are essential considerations when performing the analytical process. Digital twins are no longer only a science fiction concept because they have a lot of real-world applications. With this method, creating a virtualized system or item is possible. One uses a DT to assess how well a physical counterpart performs. Creating DT in the healthcare industry involves compiling a patient's complete medical history and combining it with AI-driven techniques that analyze the data analyzer to answer particular clinical concerns. When biological entities replace non-living machinery and equipment, digital twin technologies will change. Businesses looking to leverage IoT for development and optimization are increasing. When engaging with a service ecosystem, users may begin their digital twin journey from the perspective of technology, problem-solving, or technology [14].

Digital twins incorporate real-world elements for testing and quality assurance. Therefore, AI is required. All sensors and data sources must function seamlessly since a larger IoT ecosystem is necessary for digital twins. To achieve optimal precision and minimize errors, miniature data testing guarantees flawless real-time live data integration from several sources. IoT testing is also essential for fulfilling the data integrity and security collected and full functionality of different sensors and devices. When drugs that target tumors are unable to penetrate their targets or "strike" healthy tissue, patients receiving aerosol-delivered chemotherapeutic medications run the risk of experiencing severe adverse effects. They could effectively use a digital twin to mimic the movement of aerosol particles via the upper respiratory tract of an adult. In addition, digital twins could aid medical research into human brain repair.

In a medical setting, digital twins virtualize and offer a safe setting that assesses how modifications affect hospital performance without endangering the physical site. Gaining access to data-driven insights about service models, staffing, capacity, and operational strategies would be possible via a hospital's digital twin enabling decision making and readiness for future problems [15]. A digital twin might keep an eye on capacity all the time. Staff schedules might be optimized, and essential resources, such as operating rooms and beds, can be promptly allocated when needed. This technology may monitor and analyze how the actual object is used. With the help of the cloud and artificial intelligence, the digital twin has become a helpful healthcare instrument. The digital twin creates a customized patient mode by integrating data from multiple sources. This makes it possible for medical professionals to carefully prepare and provide accurate predictions and suggestions for specific patients relying on the DT. Cloud technology enables the collection of patient data in real time. Artificial intelligence (AI) components execute algorithms on enormous quantities of information to make precise forecasts.

The operations of medical devices or systems, healthcare providers, and patients are just a few of how the healthcare sector uses digital twins. With digital twins—very detailed virtual replicas of real-world objects like machinery, locations, or systems—information technology and data specialists can simulate how an entity will function and track an object live or even before it is created. Moreover, the twin facilitates visualizing the relationship to the object under the model. Digital twin technology has come to light as the ideal approach to solving these issues because of its potential to radically revolutionize other industries like the automotive industry. Cloud virtual twins offer extended collaboration and critical technological advantages, including improved research efficiency, predictable production, and appropriate patient care. The creation of immunizations, instead of more than 10, has been made feasible by the current improvement in teamwork brought about by common goals [16]. Digital twins have been commercially deployed in several industries, including manufacturing, engineering, energy, and others, with changing success degree in cost reduction, value generation, and efficiency improvement. While not entirely new, the concept of a "digital twin" has recently gained traction, particularly in the automotive, industrial, and healthcare industries. Owing to the potential competitive advantage, many businesses are implementing digital twins to increase efficiency, streamline processes, and reduce risks. New and more powerful techniques are being used to construct digital twins [17].

Millions of simulation programs may now be developed and run by systems with greater productivity and less anxiety. Technology related to digital twins can advance if more suppliers and substitutes become accessible as digital twins are utilized more. Function and ML have also led to an expansion in the breadth and depth of findings. Prototyping can be sped up, and diverse prototype components can be eradicating by utilizing digit-utilizing capabilities and human–computer interfaces like virtual and augmented reality. Before completing designs, engineers can use this to compare possible problems with quality, durability, and manufacturability. Traditional prototyping may be sped up, and products can go into production at a lower cost more quickly. With the help of data, machine learning, and the IoT, digital twins improve the efficacy of businesses and systems and yield superior results. A digital twin's real-time data makes it valuable, facilitating thinking, learning, and understanding of how things and systems work [18]. With its assistance, users can evaluate, model, and optimize the optimizer of a physical entity throughout its life. Table 12.1 depicts the comparison of diverse digital technologies in healthcare sectors.

12.3 Methodology

Like other fields, digital technology is essential to innovation in healthcare. Digitalization is still in its infancy because of several complex issues. The introduction of software that increases patient access to health-related data

Table 12.1 Digital technologies implemented in healthcare sectors.

Technology	Explanation	Characteristics	Platforms	Issues
EHR	Digital system to manage and store patient health	Proper sharing of information among healthcare providers	NextGen healthcare, medicine, and centricity	Data exchange and interoperability among various systems
Artificial intelligence	Improved healthcare results	Merged remote monitoring and EHR	Cloud-based mobile devices and wearables	Data security, privacy, interoperability and merged healthcare
Blockchain	Technology for preserving healthcare datasets via distributed ledgers	It avoids requirement for authority to deal with data	Corda, Hyperledger and Ethereum	Decentralized characteristics based on blockchain technology represent challenges in preserving data privacy
mHealth	Mobile technology-based treatment, diagnosis and health monitoring	Data management, remote monitoring and analysis	Web-based, iOS and android	It is related to the security and privacy of sensitive health information preserved on cloud and mobile devices
Wearable devices	Device for health tracking	Constant health monitoring via fitness health tracking	Google OS and Fitbit OS	Constrained battery life, security, and privacy

(Continued)

Table 12.1 Digital technologies implemented in healthcare sectors. (*Continued*)

Technology	Explanation	Characteristics	Platforms	Issues
Robotic automation	Task automation in healthcare	Real-time data analysis and pre-processing	Blue Prism, automation, and work fusion	Data security and privacy
Federated learning	Diminishing communication costs and prevailing data privacy	Updated in real-time, where data is acquired from various devices	PySysft and Tensorflow	Device battery life is influenced by higher energy consumption using federated learning

and secure centralization are just two examples of the tools and techniques that digitization of digitization has brought forth to improve healthcare services. The World Health Organization (WHO) regularly performs studies throughout states to perform a structural system inventory and the healthcare digitization expansion. Digitization research conducted in France on innovation in digital healthcare shows that a continued innovation integration hinders the growth of healthcare digitization. Mobile health services provided by the National Health Service (NHS) must be scaled up because they are primarily limited to pilot studies and adoptions. According to researchers, integrating technology into healthcare has benefits and drawbacks [19]. Advantageously, the new technology fosters creative administrative and medical procedures that save healthcare costs and increase the effectiveness of in-hospital and inter-hospital services. However, there are challenges, such as a better awareness of social boundaries and disputes about hospital policy and medical staff behavior. Information security threats constitute the primary underlying technical hazard.

12.3.1 IoT in Healthcare

The authorization evolved from static desktop settings to dynamic cloud environments due to the massive flow of data and services brought forth by IoT: data-driven expenses and organizational ease. Medical professionals can quickly expedite treatment in an emergency by easily accessing personal and patient data. Because of the IoT development, individuals can now get high-quality telemedicine and data analytic services for those living in remote locations. Over time, the healthcare business has evolved egalitarian, comprehensive, and integrated tactics to accommodate these changes. Prioritizing each patient can improve their outcomes. As a result, emphasizing integrating digital technologies benefits holistic healthcare [19]. Several countries have employed the Internet of Medical Things (IoMT) with other tactics to curb COVID-19 pandemic's spread, boost productivity by lessening the disease's impact on human life, enhance frontline personnel safety, and decrease fatality rates. The rapid and widespread use of IoMT worldwide has brought significant benefits in technology, applications, and security. The adoption of safe IoMT applications is made possible by the volume of research on technological security protocols. More realistic possibilities are also being made available by developing innovative IoMT technologies (see Figure 12.1) that combine artificial intelligence, big data, and blockchain [20].

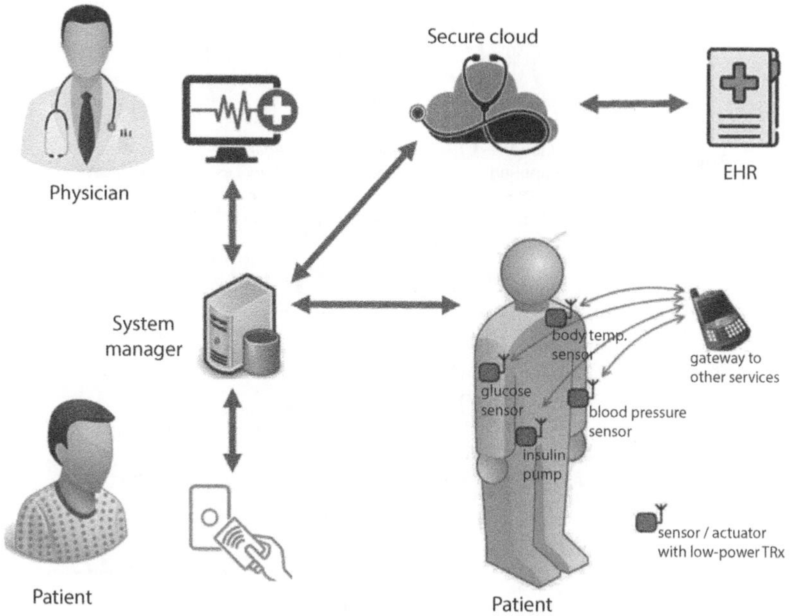

Figure 12.1 IoMT in the healthcare sector.

12.3.2 IoT in Digital Healthcare

The term "Internet of Medical Things" (IoMT) describes using wearable technology, sensors, and other networked medical equipment to collect, store, and analyze data. Tanalyzegration of health data is made feasible by the four distinct layers that comprise the architecture of IoMT. As shown in Figure 12.2, these levels are Perception, Edge, Networking, and Cloud Computing Layers. We will look closely at each layer and how it fits into the overall structure of IoMT in this part.

a) **Perception Layer**
The initial layer of the Internet of Health Things architecture, known as the Perception Layer, is in charge of compiling data from a range of medical equipment and health sensors. This layer comprises many sensors affixed to the user's body, including glucose detectors, blood pressure monitors, and heart rate sensors. These sensors provide data, and transmission to the next layer occurs for processing [21].

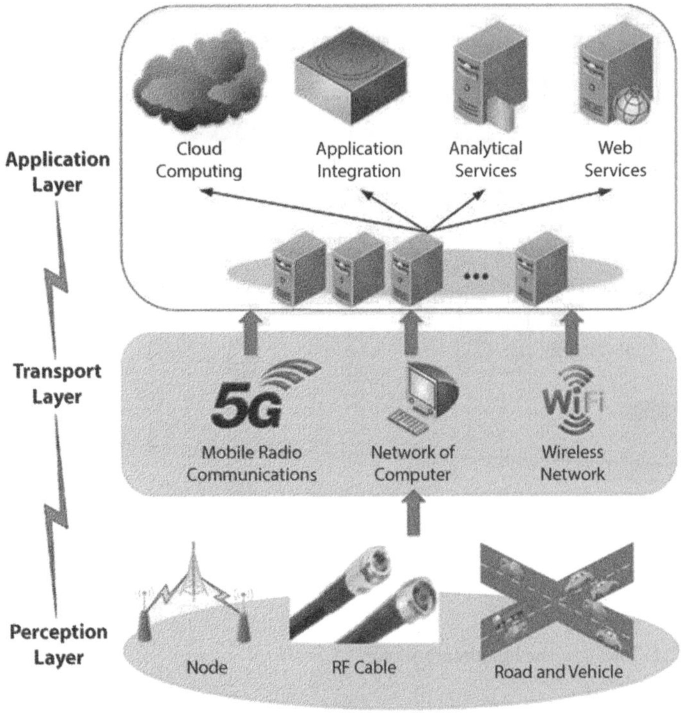

Figure 12.2 IoT-based layers for healthcare applications.

b) **Edge Layer**
Edge Layer is the second tier of the IoHT Technologies architecture. This layer receives data from the sensors, processes it, and prepares it to be sent over the Internet. This layer can handle large-scale data processing due to its scalable nature.

c) **Networking Layer**
The third tier of the Internet of Health Technology design is called the Networking tier, and its job is to send the information collected from the layer of perception to the layer of cloud computing. Several networking protocols and technologies, including Bluetooth, Zigbee, and Wi-Fi, are contained at this layer and are utilized for data transport. To make sure that no data are lost or distorted during the transmission of data from the Edge to the CC layer, the Networking Layer operates quickly, reliably, and securely [22].

Table 12.2 Comparison of various existing approaches.

Device	Functions	Metrics	Pros	Cons
Wearable devices	Wearable activity trackers, motion sensors, clinical-grade wearables, medication reminders, eye tracking devices, pain management devices, wearable patches, and wearable wearables with the ability to monitor blood pressure, heart rate, glucose, ECG, breathing rate, and sleep are more examples of wearable technology	Important health metrics including cardiovascular health, heart rate, sleeping patterns, and level of exercise are monitored by the gadget, which can also instantly connect with medical experts	Important health metrics including cardiovascular health, heart rate, sleeping patterns, and level of exercise are monitored by the gadget, which can also instantly connect with medical experts	Wearable devices collect critical medical data. Hence, it is essential to consider the security and privacy of such data

(Continued)

Table 12.2 Comparison of various existing approaches. (*Continued*)

Device	Functions	Metrics	Pros	Cons
Smart medical devices	These features can be found in various devices, such as wearable ECG monitors, intelligent insulin pumps, wireless blood pressure monitors, wireless spirometry devices, innovative body composition analyzers, monitors, telemedicine video consultation devices, linked neurological monitors, portable ultrasound devices, etc.	This instrument was designed with the medical industry in mind. It monitors various health indicators, including temperature, oxygen saturation, and glucose levels. It also makes it possible to communicate with healthcare professionals in real time	Intelligent medical devices provide vast volumes of data that can be used to improve patient care and promote medical breakthroughs. These intelligent devices can reduce healthcare costs by reducing the frequency of hospital stays, ER visits, and doctor consultations Intelligent medical devices	They may experience technical problems like connectivity, malfunction, and software mistakes

(*Continued*)

Table 12.2 Comparison of various existing approaches. (*Continued*)

Device	Functions	Metrics	Pros	Cons
Telemedicine devices	Some gadgets can be used for healthcare, including telemedicine cameras, digital stethoscopes, wearable fitness trackers, thermometers for telehealth, wireless health monitors, and remote patient monitoring devices and virtual reality tech	Mobile health apps, video conferencing, and remote monitoring technologies allow patients to get care in the comfort of their own homes	Healthcare can now be received in the convenience of one's home, saving time and money by removing the need to travel to a facility. Better overall health outcomes are attained because healthcare providers can attentively observe a patient's condition through remote monitoring and tracking and can react rapidly to any changes	Because these devices are susceptible to hacking and cyber-attacks, using telemedicine technologies and the associated data collection gives rise to security and privacy issues

(*Continued*)

Table 12.2 Comparison of various existing approaches. (*Continued*)

Device	Functions	Metrics	Pros	Cons
Smart home devices	Several smart gadgets are included in the list, such as an insulin dispenser, blood glucose level, body scale, blood pressure monitor, and pill dispenser temperature, medicine reminder, ECG, oxygen, and heart rate monitor	With the integration of smart home technologies, these devices can monitor a patient's condition and inform medical personnel of any issues	With these gadgets, people can better control their health and live better lives	The usage of smart home gadgets increases privacy and security since they can be targets of cyberattacks and hacking

d) Cloud Computing Layer

The last tier of the Internet of Health (IoHT) architecture is called the CC tier, and its job is to store and process the information gathered from the Perception Layer. This layer comprises several cloud computing services for processing and storing data, like Microsoft Azure and Amazon Web Services (AWS). Researchers and healthcare professionals have access to a wealth of data through the Cloud Computing Layer, which they can use to create novel cures and treatments for various illnesses. Table 12.2 shows the comparison of various existing approaches.

12.3.3 Internet of Medical Things (IoMT) Devices

IoMT aims to enhance patient care and health results by setting up medical systems, devices, and technologies for Internet access. Because of the improved affordability and accessibility of IoMT brought about by the advancement of IoT technology, we are witnessing the dawn of a new age in healthcare services [23]. It is possible to gather, store, and analyze data when IoT devices are connected to the Internet. The IoT devices that are appropriate for the Internet of Healthcare are the focus of this section, along with an overview of their features and potential benefits for improving healthcare delivery.

a) Wearable Devices

Popular technologies, like fitness trackers, bright clothes, and smartwatches, are examples of IoT wearables intended to be worn on the body. Blood pressure, heart rate, sleeping patterns, and physical activity are just a few of the health-related variables that these devices may monitor. Wearable technology allows for the real-time monitoring of patients' health through communication with healthcare practitioners. When a wearable gadget detects blood pressure readings higher than usual, it can notify medical professionals of a possible health issue [24].

b) Smart Medical Devices

One of the main goals of IoT-based medical devices, as in Figure 12.3, or innovative medical devices, is to offer medical support. They can remain in close contact with medical personnel and monitor critical health metrics like blood sugar, oxygen levels, and body temperature. The patient's health is thus tracked in real time. An intelligent

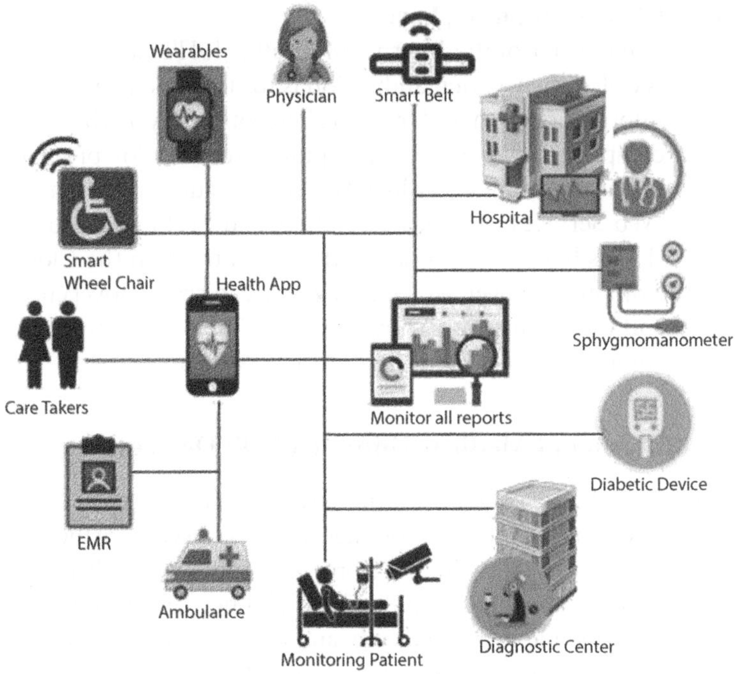

Figure 12.3 Internet of medical devices.

insulin pump can adjust insulin dosage based on glucose measurements to lower the risk of both low and high blood sugar [25].

c) **Telemedicine Devices**
With IoT technology, thanks to telemedicine, people can obtain medical care without ever leaving their homes. These devices include programs for mobile health, technologies for video conferences, and remote monitoring. By removing the requirement for in-person clinic visits, telemedicine can help those who live in remote or rural areas have better access to healthcare services. Patients might minimize travel from the office using video conferencing to have remote consultations with healthcare providers [26].

d) **Smart Home Devices**
IoT gadgets, sometimes called smart home gadgets, are incorporated into houses to improve convenience, security, and comfort. Among other things, these gadgets

include smart locks, lighting, and thermostats. Smart home technology can also wholly transform healthcare delivery by monitoring patient health and alerting medical professionals to irregularities. An intelligent bed, for example, can monitor sleep patterns and notify medical professionals if any abnormalities could raise questions about health.

12.3.4 Security and Privacy Solutions

a) **Mutual Authentication Solution**
IoT-based protocol was created by ref. [27] to solve security flaws commonly seen in healthcare systems. It includes key negotiation and authentication to ensure access control and privacy. The work also considers biometrics to safeguard user privacy and enhance user experience. Higher security is achieved via the protocol's use of asymmetric encryption and decryption, and security analysis is employed to compute the session key and the protocol's integrity, security, and soundness. The study also compares the suggested protocol to other protocols to assess its performance. The protocol performs significantly better regarding computing cost, time effectiveness, and security. Table 12.3 depicts the comparison of security frameworks.

b) **Digital Technologies' Effects on the Healthcare Industry**
Given the increasing diseases and pressures on the world healthcare system, greater focus should be placed on PCC encouraging patient participation in self-care. The prevalence of chronic diseases is rising due to demographic shifts. Thus, PCC is an essential component of long-term care. They are considering the pandemic scenario that COVID-19 has caused and the entire civilization's innovative remedies to the epidemic. Many businesses, most notably the healthcare sector, have seen global digital shifts brought on by the COVID-19 pandemic [28]. In reaction to the pandemic's initial stages, healthcare institutions swiftly embraced cutting-edge technologies and digital solutions. Patients can now readily get advice at their convenience and from any location because of the availability of health-related data. A biosensor known as a

Table 12.3 Comparison of security frameworks.

References	Network model	Techniques	Security	Advantages	Disadvantages
[27]	It includes patients, telecare servers, and a registration center	ECC	Patient anonymity	It is resistant to stolen medical equipment and attacks and privileged and resistant insiders	It has higher energy costs than prevailing protocols owing to cryptographic methods
[29]	IoT-based health model	Federated learning	Data privacy	Deals with security and privacy concerns via federated learning and differential privacy factors	It involves the utilization of complex decryption and encryption techniques
[31]	IoMT	Blockchain-based model	Untraceability and anonymity		

pulse oximeter simultaneously gauges blood oxygen levels and heart rate. Hemoglobin saturation is a sign that the respiratory system can oxygenate blood. The latest low-cost devices can transfer and record measurements via conventional connections. During the current pandemic, it would be incredibly beneficial to keep an eye on symptomatic patients at home so that they could act quickly if their saturation worsened. Consequently, the launch of these digital gadgets and applications helps to correspond with the growing trend of on-demand healthcare that has been noted, particularly since the COVID-19 outbreak.

c) **Big Data in Healthcare**

Big data analytics (BDA) has affected healthcare businesses in recent years (see Figure 12.4). Clinical data significantly impacts healthcare organizations and is the basis for many digital solutions developed in this field. After 10 years of development in digitization, the public and private sectors are working together to continue this period of accessible healthcare data. To help the healthcare industry take more effective action, throughout the years, federal authorities and various members of the public have made worth of data accessible to the public. However, as more data become available to the public, safeguarding patient privacy becomes more crucial [29]. It is imperative to guarantee appropriate security measures for the entities disclosing personal data. Clinical stakeholders are becoming more and more familiar with the idea of evidence-based medicine. This method uses

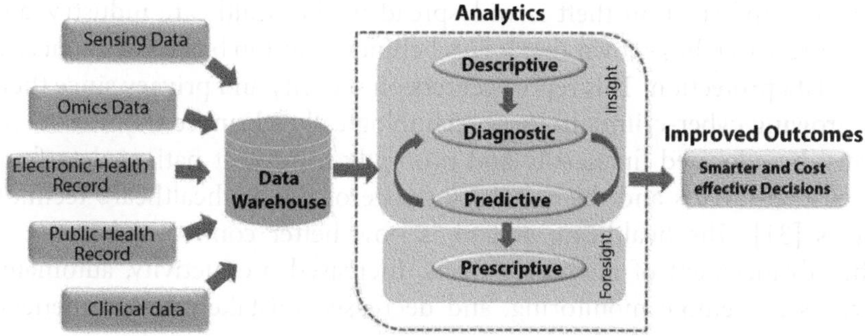

Figure 12.4 Big data in healthcare management.

the best available scientific information to inform decisions about a particular treatment. Big data algorithms are derived from large data sets. They are the most reliable source of proof for accurate patient information compared to individual patient data sets with smaller data sets. According to this research, organizations working on their BDA more quickly should see favorable outcomes sooner. Because they want to stay caught up, this is pushing other companies to explore the analytics field. Healthcare values must be consistently improved by BDA partners and providers while maintaining or raising the caliber of services rendered. There are several strategies to add value to this system, including making sure that care is affordable and getting rid of fraud, abuse, and waste [30].

12.4 Discussion

In today's corporate world, digital technology is advancing quickly. Keeping up with the digital transition can be too much for healthcare administration. The security and privacy of patients and other stakeholders in the healthcare system may suffer in the interim as new digital technologies are incorporated and used. Although management is crucial in many fields, it is particularly vital in the medical field since patient safety is the most critical factor. International standards for medical device production are being created due to the active worldwide research conducted to gauge this process's security measures.

12.4.1 Risks to the Healthcare Industry

Medical information theft is widespread in the healthcare industry, and prior research has shown that it lags behind other top businesses concerning data protection. This report centers on security and privacy since there is growing cyber-crimes in these technologically advanced day. Resources must be allocated financially and promptly to protect patient data from unwanted access and the security of state-of-the-art healthcare technologies [31]. The healthcare system is now better connected because of the advancement of medical gadgets. Increased productivity, automated processes, remote monitoring, and decreased mistake rates are benefits of interconnection. These benefits are altering the way long-term, severe illnesses are treated. Interconnected technology allows medical personnel to properly monitor and adjust implanted devices outside the hospital, removing the need for medical trips to the hospital or other treatments. According to the weekly security poster, the healthcare sector has more significant cyber risks than other businesses and is more susceptible to cyber-attacks worldwide. Almost 110 million patient records were exposed in 2015 alone, impacting more than 81% of the 223 US businesses examined. Only 50% of US healthcare workers believe they can defend themselves against cyber-attacks, even though there has been a 300% rise in these attacks in the preceding 3 years. Cyber-attacks are particularly appealing to the healthcare industry for two key reasons: their informational vulnerability and their soft target status [32].

Until now, financial gain and political influence have been the main drivers behind attacks on healthcare. However, cyber-attacks might be deliberate or accidental in the future and could contaminate test findings or blood types. Cyber-attacks on medical devices are another worrying prospect. Patients use IoT technology and have experienced compromised cyber security may be less willing to divulge information to researchers and physicians. This could further impede the therapeutic process and result in less precise and high-quality care [33].

12.4.2 Creating Management Programs for Medical Equipment

The possibility that many cyber-attacks would go unreported or undiscovered poses a severe risk to cyber-attack detection. Biomedical engineering teams in hospitals design and manage medical equipment management programs (MEMPs). MEMPs protect the security and safety of medical devices against cyber-attacks that compromise privacy and digital device trust. The fast progress in technology has led to the creation of medical gadgets that are now integrated with data and communication technologies [34]. However, due to these dissimilar technologies being connected, security risks are constantly growing from the inside out. Critical systems must, therefore, be prioritized to reduce these risks from medical devices. Healthcare organizations have organized numerous Medical Equipment Plans (MEMPs) for over 30 years with great care. However, studies have yet to be conducted to provide an optimal notion that considers safety, reliability, and cost for the service delivery of medical equipment devices.

12.4.3 Data Stored in EHR

EHRs make health-related data widely available; the facts above are supported by their potential to enhance patient care, as in Figure 12.5. Cyber-security protects computer systems and their data from malicious or unintended disruption and intrusion. The absence of confidentiality and integrity in medical information has highlighted concerns over the healthcare industry's insufficient cyber-security. EHRs are tangible objects that are spread over several geographical areas. As a result, it is feasible for unauthorized platforms and devices to corrupt all the data kept on them or even remove the security keys and program the device [18]. This study draws attention to digital technologies' security and privacy threats. There is still more work to be done before the healthcare sector can ultimately benefit from current technology in improving patient care.

Well-structured, semantically standardized, unstructured data, clever, flexible medical information extraction techniques, and highly accurate rule-based systems are needed. Instead of just being used for coding and code translation, clinical data warehouses need to grow into comprehensive knowledge discovery platforms that primarily use ontologies for methods of semantic reasoning leading to the formulation of hypotheses and knowledge discovery. It is more critical to use predictive analytics than

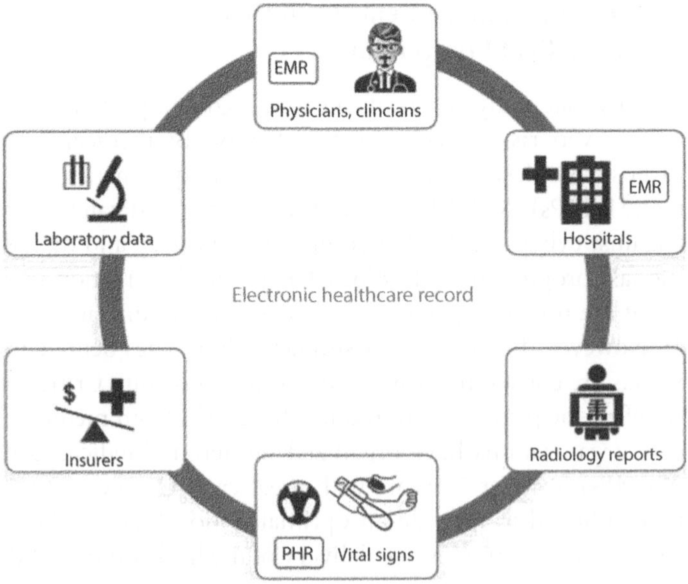

Figure 12.5 EHR connected with digital technologies.

simple analytical reporting. Caretakers must acquire new skills in providing care and understand ways to (at least partially) harvest healthcare data and train machine learning systems. Ontologies, which offer codification services and categorize medical ideas according to their similarities and differences, must also be heavily relied upon by knowledge systems [35]. Many companies are currently concentrating on ways to reduce costs. Creating and maintaining on-premise copies of software and data are the best ways to guarantee data management and security. With the many benefits of cloud technologies, things might be different. Cloud computing brings a few advantages to the healthcare industry: improved patient data usage and archiving, reduced storage costs, faster innovation cycles, easier teamwork, and more telemedicine potential. The healthcare industry will gradually adopt cloud-based technologies at different costs considering the four stages of digitization. Many program iterations will continue to be utilized, some on-site and others on the cloud. Additional potential for operating intelligence, optimizing business, improving patient care, and cutting costs is provided by big data processing using AI and ML. The FDA recently approved an AI program for diagnosis [36]. A few applications of machine learning include:

- Chat-bots and digital assistants that will transform the way medical personnel interact with patients and give them more time to concentrate on challenging tasks [37, 38].
- When it comes to helping healthcare professionals make decisions and predict a range of medical outcomes, such as length of stay, readmissions, and death, clinical decision support will be essential [39].
- Text translation should be done carefully to simplify technical, scientific terminology into plain language, according to ML-enabled NLP [40].
- Automated and more accurate billing and invoicing will expedite handling claims and maybe stop fraud.
- Clinical information retrieval systems with machine learning capabilities that learn from the facility where they are installed and offer more excellent knowledge based on clinical narratives [41].

12.4.4 Limitations

All firms must implement digital twin technology; however, adoption and installation expenses must be minimal, or other affordable solutions must be provided for all businesses. When digital twins are in their physical form, it is feasible to recognize various threats and hazards. To address these problems, 5G technology can be used, for example, to gather additional data and keep the DT up to date with recent knowledge. Updates are required to comply with security protocols where data from sensors connected by shaky networks power DT models. Businesses that use DT technology can able to handle gaps in their data streams and reject incomplete data. DT users pick up new technological abilities but must get used to new working techniques, which could provide challenges. Employers must ensure that staff members are equipped with the skills and tools required to operate with models of digital twins [42, 43].

12.4.5 Future Scope

Digital twins could be advantageous to any industry in the future. Digital twins can accelerate production's transition to automated and iterative processes meeting modern standards. Thanks to the deployment of digital twins, previously divided divisions managing maintenance, operations, finance, sales, and marketing can access a single source of data for improved design, use analysis, and pricing adjustments. One of the most crucial IT instruments for the digitalization of the digitalization marketplace is the digital twin, which has the power to drastically change many nations' social and political environments [7]. Beyond symptom treatment and environmental issues, digital twins hold great promise for the healthcare sector. Digital twins can also be utilized to unutilized ideas, speed up procedures, raise production, and detect issues early on. Hospitals use real-time health systems more frequently due to these difficulties to address problems thoroughly. Digital twin application in healthcare has great potential, but its impact will become apparent once it can reliably and broadly convert data into clinical recommendations [44]. Integrating digital twin technology with medical tablets and cart computers facilitates mobility during inpatient treatment. A digital twin for an intelligent hospital needs to integrate real-time interactions between people, processes, and linked objects with data from several subsystems [45]. The development of AI/ML offers a contextual model that can be updated, examined, and improved, representing a hospital's past, present, and anticipated future conditions. The digital twin will require collaboration from several internal and external stakeholders [46]. Clinical professionals, hospital staff, administrative team members, receptionists, appointment setters, and a dedicated, experienced technology partner will all benefit from a practical digital twin [47, 48].

12.5 Conclusion

A digital twin is a simulated copy of something that can be tracked, examined, and improved. Digital representations of material entities are "live" and "dynamic," updating the central object in response to environmental changes. It can also absorb information from its surroundings, other people, and machines. Data collected from IoT devices and embedded sensors are displayed in the model through visualization, and big data analytics, which are then employed for analysis. Digital twin technology significantly improves patient care by providing trustworthy medical advice, the ability to schedule appointments with licensed medical experts, the electronic transfer of prescriptions to pharmacies, and internet access to video recordings and doctor's notes. Using digital twins, patients' medical treatments could be more easily tailored to their unique genetic composition, physiology, family history, past behaviors, and other attributes. Healthcare workers can reorganize resources using a digital twin to observe how those changes impact the virtual environment. Because it mimics numerous features, the twin thoroughly understands the hospital's operations. The effectiveness of a healthcare institution's digital twin could be enhanced by utilizing reliable resources such as Real-Time Locating Systems. It is possible to estimate the availability of equipment and resources and quickly assess the impact of simulation-recommended alterations in the actual world using the data generated by this technology. The healthcare industry is rapidly adopting digital technologies. Instead of only being passive healthcare consumers, patients today actively seek value. The advancements and increasing popularity of smartphones are made possible by this technology. Information about medicine is more accessible than ever to patients and their families.

References

1. Redelinghuys, A.J.H., Kruger, K., Basson, A., A six-layer architecture for digital twins with aggregation, in: *Proc. Int. Workshop Service Orientation Holonic Multi-Agent Manuf*, Springer, Berlin, Germany, pp. 171–182, 2019.
2. Botín-Sanabria, Mihaita, A.-S., Peimbert-García, R.E., Ramírez-Moreno, M.A., Ramírez-Mendoza, R.A., Lozoya-Santos, J.D.J., Digital twin technology challenges and applications: A comprehensive review. *Remote Sens.*, 14, 6, 1335, Mar. 2022.
3. Shafto, Conroy, M., Doyle, R., Glaessgen, E., Kemp, C., LeMoigne, J., Wang, L., Modeling, simulation, information technology & processing roadmap. *Technol. Area*, 11, TA 11-1–TA 11-170, 2015.

4. Schleich, Anwer, N., Mathieu, L., Wartzack, S., Shaping the digital twin for design and production engineering. *CIRP Ann.*, 66, 1, 141–144, 2017.
5. Pylianidis, Osinga, S., Athanasiadis, I.N., Introducing digital twins to agriculture. *Comput. Electron. Agricult.*, 184, 105942, May 2021.
6. Răileanu, Borangiu, T., Ivanescu, N., Morariu, O., Anton, F., Integrating the digital twin of a shop floor conveyor in the manufacturing control system, in: *Proc. Int. Workshop Service Orientation Holonic Multi-Agent Manuf.*, Springer, pp. 134–145, 2019.
7. Zheng, Yang, S., Cheng, H., An application framework of digital twin and its case study. *J. Ambient Intell. Hum. Comput.*, 10, 3, 1141–1153, Mar. 2019.
8. Borangiu, Oltean, E., Raileanu, S., Anton, F., Anton, S., Iacob, I., Embedded digital twin for ARTI-type control of semi-continuous production processes, in: *Proc. Int. Workshop Service Orientation Holonic Multi-Agent Manuf.*, Springer, Berlin, Germany, pp. 113–133, 2019.
9. Kritzinger, Karner, M., Traar, G., Henjes, J., Sihn, W., Digital twin in manufacturing: A categorical literature review and classification. *IFACPapersOnLine*, 51, 11, 1016–1022, 2018.
10. Campos-Ferreira, Lozoya-Santos, J.D.J., VargasMartínez, A., Mendoza, R., Morales-Menéndez, R., Digital twin applications: A review, in: *Proc. Mem. Del Congr. Nac. Control Autom*, vol. 2, pp. 606–611, 2019.
11. Evans, Savian, C., Burns, A., Cooper, C., Digital twins for the built environment: An introduction to the opportunities, benefits, challenges and risks. *Built Environ. News*, IET Press, U.K, Tech. Rep., 2019.
12. Barricelli, Casiraghi, E., Gliozzo, J., Petrini, A., Valtolina, S., Human digital twin for fitness management. *IEEE Access*, 8, 26637–26664, 2020.
13. Pang, Huang, Y., Xie, Z., Li, J., Cai, Z., Collaborative city digital twin for the COVID-19 pandemic: A federated learning solution. *Tsinghua Sci. Technol.*, 26, 5, 759–771, Oct. 2021.
14. Laamarti, Badawi, H.F., Ding, Y., Arafsha, F., Hafidh, B., Saddik, A.E., An ISO/IEEE 11073 standardized digital twin framework for health and well-being in smart cities. *IEEE Access*, 8, 105950–105961, 2020.
15. Liu, Zhang, L., Yang, Y., Zhou, L., Ren, L., Wang, F., Liu, R., Pang, Z., Deen, M.J., A novel cloud-based framework for the elderly healthcare services using digital twin. *IEEE Access*, 7, 49088–49101, 2019.
16. Carvalho, Melo, P., Oliveira, M.A., Barros, R., The 4-corner model as a synchromodal and digital twin enabler in the transportation sector, in: *Proc. IEEE Int. Conf. Eng., Technol. Innov. (ICE/ITMC)*, Cardiff, U.K, Jun. 2020, pp. 1–8.
17. Pan, Zhou, W., Piramuthu, S., Giannikas, V., Chen, C., Smart city for sustainable urban freight logistics. *Int. J. Prod. Res.*, 59, 7, 2079–2089, Apr. 2021.
18. Qi, Tao, F., Hu, T., Anwer, N., Liu, A., Wei, Y., Wang, L., Nee, A.Y.C., Enabling technologies and tools for digital twin. *J. Manuf. Syst.*, 58, 3–21, Jan. 2021.
19. Zhou, Yan, J., Feng, D., Digital twin framework and its application to power grid online analysis. *CSEE J. Power Energy Syst.*, 5, 3, 391–398, Sep. 2019.

20. Rassõlkin, Orosz, T., Demidova, G.L., Kuts, V., Rjabtšikov, V., Vaimann, T., Kallaste, A., Implementation of digital twins for electrical energy conversion systems in selected case studies. *Proc. Est. Acad. Sci.*, 70, 1, 19–39, 2021.
21. Singh, Weeber, M., Birke, K.-P., Advancing digital twin implementation: A toolbox for modelling and simulation. *Proc. CIRP*, Jan. 2021, vol. 99, pp. 567–572.
22. Oyekan, Farnsworth, M., Hutabarat, W., Miller, D., Tiwari, A., Applying a 6 DoF robotic arm and digital twin to automate fan-blade reconditioning for aerospace maintenance, repair, and overhaul. *Sensors*, 20, 16, 4637, Aug. 2020.
23. Gopinath, N. and Prayla Shyry, S., Enhancing the cloud security using side channel attack free QKD with entangled fuzzy logic. *J. Intell. Fuzzy Syst.*, 43, 6, 8359–8369, 2022.
24. Rezaei, Shirazi, M.A., Karimi, B., IoT-based framework for performance measurement: A real-time supply chain decision alignment. *Ind. Manage. Data Syst.*, 117, 4, 688–712, May 2017.
25. Kang, Lee, J.Y., Choi, S., Kim, H., Park, J.H., Son, J.Y., Kim, B.H., Noh, S.D., Smart manufacturing: Past research, present findings, and future directions. *Int. J. Precis. Eng. Manuf. Green Technol.*, 3, 1, 111–128, 2016.
26. Xiong, Wang, F.-Y., Nyberg, R.T., Shang, X., Zhou, M., Shen, Z., Li, S., Guo, C., From mind to products: Towards social manufacturing and service. *IEEE/CAA J. Autom. Sin.*, 5, 1, 47–57, Jan. 2018.
27. Osterrieder, Budde, L., Friedli, T., The smart factory as a key construct of industry 4.0: A systematic literature review. *Int. J. Prod. Econ.*, 221, 107476, Mar. 2020.
28. Zancul, Takey, S.M., Barquet, A.P.B., Kuwabara, L.H., Miguel, P.A.C., Rozenfeld, H., Business process support for IoT based product-service systems (PSS). *Bus. Process Manage. J.*, 22, 2, 302–323, Apr. 2016.
29. Culot, Nassimbeni, G., Orzes, G., Sartor, M., Behind the definition of industry 4.0: Analysis and open questions. *Int. J. Prod. Econ.*, 226, 107617, Aug. 2020.
30. Wan, Tang, S., Li, D., Wang, S., Liu, C., Abbas, H., Vasilakos, A.V., A manufacturing big data solution for active preventive maintenance. *IEEE Trans. Ind. Informat.*, 13, 4, 2039–2047, Aug. 2017.
31. Humayed, Lin, J., Li, F., Luo, B., Cyber-physical systems security—A survey. *IEEE Internet Things J.*, 4, 6, 1802–1831, Dec. 2017.
32. Tao, Qi, Q., Wang, L., Nee, A.Y.C., 'Digital twins and cyber-physical systems toward smart manufacturing and industry 4.0: Correlation and comparison. *Engineering*, 5, 4, 653–661, Aug. 2019.
33. Liao, Deschamps, F., Loures, E.D.F.R., Ramos, L.F.P., Past, present and future of industry 4.0—A systematic literature review and research agenda proposal. *Int. J. Prod. Res.*, 55, 12, 3609–3629, Jun. 2017.
34. Piccarozzi, Aquilani, B., Gatti, C., Industry 4.0 in management studies: A systematic literature review. *Sustainability*, 10, 10, 3821, Oct. 2018.

35. Rathore, Shah, S.A., Shukla, D., Bentafat, E., Bakiras, S., The role of AI, machine learning, and big data in digital twinning: A systematic literature review, challenges, and opportunities. *IEEE Access*, 9, 32030–32052, 2021.
36. Gopinath, N., Enhanced cloud security protocols for data protection in the Internet of Healthcare Things (IoHTs) using Entangled Fuzzy Logics, 2022.
37. Bordeleau, Mosconi, E., Santa-Eulalia, L.A., Business intelligence in industry 4.0: State of the art and research opportunities, in: *Proc. 51st Hawaii Int. Conf. Syst. Sci.*, pp. 1–10, 2018.
38. Sezer, Dogdu, E., Ozbayoglu, A.M., Context-aware computing, learning, and big data in the Internet of Things: A survey. *IEEE Internet Things J.*, 5, 1, 1–27, Feb. 2018.
39. Sadiku, Wang, Y., Cui, S., Musa, S.M., Industrial Internet of Things. *Int. J. Adv. Sci. Res. Eng.*, 3, 11, 1–4, 2017.
40. Grieco, Caricato, P., Gianfreda, D., Pesce, M., Rigon, V., Tregnaghi, L., Voglino, A., An industry 4.0 case study in fashion manufacturing. *Proc. Manuf.*, 11, 871–877, Jan. 2017.
41. Tendulkar, Le, D.T., Berger, U., A multi-case study on industry 4.0 for SMEs in Brandenburg, Germany, in: *Proc. 51st Hawaii Int. Conf. Syst. Sci.*, pp. 1–10, 2018.
42. Noura, Atiquzzaman, M., Gaedke, M., Interoperability in Internet of Things: Taxonomies and open challenges. *Mob. Netw. Appl.*, 24, 3, 796–809, 2019.
43. Rathore, Son, H., Ahmad, A., Paul, A., Real-time video processing for traffic control in the smart city using Hadoop ecosystem with GPUs. *Soft Comput.*, 22, 5, 1533–1544, Mar. 2018.
44. Alam, and El Saddik, A., C2PS: A digital twin architecture reference model for the cloud-based cyber-physical systems. *IEEE Access*, 5, 2050–2062, 2017.
45. Tao, and Zhang, M., Digital twin shopfloor: A new shopfloor paradigm towards smart manufacturing. *IEEE Access*, 5, 20418–20427, 2017.
46. Zaccaria, Stenfelt, M., Aslanidou, I., Kyprianidis, K.G., Fleet monitoring and diagnostics framework based on the digital twin of aero-engines. *Turbo Expo, Power Land, Sea, Air*, Aug. 2018, vol. 51128, p. 10.
47. Gopinath, N. and Shyry, S.P., Side Channel Attack Free Quantum Key Distribution Using Entangled Fuzzy Logic. *Braz. J. Phys.*, 53, 2, 35, 2023.
48. Zhang, Liu, Q., Chen, X., Zhang, D., Leng, J., A digital twin-based approach for designing and multi-objective optimization of hollow glass production line. *IEEE Access*, 5, 26901–26911, 2017.

13

Smart Medication Dispensing: IoT Innovations in Drug Development

Sapna Singh Kshatri[1]*, Mukesh Kumar Chandrakar[2], Devanand Bhonsle[3], Manjushree Nayak[4], Prashant Tamrakar[5] and Pramisha Sharma[6]

[1]*Computer Science and Engineering, Shri Shankaracharya Institute of Professional Management and Technology, Raipur, Chhattisgarh, India*
[2]*Electrical Engineering, Bhilai Institute of Technology, Durg, Chhattisgarh, India*
[3]*Electrical Engineering, Shri Shankaracharya Technical Campus, Bhilai, Chhattisgarh, India*
[4]*Department of Computer Science and Engineering, NIST University, Berhampur, Odisha, India*
[5]*Department of Computer Science and Engineering, RSR Rungta College of Engineering and Technology, Bhilai, Chhattisgarh, India*
[6]*Department of Chemistry, Shri Shankaracharya Institute of Professional Studies, Raipur, Chhattisgarh, India*

Abstract
India was placed under quarantine in March 2020 due to the COVID-19 pandemic. A scarcity of vaccines was observed. As the case developed, the healthcare professional providing care for the patient assumed an increasingly demanding role necessitating more frequent and thorough patient assessments. Although medication is essential for mitigating the symptoms caused by the virus, the interaction between the patient and the attendant can transfer the virus from an infected individual to a non-infected staff. In light of this, a contactless medication dispenser would be the most beneficial option. Furthermore, an infrared sensor is incorporated to track the patient's body temperature and medication ingestion. Placing this design close to the patient's preferred location or storing it in a conveniently accessible area, would enable refilling if the medication box runs low. In addition, the design incorporates an LCD and alarm circuit to provide the patient with a reminder. In addition, audio amplifiers may be employed to enhance the volume of the alarm system to accommodate users with hearing impairments.

**Corresponding author*: sapna.singh@ssipmt.com

Parul Dubey, Mangala Madankar, Pushkar Dubey and Bui Thanh Hung (eds.) The Impact of Algorithmic Technologies on Healthcare, (255–278) © 2025 Scrivener Publishing LLC

The data acquisition system of the IoT module notifies the healthcare provider or caregiver that the patient has completed the medication administration. IoT-based applications are additionally utilized to facilitate communication between machines and humans. The diagram illustrates how a port is allocated to each module on the microcontroller.

Keywords: IoT, medicine despenser, pill dispenser, arduino uno

13.1 Introduction

The researchers in refs. [1–3] had previously examined a range of wearable, portable, lightweight, and compact sensors that were all created to monitor physiological parameters in humans. The Body Sensor Network (BSN) comprises a variety of physiological and biomedical sensors, including electrocardiogram (ECG), blood pressure, and electrodermal activity (EDA) sensors, all of which are implantable in the human body for real-time health monitoring. Gondaliaa *et al.* (2018) proposed an IoT-based Healthcare Monitoring System for War Soldiers, which envisioned a mechanism to allow wounded and missing soldiers to monitor their health and location in real time. It aids in decreasing the amount of time required for an army control unit to locate and rescue [4]. Due to the swift advancements in technology, the implementation of the Internet of Things has become a significant focal point for every nation. One of the subsequent revolutionary developments in internet-based computing, the Internet of Things (IoT), is positively impacting various applications, smart cities, disciplines, engineering, healthcare, and helping others [5].

This study investigates the advantages and disadvantages of IoT and WSN technologies. It explores various applications and benefits associated with IoT and WSN research. A comparative analysis of apps is provided, evaluating performance, publication year, technologies, and outcomes. This paper seeks to enhance readers' understanding of IoT and WSN uses, benefits, and limitations, ultimately promoting more effective WSN-IoT [6]. Medicine adherence is an increasing problem for doctors, healthcare systems, and other stakeholders (insurance companies) in the healthcare business since an aged or senior patients' medication has a high rate of drug abuse [7]. They are exceptionally susceptible to medication omissions. Individuals concurrently consuming multiple medications may inadvertently consume an incorrect dosage, which can have severe consequences, including fatalities. This unequivocally illustrates that it is a prevalent issue correlated with unfavorable patient outcomes and escalated healthcare expenditures.

A cloud-based system, as proposed by Rolim *et al.*, assists medical administration in monitoring the medication ingestion of patients. This system has demonstrated potential in monitoring and documenting patients' medication intake [8]. Combining an Arduino microcontroller with an infrared sensor creates a pill dispenser with an alert system to assist patients in taking their medication on time. A smartphone-based pop-up notification initiates the alarms [9]. Jabeena *et al.* put forth a system designed to assist individuals afflicted with heart and brain diseases that can worsen significantly in the event of medication non-compliance. By utilizing it, the divide between technology and medical care is closed. GSM is for communication between modules like IR sensor and humidity sensor. GSM module sends a message to the person to take medicine, which is kept in a box [9].

Abdul Kader and his colleagues utilized the Atmega 329p microcontroller to create a medication reminder system for elderly individuals. The project utilizes an SD card to record drug intake data, while the actual clock is used to configure the sleep schedule. Subsequently, an LCD is utilized for visual output, while an amplifier circuit is employed to enhance the auditory output generated by the buzzer. Additionally, it includes resetting and confirming medication administration by utilizing a push button [10]. The prototype suggested by Al-Shammary *et al.* utilizes the Arduino UNO as its microcontroller. Therefore, the programming is conducted using the C programming language. Additionally, the box is equipped with an infrared sensor that may identify the presence of narcotics. LEDs and buzzers are employed as reminders for individuals to consume medication. The Xbee module (2 GHz) was used to establish communication between the device and the output device [11]. P. Ranjana and E. Alexander suggested an idea for an Internet of Things (IoT)-enabled medicine container. The device also identifies anomalies in the individual's health using tensor technology. They proposed a concept of a pharmaceutical box using IoT. The device also detects abnormalities in the person's health via tensor. A database system stores or alters exceptional situations. This approach is especially advantageous for unwell children. For instance, it enables real-time monitoring and tailored treatment plans, leading to improved health outcomes and enhanced quality of life. Additionally, the use of IoT and tensor technology in healthcare has the potential to revolutionize patient care and disease management [12]. A database system saves or modifies the abnormality conditions. This method is particularly beneficial for sick children. A prototype provides a drug remainder system using weight sensor to trace pills or medication for patients. It also provides a safety system, which enables to regulate the lock on and off through mobile application. This technique has shown that it might be helpful for people affected by neurodegenerative diseases [7].

A patient is given an RFID bracelet at the beginning of therapy. Additionally, it employs an anti-theft alarm system that transmits a signal to the proprietor or custodian via Wi-Fi or LAN [14]. It is an exceptionally dependable surveillance system for monitoring the consumption of medications by elderly individuals or patients. The system utilizes a Wi-Fi module (EPS8266) to synchronize and update the medical administration database. A Magnetic Reed switch is used to open or close the box. Arduino delivers control signals to the system's modules [15]. The proposed Internet of Things (IoT)-based SMD system enhances the idea of an automated dispenser by incorporating novel characteristics absent in earlier computerized dispensers. Every patient is allocated an account that is only accessible to the patient and the caregiver who has been provided with the necessary credentials. In addition, statistics are presented for the medications consumed, together with their corresponding alarms and pre-existing alerts. We presented a model of an advanced medication dispenser that operates without physical contact and includes a temperature sensor to guarantee accurate medication intake and monitor the user's body temperature. The IoT module is employed in a prototype to identify medication consumption and quantify temperature. The data are transferred over Bluetooth to any compatible device, such as a mobile phone or PC.

13.2 Problem Identification

A contactless method for replenishing medicine boxes would be highly beneficial during these challenging times. Utilizing a servomotor for the dispenser system of the medicine box is the most effective approach to achieve this. Nevertheless, as the different prototypes show, the interaction between individuals and machines is further emphasized [16]. Sometimes, a weight sensor is employed to determine the quantity of medicine in the box, as demonstrated by Tariq *et al.* However, the sensitivity of the weight sensor system might lead to issues, such as locking the prototype itself, thereby rendering it unable to dispense medication [17].

Using magnetic reed switches to open and close containers can be a great way to ensure security, as suggested by Srinivas *et al.* [18]. However, it is worth noting that these switches are pretty delicate and can easily malfunction or break if something unusual occurs.

"Now, let us explore some practical situations:"

- **Health-Oriented Pill Dispenser:** Envision a drug dispenser that aids individuals in medication management and mitigates the likelihood of chronic illnesses. This invention has the potential to revolutionize the healthcare industry.
- **Cease Confusions:** Worried about accidentally mixing up our medicines? An automated system has the potential to alleviate our concerns, enhance our trust in medication administration, and eventually improve our overall wellbeing.
- **Visual Impairments:** Individuals with visual impairments can face difficulties distinguishing between various areas of their medication box daily. This can result in administering incorrect medication at inappropriate times highlighting the critical importance of innovation in this field.
- **Enhancement of Memory:** Individuals grappling with dementia or Alzheimer's encounter difficulties with remembering. Individuals may inadvertently neglect to adhere to their prescription regimen, consume excessive amounts, or fail to recall that they have previously ingested a dose.

Based on the presented situations, our research suggests an innovative resolution: a medication box that operates without physical contact. This intelligent device dispenses medication into a protected compartment only accessible to the patient. The device is outfitted with an infrared (IR) sensor that detects drug consumption and monitors the patient's body temperature. This breakthrough holds the capacity to transform medication management and healthcare.

13.3 Proposed Method

A. System Overview

The entire configuration comprises five pill compartments used to store medication. Each blank is organized to facilitate the segregation of medication for the morning, afternoon, and evening. An essential characteristic of this dispenser is its contactless nature; meaning, there is no physical interaction between the patient and worker, even throughout the refilling process. As shown in Figure 13.1, the sensors and keypad provide inputs to the microprocessor, which then takes appropriate actions like activating the motor to dispense pills or sounding the buzzer for alerts and displays relevant info on the LCD screen.

- **Microprocessor:** A microprocessor is the main processing unit of a system responsible for handling all inputs and controlling the outputs accordingly.
- **Temperature Sensor:** A temperature sensor measures the surrounding temperature to maintain the ideal storage conditions for medication.
- **IR Sensor:** An IR sensor is commonly employed to detect barriers or motion but can also be utilized to detect medication dispensing.
- **Power Supply:** Enables users to enter parameters for medicine timings or dosages improving the ability to customize and adapt.

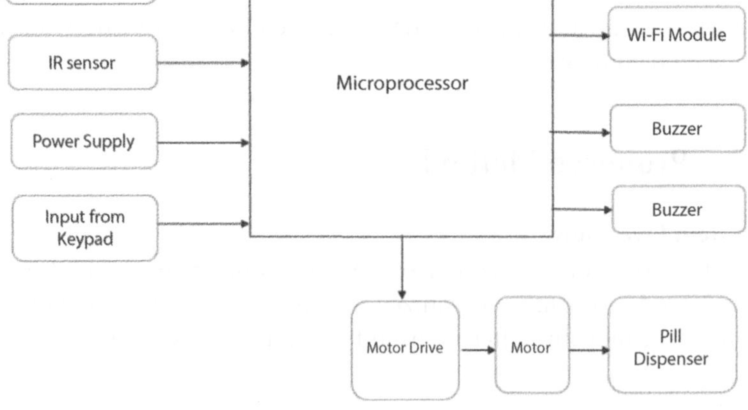

Figure 13.1 Working of pill dispenser.

- **Keypad Input:** Allows users to input settings for medication timings or dosages, enhancing customization and flexibility.
- **Wi-Fi Module:** Enables connectivity to a network for remote monitoring and control facilitating access for caregivers or healthcare providers.
- **Buzzer:** Emits signals or sounds to promptly inform users of significant occurrences, such as reminders for taking medication or problems in the system.
- **Motor Drive and Motor:** The motor drive and motor are responsible for operating the mechanism that dispenses the pills from the compartments to the user.
- **Pill Dispenser:** The physical compartments that store and distribute pills offer a systematic and practical approach to managing medication.
- **LCD Screen:** The LCD screen presents consumers with pertinent information or updates regarding medication scheduling, temperature readings, and system status, thereby offering feedback.

The working mechanism of a pill dispenser, which is intended to regulate and dispense medication in an organized way, is depicted in Figure 13.1. The diagram illustrates a conventional design, which includes compartments for storing individual volumes of medicines and a programming interface for schedules. The user generally enters the timing and dosage instructions and retains them in the device's memory. The dispenser releases the corresponding medications at the designated periods ensuring that patients comply with their prescribed regimens. Specific models might incorporate supplementary functionalities, such as alarms or reminders, augmenting users' adherence to prescribed medication regimens. In general, the illustration presented in Figure 13.1 illustrates how pill dispensers streamline and automate the medication management process consequently fostering patient health and medication adherence.

The dispenser comprises a transformer. The first aspect transformer (HV aspect) has the option of a bigger variety of turns than the secondary side (LV side), which means inpourings from the HV to the LV aspect.

- The voltage is stepped down from primary voltage (input voltage) to secondary voltage (output voltage).
- A transformer is employed to convey this low voltage price, which is appropriate for electronics supply.

- It transforms home voltage (230/120 V) from primary to low voltage on the secondary aspect, which is utilized for electronic supply.

The reduction transformers have a very vital performance throughout an influence grid as shown in Figure 13.2. They lower the voltage level and adapt it to energy customers.

1) LCD

LCD stands for liquid crystal display. These are used in devices like mobile phones, calculators, computers, TV sets, etc. The main advantages of using this module are as follows: It offers a cost-effective solution, simple programming, and flexible display capabilities, including custom characters and special symbols. Additionally, it supports popular display types, such as multi-segment and seven-segment light-emitting diodes. When interfacing with microcontrollers, data transfer is facilitated through the data bus pins (D0–D7), while the RS, RW, and E pins control the transfer mode and direction.

In simpler terms, this module allows electronic devices to display information to the user, and the various pins help control what and how this information is displayed. Figure 13.2 depicts a **16x2 LCD Screen** module

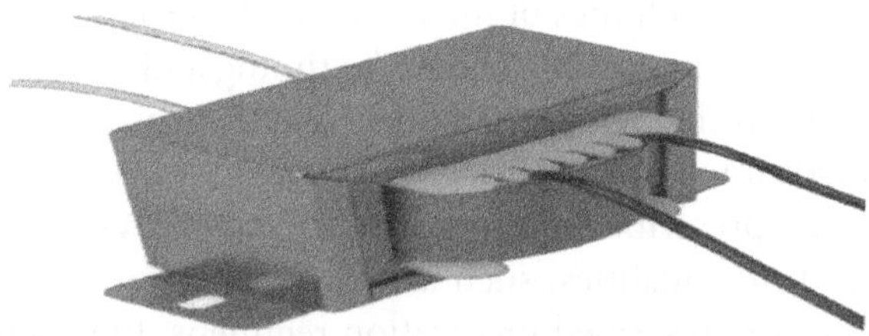

Figure 13.2 Transformer diagram.

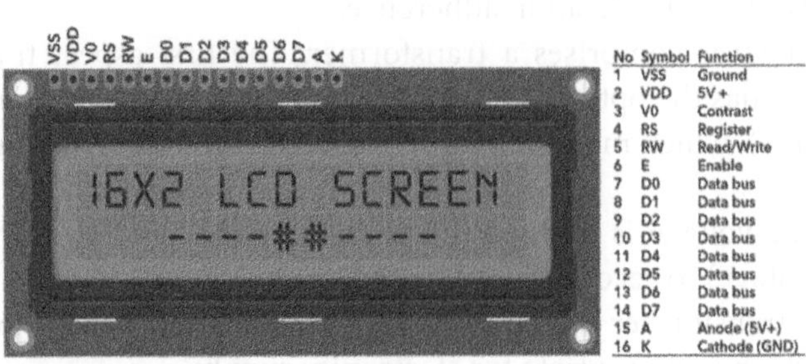

Figure 13.3 Liquid crystal display (LCD).

commonly used in electronics for displaying alphanumeric characters. The "16x2" indicates that it can display 16 characters per row with two such rows.

The circuit schematic below is illustrated in Figure 13.3, which is the liquid shown in conjunction with the Arduino module. The circuit schematic is illustrated in Figure 13.3, which shows the LCD connected to the Arduino module. As shown in the diagram, the LCD's RS pin is connected to Arduino's pin 12, and the R/W pin is connected to ground. Figure 13.3 also shows that Arduino's pin 11 is connected to the LCD module's enable pin. In this project, the LCD and Arduino modules are interfaced in 4-bit mode, utilizing four input lines to control the LCD's DB4 to DB7 values. This approach simplifies the connection process, reduces wiring, and optimizes the use of the LCD module's capabilities.

Figure 13.4 likely shows an LCD's port arrangement when attached to an Arduino Uno microcontroller board. LCDs display data in many electronic applications. The diagram usually shows LCD module ports and Arduino Uno pin connections. These connections let the Arduino Uno control the display and send data or feedback. GND, VCC, RS, RW, E pins, and D4 to D7 data lines are expected for LCD commands and data. Understanding this circuit arrangement is crucial to properly integrating the LCD with the Arduino Uno allowing users to create simple text displays and complex graphical interfaces.

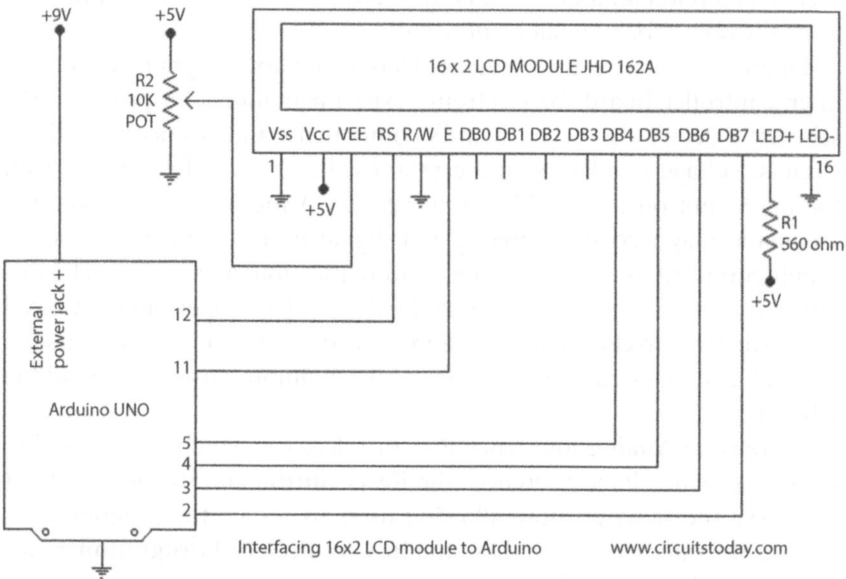

Figure 13.4 Pin configuration of LCD with Arduino Uno.

The square measure was interfaced with Arduino pins 5–2 through the digital input lines (DB4–DB7). To control the show's distinctiveness, we often use a 10K potentiometer to square measure. The current flowing through the rear LED, a 560-ohm electrical device, supplies light. The board provides power to the Arduino through the external power port utilizing the computer's USB connector to power the Arduino. Specific components of the circuit will require a +5-V power supply, which is drawn from the Arduino board's 5-V supply.

2) Arduino Uno

The Arduino Uno is an ASCII text file microcontroller board designed by Arduino. It is supported by the semiconductor unit ATmega328P microcontroller. The board has sets of digital and analog input/output (I/O) pins that may be used to interact with various expansion boards (shields) and circuits. The board features 14 digital I/O pins (six of which are capable of PWM output), six analog I/O pins, and is programmable through a USB type B connector using the Arduino IDE (Integrated Development Environment). As we can see, Figure 13.5 illustrates an **Arduino Uno** board, a popular open-source microcontroller platform. At the heart of the Arduino Uno is the **ATmega328 Microcontroller**, a versatile chip designed for embedded applications. On one side, there is a **USB Plug**, which allows for interfacing with computers for programming and power. Additionally, there is an option for an **External Power Supply** offering flexibility in powering the board for standalone projects.

Figure 13.5 shows the Arduino Uno schematic diagram, a popular microcontroller board for electronic experimentation and projects. The schematic details the circuit board's components and connections. Reset circuits, voltage regulators, and crystal oscillators are often shown with the microcontroller unit (MCU), usually an Atmel AVR processor. The schematic may also show analog and digital input/output ports, power supply connections, UART, SPI, I2C communication interfaces, and board-integrated components like LEDs and switches. Developers and advanced users who want to change the Arduino Uno board's functionality, fix issues, or build custom circuits that interface with Arduino must understand the schematic.

There is an **Analog Reference Pin** for reference, which can be used to set an external voltage reference. The **Reset Button** and the nearby **Reset Pin** serve the same purpose allowing users to restart the program running on the microcontroller. Last, the **In-Circuit Serial Programmer** aids in burning the bootloader or directly programming the microcontroller bypassing the typical Arduino bootloader.

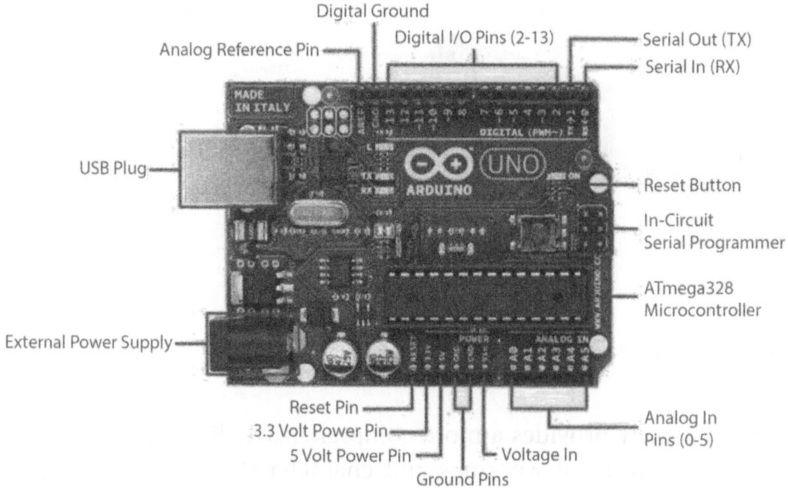

Figure 13.5 Schematic diagram of Arduino Uno.

The Arduino Uno provides an accessible platform for hobbyists, educators, and professionals to prototype and develop electronic projects, thanks to its user-friendly design and a vast online community.

• *Atmega328P Microcontroller*

Atmega328 is a low-power, high-yielding 8-bit microcontroller. It features an Advance Virtual (AVR) computer with an RISC architecture, long-lasting and non-volatile memory segments, peripheral choices, and a unique microcontroller. As shown in Figure 13.6, the **ATmega328P** is a microcontroller developed by Atmel, now a part of Microchip Technology. It is an 8-bit microcontroller based on the AVR-enhanced RISC (Reduced Instruction Set Computing) architecture. The **ATmega328P** microcontroller, due to its versatility, efficiency, and low power consumption, can be effectively utilized in a medical dispenser system. The ATmega328P is an intelligent core for a medical dispenser ensuring accurate, timely, and efficient medication delivery. Its flexibility allows it to be adapted for various requirements, from simple pill dispensers to more complex, connected medical devices [19]. Visual representations of the Atmega328P microcontroller are depicted in Figure 13.6. Part (A) probably illustrates the package outline or tangible presentation of the Atmega328P, including its form factor and pin arrangement. Designers and engineers may find this information advantageous when devising circuit board layouts or physically connecting to the microcontroller.

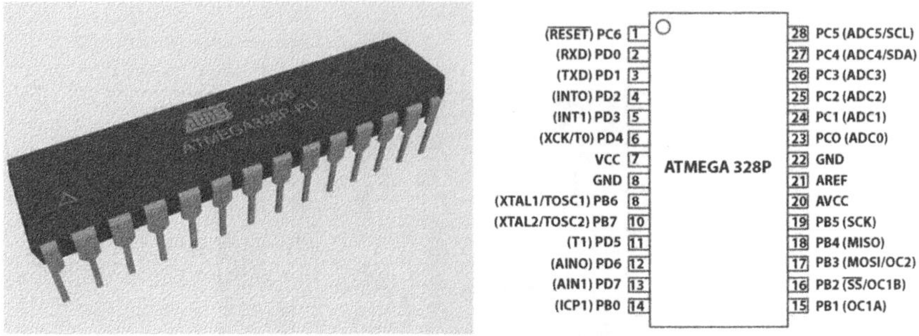

Figure 13.6 Atmega328P Microcontroller and (B) ATMEGA 328P.

Part (B) likely provides a more comprehensive diagram or illustration depicting the internal workings and characteristics of the Atmega328P microcontroller. This may encompass intricacies such as the configuration of pins, the organization of memory, peripheral interfaces (e.g., UART, SPI, I2C), and additional functional modules that are incorporated into the microcontroller.

Given its extensive application and versatile functionality, a comprehensive grasp of the Atmega328P microcontroller is imperative to design microcontroller-based projects and embedded systems.

13.4 Applications

Input integrates Arduino, HC-SR04, and Infrared Line Tracking sensors. Set up the Arduino with a beard board, jumper wires, and LED illumination to work with the HCSR 04 and Line Tracking sensors. Include sensors and other instruments [20]. To remotely monitor the prototype's mobility via smartphone or laptop, where are the Arduino board and ESP8266?

These applications exemplify the adaptability and extensive usefulness of the technology or component under consideration. Now, let us analyze each point:

- **Compatible with ARDUINO UNO, ARDUINO NANO, and other mini-ARDUINO boards:** Arduino is a widely used electronic platform that is open source and relies on user-friendly hardware and software. The listed components are several iterations of Arduino boards, commonly utilized in DIY projects, prototyping, and small-scale automation.

- **Industrial Management Systems:** Industrial management systems are essential for monitoring and efficiently controlling numerous industry activities. The indicated technology is likely involved in integrating sensors, processing data, and implementing control logic in these systems.
- **Switched Mode Power Supplies (SMPS) and Power Regulation Systems:** Precise control and monitoring of electrical parameters are necessary for Switched Mode Power Supplies (SMPS) and power regulation systems. The indicated technology can be utilized for voltage regulation, current sensing, and feedback control in these systems.
- **SMPS and Power Regulation Systems:** Digital processing encompasses a broad spectrum of digital signal activities, including data manipulation, signal processing, and communication protocols. The technique can be employed in devices requiring digital processing capabilities, such as microcontrollers or DSP (Digital Signal Processor) units.
- **Analog Signal Activity and Manipulations:** Analog signals are widely used in many applications from audio processing to sensor interfacing. The indicated technique could be used for signal conditioning, amplification, filtering, or analog-to-digital conversion.
- **Embedded Systems Like Coffee Machine, Slot Machine:** The technologies mentioned above could be incorporated into embedded systems, such as coffee or slot machines, to control logic, communicate with sensors, or manage the user interface.
- **Motor Management Systems:** Motor management systems are extensively utilized in the fields of automation and robotics. The described technology can be used in motor control systems to regulate speed, detect position, or manage torque.
- **Units of Measurement to be Shown:** Display units comprise various devices, such as LED/LCD screens, OLED displays, or primary alphanumeric displays. The technology can be employed for duties such as operating driving display modules, managing graphics rendering, or connecting with touch panels.
- A Peripheral Interface system often denotes the connection between the central processing unit and peripheral devices such as sensors, actuators, or communication modules.

The proposed technology could offer the required hardware interfaces and protocols for smooth communication between the central system and peripheral devices.

These applications exemplify the adaptability and extensive usefulness of the technology or component under consideration. Now, let us analyze each point.

13.5 Use of ATMEGA328P Using Arduino

Because the ATmega328P is used in the Arduino Uno and Arduino mini boards, you may immediately replace the Arduino board with the ATmega328 chip. For that initial, you will want to flash the chip using the Arduino bootloader. This IC with bootloader may be plugged into an Arduino Uno board and programmed. Once the Arduino software has been burned into the IC, it may be removed and used instead of the Arduino board, a quartz oscillator, and other project components. The pin configuration between the Arduino Uno board and the Atmega328P microcontroller is possibly depicted in Figure 13.7. A comprehensive grasp of the correlation between the physical pins of the Arduino Uno and the pins of the Atmega328P microcontroller requires this diagram.

The primary microcontroller processor integrated into the Arduino Uno board is the Atmega328P. Nevertheless, because of the additional components and circuitry on the board, the pins of the Arduino Uno do not correspond precisely to the pins of the Atmega328P.

In general, the diagram would present the pins of the Arduino Uno on one side and the corresponding pins of the Atmega328P on the other in the form of a table or grid. This mapping lets users discern which Atmega328P pins are connected to which Arduino pins. This knowledge empowers them to interface with peripherals and compose codes effectively.

A comprehensive comprehension of this pin mapping is imperative for sophisticated Arduino endeavors, as it enables users to directly access the diverse features and peripherals of the Atmega328P microcontroller and utilize its complete capabilities.

A. Servomotor

A servomotor could be a Rotary actuator or Linear actuator that enables precise management of angular or linear position, rate, and acceleration. It consists of an acceptable motor coupled to a detector for position feedback.

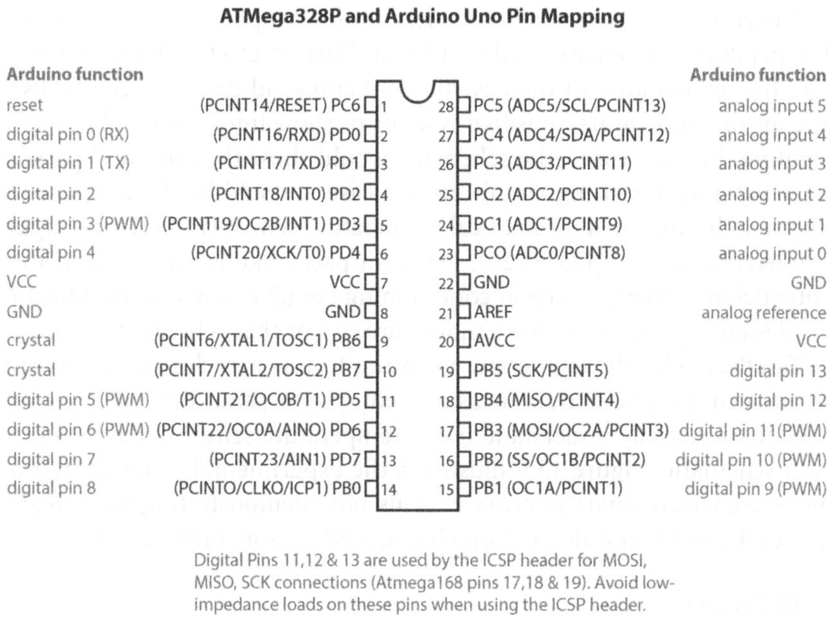

Figure 13.7 Pin mapping b/w Arduino Uno and Atmega328P microcontroller.

It conjointly needs a comparatively subtle controller, usually a zealous module explicitly designed to be used with servomotors.

Here, it is used to control the angular position of the void. When the supply is given, the void will rotate angularly as per instruction fed to the motor. A glass cylinder shields the motor to provide surface area to the dropped pill.

B. Temperature Sensor

LM35 is a temperature-measuring instrument having an analogy output voltage proportional to the temperature.

- It provides output voltage in Centigrade (Celsius).
- It does not need any external standardization calibration equipment.
- It is a three-terminal detector accustomed live encompassing temperature ranging from −55°C to 150°C.
- LM35 offers temperature output that is additionally precise than thermistor o/p.
- Small and hence suitable for remote applications.

Figure 13.8 shows a schematic design of a temperature sensor circuit. Temperature sensors are used in a lot of different electrical tasks to measure the temperature of the environment and send data that can be used to control temperature-sensitive systems or show information about temperature. In most cases, the schematic would show the links and parts of the temperature-sensing circuit. In this case, it could be the temperature sensor, a thermistor, a mechanical temperature sensor (LM35), or a digital temperature sensor (DS18B20). Different parts, like resistors, capacitors, potential amplifiers, or signal conditioning circuits, may also be added to the design depending on the temperature sensor that is being used.

To effectively add temperature-sensing features to electronic projects, create accurate temperature measurement systems, and adjust sensors, you need to thoroughly understand how a temperature sensor circuit is shown on a schematic. Figure 13.9 illustrates the experimental setup for testing the IoT-enabled smart pharmaceuticals box, demonstrating the integration of the LCD module, Arduino board, and sensor components.

C. IR Sensor

An infrared (IR) sensor is a device that measures and detects infrared in its surrounding environment. When an object comes on the brink of the sensor, the infrared from the LED reflects off of the thing and is detected by the receiver, i.e., it senses whether the tray has moved out or not.

Thermocouples, resistance temperature detectors (RTDs), and semiconductor temperature sensors are examples of infrared temperature sensors used in contact-type instrumentation. Because contact detectors maintain

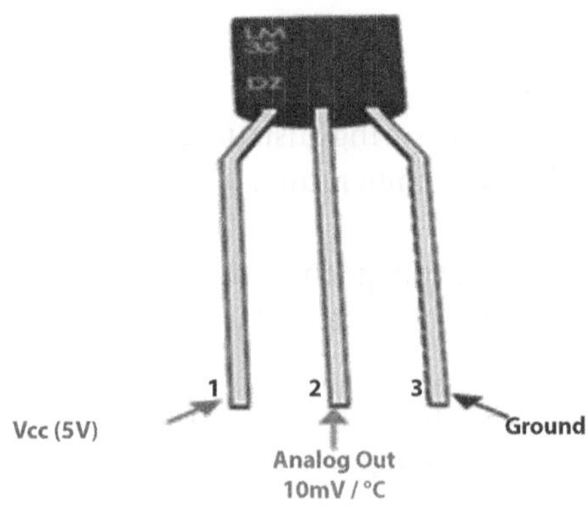

Figure 13.8 Schematic diagram of a temperature sensor.

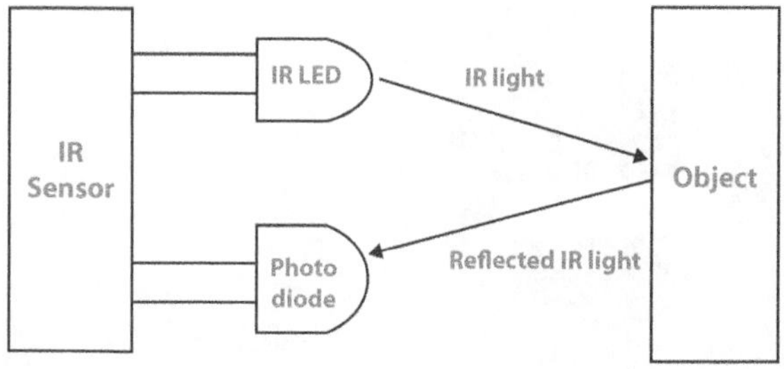

Figure 13.9 Working principle of infrared sensor.

their temperature, they require physical contact with the measured item to raise the sensor body's temperature to that of the object.

D. Buzzer

A buzzer is a small yet cost-effective component that may use to add sound choices to a project/system. Its microscopic and compact two-pin structure makes it ideal for usage onboard, perf board, and even on PCBs, making it a widely utilized component in most electronic applications. It is a portable equipment, thanks to its compact size.

E. Resistor, Transistor, Diode, and Capacitor

Resistance is a passive two-terminal electrical device that acts as a circuit component by implementing electrical phenomena. Resistor square measures are used in electronic circuits to reduce current flow, adjust signal levels, divide voltages, bias active components, and terminate transmission lines, among other things.

F. Switch and Connecting Wire

In electrical engineering, a switch is an electrical device that connects or disconnects the conducting channel in an electric circuit, interrupting or entertaining the electrical current between conductors. The most often used type of switch is a 37-mechanical device composed of one or more sets of movable electrical contacts coupled to external circuits. When two references are in contact, current flows between them; however, when the contacts are separated by a square measure, no current flows.

Figure 13.10 show that the connecting wires enable electrical current to flow from one point on a circuit to another; as a result, electricity needs a medium to go through. In computers, square wires are inserted into circuit boards conveying electrical pulses interpreted as binary messages of zeros and ones.

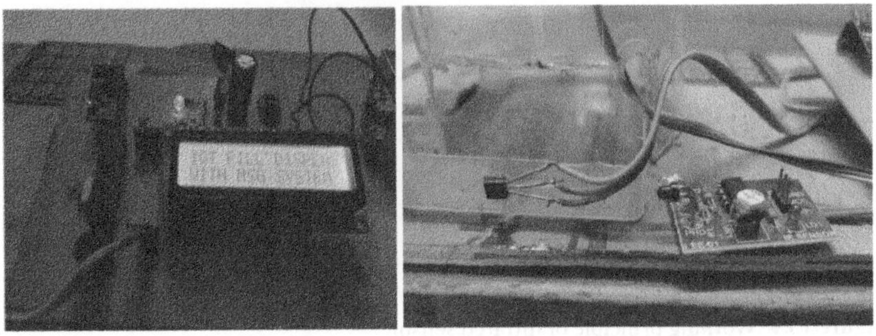

Figure 13.10 Top view of transformer, LCD, ESP8266, Atmega328, buzzer top view of IR sensor, and temperature sensor.

13.6 Software Used

Blynk: Blynk App is a cloud platform designed for IOT. It has three major components in it from which Blynk Server is used for the communication between a hardware and your Smartphone [21]. Blynk is a specialized cloud platform designed exclusively for applications related to the Internet of Things (IoT). The software provides an intuitive interface and features facilitating smooth connection between hardware devices and smartphones. The platform comprises three primary components, with the Blynk Server playing a vital role in enabling connectivity between hardware devices and smartphones. This component functions as a mediator for data exchange allowing the users to remotely engage with their smartphones using their Internet of Things (IoT) devices.

An essential feature of Blynk is its capability to store and present data gathered from Internet of Things (IoT) devices. This functionality allows users to continuously track and analyze different characteristics or metrics in real time offering essential observations regarding the performance and state of their interconnected devices. In addition, Blynk can establish connections with cloud services through Wi-Fi, Bluetooth, and other communication protocols. This ensures versatility and compatibility with a diverse array of IoT devices.

Blynk is compatible with Android and iOS smartphones, ensuring accessibility to a wide range of users. This product's straightforward interface and diverse capabilities make it an excellent option for anybody interested in IoT, whether they are enthusiasts, hobbyists, or professionals. Blynk facilitates data visualization and supports messaging and push notifications, enabling users to receive alerts and messages directly on their smartphones.

Many software tools are typically used when setting up hardware to work with Blynk. An example of such a tool is the Arduino IDE (Integrated Development Environment), which is extensively employed for programming and customizing Arduino microcontrollers. The Arduino IDE allows users to conveniently customize the ports and configurations of their Arduino boards, facilitating smooth integration with Blynk-enabled IoT projects. Furthermore, the Arduino IDE enables project simulation, offering customers a more comprehensive comprehension of the functioning of their IoT devices in real-life situations.

NI Ultiboard is a beneficial software tool for customizing hardware components. NI Ultiboard is a software tool that is used to create circuit layouts for hardware projects. It is similar to the Arduino IDE and can be used to design circuits that include components such as ATmega microcontrollers, transformers, servomotors, and temperature sensors. NI Ultiboard provides a user-friendly interface and robust functionality for creating and testing intricate circuit layouts making it an essential tool for IoT projects that demand accurate hardware configuration.

To put it concisely, it is an aflexible cloud platform created explicitly for the Internet of Things (IoT) applications enabling seamless connectivity between hardware devices and smartphones. The tool is equipped with data storage and visualization capabilities as well as messaging and push notifications functionalities making it indispensable for IoT enthusiasts. Furthermore, the Arduino IDE and NI Ultiboard frequently employ software tools for setting hardware components and creating circuit layouts for Blynk-enabled IoT applications.

A. Software Used to Configure the Hardware

- ***Arduino Ide***: It is an open-source software used to configure the ports of the Arduino. It is used to connect the hardware and IOT module for smooth running of the system. A simulation of the project can be done into this software, which provides better understanding of its work.
- ***NI Ultiboard***: Similar to the Arduino's software, this is used to for designing the circuit layout of the hardware part of the project (ATmega, transformer, servomotor, temp sensor). It is a very useful tool for this type of projects and easily available.

13.7 Result and Discussion

A. Working Principle of Pill Dispenser

The dispenser works on the principle that when the whole circuit is made "ON," power supply is given to the system, and the controlling element comes into play. It is connected to a Wi-Fi module, which sends data on the phone.

Upon completion of the circuit, the servomotor will return to its initial position. The health worker will then place the medicine in the void and insert the order of the pill with the help of a keypad, and the timer is set. When the allotted time comes, the system notifies the patient with the help of a buzzer. When the receiver reaches the tray to get hold of their medicine, the IR sensor checks for the proximity of the object, and the LM35 temperature sensor, which is attached to the tray, notes down the temperature and displays it on LCD. At the allotted time, the allotted sequence of medicine is taken, and the worker gets to monitor the schedule.

The Result and Discussion section elucidates the operational philosophy of the pill dispenser, which amalgamates diverse components and capabilities to guarantee effective medication administration and patient safety. The dispenser functions in the following manner:

- **Power Activation and Control Element:** The Power Activation and Control Element supplies power to the system upon circuit activation activating the controlling element. This component supervises the dispenser's operation.
- **Wi-Fi Connectivity:** The controlling element is linked to a Wi-Fi module allowing for connection with a smartphone. This connectivity enables the dispenser to be monitored and controlled from a distance and allows for data transmission to healthcare practitioners or carers.
- **Servomotor Initialization:** When the circuit is activated, the servomotor automatically adjusts to its starting position preparing the dispenser mechanism for placing medication.
- **Medication Placement and Schedule Entry:** A healthcare professional inserts medication into the compartments of the dispenser and enters the pill schedule using a keypad. This function establishes the timer for the dispensation of drugs.
- **Patient Alert:** The system emits a buzzer to notify the patient when it is time to take their medication asking them to get it from the dispenser tray.

- **Object Proximity and Temperature Sensing:** The system utilizes an infrared (IR) sensor to detect the proximity of the patient's hand or object as they approach the dispenser. At the same time, a tray incorporates an LM35 temperature sensor to measure the temperature of the medication or the surrounding environment. The temperature data are exhibited on an LCD panel for monitoring purposes.
- **Medication Dispensing:** The patient obtains their medication in the prescribed order. Simultaneously, the healthcare practitioner can oversee the medication timetable and compliance.
- The system utilizes the LM35 sensor to monitor temperature levels. If the temperature surpasses a pre-established threshold, it signifies possible degradation of medication or environmental problems. In such cases, the system promptly notifies the guardian through a cloud-based service like the Blynk App. This guarantees prompt intervention to mitigate any potential hazards.
- **Emergency Communication:** During emergencies, the patient can utilize the keypad to transmit an urgent message to their designated guardian. This feature improves patient safety by allowing prompt aid and action if necessary.

The talk will explore each component's efficacy and the pill dispenser's overall functioning in promoting prescription adherence, guaranteeing patient safety, and enabling remote monitoring capabilities. Furthermore, it is worth considering the possibility of investigating new enhancements or optimizations to improve the performance and usefulness of the dispenser. In summary, the operational concept of the pill dispenser showcases its capacity to enhance medicine administration for patients while also offering reassurance to carers and healthcare personnel.

13.8 Conclusion

In this paper, we have exhibited a prototype of smart medicine dispenser, which is a contactless medicine dispenser with a temperature sensor to ensure the intake of medicine and displays the temperature of the individual. The IOT module is used in prototype for the purpose of tracking medicine in-take and temperature recording. These data are logged into any device (such as a cellphone, computer) via Bluetooth. Possible improvements can be done in this prototype: when medicine is placed in the dispenser box, some medicines oxidize in open air. To get rid of this problem, an airtight box or vacuum-sealed container is to be used. A memory module can be introduced so that the information from the prototype is automatically stored in the micro-SD card. A safety lock with automatic locking and opening of medicine can also be implemented to ensure the intake of medicine by the intended person. For a large number of patients, a server can be installed so that the tracking record can be stored online and shared among the Medical Administration. For example, the hospitals can implement a server, which is connected to all these devices via Wi-Fi, and all the data are stored in the server.

References

1. Sailesh, M.P., Kumar, C.V., Cecil, B., Mangal Deep, B.M., Sivraj, P., Smart soldier assistance using WSN, in: *2014 International Conference on Embedded Systems (ICES)*, pp. 244–249, 2014, doi: 10.1109/EmbeddedSys.2014.6953166.
2. Walker, W., Aroul, A.L.P., Bhatia, D., Mobile health monitoring systems, in: *2009 Annual International Conference of the IEEE Engineering in Medicine and Biology Society*, pp. 5199–5202, 2009, doi: 10.1109/IEMBS.2009.5334583.
3. Lim, H.B., Ma, D., Wang, B., Kalbarczyk, Z., Iyer, R.K., Watkin, K.L., A Soldier Health Monitoring System for Military Applications, in: *2010 International Conference on Body Sensor Networks*, pp. 246–249, 2010, doi: 10.1109/BSN.2010.58.
4. Gondalia, A., Dixit, D., Parashar, S., Raghava, V., Sengupta, A., Sarobin, V.R., IoT-based Healthcare Monitoring System for War Soldiers using Machine Learning. *Procedia Comput. Sci.*, 133, 1005–1013, 2018, doi: https://doi.org/10.1016/j.procs.2018.07.075.
5. S.S., M.J.R., B.R.K., L.R.K., Rout, S., Patra, Energy Aware Task Consolidation in Fog Computing Environment, in: *Intelligent Data Engineering and Analytics*, Y.-D., B.V., M.R., S.C. Satapathy, Zhang (Eds.), pp. 195–205, Springer Singapore, Singapore, 2021.
6. Bajaj, K., Sharma, B., and Singh, R. Integration of WSN with IoT applications: a vision, architecture, and future challenges. *Integration of WSN and IoT for Smart Cities*, 79–102, 2020.
7. Bahman, S., & Shamsollahi, M. B., Robot Control Using an Inexpensive P300 Based BCI. In *2019 26th National and 4th International Iranian Conference on Biomedical Engineering (ICBME)* pp. 204–207, IEEE, 2019, November.
8. Rolim, C.O., Koch, F.L., Westphall, C.B., Werner, J., Fracalossi, A., Salvador, G.S., A cloud computing solution for patient's data collection in health care institutions, in: *2nd International Conference on eHealth, Telemedicine, and*

Social Medicine, eTELEMED 2010, Includes MLMB 2010; BUSMMed 2010, pp. 95–99, 2010, doi: 10.1109/eTELEMED.2010.19.

9. Joshi, J.B.D., Institute of Electrical and Electronics Engineers, and IEEE Computer Society, Proceedings. In *2016 IEEE International Conference on Big Data,* Dec 2015.
10. Shaik, M.N. and Abdul-Kader, W., A hybrid multiple criteria decision making approach for measuring comprehensive performance of reverse logistics enterprises. *Comput. Ind. Eng.*, 123, 9–25, Sep. 2018, doi: 10.1016/j.cie.2018.06.007.
11. Al-Shammary, A.A.G., Kouzani, A.Z., Kaynak, A., Khoo, S.Y., Norton, M. and Gates, W., Soil Bulk Density Estimation Methods: A Review. *Pedosphere*, 28, 4, 581–596, Aug. 2018, doi: 10.1016/S1002-0160(18)60034-7.
12. Ranjana, P., and Alexander, E., Health alert and medicine remainder using internet of things. In *2018 IEEE International Conference on Computational Intelligence and Computing Research (ICCIC)*, pp. 1–4, IEEE, 2018, November.
13. Zeidan, H., Karam, K., Abi, R., Daou, Z., Smart Medicine Box System.
14. Zhang, T., Liu, Z., Cao, X., Xia, W., Intelligent Medicine Box Monitoring and Management System, in: *Proceedings - 2015 International Conference on Computer Science and Mechanical Automation, CSMA 2015*, Jan. 2016, Institute of Electrical and Electronics Engineers Inc., pp. 153–156, doi: 10.1109/CSMA.2015.37.
15. Srinivas, A., Jabri, A., Abbeel, P., Levine, S., Finn, C., Universal Planning Networks, 2018, [Online], Available: https://sites.google.
16. Guerrero-Ulloa, G., Hornos, M.J., Rodríguez-Domínguez, C., and Fernández-Coello, M.M., IoT-based smart medicine dispenser to control and supervise medication intake. In *Intelligent Environments*, pp. 39–48, IOS Press, 2020.
17. Tariq, R.A., Vashisht, R., Sinha, A., Scherbak, Y., *Medication Dispensing Errors And Prevention*, StatPearls Publishing, Treasure Island (FL), 2022, [Online], Available: http://europepmc.org/books/NBK519065.
18. Srinivas, M., Durgaprasadarao, P., Raj, V.N.P., Intelligent medicine box for medication management using IoT, in: *2018 2nd International Conference on Inventive Systems and Control (ICISC)*, pp. 32–34, 2018, doi: 10.1109/ICISC.2018.8399097.
19. Ocampo, J.U. and Kaminski, P.C., Medical device development, from technical design to integrated product development. *J. Med. Eng. Technol.*, 43, 5, 287–304, 2019, doi: 10.1080/03091902.2019.1653393.
20. Nursakinah, B., Implementation of IoT (Internet of Thing) In The Design of a Smart Robot Prototype For Automatic Waste Disposal Based on Arduino At Mega. *Int. J. Intgr. Sci.*, 3, 2, 209–222, Feb. 2024, doi: 10.55927/ijis.v3i2.8203.
21. Suryaningrat, I.B., Darmawan, A.H., Amilia, W., Suryadharma, B., Developing of Tomato Distribution Process Monitoring System Using Internet of Things (IoT). *J. Ilmiah Rekayasa Pertanian Biosistem*, 12, 1, 147–166, Mar. 2024, doi: 10.29303/jrpb.v12i1.445.

14

Telemedicine and Virtual Health: Pioneering Innovation and Future Frontiers in Personalized Patient Care

R. Rahul, R. Raghul Jayaprakash, M. Shibhi Varmaah and S. Velmurugan*

Department of Biomedical Engineering, Dr. N.G.P. Institute of Technology, Coimbatore, Tamil Nadu, India

Abstract

Healthcare providers are on the search for approaches to lower costs and enhance accessibility for patients to healthcare as that of their organization develops significantly. One of digitalization's most significant benefits is that emerging technologies enable the interactions between patients and providers and facilitates patients' access to health through the elimination of boundaries, the services they require. Patients can currently communicate with medical professionals owing to digital technology; customers may obtain services through an interface that provides them at any time wherever they are. Technological advances include audio, video, and instant messaging in real time. The continual development of health care and innovation has effectively increased people's lifespan. This work provides one of the best methods to get around this issue, whereas progressively, it is developed into a useful tool for those who find it difficult to find the time to travel to a doctor's appointment and wait in a waiting area. There is a great deal of uncertainty in the health profession due to new concepts like telemedicine and virtual care. The practical guidance provided in this article will concentrate on using virtual care and telemedicine. This study offers consequences on the likelihood of combining virtual care options in the near future to support the use of digital technology in healthcare.

***Keywords*:** Data security, digital technology, healthcare accessibility, patient care, reimbursement, remote monitoring, telemedicine, virtual health

**Corresponding author*: velmurugan.s@drngpit.ac.in

Parul Dubey, Mangala Madankar, Pushkar Dubey and Bui Thanh Hung (eds.) The Impact of Algorithmic Technologies on Healthcare, (279–312) © 2025 Scrivener Publishing LLC

14.1 Introduction to Telemedicine and Virtual Health

The provision of health-related information and services through electronic communication is known as telehealth. Although they have different meanings, the terms "telehealth" and "telemedicine" can be used interchangeably [2]. The term "telemedicine" refers especially to the use of telecommunications technologies, including the internet, wireless, satellite, and telephones, to provide clinical information and healthcare services remotely. The use of electronic communications to transfer medical information across locations with the goal of enhancing patient care is known as telehealth. Telehealth is an extension of telemedicine; however, in contrast to telemedicine, which concentrates on curative elements of health, telehealth covers preventive, promotive, and curative aspects of health and involves a wide range of healthcare professionals in its delivery. Because it is a general term, it can refer to patient education as well as that of healthcare professionals.

14.1.1 Telemedicine

Imagine a society in which sterile clinics are not the only place where people can receive treatment. Just picture being able to visit a doctor from the comfort of your couch for regular examinations or consultations. With the advent of telemedicine, a quickly developing area that uses technology to provide healthcare remotely, this vision is starting to come true. A phone conversation with your doctor is not the only aspect of telemedicine [4]. It makes use of many telecommunication technologies, including secure messaging services, video conferencing, and even remote patient monitoring equipment.

Studies in this topic are expanding, despite the fact that it is yet early. Telemonitoring vital signs and providing treatment over the phone were two such interventions that decreased mortality and hospitalization risk while also improving quality of life in people with heart disease. For several good reasons, it is important to get a diagnosis or treatment plan. Patients are reassured in addition to receiving the best care possible. Telemedicine is a great alternative for addressing mental health issues. It takes away some of the reasons why people are unable to access this essential form of treatment.

Safe, convenient care can be provided to patients at their convenience by their doctor using telemedicine. This could mean that making childcare arrangements or taking time off from work are not essential. A doctor's office is an infection-prone place to sit close to other individuals. This should be especially cautiously considered by those with weakened immune systems or long-term medical issues. It removes the possibility that the doctor may contract a disease at the hospital where they work. Telemedicine service providers may be able to reduce their overhead expenses. Clinical professionals may be able to augment their income through telemedicine by treating additional patients. By interacting with patients online, caregivers are protected from viruses that patients might carry. Take a trip if receiving treatment does not need waiting.

Telemedicine is the term for health-related services delivered via electronic information and communication technologies [1]. It outlines the complete package of deliverables meant to empower patients and their physicians or other healthcare providers. It can be used for many different things, including online patient consultations, telehealth nursing, remote control, and remote psychiatric and physical rehabilitation. Through the simplification of clinical procedures and reduction of hospital travel expenses, it facilitates better decision making regarding health care, enhances the efficacy and caliber of emergency services, expedites the diagnosis process, and decreases costs for patients and clinicians alike.

14.1.2 Virtual Health

Virtual health extends beyond remote doctor consultations. It is an all-encompassing ecosystem that uses technology to completely transform the way that healthcare is obtained, administered, and provided. Patients can maintain their medical records, check test results, make appointments, and message doctors securely via secure online platforms. This encourages a more team-based approach to healthcare. Ignore phone calls! Through the use of virtual health platforms, patients may conveniently schedule appointments online, saving time and providing more flexibility. By providing refill requests, reminders, and potential medication interactions, these applications assist patients in adhering to their prescribed regimens. Health information such as blood pressure, heart rate, and sleep patterns can be remotely collected and transmitted to healthcare practitioners by fitness trackers, smartwatches, and other wearables.

Virtual health, sometimes referred to as telehealth or telemedicine, is a revolutionary method of delivering healthcare that uses technology to deliver treatments remotely. Technological developments in communication, such as smartphones, wearables, and high-speed internet, have sped up this paradigm change [5]. Virtual consultations, remote monitoring, digital prescriptions, and telesurgeries are just a few of the many services that fall under the umbrella of virtual health. Some of the elements that have accelerated its popularity are the need for more affordable, accessible healthcare solutions as well as cost effectiveness. Virtual health's capacity to transcend geographic boundaries is one of its main benefits. Patients can communicate with medical specialists virtually negating the need for travel, especially in underserved or rural areas where access to healthcare institutions may be limited.

For those who live in rural areas, have chronic illnesses, or have mobility challenges, this is very helpful. Virtual health facilitates equitable and inclusive access to healthcare by expanding the reach of healthcare services. For consumers and doctors alike, virtual health also provides ease and flexibility [6]. Patients can book consultations, get medications, and get medical advice from the comfort of their homes with the help of safe video conferencing platforms and smartphone apps. Long wait periods are no longer necessary, and the administrative difficulties brought on by in-person visits are diminished. Healthcare professionals can also better manage their calendars with virtual consultations, which boosts productivity and enhances patient results. Potential cost savings in healthcare is another important benefit of virtual health.

14.1.3 Benefits of Telemedicine and Virtual Health

The healthcare industry is changing dramatically thanks to the many advantages that telemedicine and virtual health offer. These technologies are revolutionizing healthcare delivery and patient experiences, from expanding access to care to improving patient outcomes.

- **Improved Access to Care**
  Patients can receive healthcare treatments no matter where they are thanks to telemedicine, which overcomes geographic limitations. People who live in remote or underdeveloped locations with little access to medical services may particularly benefit from this. Patients can communicate virtually with medical professionals, eliminating the need for travel and removing geographical and transportation-related barriers.
- **Convenience and Flexibility**
  Services for virtual health are incredibly convenient for both individuals and medical professionals. Long drives and

waiting room waits are avoided when patients use telemedicine to book appointments, get medical advice, and access medicines from the comfort of their homes. Moreover, virtual consultations allow medical professionals to better accommodate patients' hectic schedules by optimizing their schedules and providing additional hours of service.

- **Personalized Care**
  Healthcare professionals can give individualized treatment based on the needs of each patient thanks to telemedicine. Providers can perform thorough examinations, go over patient histories, and create individualized treatment programs via virtual consultations. Continuous data collection is made possible by remote monitoring technologies, which give healthcare professionals the ability to watch patients' progress, spot trends, and take proactive measures to improve their results.
- **Cost Effectiveness**
  Telemedicine has the potential to lower healthcare costs for patients, providers, and healthcare systems alike. By reducing the need for physical infrastructure and streamlining administrative processes, virtual health services can be more cost effective than traditional in-person care. Moreover, virtual consultations can prevent unnecessary emergency room visits and hospitalizations leading to overall savings for healthcare systems and patients.
- **Reduced Wait Times and Improved Efficiency**
  Patient satisfaction and efficiency are increased when telemedicine eliminates wait times for consultations and appointments. Virtual consultations facilitate faster patient visits, minimizing scheduling conflicts and streamlining workflow for healthcare practitioners.

14.2 Challenges in Telemedicine

The COVID-19 pandemic has pushed the rise of telemedicine, which is the remote provision of healthcare services via telecommunications technology, in recent years. While there are many advantages to telemedicine, including cost effectiveness, convenience, and improved access to treatment, there are also some drawbacks.

Even while cell phones and internet connectivity are widely available, not everyone has the equipment or internet connectivity needed for telemedicine consultations. This is especially true in low-income or rural locations where there may not be as much access to broadband internet. A "digital divide" has been identified, whereby specific groups, such the elderly or those from poorer socioeconomic backgrounds, may have less access to technology or digital knowledge [7]. Figures 14.1 show the major challenges faced in telemedicine. To keep people confident in telemedicine systems, patient data security and privacy must be guaranteed. There is an extra layer of complexity associated with complying with rules like the Health Insurance Portability and Accountability Act (HIPAA) in the United States.

The licensing laws that apply to the various jurisdictions where healthcare providers work must be followed. Crossing national or even international borders is a common practice in telemedicine, which raises complicated legal concerns about compensation, malpractice, and licensing. Policies for telemedicine service reimbursement are currently being developed. Healthcare practitioners may face financial difficulties as a result of telemedicine consultations not always receiving the same reimbursement as in-person appointments. Navigating the complexities of insurance coverage and telemedicine service pricing schemes can also be challenging. Some contend that by reducing in-person encounters and physical examinations, telemedicine could lower the standard of care for patients and medical professionals. It is crucial to guarantee that telemedicine platforms provide patients with the same level of care and happiness as traditional in-person sessions. Platforms for telemedicine depend on reliable internet connections and working technologies. Technical issues that affect the patient experience include dropped calls, poor audio or video quality, and system outages. These can cause disruptions to consultations. Numerous

Figure 14.1 Challenges in telemedicine.

medico-legal concerns are brought up by telemedicine, like as documentation requirements, informed consent protocols, and malpractice responsibility. To reduce these hazards and guarantee patient safety, certain rules and procedures are required. Effective communication with patients who speak different languages or come from distinct cultural backgrounds may be difficult while using telemedicine. Delivering fair telemedicine services requires offering culturally aware treatment as well as language interpretation services.

14.2.1 Reimbursements

The issue of reimbursement in telemedicine is complicated and involves a number of interrelated elements, including as patient preferences, insurance laws, healthcare policies, and technical developments. The reimbursement landscape can be complex and complicated, despite the fact that telemedicine has several advantages, including cost effectiveness and improved access to care.

The lack of consistency and uniformity throughout payers and healthcare systems is one of the main issues with telemedicine reimbursement. Private insurance companies, Medicare, Medicaid, and other government programs all have very different reimbursement policies, which causes uncertainty and discrepancies for consumers and providers alike. Widespread acceptance and implementation may be hampered by payers' differing coverage of different telemedicine services and their associated constraints.

Furthermore, the requirements for payment may vary depending on the kind of telemedicine service rendered, the communication method (such as video conferencing or remote monitoring), and the particular medical condition being treated. For instance, some payers would fund the cost of virtual consultations with medical professionals, but they might not pay for digital health apps or remote monitoring equipment. The reimbursement procedure is made more difficult by the absence of standardized criteria, which may discourage providers from providing telemedicine services.

Reimbursement policies for telemedicine may also not always keep up with changes in healthcare delivery methods and technology improvements. Reimbursement rules need to change to reflect these new care modalities as telemedicine continues to advance with the introduction of smart devices, virtual reality, and artificial intelligence. Nonetheless, providers facing difficulties in being paid for state-of-the-art telemedicine services may find it difficult to keep up with the speed at which regulations are changing.

14.2.2 Technical Issue

The provision of care, patient happiness, and clinical outcomes can all be adversely affected by technical problems in telemedicine [18]. Telemedicine is dependent on technology, which is prone to a variety of technical problems, even while it has the ability to expand access to healthcare services and get around geographical constraints. To guarantee the dependability, efficiency, and scalability of telemedicine systems and services, it is imperative to address these issues. Connectivity problems are one of the main technological obstacles in telemedicine. To conduct virtual consultations, send medical data, and retrieve electronic health records, one needs dependable internet access. The efficiency of telemedicine consultations, however, can be jeopardized by differences in internet infrastructure and bandwidth restrictions, which can lead to poor video quality, audio lag, or failed connections.

Furthermore, malfunctions, defects, or system failures might have an impact on the dependability of telemedicine platforms and software applications. From small annoyances like brief audio or visual disturbances to more significant concerns like crashes or data breaches, these problems can vary widely. To safeguard patient privacy and data integrity, telemedicine technology must have a strong infrastructure, frequent software updates, and adherence to cybersecurity best practices.

To facilitate the widespread adoption and integration of telemedicine into mainstream healthcare delivery, stakeholders must make investments in infrastructure, technology, and training to address these technical hurdles [11]. The aforementioned measures encompass broadening the reach of broadband internet connectivity, creating telemedicine platforms that are easy to use, guaranteeing compatibility with current healthcare systems, and offering patient and provider education and assistance. Telemedicine has the potential to improve patient outcomes, increase access to care, and revolutionize healthcare delivery in the digital era. Some goals can be realized by resolving some technical obstacles.

14.2.3 Privacy

The safeguarding of private patient data, maintaining communication secrecy, and complying with legal requirements are all important aspects of electronic health care privacy. In addition to posing special privacy problems with data security, patient permission, and the transmission of private medical information, telemedicine also presents opportunities for easy and remote delivery of healthcare services. Making sure that patient data are securely sent over digital channels is one of the main privacy challenges in telemedicine. Exchanges of private medical data, including diagnoses, treatment plans, and medical histories, are common in telemedicine interactions. These data need to be protected against unwanted access or disclosure. Identity theft, financial fraud, and reputational damage are just a few of the serious hazards to patient privacy posed by data breaches, cyberattacks, and hacking incidents.

To preserve the security and integrity of patient information, telemedicine platforms and communication tools also need to abide by strict data protection laws, like the US's Health Insurance Portability and Accountability Act (HIPAA) [9]. Healthcare providers and business partners are required under HIPAA to put in place security measures to secure patient data. HIPAA also sets criteria for the privacy and security of protected health information (PHI). Concerns concerning the security and privacy of patient data are raised by the possibility that some telemedicine platforms are not HIPAA compliant. Furthermore, to provide services, telemedicine encounters may require third-party service providers like software suppliers, cloud service providers, or telecommunications firms. As part of this process, these providers may have access to patient data.

To ensure patient confidentiality and prevent hazards, strong contractual agreements, data encryption procedures, and oversight systems are necessary when outsourcing telemedicine services and need to guarantee the privacy and security of patient information. The secrecy of patient and healthcare provider conversations is another issue that telemedicine brings to light. Even while most telemedicine platforms use encrypted messaging apps and secure video conferencing, there is still a chance that uninvited parties will intercept or listen in. To safeguard against unwanted access or interception, telemedicine privacy must be ensured through the use of access controls, authentication methods, and encryption protocols. Getting informed consent from patients for the gathering, use, and sharing of their personal health information is another privacy concern in telemedicine.

Building trust in telemedicine services and improving patient engagement can be achieved by giving patients clear information about how their data are gathered, used, and protected during telemedicine encounters; obtaining informed consent for the use of personal health information; and enabling patients to make educated decisions about their privacy preferences. In summary, protecting patient privacy in telemedicine is a serious issue that needs to be carefully considered to maintain the security, confidentiality, and integrity of patient data. Stakeholders can reduce risks and increase confidence in telemedicine as a secure and reliable method of providing healthcare remotely by putting strong security measures in place, abiding by legal requirements, and informing patients of their rights regarding privacy.

14.2.4 Regulations

There are many different legal, ethical, and technical factors that are taken into account in the complicated and dynamic world of telemedicine regulations [5]. In addition to posing special issues with regard to privacy, licensure, payment, and the standard of care, telemedicine also presents opportunities to increase patient outcomes and access to healthcare. Credentialing of providers and licensure are two of the main issues with telemedicine regulations. It might be difficult to implement telemedicine if medical professionals are not licensed to operate in the state where their patients are situated. This is especially true for cross-state practitioners. Due to the disparities in state-by-state licensing standards, it is more difficult for these professionals to obtain the necessary credentials to practice across multiple states, navigate varying regulatory requirements, and ensure compliance with each state's unique legal and medical guidelines.

Furthermore, clinicians looking to get paid for telemedicine services face confusion and inconsistency due to differing telemedicine payment policies across payers, including commercial insurers, Medicare, Medicaid, and other government programs. Amidst the COVID-19 pandemic, certain payers have extended their coverage for telemedicine; nevertheless, these modifications can be momentary or contingent on particular eligibility requirements, thereby restricting the telemedicine programs' capacity to persist and grow over time. Policies like the United States' Health Insurance Portability and Accountability Act (HIPAA) mandate that healthcare providers and business associates put in place security measures to secure patient data. They also set requirements for the privacy and security of protected health information (PHI). Maintaining HIPAA compliance and ensuring that all patient data is securely stored and transmitted is crucial for protecting patient privacy and avoiding legal penalties.

In addition, to guarantee the security and efficacy of telemedicine consultations, telemedicine rules had to tackle professional responsibility and quality of care requirements [6]. The same ethical and medical norms that apply to in-person visits must also apply to telemedicine providers. These include doing thorough evaluations, getting informed consent, and keeping up-to-date medical records. Regulators must give considerable thought to and supervise telemedicine contacts because of the potential special difficulties they may provide for patient assessment, diagnostic accuracy, and follow-up care due to their virtual nature. Policymakers, payers, healthcare providers, technology vendors, and patient advocacy organizations must work together to tackle the problem of telemedicine laws.

Regulatory frameworks can promote the safe and efficient delivery of telemedicine services and facilitate the integration of telemedicine into mainstream healthcare delivery by addressing concerns relating to licensure, payment, privacy, quality of treatment, and patient access. Telemedicine holds the ability to revolutionize the healthcare industry and enhance global patient outcomes via sustained innovation and collaboration.

Similar to electronic medical records, telehealth systems have associated expenses for both software and hardware, and substantial resources are presently being allocated to enhance the user's "quality of experience [18]." Furthermore, the maintenance of clinical productivity through telemedicine is placing further strain on healthcare systems and providers. Uncertainty surrounds the commoditization of these new expenses; there is a chance that some of them will be passed on to vulnerable groups, such as those with impairments, who might not be able to pay them. Furthermore, unlike several private practices, telemedicine has not been as smoothly incorporated into the daily operations of many healthcare institutions, especially academic institutions and hospitals that primarily rely on graduate medical trainees. Access to telemedicine has been severely damaged for communities like people with disabilities, who frequently depend on treatment provided by trainees (under safety net health insurance systems like Medicaid and Medicare). Ancillary healthcare services, such diagnostic investigations and laboratory tests, are frequently smoothly integrated with traditional in- person healthcare appointments, albeit they frequently need scheduling ahead of time. Navigating and organizing such arrangements can be especially difficult because these supplementary services still need people with disabilities to physically visit a testing location.

14.3 Artificial Intelligence in Telemedicine

To help medical professionals diagnose illnesses and ailments, AI-powered algorithms can evaluate medical pictures like X-rays, MRIs, and CT scans. Diagnoses made with greater accuracy and speed are possible, thanks to these algorithms' ability to identify anomalies and patterns that human eyes might miss. Artificial intelligence (AI)-powered chatbots or virtual health assistants can help patients make appointments, respond to questions about health, and offer individualized medical advice. Patients can benefit from the ease and accessibility of these virtual assistants, who are on call around-the-clock. AI-enabled gadgets are able to remotely monitor patients' health indicators and vital signs on a continuous basis. Healthcare professionals may keep tabs on their patients' health state outside of conventional clinical settings, thanks to this real-time monitoring, and they can take swift action if any irregularities are found. AI systems are able to find trends and forecast health outcomes by analyzing massive patient data sets.

14.3.1 Risk Prediction and Stratification

To estimate the likelihood of contracting specific illnesses or consequences, AI algorithms can examine test results, electronic health records (EHRs), and other patient data [15]. Healthcare professionals can use individual risk profiles to identify high-risk patients and stratify them based on those profiles to execute tailored treatment plans and preventive measures to reduce risks and enhance treatment outcomes. Healthcare service allocation and resource prioritization can be improved with the use of AI-driven risk prediction models, especially in environments with limited resources.

14.3.2 Personalized Treatment Planning

AI provides individualized treatment planning by evaluating clinical guidelines, medical literature, and patient data to suggest the best course of action based on each patient's unique needs and preferences. Based on the patient's medical history, genetic composition, and other pertinent variables, AI-driven decision support systems can help healthcare professionals choose the right drugs, doses, and treatment plans. Treatment efficacy is increased, side effects are reduced, and patient adherence and satisfaction are raised using this individualized approach to treatment planning.

14.3.3 Virtual Assistants and Chatbots

Personalized information and support are offered to patients, caregivers, and healthcare providers using AI-powered chatbots and virtual assistants via conversational interfaces and natural language processing (NLP) [14]. By facilitating communication between patients and physicians, setting up appointments, responding to inquiries, and offering educational materials, these virtual agents can raise patient happiness and participation. Automating administrative duties like prescription refills, appointment reminders, and paperwork can help healthcare providers by freeing up time for deeper patient encounters. This is another way that virtual assistants can help.

AI-powered telepresence technologies allow for real-time remote consultations between medical professionals and patients. To promote efficient communication and teamwork, these systems frequently include functions like video conferencing, interaction with medical devices, and decision assistance tools. Figures 14.2 show the wide applications of AI in telemedicine where it has many applictions in telemedicine. To expedite the identification of viable therapeutic candidates, forecast their safety and efficacy profiles, and improve clinical trial design, artificial intelligence (AI) algorithms are being employed in the drug research and development processes. Healthcare firms can enhance operational efficiency and patient care delivery by optimizing resource allocation through AI-driven predictive models. Examples of these resources include hospital beds, staff scheduling, and inventory management. All things considered, AI has the potential to greatly increase the efficacy, efficiency, and accessibility of telemedicine services, which would eventually improve patient outcomes and their overall quality of life.

Care delivery is becoming more complex and is now outside the purview of any one healthcare professional due to increased innovation and discovery. AI can aid in the advancement of knowledge about therapeutic processes. Take the example of leveraging new advances in medicines and procedures by tailoring them to the specific needs of particular patients or

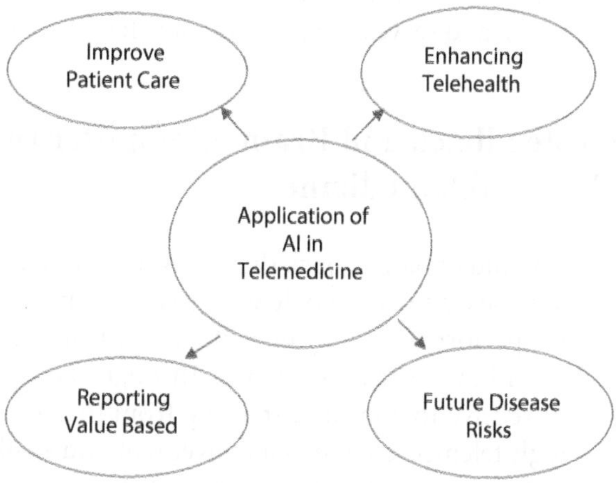

Figure 14.2 Applications of AI in telemedicine.

cohorts. A multidisciplinary team approach is required to increase longevity and treat chronic diseases in multimorbidity settings. The care should be continued in the community, preferably at home. Health care equity and quality are negatively impacted when integrated care and continuum of care routes are not adhered to. Across all facets of health care delivery, there must be smooth linkages and communication. Since some team members are not always able to be there, tele-support or remote care is required. AI might once more assist in meeting this need by facilitating the intelligent information and communication environment that would allow physicians to collaborate and by maintaining a comprehensive virtual knowledge base for the continuous education and support of healthcare professionals.

RPM is a method of gathering and transmitting patient health data to medical specialists outside of a clinic or doctor's office using linked technology. This kind of technical breakthrough can result in better health outcomes and lower healthcare costs by enabling patients and healthcare professionals to manage conditions, including chronic diseases, proactively [13]. Monitoring gadgets like the Apple Watch, Google Fit, and other wearables are collecting patient data as well as other crucial indicators, such as heart rates, sleep patterns, and levels of physical activity. One of the most significant and challenging tasks for patients is this one. To solve this issue, several hospitals are employing chatbots driven by artificial intelligence (AI) to plan and remind patients of their next in-person appointments or to just inform connected patients of critical health reminders. A case in point is the chatbot myCheck-in, created by Myriad Genetics. By utilizing information from the patient's electronic health record, this chatbot assists patients with check-in and serves as a reminder for their next appointment.

14.4 Neurofeedback and Brain–Computer Interfaces (BCIs) in Telemedicine

Neurofeedback is a kind of biofeedback that gives the user feedback in real time based on brainwave activity. People with ADHD, anxiety, depression, and even cognitive performance may benefit from this input as it teaches them how to control how their brains work. Through remote neurofeedback, patients can receive therapy and training from the comfort of their own homes through telemedicine. It is a convenient and easily accessible choice for many patients, as therapists may evaluate progress remotely and modify treatment regimens accordingly. With the use of brain–computer interfaces (BCIs), people can operate computers and other gadgets with just their brain activity.

14.4.1 Understanding Neurofeedback and BCIs

Electroencephalography (EEG) sensors put on the scalp are commonly used in neurofeedback to measure brain activity in real time. Through processing and analysis, the electrical impulses produced by the brain's neurons are detected by these sensors, and the user receives feedback. Neurofeedback has proven to be an effective treatment for a number of neurological and psychiatric disorders, such as traumatic brain injury, ADHD, anxiety, depression, and epilepsy, by teaching patients to alter their brainwave patterns.

Brain–computer interfaces (BCIs), on the other hand, allow direct communication between the brain and external devices without going through conventional channels like muscles or nerves [10]. Functional near-infrared spectroscopy (fNIRS), EEG, and invasive neural implants are just a few of the techniques that BCIs can use to identify brain activity.

Following decoding, these signals are converted into commands that operate prosthetic limbs, computers, and other equipment. Applications for BCIs are numerous and include neuroprosthetics, cognitive enhancement, and assistive technologies for paralyzed people.

In conclusion, novel approaches to brain interaction are provided by neurofeedback and brain–computer interfaces (BCIs), which provide real-time monitoring, feedback, and regulation of brain activity. It is crucial to comprehend these technologies to take use of their potential in telemedicine, where they can be included into platforms for remote healthcare to provide individualized interventions and enhance patient outcomes.

14.4.2 Integration of Neurofeedback and BCIs into Telemedicine Platforms

The incorporation of neurofeedback and brain–computer interfaces (BCIs) into telemedicine systems signifies a noteworthy progression in the provision of remote healthcare services providing tailored and efficacious interventions for neurological and psychiatric ailments. Figure 14.3 shows how the brain computer have interfaced. The goal of this integration is to improve monitoring, therapy, and diagnostic capacities by smoothly integrating these technologies into telemedicine systems.

14.4.2.1 *Software Development*

Telemedicine platforms need to be equipped with specialized software that can interface with Neurofeedback and BCI devices. This software should be user friendly for both healthcare providers and patients allowing for easy setup, calibration, and data visualization during remote sessions.

14.4.2.2 *Device Compatibility*

The compatibility of telemedicine platforms with various Neurofeedback and BCI devices is crucial. These devices may include brain implants, fNIRS sensors, and EEG headsets. For patients and healthcare professionals, flexibility and accessibility are made possible by ensuring compatibility with various hardware choices.

14.4.3 Remote Neurofeedback Sessions: Accessibility and Convenience

A new way to get and benefit from neurofeedback therapy without having to travel in person to medical institutions is through Remote Neurofeedback Sessions. This section examines the ways in which telemedicine platforms that incorporate neurofeedback can improve patient accessibility and convenience.

14.4.3.1 *Geographical Accessibility*

Geographic accessibility: Patients can receive remote neurofeedback sessions without having to travel to clinics or hospitals. This is especially advantageous for people who live in distant or underdeveloped locations. Patients can overcome geographic limitations to healthcare access by attending therapy sessions from the comfort of their homes.

14.4.3.2 *Reduced Travel Burden*

Decreased Travel Burden: Remote neurofeedback sessions make traveling to medical facilities less taxing for people with limited mobility, trouble getting around, or hectic schedules. As a result, patients stick to treatment plans more closely and experience less stress from traveling to and from appointments.

14.4.4 Challenges in Telemedicine Implementation

Many people may not have access to dependable internet connections or the right equipment for telemedicine consultations, which makes it difficult for them to take part in remote healthcare, especially in underdeveloped or rural locations. Due to the fact that underprivileged communities may find it difficult to use telemedicine platforms or obtain remote healthcare, disparities in access to technology and digital literacy may make already existing healthcare inequalities worse. Healthcare providers face ambiguity over licensure, reimbursement, liability, and privacy compliance due to the variability of telemedicine rules across different countries and their constant development. Data security and privacy violations are problems when transmitting sensitive patient information across digital networks. To protect patient data and adhere to laws like HIPAA, healthcare providers need to have strong cybersecurity protections in place.

14.4.5 Opportunities in Telemedicine Implementation

Especially for those who reside in rural or isolated places, telemedicine provides a way to get over geographic restrictions and improve access to healthcare services. No travel is required for patients to visit with professionals and receive specialized care. Healthcare providers can obtain objective neurophysiological data through BCI-enabled telemedicine platforms, which can then be used to inform the creation of individualized treatment programs for patients. Clinicians can maximize therapeutic results, evaluate progress over time, and customize interventions to address specific cognitive or motor deficiencies by evaluating brain signals. In particular, for those with long-term neurological disorders, BCI technology offers a promising approach to enhance therapeutic outcomes.

Cognitive deficits, epilepsy, and Parkinson's disease can all be remotely monitored with the help of BCI. Using brain–computer interface (BCI) equipment, patients can record brain signals that can be sent, remotely, to medical professionals for diagnosis and study. BCI technology makes it possible for people with motor difficulties to receive rehabilitation remotely. Distance-based individualized rehabilitation programs are made possible by the ability for patients to engage with virtual worlds and complete exercises under the supervision of medical specialists using BCI-controlled equipment. BCI facilitates successful communication for those with significant motor limitations, including locked-in syndrome or ALS [17].

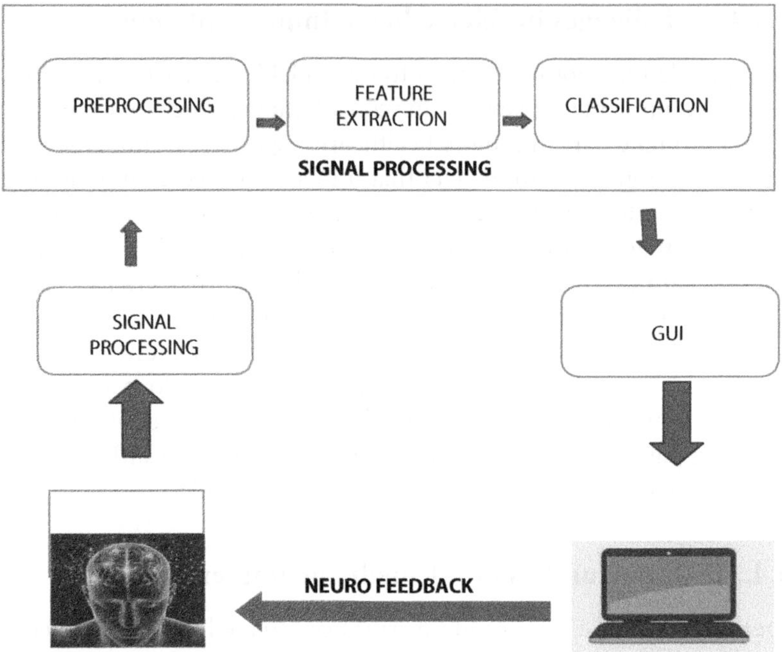

Figure 14.3 Brain–computer interface.

BCI technologies enable patients to communicate with caregivers and healthcare providers remotely by converting brain signals into text or speech. This increases patient autonomy and facilitates communication. More diagnostic data based on brain activity can be provided by BCI, which can improve teleconsultation experiences. For example, BCI enables doctors to monitor patients' emotional states or cognitive reactions in real time during mental health consultations offering insightful information for diagnosis and therapy planning. Reducing the need for frequent in-person visits, patients can participate in cognitive training and mental health interventions from the comfort of their homes by obtaining real-time feedback on their brain signals.

BCI can give crucial information regarding a patient's neurological condition in emergency scenarios when they are unable to communicate vocally or physically. When emergency responders have portable BCI equipment at their disposal, they can evaluate brain function fast and make well-informed judgments about the severity of neurological injuries or impairments. Researchers can obtain neurophysiological data from participants who are spread out geographically using BCI technology to enable remote data collection for clinical research and trials. By widening the scope of research and improving the diversity of participant groups, this accelerates the development of novel treatments and produces more thorough results. Those with severe motor limitations or communication difficulties can now receive telemedicine treatments because of BCI technology. BCI-controlled interfaces improve accessibility to healthcare by enabling patients who would have trouble using conventional input devices, such as keyboards or touchscreens, to interact with medical professionals and take part in remote counseling. With BCI, brain activity can be continuously monitored giving telemedicine practitioners important information about a patient's neurological condition. The ability to remotely evaluate mental health, emotional condition, and cognitive performance allows medical professionals to make more precise diagnoses and individualized treatment regimens [1]. This continuous feedback loop makes this possible. BCI is an essential communication tool in telemedicine for individuals with illnesses like locked-in syndrome or ALS. BCI improves communication and encourages greater patient participation in remote consultations by converting brain signals into text or spoken output, allowing these people to communicate their feelings, ideas, and medical concerns to healthcare professionals. Neurological rehabilitation patients can engage with virtual environments, carry out motor tasks, and get real-time feedback on their progress using BCI-controlled devices. This allows for improved rehabilitation results in terms of independence and continuity of treatment.

14.5 Blockchain Technology in Virtual Healthcare

Sensitive patient data are extremely safe to be stored on blockchain due to its decentralized and unchangeable nature. Data integrity is guaranteed by the fact that every block in the blockchain has a cryptographic hash of the one before it. The Blockchain opportunities in healthcare was shown in Figure 14.4. Patients can improve privacy by having more control over their health information and allowing healthcare providers access when needed. Many parties, including patients, healthcare professionals, insurers, and pharmacists, are frequently involved in virtual healthcare. Blockchain can help with interoperability by offering a safe, standardized platform for health data exchange between various systems. In addition to lowering administrative burden, this can enhance care coordination.

14.5.1 The Role of Blockchain in Virtual Healthcare

Blockchain technology is revolutionizing a number of industries, and its promise in healthcare—especially in the area of virtual care—is becoming more widely acknowledged. Blockchain essentially provides an immutable, decentralized ledger system that allows safe, open transactions without the need for middlemen [21]. This special combination of characteristics addresses important issues with data security, interoperability, and patient-centered care, and has the potential to transform virtual healthcare. Safeguarding patient data confidentiality and privacy is one of the main uses of blockchain in virtual healthcare. Vulnerabilities in traditional healthcare systems include centralized databases that are open to intrusions and hacks. Additionally, blockchain helps various healthcare systems communicate with each other, which is essential for smooth information sharing in virtual care settings. Smart contracts, or self-executing contracts with the terms of the agreement explicitly put into code, are another application made possible by blockchain technology. Smart contracts have the potential to automate a number of patient care tasks in the virtual healthcare setting, including making appointments, processing insurance claims, and billing.

Blockchain can help with the safe and unchangeable transfer of diagnostic pictures and medical records during telemedicine sessions. The information shared during virtual encounters is private and unmodified, so patients and clinicians can feel secure in that knowledge. Blockchain facilitates the ownership and control of health data by patients, hence supporting a patient-centric approach to healthcare delivery. Individualized and well-coordinated care might result from patients' ease of sharing their medical history with several physicians. Although incorporating blockchain technology into virtual healthcare has many potential advantages, there are drawbacks as well, including scalability, regulatory compliance, and interoperability with current systems.

14.5.2 Enhancing Virtual Health Practices with Blockchain

Blockchain technology's potential to improve virtual health practices signifies a profound paradigm shift in the administration, accessibility, and security of medical data. The distributed ledger technology known as blockchain—which is frequently confused with cryptocurrencies like Bitcoin—offers decentralization, immutability, and transparency. Blockchain has the potential to completely transform the virtual healthcare space in a number of ways, including telemedicine services and patient data management.

Blockchain uses decentralization and cryptographic techniques to protect privacy and security of data. It is very difficult for unauthorized parties to access or tamper with patient health records stored on a blockchain since the data are encrypted and dispersed across a network of computers [20]. An unchangeable audit trail of all transactions with the data is produced by the blockchain, where every transaction is time stamped and connected to every other one. By doing this, the risk of data breaches is decreased, and patient confidentiality is improved. A transparent and auditable platform for exchanging research data and clinical trial findings is what blockchain promises to provide for medical innovation and research. Novel cures and therapies can be discovered more quickly because of researchers' safe access to anonymized patient data kept on the blockchain. Patients' involvement and participation in research projects can also be promoted by blockchain-based incentives, such as token prizes for providing data or taking part in clinical trials.

Blockchain's core features, including decentralization, cryptographic hashing, and immutable recordkeeping, address the critical issues of data security and privacy in virtual healthcare. Patient health records, treatment histories, and other sensitive medical information are securely stored and encrypted on a decentralized ledger making it nearly impossible for unauthorized parties to access or tamper with the data. This heightened level of security instills trust among patients and healthcare providers fostering a more secure virtual healthcare ecosystem. Interoperability remains a significant challenge in healthcare, particularly in virtual health settings where multiple platforms and systems need to seamlessly exchange data. Blockchain technology facilitates interoperability by providing a standardized, secure, and transparent framework for sharing healthcare data across disparate systems and stakeholders.

The main issues that blockchain addresses are tracing pharmaceuticals and medications along the supply chain, monitoring the whereabouts of infected patients, confirming the qualifications of doctors, and safeguarding medical information. To promote the sharing and viewing of patient data and the creation of a collaborative treatment plan, the decentralized application enabled by blockchain features an easy-to-use website. By utilizing digital IDs, participants' identities are authenticated and verified [5]. Digital health identities of patients and healthcare professionals that register with telemedicine applications are preserved by means of a Registry smart contract. Public encryption and signing keys generated after user registration are used by the registry to save provider phone numbers and email addresses.

To grant authorization for data access, blockchain employs an exchange system based on tokens. Logging all user requests and interactions on the portal is done by smart contracts for data access. It records which users, by whom, and when, exchange or stop sharing certain data with one another.

A face-to-face meeting between patients and physicians is necessary for effective remote treatment. Direct-to-consumer and business-to-business business formats are used in telemedicine services [16]. While the later model involves caregivers participating in consultation and medical education services by utilizing systems that permit audio and video conferencing, the previous approach allows patients to speak with doctors directly about their health concerns. Additionally, blockchain allows telemedicine applications to give all involved parties a unified and consistent picture of electronic documents. EHR transparency and visibility help in tracking down patients' medical histories to provide appropriate care. Physicians have traditionally viewed the use of in-home medical kits and gadgets to aid in self-diagnosis in a non-clinical setting as less reliable due to the lack of transparency and awareness regarding the provenance of medical equipment. This problem was resolved by blockchain technology, which offers fully visible and unchangeable record transactions for testing kit ownership and performance on a distributed ledger. Smart contracts are used to track the reputation scores of all medical equipment and test kits. Due to their single point of management, personal records on typical cloud-based telemedicine systems are vulnerable. The data owner has the ability to control their own data thanks to the decentralized blockchain technology. Smart contracts, in compliance with the patient consent policy, register patients' data and grant users access to it.

To guarantee non-repudiated safe transactions, blockchain facilitates digitally signed automatic payments. Blockchain eliminates the need for a third party in the payment settlement process when compared to

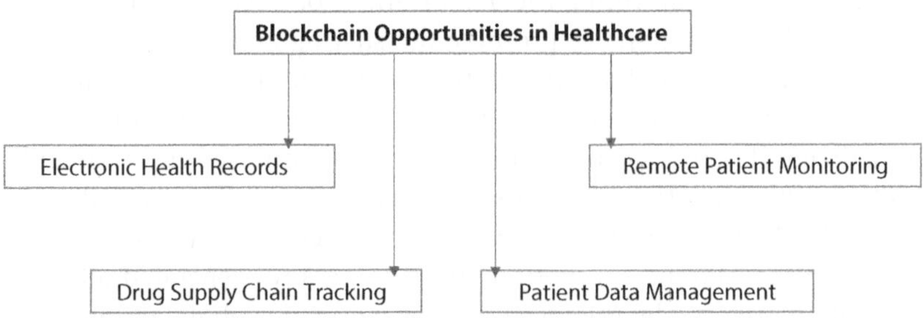

Figure 14.4 Blockchain opportunities in healthcare.

conventional centralized systems. By doing this, Blockchain hopes to win over patients' trust. Furthermore, blockchain facilitates micropayments through the provision of cryptocurrency tokens for payment. The method is improved to be more safe, quick, auditable, and transparent via the direct transfer of cryptocurrency tokens to the service providers' wallets. Maintaining patient data security and privacy is one of the primary issues facing the healthcare industry. An immutable, transparent, and better security distributed ledger system is provided by blockchain technology. To lower the danger of data breaches and illegal access, patient information, clinical trial data, and medical research findings can be safely maintained on the blockchain [20]. By allowing researchers and healthcare professionals to safely access patient data, this technology gives patients autonomy over their health information. Blockchain makes it easier for various healthcare stakeholders to exchange data and work together seamlessly. Accurate and current patient data are accessible in real time, thanks to its ability to integrate diverse systems, including insurance providers, laboratory systems, and electronic health records (EHRs). Efficient data exchange has the potential to enhance patient outcomes, decrease medical errors, and improve care coordination. Clinical trials and medical research could undergo a Transformation, thanks to blockchain technology. Researchers can automate payment, data gathering, and consent management procedures by utilizing smart contracts. This improves transparency and confidence in the research process while also cutting down on administrative overhead. Additionally, blockchain makes it possible for study findings to be shared safely and effectively encouraging international researcher collaboration. Because blockchain is decentralized, it can improve supply chain management in the pharmaceutical sector. Blockchain maintains transparency and prevents fake goods from reaching the market by recording a drug's complete lifecycle, from production to delivery. While authorities can quickly identify and recall tainted or defective drugs, patients can feel confident in the genuineness and quality of the medications they get. Medical records may be accessed securely and easily by patients and healthcare professionals, thanks to blockchain-based EHR solutions.

14.6 Telemedicine for Personalized Patient Care

Patients can consult with doctors online, thanks to telemedicine, which eliminates the need for in-person appointments and allows for more individualized interactions. People who have trouble moving around, live in remote locations, or need frequent follow-ups can especially benefit from this [17]. Connecting patients with medical professionals who might not be available locally through telemedicine increases access to specialist treatment. In spite of the fact that the necessary knowledge may not always be easily accessible, this guarantees that patients receive individualized care catered to their unique medical needs. Providers can monitor patients' vital signs, symptoms, and adherence to treatment plans from a distance with the use of telemedicine systems, which frequently come equipped with remote monitoring features. Better health results result from the ongoing monitoring's ability to tailor treatment regimens depending on current data [3]. Telemedicine allows medical professionals to create individualized treatment programs based on the medical history, preferences, lifestyle, and specific requirements of each patient. Better patient outcomes result from these customized strategies' increased patient participation and treatment adherence. Tools and educational materials that enable patients to actively manage their health are frequently included in telemedicine platforms. Telemedicine supports better patient participation and health literacy, which results in better-informed healthcare decisions, by offering individualized education and support. Without requiring face-to-face consultations, telemedicine allows medical professionals to electronically prescribe drugs and schedule refills.

14.6.1 The Personalized Touch of Telemedicine

"The Personalized Touch of Telemedicine" describes how patients can receive customized and individualized care using telemedicine, even if it is a digital and remote modality. In the past, receiving medical care has frequently been linked to in-person consultations and direct communication between patients and healthcare professionals. But by using technology to provide individualized treatment from a distance, telemedicine has completely changed this paradigm [18]. Based on each patient's particular requirements and preferences, telemedicine enables medical professionals to design individualized treatment programs. Virtual consultations enable healthcare providers to perform comprehensive evaluations, talk about medical histories, and work with patients to create individualized care plans that suit their needs and objectives. Telemedicine enables multidisciplinary collaboration among healthcare experts, hence facilitating holistic and thorough care. By means of virtual care team meetings and teleconsultations, healthcare professionals from diverse specializations can exchange ideas, synchronize treatment plans, and guarantee that every facet of the patient's health is attended to in a coordinated fashion, thereby delivering a customized and comprehensive approach to patient care. Telemedicine solutions encourage patient-centered communication and engagement even in the absence of in-person interactions. To connect with patients, address their issues, and develop trust—all of which are crucial for the development of successful therapeutic relationships—providers use secure texting, video conferencing, and virtual visits.

14.6.2 Personalized Telemedicine Services

The healthcare sector is always changing to meet the needs of the contemporary world. The advancements in medical technology present great opportunities for bettering lives from telemedicine and AI-assisted diagnosis to personalized treatment. We will look at how these new technologies are influencing healthcare in the future as well as the advantages they offer to both patients and physicians in this blog article. Undoubtedly, advancements such as these will have a significant influence on every facet of the patient experience ranging from the precision of diagnosis to the prevention of illness and the results of therapy. This includes closing gaps in access to technology that can significantly enhance care capacity. With the development of personalized medicine in recent years, the field of medicine has advanced quickly. Using their distinct genetic composition, way of life, and medical background, these individuals receive customized therapy [19]. Improving patient outcomes through more effective therapies with fewer side effects is one of the main advantages of personalized medicine. By preventing needless surgeries and treatments, this technology can also aid in the efficient use of healthcare resources. Additionally, personalized medicine has created new opportunities for investigation and learning, which will help in the development of novel medications and treatments.

Nowadays, patients who have transportation or distance-related obstacles can receive better care because of technological breakthroughs that enable remote consultations and testing. Through the elimination of in-person visits and a decrease in hospital readmissions, telemedicine can lower healthcare expenses [8]. Further, if access to healthcare is scarce, telemedicine may be able to help with medical needs in underserved or rural areas. With its ability to provide high-quality care to a wider spectrum of patients and guarantee treatment access for all, telemedicine is quickly emerging as a crucial instrument in contemporary healthcare. Healthcare providers are using telemedicine increasingly frequently to expand their services outside of typical hospital settings because of its accessibility and cost-saving advantages.

The utilization of state-of-the-art technology in conjunction with superior network services enables individuals to enhance healthcare delivery and expand accessibility. A more beneficial technological advancement is telemedicine, which can help people receive preventive care and enhance their long-term health. People who are unable to pay for or receive high-quality care because of financial or local obstacles should particularly be aware of this. The accessibility, effectiveness, and structure of healthcare could all be enhanced by using telehealth. This field of study is expanding, although being quite young. For example, telemonitoring vital signs and telephone-based treatment lower hospitalization and mortality rates while enhancing quality of life in patients with heart disease. When it is convenient for both the patient and the physician, telemedicine can provide medical treatment.

- **Convenience and Accessibility**
  The greater accessibility and convenience that telemedicine provides is one of its most noticeable effects on the patient experience. For their medical appointments, patients no longer need to drive great distances or wait in packed waiting rooms. People can now obtain healthcare services from the convenience of their homes or places of employment, which will save them time and lessen the anxiety that comes with going to the doctor on a regular basis.
- **Personalized Care Experiences**
  Healthcare professionals can tailor patient care experiences via telemedicine by taking into account the requirements and preferences of each patient. More focused interactions between patients and doctors during virtual consultations enable the creation of individualized treatment plans and treatments that take into account the needs and goals of each patient. The primary goals of digital transformation in healthcare are to enhance patient outcomes, experience, and engagement. Using cloud-based calling, meeting, messaging, and video solutions—ideally combined into a single application—to improve access between healthcare providers and their patients is a crucial component of this [7]. This is important since the focus of care is not always where the doctor is, but rather where the patient is. By doing this, doctors may reach a wider audience and serve patients anywhere there is an internet connection. Three major factors

> determine how telehealth is being adopted. Enhancing patient access to care is the first priority. Providers can safely interact with patients via their preferred channel eliminating distance through telehealth [8]. It facilitates real-time consultations between physicians and patients as well as virtual check-ins and distant evaluation services. Second, it eliminates obstacles like patient travel and other elements (like packed waiting areas) that cause appointment start times to be delayed enabling healthcare providers to assess a greater number of patients in less time. Third, telehealth is socializing and connecting doctors and patients in ways that are distinct from an in-person visit, which can improve the doctor–patient relationship. A doctor can evaluate patients' problems and physical environs during a more concentrated and immersive interaction.

Physicians, many of whom are seeking a more balanced work–life balance and the ability to assist telehealth sessions remotely themselves, also benefit from this personalization in addition to the patient. When choosing a telehealth solution, seek out those with dynamic call-routing capabilities. These will allow specialized teams to handle all calls linked to telehealth services, such as in-person consultations, future scheduling, or inpatient requirement triage evaluation. A technology that enables voicemails to be transcribed and read rather than just heard will also contribute to a quicker response time from patients [5]. By automating patients' access to recorded FAQ responses or current information, multi-level IVR solutions let providers support patient self-service and contribute to better patient experiences. It is also critical to provide support for remote workers. Clinic employees will find it simple to move to a temporary or permanent work-from-home arrangement, thanks to a flexible telehealth platform that offers the same in-office phone, video, and messaging capabilities. Modern healthcare is starting to rely heavily on telemedicine or the distant provision of medical treatments via digital communication. Benefits from it go beyond boundaries; patients can consult with doctors from the comfort of their own homes.

Telemedicine has grown significantly as a result of the widespread use of cellphones and high-speed internet, and it is now a practical choice for primary care, managing chronic illnesses, providing mental health assistance, and even after surgery. Patients now have unprecedented access to healthcare services, thanks to telemedicine, especially when it comes to virtual visits and remote consultations [12]. With the development of telemedicine technology, people may now consult with their doctors without leaving their homes saving time spent in waiting rooms and avoiding travel. This convenience is particularly helpful for people who have trouble moving around or who live in rural, underdeveloped areas with little access to medical facilities. Furthermore, by facilitating real-time direct communication between patients and healthcare providers, telemedicine promotes tailored care. Patients can have open and honest conversations about their symptoms, medical history, and concerns during virtual sessions.

Further improving continuity of treatment is telemedicine, which allows patients to continue seeing their doctors for follow-ups and check-ups without physically visiting the clinic. Patients who have chronic diseases that need for constant monitoring and care will find this feature especially beneficial. To further enhance comprehensive and individualized care, telemedicine platforms frequently interface with electronic health records (EHRs) enabling doctors to easily access and update patient data during virtual consultations. AI-driven chatbots and virtual assistants are revolutionizing patient interaction and communication within the healthcare sector. These smart digital tools are always on call, offering prompt answers to patient questions and customized health recommendations based on patient information and pre-programmed algorithms. Chatbots can help patients comprehend their symptoms, make recommendations for self-care, and advise them on when to seek emergency medical intervention. Additionally, they can point patients in the direction of relevant materials that are catered to their particular medical issues, including educational articles, films, or support groups. Chatbots save healthcare professionals time by automating these exchanges, freeing them up to concentrate on more complicated patient cases, and providing more individualized treatment for patients with urgent needs [11]. The way healthcare organizations monitor and maximize health outcomes is being revolutionized by data analytics. Healthcare professionals can learn about patient trends, risk factors, and common health conditions by analyzing massive datasets from insurance claims, electronic health records, and other sources. Healthcare providers can intervene with tailored support and reminders when they see trends of non-adherence to treatment regimens through data analytics. This strategy saves money for both the patient and the healthcare provider by lowering needless medical expenses and improving patient outcomes. Healthcare practitioners can increase patient engagement, contentment, and overall health outcomes by utilizing technology in these ways to provide more individualized and patient-centered experiences.

14.7 Future Directions of Telemedicine in Healthcare

Particularly in reaction to the COVID-19 epidemic, telemedicine has grown and been adopted quite quickly; nonetheless, its evolution is far from complete. The use of telemedicine in healthcare could go in the following areas in the future. A more proactive and individualized approach to healthcare delivery will be possible as wearable technology advances and becomes more widely used [10]. Patients' vital signs, activity levels, and other health indicators can be monitored in real time with the help of telemedicine platforms that can easily interact with these gadgets. Telemedicine platforms can benefit from the assistance of AI-powered algorithms in areas like patient monitoring, treatment recommendations, and diagnosis. The quality and effectiveness of care delivery can be eventually improved by these systems' ability to analyze massive datasets, find trends, and forecast results. With their ability to create immersive experiences for both patients and clinicians, VR and AR technologies hold the potential to completely transform telemedicine. By removing geographical obstacles and improving the delivery of specialized care, these technologies can enable virtual consultations, medical training simulations, and even remote surgery. Primary care and mental health services have been the traditional areas of concentration for telemedicine; nevertheless, there is increasing room for growth into specialist care settings including cardiology, dermatology, and cancer. Improved access to expertise for patients in underserved areas can be achieved through advanced telemedicine technologies that provide virtual consultations with professionals [6]. For patients recovering from surgery or those with chronic diseases, telemedicine can be extremely helpful in providing remote patient monitoring. To enable preventive interventions and lessen the need for frequent in-person visits, connected devices and mobile apps can gather patient data and securely communicate it to healthcare providers. Further legislative support and payment for telemedicine services could result from persistent lobbying and policy modifications. Encouraging healthcare professionals to utilize telemedicine more extensively can be achieved by providing greater financial incentives and clear guidelines, which will ensure that all patients have equitable access to care.

The COVID-19 pandemic has provided valuable insights that could guide future approaches to public health emergencies. One such lesson is the critical role that telemedicine plays in preserving continuity of treatment while reducing the spread of infectious diseases. As a crucial part of providing healthcare during emergencies, preparedness plans may include telemedicine. Global access to healthcare treatments for those living in distant or underdeveloped areas is possible with telemedicine's capacity to cross national borders. The global expansion of telemedicine efforts can be facilitated by partnerships among governments, technology corporations, and healthcare professionals.

Significant advancements in telemedicine have been made, with the COVID-19 pandemic serving as a major catalyst [3]. As more people and healthcare professionals become aware of the affordability, ease, and convenience of virtual care, this trend is anticipated to continue. Growing throughout different medical specialties and geographical areas, telemedicine is anticipated to become a crucial component of healthcare delivery [13]. Technological developments will be a major factor in how telemedicine develops in the future. Future of telemedicine in healthcare was shown in the Figure 14.5.These developments in technology will improve the range and caliber of telemedicine services, allowing for the provision of more thorough and individualized care. Integrations between telemedicine and other healthcare technologies, including data analytics platforms, AI algorithms, remote patient monitoring systems, and electronic health records (EHRs), are anticipated. Care that is more thorough and well coordinated will result from this integration's ability to facilitate easy information sharing, real-time monitoring, and data-driven insights. Although primary care settings were where telemedicine first became popular, specialist care settings are starting to utilize it more and more. Telemedicine is being embraced by specialties like cardiology, radiology, psychiatry, and dermatology to decrease wait times and provide access to expert care. Hybrid care models, which integrate in-person and virtual visits, are anticipated to play a significant role in the future of telemedicine [14]. Using telemedicine for routine follow-ups, chronic disease management, post-operative care, and patient education, along with in-person visits saved for more complex cases or procedures requiring physical examinations, is a blended approach that healthcare providers can adopt to improve specialist collaboration.

Concerning their adaptation to the telemedicine scenario, regulatory organizations and insurers have made great progress. Future legislation and payment practices to encourage and promote the use of telemedicine are probably going to see additional developments. Standardized protocols, higher reimbursement rates for telemedicine services, and broader coverage are a few examples of this. By facilitating access to care for marginalized populations—such as those living in rural or isolated places or in areas with inadequate healthcare resources—telemedicine offers the potential to reduce healthcare.

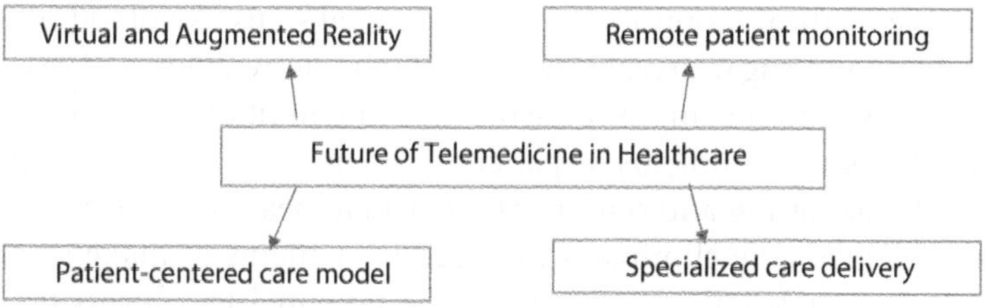

Figure 14.5 Future of telemedicine in healthcare.

14.7.1 Virtual Reality and Augmented Reality

Users can engage with and experience a simulated world by submerging themselves in a computer-generated environment through virtual reality. Virtual reality technology has various applications in telemedicine. Virtual reality simulations offer immersive learning opportunities for medical students, residents, and healthcare professionals. In a lifelike virtual setting, they can rehearse surgeries, medicinal interventions, and diagnostic procedures, building their confidence and skills without endangering patient safety. Through immersive experiences, virtual reality (VR) is utilized to help patients who are in pain during medical operations or to manage chronic pain. Additionally, by involving patients in interactive exercises and activities customized to meet their needs, VR-based rehabilitation programs aid in the recovery of patients following operations or accidents.

Telemedicine is becoming more and more commonplace, thanks to rapid breakthroughs in big data, analytics, and connected care technology [12]. Consumer-to-provider telemedicine is finally emerging as a result of the widespread use of smart devices and the growing accessibility of the internet, which is greatly facilitating teleconsultations. As smart and connected fitness wearables and telehealth programs, like Practo, Portea, Lybrate, and others, gain popularity, it is clear that the market is growing beyond the confines of basic healthcare access. While Sweden, the Netherlands, and Singapore already have high rates of adoption of connected care technology, other developing markets, such as Brazil, Russia, and India, are seeking to improve their electronic health records (EHRs) and clinical decision support systems (CDS).

14.7.2 Remote Patient Management

Using a variety of tools and sensors, RPM enables medical professionals to remotely monitor patients' vital signs, health measures, and factors unique to their particular diseases. These could be fitness trackers, smartwatches, or wearable medical monitors that measure vital signs like blood pressure, heart rate, blood sugar, oxygen saturation, and activity level. RPM facilitates proactive monitoring of patients' health condition and early identification of possible problems or patterns that may call for intervention by consistently gathering and sending these data to healthcare providers.

Since telemedicine eliminates the need for patients to make in-person hospital visits or lengthy travel, it has the potential to address the issue of patients always having access to high-quality healthcare at their leisure [2]. Telemedicine, a patient-centered approach to high-quality healthcare services, has made it possible to provide healthcare more consistently and fairly across national borders as well as across continents. Apart from enabling remote access, telemedicine also facilitates doctor-to-doctor consultations and allows practitioners to consult with specialists from any location. By assisting patients in keeping up with care plans and check-ups, it also plays a critical role in fostering patient involvement. This improves patient care and lowers expenses for both the patient and the healthcare service provider.

While its applications were primarily used to connect healthcare providers with specialists, referral hospitals, and tertiary care centers, telemedicine has historically been associated with improving healthcare access to low-income populations, underserved communities, and rural populations. Scaling up the use of low-cost telemedicine applications is necessary, despite the fact that these applications have shown to be workable, therapeutically beneficial, and sustainable in these kinds of settings [20]. A few issues still need to be resolved. Delivering efficient and seamless telemedicine services requires ICT literacy as well as the capacity to operate the equipment in accordance with timetables and patient needs. To guarantee a well-organized and reliable system, it is also essential to document usage, treatment methods, and results. Consequently, educating staff members on how to provide telemedicine services and how to set up and maintain telemedicine equipment will help the sector to grow. Second, it is imperative to address human and cultural variables, such as patients' and healthcare professionals' reluctance to accept services that deviate from customs or native norms. The benefits of these technology developments and the evolving healthcare landscape can be raised awareness of through education. The absence of a global legal framework and varying government regulations that permit medical practitioners to provide care across borders is an additional barrier impeding the broad implementation of telemedicine.

To increase the prominence of telemedicine market trends in the future, a global effort is being made to solve difficulties driven by law and policy, investment and reimbursement, adoption, and cyber-security. Ayushman Bharat Scheme, the largest health financing scheme launched by the Indian government, along with the establishment of NITI Aayog in several states and ISRO's support for advanced satellite technology, have all contributed to the country's push for improved patient care practices and outreach.

References

1. Hajesmaeel-Gohari, S. and Bahaadinbeigy, K., The most used questionnaires for evaluating telemedicine services. *BMC Med. Inf. Decis. Making*, 21, 87–88, 2021 Dec.
2. Wilson, L.S. and Maeder, A.J., Recent directions in telemedicine: review of trends in research and practice. *Healthcare Inf. Res.*, 21, 14, 2015 Oct.
3. Lupton, D. and Maslen, S., Telemedicine and the senses: a review. *Sociol. Health Illness*, 56–56, 2017 Nov.
4. Sarhan, F., Telemedicine in healthcare. 1: exploring its uses, benefits and disadvantages, *Nurs. Times*, 2009 Oct 1.
5. Sapci, A.H. and Sapci, H.A., Digital continuous healthcare and disruptive medical technologies: m-Health and telemedicine skills training for data-driven healthcare. *J. Telemed. Telecare*, 25, 78–78, 2019 Dec.
6. Magann, E.F., McKelvey, S.S., Hitt, W.C., Smith, M.V., Azam, G.A., Lowery, C.L., The use of telemedicine in obstetrics: a review of the literature. *Obstet. Gynecol. Surv.*, 32–32, 2011 Mar 1.
7. Palozzi, G., Schettini, I., Chirico, A., Enhancing the sustainable goal of access to healthcare: findings from a literature review on telemedicine employment in rural areas. *Sustainability*, 12, 18–19, 2020 Jan.
8. Brown, E.M., The Ontario telemedicine network: a case report. *Telemed. e-Health*, 67–68, 2013 May 1.
9. Jampani, N.D., Nutalapati, R., Dontula, B.S., Boyapati, R., Applications of teledentistry: a literature review and update. *J. Int. Soc. Prev. Community Dent.*, 21–22, 2011 Jul.
10. Daniel, S.J. and Kumar, S., Teledentistry: a key component in access to care. *J. Evid. Base Dent. Pract.*, 45–45, 2014 Jun 1.
11. Kamsu-Foguem, B. and Foguem, C., Telemedicine and mobile health with integrative medicine in developing countries. *Health Policy Technol.*, 2014 89–90, Dec 1.
12. Bashshur, R., Shannon, G., Krupinski, E., Grigsby, J., The taxonomy of telemedicine. *Telemed. e-Health*, 34–34, 2011 Jul 1.
13. Weinstein, R.S., Lopez, A.M., Joseph, B.A., Erps, K.A., Holcomb, M., Barker, G.P., Krupinski, E.A., Telemedicine, telehealth, and mobile health applications that work: opportunities and barriers. *Am. J. Med.*, 56–56, 2014 Mar 1.

14. Wang, X., Zhang, Z., Zhao, J., Shi, Y., Impact of telemedicine on healthcare service system considering patients' choice. *Discrete Dynam. Nat. Soc.*, 2019, 94–95, 2019 Jan 1.
15. Kadir, M.A., Role of telemedicine in healthcare during COVID-19 pandemic in developing countries. *Telehealth Med. Today*, 89–90, 2020 Apr 3.
16. Mars, M., Telemedicine and advances in urban and rural healthcare delivery in Africa. *Prog. Cardiovasc. Dis.*, 156–157, 2013 Nov 1.
17. Heinzelmann, P.J., Lugn, N.E., Kvedar, J.C., Telemedicine in the future. *J. Telemed. Telecare*, 11, 143–145, 2005 Dec.
18. Bajowala, S.S., Milosch, J., Bansal, C., Telemedicine pays billing and coding update. *Curr. Allergy Asthma Rep.*, 20, 67–68, 2020 Oct.
19. Lin, J.C., Kavousi, Y., Sullivan, B., Stevens, C., Analysis of outpatient telemedicine reimbursement in an integrated healthcare system. *Ann. Vasc. Surg.*, 120–122, 2020 May 1.
20. Javaid, M., Haleem, A., Singh, R.P., Suman, R., Significance of Quality 4.0 towards comprehensive enhancement in manufacturing sector. *Sens. Int.*, 134–134, 2021 Jun 24.
21. Salehahmadi, Z. and Hajialiasghari, F., Telemedicine in Iran: chances and challenges. *World J. Plast. Surg.*, 67–68, 2013 Jan.

15

Blockchain Algorithm: Revolutionizing Healthcare Systems

Ritika Awasthi[1,2*] **and Arvind Tiwari**[2†]

[1]*Department of Computer Science, GD Rungta College of Science and Technology, Bhilai, India*
[2]*Department of IT and Computer Science, Dr. C.V. Raman University, Bilaspur, India*

Abstract

Over the past few years, there has been a notable growth of interest in applying blockchain technology to the healthcare sector, with the potential to address significant challenges in electronic health record systems. This chapter sheds light on existing facts of blockchain applications in healthcare that excavate the benefits and limitations of integrating blockchain technologies to enhance healthcare operations. The primary aim is to showcase the diverse applications of this technology highlighting current research themes and identifying potential areas for future exploration in the healthcare domain. The chapter initiates with a thorough background study of blockchain and its features, followed by a comprehensive literature review of selected articles to illuminate prevalent research themes in blockchain-driven healthcare systems. Further, it discusses different algorithms, such as POA and POW, their attributes and level of accuracy, and then proceeds to outline major application areas and the corresponding solutions that blockchain presents within healthcare systems. In the final section of the chapter, the discussion provides valuable insights into the constraints and challenges associated with the integration of blockchain technology into healthcare. Furthermore, it offers a glimpse into future directions for research in this dynamic field emphasizing the need for ongoing exploration and innovation. As the healthcare sector stands on the edge of a technological revolution, understanding the heterogeneous implications of blockchain technology becomes paramount for shaping a more efficient and secure healthcare ecosystem.

**Corresponding author*: ritikaawasthi1612@gmail.com
†*Corresponding author*: Arvind.tiwari@cvru.ac.in

Parul Dubey, Mangala Madankar, Pushkar Dubey and Bui Thanh Hung (eds.) The Impact of Algorithmic Technologies on Healthcare, (313–348) © 2025 Scrivener Publishing LLC

Keywords: Blockchain technology, healthcare, POA algorithm, POW algorithm, hyperledger fabric consensus

15.1 Introduction

Blockchain is an instance or accounting system that assists with organizing and storing information in time-stamped blocks. It works primarily in a decentralized fashion across all computing networks that are connected via cryptography. The blockchain's abilities were first introduced in the financial space, but they may eventually find applications in other sectors. However, there is still a lack of development in application settings with effective solution design. Blockchain holds the potential to significantly alter an array of sectors, including the supply chain, wellness, governance, and finance [1]. Potential advantages include decreased expenses and transaction complexity between parties, more security, better regulation, and improved transparency.

Due to the reality of change, the healthcare industry is characterized as being quite traditional, hard to measure, and resistant to new ideas. Privacy concerns, the norms of care, and information security in the healthcare industry have attracted worldwide interest in recent years. The potential of blockchain technologies to solve present issues with information attribution has become increasingly recognized. It could improve current healthcare processes, such as boosting the provision of healthcare services and the standard of care delivered. Blockchain technology in the healthcare industry is predicted to create over 42 million in value and expand at a compound annual growth rate of 71.8% by 2023, in accordance with a recent Market Research Future (MRFR) analysis [2].

There are a number of benefits and challenges associated with the Internet of Things' (IoTs') recent advancements for smart city applications inside the Industry 4.0 framework. One of the key uses of Industry 4.0 that is quickly becoming the standard for Healthcare 4.0 for remote health monitoring is e-healthcare. Industry 4.0 originally included Healthcare 4.0 as a subclass. Several layers make up the Healthcare 4.0 standard, including the edge, fog, cloud storage, and blockchain levels. The primary concerns for e-healthcare systems are privacy preservation and medical data security when processing data via fog computing from the edge layer to the cloud storage layer. Strong security features are provided by the development of blockchain technology in conjunction with edge layer and cloud storage [3].

With numerous built-in features—including distributed ledgers, decentralized storage, authentication, security, and immutability—blockchain technology has transcended hype and found real-world uses in fields like healthcare. Due to strict regulatory requirements like the Health Insurance Portability and Accountability Act of 1996 (HIPAA), blockchain applications in the healthcare industry typically require additional authentication, interoperability, and record-sharing access requirements. Researchers in academia and business are beginning to investigate applications targeted at the healthcare sector, building on the blockchain technologies that are now in use. These uses include identity verification, fraud detection, and smart contracts. Despite these advancements, worries remain since blockchain technology has unique flaws and problems that need to be solved, like mining incentives, mining attacks, and management [4].

However, there is a dearth of experimental work tackling lightweight cryptography with blockchain incorporation. This research proposes an effective structure for protecting medical data processing via the use of blockchain integrated with a cloud storage system. The medical data that was collected at the edge layer was first encrypted with Elliptic Curve Diffie Hellman (ECDH) cryptography. The blockchain then presents the encrypted data that has been stored in cloud storage. The Elliptic Curve Digital Signature Algorithm (ECDSA) has been created with the purpose of creating identities and verifying medical data. The proposed structure performs better in experiments than the most advanced approaches [3].

15.2 How Blockchain can Relate to Healthcare

Blockchain technology's advances in data security, transparency, and efficiency have the potential to completely reshape the healthcare sector. Several applications for it exist, including prescription tracking, health insurance, and device tracking [5]. In addition to improving performance and security, technology can also improve the sharing and maintenance of patient data [6]. However, problems like expenses for implementation and model performance must be rectified [7]. Despite these obstacles, the application of blockchain technology has enormous potential in the healthcare industry; nevertheless, more study is required to completely reap these rewards [8].

Industry experts believe blockchain, a digital ledger technology that securely records constantly growing lists of data recordings and transactions, has the potential to transform the healthcare system. Blockchain has the potential to significantly lower the back office information entry and maintenance costs, improve data accuracy and security, and accelerate the way the medical industry processes data in areas like revenue cycle management, supply chain confirmation, and health information experts believe blockchain, a digital ledger technology that securely maintains ever-expanding lists of data records and transactions, has the potential to completely transform the healthcare system [2].

With its many built-in features—including distributed databases, decentralized storage, authentication, security, and immutability—blockchain technology has transcended hype and found real-world uses in fields like healthcare. Because of strict laws like the Healthcare Insurance Portability and Accountability Act of 1996 (HIPAA), blockchain applications in the healthcare industry usually need stricter authentication, connectivity, and record-sharing requirements. Researchers in academia and business are beginning to investigate applications targeted at healthcare providers, building on the blockchain technologies that are now in use. These uses include identity verification, fraud detection, and smart contracts. Despite those developments, worries remain since blockchain technology has unique drawbacks and issues that need to be resolved, like extraction incentives, mining attacks, and managements [9].

The intricate web of intermediary firms and a lack of transaction traceability are the root causes of numerous issues in the healthcare industry. To name a few: the price of drug discovery continues to rise, 50% of clinical trials are never released, fragmented healthcare data across several silos significantly affects research and services, and counterfeit and subpar medications continue to be a major issue. These issues could be resolved by blockchain since it offers trust without the need for intermediaries, makes traceability a default characteristic, and unlocks up the possibility to new industries by enabling innovative incentive systems [10]. Blockchain has generated a lot of interest in the field of healthcare due to its potential.

Since its debut nearly a decade ago, the technology known as blockchain has attracted significant interest from a variety of industries, including banking, energy, cybersecurity, and cryptocurrencies. An overview of blockchain's use in healthcare information management and protection is provided in this study. Healthcare researchers benefit from electronic ledgers because it makes it easier for them to securely share patient medical records. Considering that the ledgers are stored on a database that is distributed, the confidentiality associated with genetic code can be guaranteed. Furthermore, patient-centric ledgers can be validated thanks to the blockchain's digital signature feature [11].

15.3 Literature Review

According to ref. [12], an irreversible and decentralized feature of the blockchain is used by the recommended approach to ensure the safety and reliability of patient data. By optimizing the allocation of blockchain resources, SSA improves the efficiency and durability of the data management system. The study demonstrates that this combination approach considerably raises the level of protection of data, reduces the possibility of unwelcome access, and improves the overall functionality of the healthcare data architecture. The viability of the indicated approach has been confirmed via the experimental results, and this further demonstrates that it may have broad opportunities for application across the healthcare sector.

Ref. [13] focuses emphasis on the potential benefits of blockchain's immutable and decentralized structure to enhance the security of information, seamless integration, along management of patients. The benefits of improved clinical trial management, supply chain verification, and lower administrative expenses are also covered in the investigation. On the contrary together, it brings out important obstacles such as costly implementations, requirements for data, compliance with regulations, and sustainability. The examination stresses how crucial it is to wrestle with these challenges when attempting to make full use of the use of blockchain in the healthcare sector. It additionally makes sense that, with careful preparation and collaboration from every relevant party, blockchain could completely change the handling of data and delivery of healthcare.

Ref. [14] suggested an approach that utilizes blockchain technology to ensure the accessibility, privacy, and reliability of personal medical data. The framework reduces vulnerabilities connected to centralized data warehouses by improving data security and privacy, though the implementation uses smart contracts and distributed storage. The research highlights how the immutable ledger of the blockchain system may protect from unwelcome changes ensuring transparency and trust. It also focuses at the challenges, such as compatibility and scaling, in combining blockchain with existing healthcare systems. The authors provide experimental results that highlight the enhanced security and information management capabilities of the framework proving its effectiveness. Overall, the research makes an excellent argument for blockchain's ability to impact medical information security, even though it recognizes that eliminating constitutional and technological barriers will be needed until blockchain is widely used.

[15] This approach greatly improves data integrity by avoiding manipulation and unauthorized modifications using the blockchain's immutable

ledger. The advantages of private blockchain are emphasized in the study, including a stronger commitment to the requirements of HIPAA as well as greater control over data access. Using instances and modeling, the study demonstrates the effectiveness of the framework showing a notable improvement in patient data protection. The research additionally addresses shortcomings such as the need for significant processing capacity and the challenge of connecting a private blockchain with healthcare IT systems. With all factors taken into account, the authors make an excellent argument for the use of confidential blockchain technology in the healthcare sector emphasizing that it has the potential to completely change data security while also bringing up the challenges that need to be solved so it can be widely adopted.

Ref. [16] outlines a blockchain-based framework that secures patient data against influence and illegal access using the distributed and irreversible characteristics of blockchain technology. The framework ensures that only authorized and approved people can access private medical data by setting smart contracts in place. The use of encryption technologies for enhancing data security and guaranteeing that all record modifications are transparent and traceable is emphasized in the research. The authors demonstrate that, when compared with traditional systems, their approach significantly improves data reliability and authenticity through extensive examination and experimental validation. The necessity of regulatory compliance, compatibility with contemporary healthcare infrastructures, and scaling issues additionally feature in the research investigation.

Ref. [17] proposes a blockchain-based approach to improve the network's security, traceability, and transparency enabling organ donation and transplantation. The structure ensures that donor and recipient data are carefully preserved and transparently dealt with by exploiting the unchangeable blockchain and decentralized features inherent in the digital currency blockchain. By automating and streamlining the combination and distribution process, the technology uses smart contracts to cut off delays and boost efficiency. Along with increased safety against fraud and information manipulation, the study involves investigations and simulations that show substantial improvements in organ-corresponding speed and accuracy. There is consideration of challenges including enforcing compliance with healthcare rules and integrating blockchain with contemporary healthcare infrastructure.

Ref. [18] proposes an approach for protecting private patient data from theft and modification by using blockchain's decentralized and irreversible characteristics. The framework guarantees only those with permission may view or modify data by automated data access limitations using the execution of smart contracts. The research emphasizes the use of innovative encryption technologies to enhance data privacy and guarantee the confidentiality of patient data. The study demonstrates significant improvements in the integrity and security of data beyond traditional methods through empirical analysis and examples. The writers additionally explore problems with blockchain networks' scalability, merging them with contemporary healthcare systems, and sticking to regulation. If everything is considered, this study presents an impressive case for the use of blockchain technology for healthcare applications demonstrating its potential to supply an effective, reliable solution.

[19] The authors propose an entirely novel system, which employs federated learning to locally retrain predictive models on mobile devices while preserving individual privacy by avoiding the transmission of raw data. The incorporation of blockchain technology secures the decentralized learning process's security, transparency, and integrity. Closest to the data source, fog computing offers reduced latency as well as efficient data processing. The research shows that the platform anticipates illnesses while maintaining the privacy and confidentiality of user data. In comparison to traditional centralized approaches, the authors' experiments indicate a lower latency and improved predictive accuracy. They also talk about concerns with integration, conformance to regulations, and system scalability. According to the results of this study, this integrated methodology has an enormous opportunity to promote wearable-based predictive healthcare and guarantee a secure and efficient option.

[3] The authors recommend an assortment of inexpensive safety precautions intended for protecting confidential patient information whenever it is being handled without compromising performance. The framework utilizes safe communication protocols and innovative encryption techniques to guarantee the privacy, reliability, and reliability of data. Scalability and decreased calculating overhead are highlighted in the study making the solutions suitable for resource-constrained functions like smartwatches and Internet of Things devices.

Ref. [20] emphasizes the value of limited computational overhead and scalability that qualified the solutions for resource-constrained use like smartwatches and Internet of Things gadgets. In-depth analyses and simulations utilized in the paper demonstrate that the recommended precautions efficiently safeguard medical data while retaining high processing efficiency. Especially compared to traditional security approaches, the results demonstrate an important reduction in processing time as well as resource use. The examination does note some obstacles though, such as connecting with the prevailing healthcare IT infrastructures and complying with extremely strict legal constraints.

15.4 Features of Blockchain

The ability of blockchain technology to enhance distributed systems' reliability, safety, and durability has tend to its growing prominence. Research employing this technique has benefited a number of fields, including data analysis, finance, satellite imagery, and healthcare. The key features of the blockchain system, which draw users in, are distributed ledgers, confidentiality, openness, decentralization, and immutability of data.

However, because there is a chance of an invasion of privacy, this method is made far harder by healthcare records that contain sensitive information about patients. The goals of the initiative is to investigate blockchain applications in the field of healthcare. It begins by going over the sharing of medical files, log management, pictures sharing, and clinical data management [21].

Below are a few features of the technology known as blockchain that are extremely beneficial in the field of healthcare.

15.4.1 Decentralized Storage

Blockchain technology has rendered decentralized storage achievable causing an important change in how that data are shared, accessed, and retained. Essentially, as shown in Figure 15.1 blockchain technology offers a distributed ledger, which stores transactions through a network of

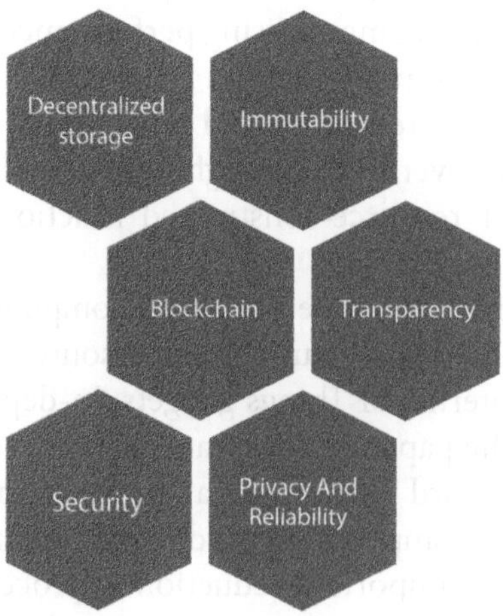

Figure 15.1 Features of blockchain.

computers, ensuring immutability, security, and transparency. Through a decentralized approach, access to data can be governed without the need of a central authority—like a government or business. Instead, data are shared near several nodes operated by various stakeholders ranging from corporations to private citizens. Every participant of the network supplies computing assets, such as processing power and space for storage, in return for payouts that are sometimes cryptocurrency tokens [21].

15.4.2 Immutability

Whenever we refer to immutability in connection with blockchain technology, we as a species mean that once material has been recorded to a blockchain, it cannot be withdrawn or altered. Because it ensures the precision and dependability of medical records and other delicate health data, this feature is crucial in the healthcare industry.

Blockchain has a chance to revolutionize data management in the healthcare industry by offering a transparent, safe, and unchangeable ledger for handling insurance information, storing medications, and preserving patient records. Blockchain, for instance, has the potential to address issues with healthcare data management, including data provenance, audit, traceability, immutability, and flexible access. The dissertation came out in Neural Computing and Applications [22].

In addition, the peer-to-peer architecture of the blockchain allows the automatic updating of patient records across multiple machines, leading to an immutable database that can be updated instantly for medical records [23]. Through the implementation of a decentralized strategy, the risks of centralized systems—like a single point of failure in natural disasters—are eliminated.

In the end, the immutability of digital currencies in the medical sector provides a means of preserving health data integrity, establishing trust between physicians and patients, and simplifying procedures to lower fraud and errors in the processing of bills and claims. One must remembers that although blockchain technology has lots of benefits, it also has pitfalls. Those include technological challenges, regulatory obstacles, and scalability issues, all of which must be resolved before blockchain can be successfully implemented in the field of healthcare.

15.4.3 Transparency

Multiple investigations indicate that the use of blockchain has an opportunity to dramatically boost healthcare transparency.

Blockchain software can aid consumers with insurance filing of claims and medical and pharmaceutical benefit calculation. Blockchain may provide a safe and auditable means of transferring genetic information, hence increasing its availability in the discipline of genomics by putting together data owners and buyers directly. While each member of a blockchain network views an immutable version of actuality, blockchain technology may provide an immutable, time-stamped recording of consent enhancing transparency in consent management. Blockchain technology can help the healthcare industry deal with several types of issues, enhance efficiency, and promote more trust in each case that this perspective addresses. An organization must evaluate the possible effect of blockchain features on its IT infrastructure. Specifically, the append-only structure of blockchain restricts the ability to remove data from the network, and distributed structures, while more secure, offer less productivity. While these trade-offs must be taken into account when evaluating alternatives to blockchain, the technology itself may maximize process optimization, reduce ineffectiveness, and increase trust in every situation [24].

15.4.4 Privacy and Reliability

Blockchain technology enhances privacy, confidentiality, and dependability in the healthcare industry. Both refs. [25, 26] stress the importance of these components; Ali proposes a novel security algorithm, whereas Sastry discusses the necessity of advanced technologies for protecting confidential medical data. Further emphasizing the potential of blockchain in addressing safety concerns like data protection and interoperability, Hamad [27] additionally points out the challenges related to data backup and privacy law compliance. Ref. [28] provides an in-depth examination of the safety and privacy of the use of blockchain in the healthcare industry,\ giving useful data for future studies.

15.4.5 Security

Preserving data from feasible perpetrators is one of the many essential requirements in today's smart healthcare systems. Therefore, it is essential to have appropriate data access procedures that ensure that the patient's medical information is only accessible to those allowed. Thus, the use of blockchain has been taken into account in the following section as a distributed way of protecting patient data in healthcare systems. This study suggests a safe and effective blockchain-based approach to both doctor and patient data accessibility within a specific healthcare system. The suggested approach is additionally effective in protecting the patients' privacy. Scheme's safety research shows that it can withstand well-known attacks while maintaining the system's integrity [29].

15.5 Blockchain Algorithms

Blockchain technology offers enormous potential to improve data management, connectivity, and security in the field of healthcare [30]. The distributed data storage and consensus processes of the technology and its algorithms may enhance the efficiency and reliability of healthcare systems [31]. In addition, data management difficulties can be addressed through the integration of the use of blockchain in machine learning ensuring data security and dependability [32]. Each of these studies demonstrates that the use of blockchain algorithms can revolutionize healthcare data security and management. Figure 15.2 highlights the name of the popular algorithm for blockchain which will be discussed in a further section.

15.5.1 POA (Proof-of-Authority) Algorithm

Many studies have looked into the Proof-of-Authority (PoA) method's application in the healthcare sector. Refs. [33, 34] both focus on leveraging PoA to improve the security and performance of healthcare data exchange. Ref. [34] offers a permission-based blockchain with PoA for safe data exchange, while ref. [33] provides an approach for optimizing PoA blockchain networks. Ref. [35] proposes a powered-by-blockchain confidentiality system for collective medical decision making, which could profit from

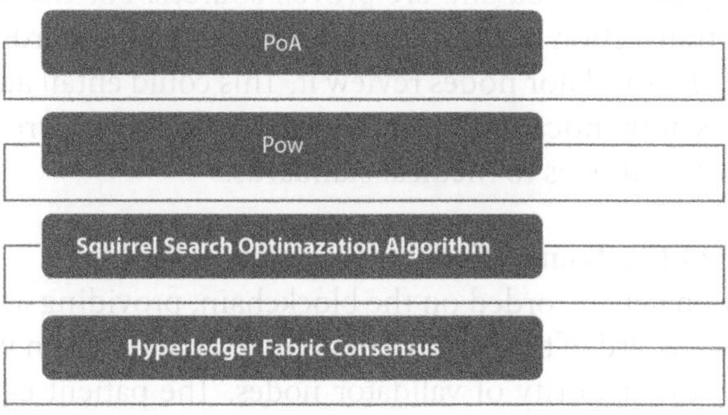

Figure 15.2 Blockchain algorithm used in healthcare.

the use of PoA. Finally, ref. [18] proposes a blockchain-based approach to preserving patient privacy when dealing with health-related information, which could benefit from PoA's security features. Together, these studies demonstrate how effective PoA might be in addressing certain challenges that arise from healthcare data administration.

One consensus technique for permission digital currencies, Proof of Authority (PoA), is preferable to typical BFT algorithms because it works better and has an additional distinctive character because of the lighter message exchange with PoA [36]. Proof of authority also has the added advantage of enabling blocks to be verified based on a person's real proof of identity, which enhances system safety and effectiveness and enables the blockchain to function at high throughput and low latency [36, 37]. PoA is basically implemented in the two forms of Aura and Clique, and it is suggested for private networks as part of the Ethereum ecosystem. Ref. [33] suggests using PoA Clique in his experiment, wherein the sequence is a node/validator identity.

Steps of POA:

Proposal for a Transaction

Client Application (e.g., Hospital A): The medical record of a patient is updated by a healthcare provider (e.g., a doctor at Hospital A). The modification is incorporated in a transaction proposal generated through the customer's application.

Acceptance and Agreements

Validator Nodes (which include Insurance Providers, Institutions B and C): The network's validation nodes receive the transaction proposal. These nodes, encompassing insurance businesses, clinics, and other hospitals, were carefully pre-selected and are proven sources. For the sake of being ensured, the transaction proposition is bound by the standards and rules of the network; the validator nodes review it. This could entail authenticating the proposer's authentication, guaranteeing the data is correct, as well as making sure it conforms to medical standards.

Finalization of the Transaction

The transaction gets recorded on the blockchain, providing an irreversible and accessible record of the medical update, when it has been validated and permitted by the majority of validator nodes. The patient can view their corrected medical record through an encrypted website once every relevant party, including the patient, healthcare providers, and insurance companies becomes aware of the update. Ensuring consistency and accuracy of medical data, the fresh data will appear in the patient's health records across all institutions that participate. To be sure that every transaction adheres to the regulations and laws that govern the healthcare network, audits have been carried out on regular schedules. For the sole purpose of preserving medical records, a system using blockchain technology guarantees enhanced privacy, efficiency, and accountability, which can be attractive to insurance companies, patients, and healthcare providers.

PoW (Proof-of-Work) Algorithm

[40] Several studies have investigated the application of the Proof-of-Work (PoW) algorithm in the field of medicine. To improve reliability [38], Mi incorporated the PoW algorithm into a combination of multi-criteria decision-making systems for healthcare waste management. Ref. [39] decreased the consumption of energy and enhanced safety in medical data management by optimizing and implementing the PoW algorithm as an IP address on an FPGA. Selvaraj integrated the Proof-of-Authority (PoA) and Proof-of-Work (PoW) algorithms to further enhance the safety and sustainability of blockchain-based healthcare systems. Game [41] utilized a divergence-based gray wolf optimization technique to improve decision tree rules while applying the PoW algorithm in a big data classification model for heart disease.

The first lottery-based consensus system used by blockchain, including Bitcoin, Ethereum, and many other networks that use blockchain today, has the acronym Proof of Work (PoW). PoW initially went live much before blockchain to lessen email spam attacks [18] and Sybil attacks, in which users are required to complete a computationally demanding activity. The primary purpose of Proof of Work (PoW) in the blockchain is to verify the blocks via a process referred to as mining, which requires enormous processing capacity. When utilizing Proof of Work (PoW), miners are in the position of accepting or rejecting transactions and conducting a validity check. Miners may extend the chain through the inclusion of new blocks from solving a series of computationally demanding tasks, which are referred to as crosswords. Every miner competes to solve a predetermined challenge, and the person who finishes it quickly won [42].

Steps of PoW

Proposal to Initiate a Transaction
Client Applications (e.g., Hospital A): The health record of a patient has been modified by a healthcare provider (e.g., a doctor at Hospital A). The modification is incorporated in a transaction proposal, which the client applications creates and sends to the network.

Mining (Workproof Documentation)
Miner Nodes: The transaction proposal is received by the network's miner nodes in included Clinics and Hospitals B and C. These nodes compete against one another to overcome an intricate crypto objection. The transaction is capable of being added to the blockchain for the first miners to solve the puzzle. To preserve the network's safety and integrity, the mining process requires an extensive amount of energy and processing power.

Block Generator and Transmission
Miner Nodes: A miner broadcasts an additional block, including the authenticated transaction, to the network following resolving a cryptographic puzzle.

Every peer in the system, including insurers, clinics, as well as hospitals: Once obtaining the most recent block, every peer in the network validates that it is genuine. They add the new block onto their local copies of the blockchain ledger when it has been established.

15.5.2 Hyperledger Fabric Consensus

Numerous research studies have examined the application of Hyperledger Fabric in the field of medicine stressing consensus methods. Both Alexandridis [43] and Antwi [44] advocate using Hyperledger Fabric in the healthcare sector; Alexandridis, in particular, recommends the RAFT consensus algorithm because of its scalability and durability. Leng [45] reviews Hyperledger applications in hospital information systems, including medical records, medicinal images, and medical prescription traceability. Barger [46] answers the growing need for a production-grade BFT ordering service by developing a Byzantine Fault-Tolerant (BFT) consensus library for Hyperledger Fabric. Both of these tests illustrate that Hyperledger Fabric and its consensus algorithms can improve healthcare systems' efficiency, security, and privacy.

It is believed that Hyperledger is the most advanced consortium chain technology. Compared with other blockchain technologies, Hyperledger focuses on developing enterprise-level uniformed applications. Hospital information systems are adopting Hyperledger more and more because of its superior transaction performance, pluggable consensus algorithm, flexible access control, and differentiated permission management. Despite the increasing amount of Hyperledger applications in the healthcare industry, no thorough classification and comparison research has yet been performed [47].

Steps of Hyperledger Fabric Consensus:

Phase of Proposals

Client Application (Hospital A, for instance): A doctor at Hospital A updates an individual's medical record. The change appears in a transaction proposal created by the client application. The request contains all the data the healthcare application requires, including the patient's ID, health records, a timestamp, and metadata.

Phase of Endorsement

Endorsement Peers (such as Hospitals B and C): The request is forwarded to endorsing, to verify the transaction's reliability, these peers, which may consist of other healthcare consortium membership hospitals or clinics. Endorsing peers resemble it (e.g., screening for conflicts or reviewing that the amendment corresponds with medical standards). If the action plan satisfies the endorsement policy—which could call for the endorsement of numerous healthcare providers to guarantee consensus—endorsing peers sign it.

Phase of Validation

Orderer Nodes: The accepted transaction is transmitted to the ordering service using the client application, and it additionally collects the endorsements. The ordering service effectively groups transactions and guarantees they happen in the correct sequence by packing them in to blocks.

Committer Peers: The sorted blocks are given out to all peers, including hospitals, healthcare clinics, and insurance firms. By checking the endorsements and making sure that there are no disputes or incidences of double spending, they authenticate the transactions. Peers upgrade the patient's medical record through the network by contributing the blocks to their local ledgers once their contents are finally approved.

Important Elements in a Healthcare Environment

Client Application: This program originates transaction proposals (e.g., revisions to health information) on behalf of contracted healthcare providers (e.g., hospitals, clinics).
Endorsing Peers: Specialized health care organizations that authenticate to and promote transactions with the objective to safeguard data integrity and conformance to medical standards.
Ordering Service Orderer Nodes: Regulate creation of blocks and transaction order, both of which are essential to protecting the order of medical modifications. Healthcare providers and other participants who evaluate and recommit the segments to their ledgers become known as committer peers. This makes certain patient records correct and uniform around all entities.

15.5.3 Squirrel Search Optimization Algorithm

A smart and secure healthcare system is proposed using the Multi-Objective Squirrel Search Optimization Algorithm (MOSSA) to protect healthcare data over an efficient blockchain network. In this case, the blockchain—a distributed, decentralized ledger comprised of multiple blocks interconnected by hashing chains, digital signature systems, and consensus procedures—offers extremely dependable capacity for storage. With the help of MOSSA, additional blockchain features, including block size, transaction size, and the amount of blockchain channels, are optimized. As MOSSA evolved, it has added extra features that enhance security and scalability. The Java platform is employed for carrying out the simulation process [48].

Steps of Squirrel Search Optimization Algorithm:

Evaluating Fitness as an Independent Function
A utility function, which can be determined based on various objectives including decreasing wait times for patients, improving treatment efficacy, or optimizing the utilization of resources, is used to evaluate each solution.

Organize and Revise Places (Squirrel Movement)
The suitability of the responses is used to sort them. The relative positions of the solutions are modified using movements comparable to the actions of a squirrel. Movements are impacted by variations in the seasons, consuming behavior, and the avoidance of predation.

Look for Termination or Convergence
Figure out whether or not a termination of the demand (which might be a maximum number of iterations) has been completed or how much the optimization process has reached convergence signifying that the outcomes are ceaselessly improving.

15.6 Network Model in Blockchain Algorithm

15.6.1 Permissioned Blockchain

Permissioned blockchain models are a primary blockchain technology used in the healthcare industry. Considering the healthcare industry has special needs for data privacy, security, and compliance with regulations, this method won out over public blockchains.

Blockchains having permissioned access: These blockchains manage sensitive medical data effectively since they limit access to trusted individuals exclusively. They give patients more control over data access and administration, which is essential for protecting patient privacy and adhering to regulatory requirements like the GDPR in Europe and the HIPAA in the United States [49].

Permissioned blockchain solutions are preferred in the healthcare sector because they can satisfy the strict requirements for data security, privacy, and regulatory compliance. Permissioned blockchains limit access to a small number of approved users, in contrast to public blockchains, which let everybody join and view transactions. This kind of management is essential in the healthcare industry since private medical information must be shielded from unwanted access. Permissioned blockchains guarantee that patient information is handled with the highest confidentiality by restricting access to only trustworthy entities. This architecture facilitates adherence to strict laws, such as the Health Insurance Portability and Accountability Act (HIPAA) in the US and the General Data Protection Regulation (GDPR) in Europe, which both impose strict guidelines for data security and privacy [21].

[50] Permissioned blockchains further give patients more control over their own healthcare information. Patients have the power to add or remove access to their medical records ensuring that only organizations and individuals with appropriate permission can access or change their information. Maintaining obedience to legislation and protecting patient privacy require such a level of control. Permissioned blockchains also

make it easier for insurers, healthcare providers, and other stakeholders to collaborate on secure data, which increases the effectiveness and precision of healthcare delivery. Blockchain records' transparency and immutability contribute to data integrity upkeep by lowering the prospect of fraud and mistakes. Permissioned blockchains successfully meet the specific requirements of the healthcare sector via providing a safe and legally authorized environment for handling sensitive medical data [51].

15.6.2 Consortium Block

Consortium Blockchains: A sort of permissioned blockchain, consortium blockchains are managed cooperatively by several entities on the blockchain network. By assuring data integrity and security, this paradigm improves interoperability and data sharing across healthcare providers, insurance companies, and other stakeholders [52].

Consortium blockchains, a type of permissioned blockchain, are designed to be managed cooperatively by multiple entities within a blockchain network. Unlike public blockchains, where anyone can participate and contribute to the network, consortium blockchains restrict access to a predefined group of organizations [17]. This collaborative management model is particularly well suited to sectors like healthcare, where data integrity, security, and regulatory compliance are paramount.

In a consortium blockchain, healthcare providers, insurance companies, pharmaceutical firms, and other relevant stakeholders collectively maintain the blockchain network. This cooperative approach ensures that no single entity has full control over the blockchain, thereby distributing trust among the participating entities. Each member of the consortium has a role in validating transactions and maintaining the ledger, which helps prevent fraud and ensures the reliability of the data recorded on the blockchain [1].

One of the significant advantages of consortium blockchains is enhanced data integrity. Because multiple entities are involved in the consensus process, the likelihood of data tampering is significantly reduced. Every transaction is validated by several independent parties ensuring that all records are accurate and trustworthy. This level of scrutiny is essential in the healthcare sector, where data integrity directly impacts patient care and outcomes. For example, accurate patient records, treatment histories, and medication logs are crucial for effective healthcare delivery [1].

Security is another critical benefit of consortium blockchains. Since the network is permissioned, only authorized entities can access and contribute to the blockchain. This restriction minimizes the risk of unauthorized access and data breaches, which are significant concerns in the healthcare industry. Furthermore, the use of cryptographic techniques ensures that data stored on the blockchain are encrypted and protected from external threats. This robust security framework helps in safeguarding sensitive health information against cyber-attacks and unauthorized disclosures [1].

Interoperability and data sharing are also significantly improved through consortium blockchains. Healthcare systems often face challenges with data silos, where patient information is fragmented across different institutions and databases. Consortium blockchains enable seamless data sharing and integration among various stakeholders fostering a more holistic view of patient health. This interoperability ensures that healthcare providers have access to comprehensive patient records, facilitating better coordination of care, more accurate diagnoses, and personalized treatment plans [1].

Moreover, the use of consortium blockchains can streamline administrative processes and reduce operational costs. By providing a single, unified platform for data exchange, these blockchains eliminate the need for intermediaries and redundant data entry, thereby reducing administrative overheads. This efficiency not only cuts costs but also speeds up processes, like insurance claims, medical billing, and patient referrals, ultimately enhancing the overall efficiency of healthcare delivery [6].

15.6.3 Applications in Healthcare

Patients may control who has access to their medical records through the utilization of blockchain technology to securely store and manage electronic health records (EHRs). As noted by BMJ Informatics, this increases patient privacy and guarantees data integrity.

15.6.3.1 Management of the Supply Chain

Electronic Health Records (EHR): Blockchain helps ensure the validity of substances, lower fraud, and track pharmaceuticals and medical supplies. This is essential to preventing the supply chain from getting contaminated with fake drugs (IBM).

Blockchain technology enhances the management of Electronic Health Records (EHRs) by ensuring the authenticity and security of medical data and tracking pharmaceuticals and medical supplies. This technology uses an immutable ledger to record each transaction within the supply chain providing a verifiable and tamper-proof history of all interactions. Here is how it works and its importance:

Validation of Substances

Blockchain ensures that all substances used in healthcare, from raw materials to finished pharmaceuticals, are validated at each step of the supply chain. This helps verify the authenticity and quality of the drugs being produced and distributed.

Reduction of Fraud

By maintaining an immutable record of every transaction, blockchain makes it nearly impossible to alter or forge documents related to the manufacture and distribution of pharmaceuticals. This transparency helps in significantly reducing fraud within the healthcare sector.

Tracking Pharmaceuticals

Each pharmaceutical product is assigned a unique identifier recorded on the blockchain. This identifier tracks the product from its origin through to its final destination ensuring that the product is genuine and has not been tampered with. This traceability helps in quickly identifying and removing counterfeit drugs from the supply chain.

Preventing Contamination With Fake Drugs

The secure and transparent nature of blockchain technology prevents the introduction of counterfeit drugs into the supply chain. Since every transaction is visible and verified by the network, any attempt to insert fake drugs can be quickly identified and stopped ensuring that only legitimate products reach patients.

15.6.3.2 Improving Supply Chain Efficiency

Blockchain can streamline supply chain operations by providing real-time visibility into the movement and status of medical supplies. This enhanced visibility can lead to better inventory management reducing shortages and overstock situations.

Overall, blockchain technology not only secures and validates EHRs but also plays a crucial role in maintaining the integrity of the pharmaceutical supply chain, protecting it from fraud and contamination, and ensuring that patients receive safe and effective medications.

- **Real-Time Visibility**

Tracking and Monitoring
Blockchain enables the continuous tracking of medical supplies from manufacturers to end users. Each transaction and movement of supplies is recorded on the blockchain creating an immutable and transparent log. This real-time tracking allows healthcare providers and supply chain managers to monitor the status and location of supplies at any given time.

Improved Forecasting and Planning
The data generated through blockchain can be analyzed to predict future supply needs more accurately. With real-time insights into supply levels, healthcare organizations can anticipate demand surges and plan accordingly ensuring that critical medical supplies are available when needed.

- **Enhanced Inventory Management**

Reduction of Shortages and Overstock
Blockchain's transparency helps balance supply and demand by providing precise data on current inventory levels across various locations. This visibility prevents both shortages, which can jeopardize patient care, and overstock situations, which can lead to wastage and increased storage costs. Efficient inventory management ensures that resources are used optimally and that supplies are available where and when they are needed most.

Automated Replenishment
Smart contracts on the blockchain can automate the reordering process when inventory levels fall below a certain threshold. This automation reduces the need for manual intervention speeding up the replenishment process and minimizing the risk of stockouts [51].

❖ Securing the Pharmaceutical Supply Chain

Fraud Prevention

Blockchain technology ensures that every step in the pharmaceutical supply chain is transparent and verifiable. This transparency makes it extremely difficult for counterfeit drugs to enter the supply chain, as each product's origin and journey are recorded and can be traced back to its source. By verifying the authenticity of drugs, blockchain helps protect patients from the dangers of counterfeit medication [20].

Contamination Control

With blockchain, any issues related to contamination or defects can be quickly traced back to their source allowing for swift action to be taken to address the problem. This traceability ensures that only safe and effective medications reach patients maintaining the integrity of the supply chain [52].

❖ Ensuring Safe and Effective Medications

End-to-End Transparency

The end-to-end transparency provided by blockchain means that all stakeholders, including manufacturers, distributors, healthcare providers, and patients, have access to the same verified information. This transparency ensures that everyone involved in the healthcare supply chain is working with accurate and reliable data enhancing overall trust and safety in the system [50].

Compliance and Reporting

Blockchain can simplify regulatory compliance by providing regulators with a transparent and immutable record of all transactions. This can help ensure that all parties comply with industry standards and regulations further protecting the safety and effectiveness of medications supplied to patients [50].

15.6.3.3 Research and Clinical Trials

By offering an unchangeable record of all trial business processes, blockchain simplifies organizing and keeping track of clinical trial data strengthening transparency and confidence in the findings [1].

Blockchain technology offers an immutable ledger that records all clinical trial activities providing a transparent and tamper-proof history of the trial process. Each step, from patient consent to data collection and analysis, is logged on the blockchain ensuring that all entries are time stamped and verifiable. This transparency helps in detecting any discrepancies or manipulations, thus bolstering the integrity of the trial data. Additionally, stakeholders, including regulatory bodies, researchers, and participants, can access a consistent and secure record facilitating trust and accountability. By reducing the likelihood of data tampering and enhancing traceability, blockchain simplifies compliance with regulatory standards and promotes confidence in the trial outcomes. The decentralized nature of blockchain ensures that no single entity can alter the records further strengthening the reliability of the data [6].

15.7 Data Collection and Storage

Blockchain technology is described as a safe, decentralized method of gathering and storing health data in the study by ref. [53]. Patient data are maintained secure because of blockchain's decentralized structure, which reduces the possibility of data manipulation and leaks. The study underscores how smart contracts aid in automating secure access restrictions ensuring that only individuals with appropriate permission can access information about patients. Blockchain-based identity verification strengthens the security construction even further preventing unauthorized entry and boosting system assurance. The report underlines how crucial these layers of protection are to preserving the confidentiality and exactness of medical data. Blockchain technology is outlined as a safe, decentralized technique for gathering and storing medical data in the study by ref. [53].

The application of attribute-based access control (ABAC) in the framework of blockchain is investigated by ref. [53] in an effort to enhance the security and integrity of health information. A blockchain with permissions technology called Hyperledger Fabric is employed in the study to guarantee strong access control and data safeguarding the environment.

Using ABAC, the likelihood of illegal access has been reduced since the system dynamically supplies access for individuals depending on specific characteristics. The study shows that by preventing tampering, this approach not only safeguards information regarding patients but also preserves data integrity. A deep analysis of how a blockchain system might strengthen healthcare data systems against frequent security threats has been given by ref. [53].

Ref. [54] focuses into how blockchain technology could enhance healthcare data management in terms of both price and resource efficiency. The study demonstrates how the decentralized nature of blockchain eliminates the need for centralized data storage, which leads to an important decrease in infrastructure expenditures pertaining to data management. Furthermore, adopting blockchain saves both money and time by eliminating the need for onerous human data verification procedures. Mengade highlights why blockchain technology makes managing information easier by offering a safe, unhackable architecture that protects data accessibility and integrity. This study establishes a strong case for the use of blockchain technology to provide affordable and effective management of medical record solutions.

Ref. [55] analyzes how blockchain technology could be used into mobile health applications to ensure data integrity and privacy protection. The study illustrates how blockchain technology could safeguard private health data on mobile platforms from illegal access and data breaches. Mobile

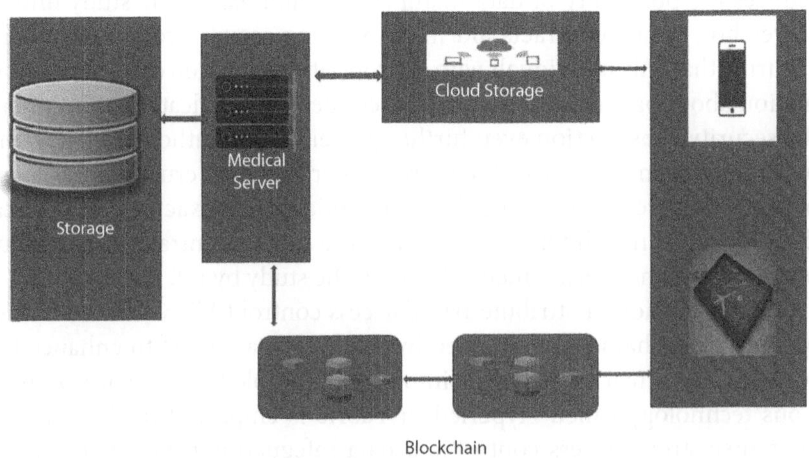

Figure 15.3 Storage in the blockchain database.

healthcare apps can improve security and trust through the use of blockchain technology to give customers an unalterable, transparent record of their data. The findings of Liang's research, the use of blockchain, plays a key role in enabling safe data exchange and compatibility among diverse mobile health apps. In line with the study's outcomes, blockchain technology is essential for preserving patient data's accuracy and confidentiality in mobile healthcare environments. Figure 15.3 shows evidence that how data is stored and how data flow takes place.

A blockchain network's decentralized, transparent, and unchangeable data storage is what defines and makes it distinctive. User-initiated transactions are assembled into blocks, which are subsequently verified for correctness and validity by nodes throughout the network. A collection of blocks that are securely connected to one another is formed by each block having a secure hash of the header form the block before it. It is rendered computationally impossible to do anything with the stored information by this chaining technique, which guarantees that any effort to change the data within a block would involve changing the hash value of that block and all complying with blocks. In addition, consensus mechanisms, like Proof of Work (PoW) and Proof of Stake (PoS), promise that every node in the network concurs on the legitimacy of fresh blocks, thus augmenting the security and integrity of the blockchain.

Once a block is added to the blockchain, it is replicated and distributed across all nodes in the network creating redundancy and resilience. This distributed storage ensures that there is no single point of failure making blockchain data storage highly resistant to censorship and attacks. Moreover, the transparent and decentralized nature of blockchain technology enhances trust among participants by providing a clear and auditable record of transactions. As a result, data stored in a blockchain are considered immutable providing a secure and reliable platform for a wide range of applications from financial transactions to supply chain management and beyond.

15.8 Diversity in Blockchain Technology

In ref. [6], the potential of blockchain technology to revolutionize the healthcare industry is emphasized, particularly in improving data security, transparency, and efficiency. The research highlights the promising applications of blockchain in healthcare, including fraud detection and identity verification, which have the potential to address critical challenges within the industry. However, while acknowledging the transformative potential of blockchain, the study also underscores the need to address challenges, such as stringent authentication and record sharing requirements, which may hinder its widespread adoption in healthcare settings.

The work in ref. [51] goes further into the uses of blockchain in healthcare highlighting the ways it might improve efficiency, transparency, as well as security. The study emphasizes how blockchain technology has an opportunity to enhance fraud detection and identity verification processes in the healthcare sector. To fully reap the benefits of the blockchain in healthcare, the research acknowledges the obstacles that must be overcome in order such as the demand for stricter authentication and record-sharing guidelines.

Ref. [22] focuses on the usage of blockchain technology in healthcare, namely, in the areas of identity verification and fraud prevention. The report highlights how blockchain-based technology has the potential to significantly enhance the medical field in several important areas. It also points out obstacles that must be removed to fully realize the beneficial effects of the technology of blockchain in the healthcare industry, such as demands for stricter authentication and record-sharing requirements.

According to ref. [2], blockchain technology offers a lot of potential in the healthcare industry. However, further research is required to completely reap these perks. The study recognizes how blockchain technology has revolutionized data security, being transparency, and effectiveness in the healthcare sector. But it also emphasizes how critical it is to deal with issues like strict authentication guidelines and record-sharing obligations.

Diversity in blockchain technology within the healthcare sector encompasses a broad spectrum of applications from data security and transparency to patient care and medical research. One aspect of diversity lies in the various use cases of blockchain ranging from fraud detection and identity verification to supply chain management and clinical trials. Blockchain's decentralized and immutable nature provides a versatile platform for addressing a wide array of challenges faced by healthcare organizations, including interoperability issues, data silos, and privacy concerns. This diversity of applications underscores the transformative potential of blockchain in revolutionizing traditional healthcare practices and improving patient outcomes.

Moreover, diversity in blockchain technology extends beyond its applications to encompass the range of stakeholders involved in its development, implementation, and adoption within the healthcare ecosystem. This includes healthcare providers, technology companies, regulatory bodies, research institutions, and patients themselves. Each stakeholder brings unique perspectives, expertise, and priorities to the table contributing to a diverse and dynamic ecosystem of innovation and collaboration. By embracing diversity in both its applications and stakeholders, blockchain technology has the potential to drive positive change in healthcare delivery, data management, and patient engagement ultimately shaping a more inclusive and equitable healthcare system for all.

15.9 Limitations of Blockchain

According to refs. [21, 31, 56], all the use of blockchain technology has the potential to completely change the medical field by providing safe, decentralized data sharing and management. The use of it in this sector of the economy is still in its infancy, nonetheless, as reflected by the absence of prototype implementations and a shortage of technical information [56]. In addition, there are practical challenges to overcome while using blockchain to safeguard cloud privacy and data security [57]. With these limitations, the blockchain system appears to be having a bright future in the healthcare sector, with potential uses in safe, personalized treatment [31].

15.9.1 Scalability Problems

Scaling is one of blockchain's disadvantages in healthcare. Blockchain networks may find it difficult to handle the load as the number of transactions rises, which could result in lengthier transaction times and higher costs. This is particularly problematic in the healthcare industry, as an enormous amount of data is generated daily from various sources including medical imaging, IoT devices, and patient records. Blockchain-based technology may not be able to serve the requirements of a large-scale healthcare ecosystem due to problems with scalability, which might stop it from becoming prevalent in the healthcare sector [19].

The primary limitation of blockchain in healthcare is scaling. As the volume of transactions increases, blockchain networks may not be able to handle the demand, which could contribute to longer transaction times and higher costs. This is especially difficult for the healthcare sector since every day, an immense quantity of data is generated from a variety of sources, such as patient records, medical imaging, and Internet of Things devices. Scalability issues may prevent blockchain-based technology from satisfying the requirements of a large-scale healthcare ecosystem, which might stop it from proliferating in the business.

15.9.2 Regulatory Difficulties

The regulatory uncertainty around blockchain technology for medical applications is another constraint. Current laws may fall short of dealing with the special features of blockchain, including interoperability, security, and data privacy. Whenever medical companies traverse complex regulatory frameworks to ensure compliance, this ambiguity can create challenges that hinder their implementation. In addition, since there are no standard regulations across jurisdictions, the implementation of distributed ledgers in healthcare has become harder to implement [58].

One major barrier to the use of blockchain technology in healthcare settings is the lack of clarity regarding rules and regulations. It is possible that current laws are inadequate in addressing the distinctive qualities of blockchain, including data privacy, protection, and interoperability. The multitude of regulatory frameworks that medical companies need to navigate to achieve compliance may create impediments to implementation efforts due to uncertainty. Distributed ledger adoption in the health care sector is further complicated by the lack of consistent regulations across different countries. The healthcare sector finds it more difficult to use blockchain solutions due to its inconsistent rules and regulations, which restricts the potential advantages of these technologies in terms of safeguarding information and management.

15.9.3 Data Privacy Issues

Blockchain technology offers data privacy problems for the field of healthcare despite its cryptographic security features. While blockchain offers immutability and transparency, it also persistently saves information to a distributed ledger, which raises security risks around illegal access to and disclosure of confidential medical data. Additionally, the pseudonymous aspect of blockchain transactions might not adhere to stringent patient privacy laws like the United States Health Insurance Portability and Accountability Act (HIPAA). Therefore, maintaining patient anonymity when taking advantage of blockchain's capabilities continues to be an important issue for stakeholders in the field of healthcare [59].

Apart from its cryptographic security features, blockchain technology raises privacy concerns regarding patient information in the medical sector. Persistent information storage on a distributed ledger increases the likelihood of unauthorized use and disclosure of personal medical data even though it provides immutability and transparency. In addition, healthcare firms can encounter compliance problems due to the anonymous nature of digital currency transactions, and this may not fit with rigorous patient privacy regulations like HIPAA. In view of this, stakeholders in the healthcare sector continue to raise serious worries about maintaining patient anonymity while leveraging blockchain's advantages. As a consequence, privacy-enhancing methods and regulatory compliance measures must be carefully weighed.

15.10 Conclusion

The work's conclusion highlights whether blockchain technology has been having an enormous effect on revolutionizing the healthcare industry. While exploring Proof of Authority (POA), Proof of Work (POW), and Hyperledger Fabric algorithms, it throws light on how different types of blockchains can be used to enhance data security, transparency, and interoperability among healthcare programs. These algorithms propose answers to problems such as guaranteeing the decentralization, immutability, and reliability of healthcare data. The conclusion does, however, also recognize the limitations that the blockchain system has in the field of healthcare, despite its enormous promise. These constraints include difficulties with scalability, privacy, compliance with rules and regulations, and interoperability with current systems. Therefore, while blockchain offers enormous potential to alter healthcare, these issues must be resolved to fully realize the benefits of the technology and advance the sector toward a future that will be more patient-centered and efficient.

The conclusion sheds insights on how blockchain technologies, such Proof of Authority (POA), Proof of Work (POW), and Hyperledger Fabric, could enhance data security, transparency, and interoperability throughout healthcare systems. These algorithms indicate how blockchain has the potential to totally change the healthcare industry by offering practical solutions for significant problems like decentralization, immutability, and trustworthiness of healthcare data.

Despite its potential, the conclusion recognizes the significant obstacles that blockchain technology in healthcare must overcome. Significant challenges include those related to scalability, privacy protection, regulatory compliance, and integration with current infrastructure. To fully realize the potential advantages of blockchain technology and advance the healthcare industry toward increased effectiveness and patient-centered treatment, these issues need to be thoroughly resolved.

The conclusion highlights the necessity of coordinated efforts to get above the limitations of blockchain technology in light of these restrictions. This calls for ongoing study, stakeholder collaboration, and legislative adaptation to support privacy concerns, promote innovation, and guarantee adherence to healthcare laws. Blockchain technology can open up new opportunities for patient interaction, data management, and healthcare delivery by tackling these issues head-on.

15.11 Future Work

In the rapidly evolving landscape of healthcare technology, blockchain has emerged as a promising solution to address critical challenges in data management, security, and interoperability. The abstract underscores the growing interest and potential of blockchain technology within the healthcare sector highlighting the need for further exploration to fully capitalize on its benefits. A key area for future research lies in the refinement and optimization of existing blockchain algorithms, such as Proof of Authority (POA) and Proof of Work (POW), to better suit the unique requirements of healthcare systems. This involves exploring variations or hybrid models of these algorithms to enhance their attributes and accuracy levels for specific healthcare applications. Additionally, as blockchain technology continues to advance, there is an opportunity to explore its integration with emerging technologies, like artificial intelligence (AI), Internet of Things (IoT), and decentralized finance (DeFi), to further enhance healthcare operations and patient outcomes.

Moreover, future work could focus on the development and implementation of practical blockchain-based applications tailored to address specific challenges in healthcare, including interoperability, data security, and patient privacy. Translating theoretical concepts into real-world solutions that can be seamlessly integrated into existing healthcare infrastructures is imperative for driving meaningful impact. Another crucial aspect of future research involves addressing the regulatory challenges associated with blockchain integration in healthcare. Collaboration with policymakers and regulatory bodies is essential to develop frameworks that ensure blockchain solutions comply with existing healthcare regulations and standards facilitating their widespread adoption and implementation across healthcare organizations. By addressing these areas of future work, researchers can contribute to the ongoing evolution of blockchain technology in healthcare paving the way for a more efficient, secure, and patient-centered healthcare ecosystem.

References

1. Agbo, C.C., Mahmoud, Q.H., Eklund, J.M., Blockchain technology in healthcare: A systematic review. *Healthcare (Switzerland)*, 7, 2, 1–30, 2019, doi: 10.3390/healthcare7020056.
2. Prokofieva, M. and Miah, S.J., Blockchain in healthcare, pp. 1–22, 2019, [Online], Available: https://nebula.org.
3. Uke, N., Healthcare 4.0 Enabled Lightweight Security Provisions for Medical Data Processing. *Turk. J. Comput. Math. Educ. (TURCOMAT)*, 12, 11, 165–173, 2021, doi: 10.17762/turcomat.v12i11.5858.
4. McGhin, T., Choo, K.K.R., Liu, C.Z., He, D., Blockchain in healthcare applications: Research challenges and opportunities. *J. Netw. Comput. Appl.*, 135, 62–75, 2019, doi: 10.1016/j.jnca.2019.02.027.
5. Bell, L., Buchanan, W.J., Cameron, J., Lo, O., Applications of Blockchain Within Healthcare. *Blockchain Healthc. Today*, 1, 1–7, 2018, doi: 10.30953/bhty.v1.8.
6. Haleem, A., Javaid, M., Singh, R.P., Suman, R., Rab, S., Blockchain technology applications in healthcare: An overview. *Int. J. Intell. Netw.*, 2, 130–139, 2021, doi: 10.1016/j.ijin.2021.09.005.
7. Tandon, A., Dhir, A., Islam, N., Mäntymäki, M., Blockchain in healthcare: A systematic literature review, synthesizing framework and future research agenda. *Comput. Ind.*, 122, 1–22, 2020, doi: 10.1016/j.compind.2020.103290.
8. Pilkington, M., Can Blockchain Improve Healthcare Management? *Technol. Innov. Manage. Rev.*, 12, 1–2, 1–13, 2022, doi: 10.22215/timreview/1480.
9. McGhin, T., Choo, K.K.R., Liu, C.Z., He, D., Blockchain in healthcare applications: Research challenges and opportunities. *J. Netw. Comput. Appl.*, 135, 62–75, 2019, doi: 10.1016/j.jnca.2019.02.027.
10. Albahri, A.S. *et al.*, A systematic review of trustworthy and explainable artificial intelligence in healthcare: Assessment of quality, bias risk, and data fusion. *Inf. Fusion*, 96, 1–63, 2023, doi: 10.1016/j.inffus.2023.03.008.
11. Raut, V., Thombare, H., Pendavle, P., Sharma, S., Patil, M., Need of Blockchain in Healthcare. *Int. J. Adv. Res. Sci. Commun. Technol.*, 2, 1, 1–2, 2022, doi: 10.48175/ijarsct-2648.
12. Wagh, S.B. and Murthy, J.K., Securing health care data for medical research using blockchain technology. *J. Adv. Electron.*, 1, 3, 17–23, 2018.
13. Gökalp, E., Gökalp, M.O., Çoban, S., Eren, P.E., Analysing opportunities and challenges of integrated blockchain technologies in healthcare, in: *Lecture Notes in Business Information Processing*, 2018, doi: 10.1007/978-3-030-00060-8_13.
14. Venugopal, L.K., Rajaganapathi, R., Birjepatil, A., Raja, S.E., Subramaniam, G., A Novel Information Security Framework for Securing Big Data in Healthcare Environment Using Blockchain †. *Eng. Proc.*, 59, 1, 1–10, 2023, doi: 10.3390/engproc2023059107.

15. Khan, S., Ahmed, F., Baig, M.S., Khan, Z.A., Yousufzai, U.A., Securing Medical Datasets using Block Chain Technology. *J. Nanoscope (JN)*, 3, 2, 205–217, 2022, doi: 10.52700/jn.v3i2.80.
16. Pandey, P. and Litoriya, R., Securing and authenticating healthcare records through blockchain technology. *Cryptologia*, 44, 4, 341–356, 2020, doi: 10.1080/01611194.2019.1706060.
17. Momaya, V.J. *et al.*, Revolutionizing Organ Donation With Blockchain Technology. *J. Comput. Mech. Manage.*, 2, 5, 31–38, 2023, doi: 10.57159/gadl.jcmm.2.5.23071.
18. Soni, M. and Singh, D.K., Blockchain Implementation for Privacy preserving and securing the Healthcare data, in: *Proceedings - 2021 IEEE 10th International Conference on Communication Systems and Network Technologies, CSNT 2021*, pp. 729–734, 2021, doi: 10.1109/CSNT51715.2021.9509722.
19. Chukwu, E. and Garg, L., A systematic review of blockchain in healthcare: Frameworks, prototypes, and implementations. *IEEE Access*, 8, 21196–21214, 2020, doi: 10.1109/ACCESS.2020.2969881.
20. Faruk, M.J.H., Basney, J., Cheng, J.Q., Blockchain-Based Decentralized Verifiable Credentials: Leveraging Smart Contracts for Privacy-Preserving Authentication Mechanisms to Enhance Data Security in Scientific Data Access, in: *Proceedings - 2023 IEEE International Conference on Big Data, BigData 2023*, 2023, doi: 10.1109/BigData59044.2023.10386360.
21. De Aguiar, E.J., Faiçal, B.S., Krishnamachari, B., Ueyama, J., A Survey of Blockchain-Based Strategies for Healthcare. *ACM Comput. Surv.*, 53, 2, 1–27, 2020, doi: 10.1145/3376915.
22. McGhin, T., Choo, K.K.R., Liu, C.Z., He, D., Blockchain in healthcare applications: Research challenges and opportunities. *J. Netw. Comput. Appl.*, 135, 62–75, 2019, doi: 10.1016/j.jnca.2019.02.027.
23. Loukil, F., Abed, M., Boukadi, K., Blockchain adoption in education: a systematic literature review. *Educ. Inf. Technol. (Dordr)*, 26, 5, 5779–5797, 2021, doi: 10.1007/s10639-021-10481-8.
24. Velmovitsky, P.E., Bublitz, F.M., Fadrique, L.X., Morita, P.P., Blockchain applications in health care and public health: Increased transparency. *JMIR Med. Inf.*, 9, 6, 1–16, 2021, doi: 10.2196/20713.
25. Ali, A. and *et al.*, Security, privacy, and reliability in digital healthcare systems using blockchain. *Electron. (Switzerland)*, 10, 16, 2034, 2021, doi: 10.3390/electronics10162034.
26. Sastry, J.B. and Banik, B.G., Imposing Security and Privacy in the Healthcare Industry Using Blockchain Technology, in: *Intelligent Interactive Multimedia Systems for e-Healthcare Applications*, 2021, doi: 10.1007/978-981-16-6542-4_13.
27. Al Hamad, N.F. and Liou, J.C., Current Cybersecurity Challenges of Applying Blockchain in Healthcare, in: *Proceedings - 2022 International Conference on Computational Science and Computational Intelligence, CSCI 2022*, 2022, doi: 10.1109/CSCI58124.2022.00305.

28. Ratta, P., Kaur, A., Sharma, S., Shabaz, M., Dhiman, G., Application of Blockchain and Internet of Things in Healthcare and Medical Sector: Applications, Challenges, and Future Perspectives. *J. Food Qual.*, 2021, 1–20, 2021, doi: 10.1155/2021/7608296.
29. Ramani, V., Kumar, T., Bracken, A., Liyanage, M., Ylianttila, M., Secure and Efficient Data Accessibility in Blockchain Based Healthcare Systems, in: *Proceedings - IEEE Global Communications Conference, GLOBECOM*, 2018, doi: 10.1109/GLOCOM.2018.8647221.
30. Tanwar, S., Parekh, K., Evans, R., Blockchain-based electronic healthcare record system for healthcare 4.0 applications. *J. Inf. Secur. Appl.*, 50, 1–13, 2020, doi: 10.1016/j.jisa.2019.102407.
31. Siyal, A.A., Junejo, A.Z., Zawish, M., Ahmed, K., Khalil, A., Soursou, G., "Applications of blockchain technology in medicine and healthcare: Challenges and future perspectives. *Cryptography*, 3, 1, 1–16, 2019, doi: 10.3390/cryptography3010003.
32. Jain, S., Anand, A., Gupta, A., Awasthi, K., Gujrati, S., Channegowda, J., Blockchain and machine learning in health care and management, in: *2020 International Conference on Mainstreaming Block Chain Implementation, ICOMBI 2020*, 2020, doi: 10.23919/ICOMBI48604.2020.9203483.
33. Yasir, A.I. and Kusuma, G.P., Deep deterministic policy gradients for optimizing simulated poa blockchain networks based on healthcare data characteristics. *Adv. Sci. Technol. Eng. Syst.*, 6, 1, 757–64, 2021, doi: 10.25046/aj060183.
34. Al Asad, N., Elahi, M.T., Al Hasan, A., Yousuf, M.A., Permission-based blockchain with proof of authority for secured healthcare data sharing, in: *2020 2nd International Conference on Advanced Information and Communication Technology, ICAICT 2020*, 2020, doi: 10.1109/ICAICT51780.2020.9333488.
35. Yang, J., Onik, M.M.H., Lee, N.Y., Ahmed, M., Kim, C.S., Proof-of-familiarity: A privacy-preserved blockchain scheme for collaborative medical decision-making. *Appl. Sci. (Switzerland)*, 9, 7, 3070, 2019, doi: 10.3390/app9071370.
36. De Angelis, S., Aniello, L., Baldoni, R., Lombardi, F., Margheri, A., Sassone, V., PBFT vs proof-of-authority: Applying the CAP theorem to permissioned blockchain, in: *CEUR Workshop Proceedings*, pp. 1–11, 2018.
37. Samuel, O., Javaid, N., Awais, M., Ahmed, Z., Imran, M., Guizani, M., A blockchain model for fair data sharing in deregulated smart grids, in: *Proceedings - IEEE Global Communications Conference, GLOBECOM*, 2019, doi: 10.1109/GLOBECOM38437.2019.9013372.
38. Mi, X., Tian, Y., Kang, B., "A hybrid multi-criteria decision making approach for assessing health-care waste management technologies based on soft likelihood function and D-numbers,". *Appl. Intell.*, 51, 10, 1–20, 2021, doi: 10.1007/s10489-020-02148-7.
39. Ktari, J., Frikha, T., Yousfi, M.A., Belghith, M.K., Sanei, N., Embedded Keccak implementation on FPGA, in: *4th IEEE International Conference on*

Design and Test of Integrated Micro and Nano-Systems, DTS 2022, 2022, doi: 10.1109/DTS55284.2022.9809847.

40. Selvaraj, A.P. and Annamalai, S., Towards Reliable Medical Transactions for Blockchain based Healthcare Systems using Hybrid Consensus Method, in: *ACM International Conference Proceeding Series*, 2022, doi: 10.1145/3590837.3590867.
41. Game, P.S., Vaze, V., Emmanuel, M., Optimized Decision tree rules using divergence based grey wolf optimization for big data classification in health care. *Evol. Intell.*, 15, 2, 971–987, 2022, doi: 10.1007/s12065-019-00267-w.
42. Al-Joboury, I.M. and Al-Hemiary, E.H., CONSENSUS ALGORITHMS BASED BLOCKCHAIN OF THINGS FOR DISTRIBUTED HEALTHCARE. *Iraqi J. Inf. Commun. Technol.*, 3, 4, 34–36, 2020, doi: 10.31987/ijict.3.4.116.
43. Alexandridis, A., Al-Sumaidaee, G., Alkhudary, R., Zilic, Z., Making Case for Using RAFT in Healthcare Through Hyperledger Fabric, in: *Proceedings - 2021 IEEE International Conference on Big Data, Big Data 2021*, 2021, doi: 10.1109/BigData52589.2021.9671934.
44. Antwi, M., Adnane, A., Ahmad, F., Hussain, R., Habib ur Rehman, M., Kerrache, C.A., The case of HyperLedger Fabric as a blockchain solution for healthcare applications. *Blockchain: Res. Appl.*, 2, 1, 1–15, 2021, doi: 10.1016/j.bcra.2021.100012.
45. Leng, Z., Tan, Z., Wang, K., Application of Hyperledger in the Hospital Information Systems: A Survey. *IEEE Access*, 9, 128965–128987, 2021, doi: 10.1109/ACCESS.2021.3112608.
46. Barger, A., Manevich, Y., Meir, H., Tock, Y., A byzantine fault-tolerant consensus library for hyperledger fabric, in: *IEEE International Conference on Blockchain and Cryptocurrency, ICBC 2021*, 2021, doi: 10.1109/ICBC51069.2021.9461099.
47. Leng, Z., Tan, Z., Wang, K., Application of Hyperledger in the Hospital Information Systems: A Survey. *IEEE Access*, 9, 128965–128987, 2021, doi: 10.1109/ACCESS.2021.3112608.
48. Jaishankar, B., Vishwakarma, S., Mohan, P., Pundir, A.K.S., Patel, I., Arulkumar, N., Blockchain for Securing Healthcare Data Using Squirrel Search Optimization Algorithm. *Intell. Autom. Soft Comput.*, 32, 3, 1815–1829, 2022, doi: 10.32604/IASC.2022.021822.
49. Yaqoob, I., Salah, K., Jayaraman, R., Al-Hammadi, Y., Blockchain for healthcare data management: opportunities, challenges, and future recommendations. *Neural Comput. Appl.*, 34, 14, 1–16, 2022, doi: 10.1007/s00521-020-05519-w.
50. Woodside, J.M., Augustine, F.K., Giberson, W., Blockchain Technology Adoption Status and Strategies. *J. Int. Technol. Inf. Manage.*, 26, 2, 65–93, 1–3, 2017, doi: 10.58729/1941-6679.1300.
51. Angraal, S., Krumholz, H.M., Schulz, W.L., Blockchain technology: Applications in health care. *Circ.: Cardiovasc. Qual. Outcomes*, 10, 9, 2017, doi: 10.1161/CIRCOUTCOMES.117.003800.

52. Baucas, M.J., Spachos, P., Plataniotis, K.N., "Federated Learning and Blockchain-Enabled Fog-IoT Platform for Wearables in Predictive Healthcare,". *IEEE Trans. Comput. Soc. Syst.*, 10, 4, 1732–1741, 2023, doi: 10.1109/TCSS.2023.3235950.
53. Sun, Z., Han, D., Li, D., Wang, X., Chang, C.C., Wu, Z., A blockchain-based secure storage scheme for medical information. *EURASIP J. Wirel. Commun. Netw.*, 2022, 1, 1–25, 2022, doi: 10.1186/s13638-022-02122-6.
54. Mengade, D., Blockchain Use in Healthcare Data Storage. *Int. J. Res. Appl. Sci. Eng. Technol.*, 7, 4, 1–9, 2019, doi: 10.22214/ijraset.2019.4452.
55. Liang, X., Zhao, J., Shetty, S., Liu, J., Li, D., Integrating blockchain for data sharing and collaboration in mobile healthcare applications, in: *IEEE International Symposium on Personal, Indoor and Mobile Radio Communications, PIMRC*, 2017, doi: 10.1109/PIMRC.2017.8292361.
56. Hölbl, M., Kompara, M., Kamišalić, A., Zlatolas, L.N., A systematic review of the use of blockchain in healthcare. *Symmetry (Basel)*, 10, 10, 1–22, 2018, doi: 10.3390/sym10100470.
57. Esposito, C., De Santis, A., Tortora, G., Chang, H., Choo, K.K.R., Blockchain: A Panacea for Healthcare Cloud-Based Data Security and Privacy? *IEEE Cloud Comput.*, 5, 1, 31–37, 2018, doi: 10.1109/MCC.2018.011791712.
58. Kuo, T.T., Kim, H.E., Ohno-Machado, L., Blockchain distributed ledger technologies for biomedical and health care applications. *J. Am. Med. Inf. Assoc.*, 24, 6, 1211–1220, 2017, doi: 10.1093/jamia/ocx068.
59. Xia, Q., Sifah, E.B., Smahi, A., Amofa, S., Zhang, X., BBDS: Blockchain-based data sharing for electronic medical records in cloud environments. *Information (Switzerland)*, 8, 2, 1–16, 2017, doi: 10.3390/info8020044.

16

Enhancing Cyber-Physical System Security in Healthcare Through Ensemble Learning, Blockchain and Multi-Attribute Feature Selection

Jagdish Pimple* **and Avinash Sharma**

Department of Computer Science and Engineering, Madhyanchal Professional University, Bhopal, MP, India

Abstract

The foundation of today's healthcare infrastructure is made up of Cyber-Physical technologies (CPS), which combine computational and physical technologies to provide effective patient care and management. But because CPS are networked in healthcare settings, they are vulnerable to a variety of security flaws; therefore, robust safety measures are needed to protect sensitive data and guarantee system integrity. We put up a thorough plan to improve CPS security in the healthcare industry by utilizing blockchain, Multi-Attribute Feature Selection (MAFS), and Ensemble Learning. We start with the particular security issues that CPS faces in the healthcare industry, such as the possibility of hostile attacks, unauthorized access, and data breaches that target medical equipment and patient records. Next, we present Ensemble Learning, a potent method for enhancing the precision of threat identification and categorization in CPS security applications. Ensemble Learning frameworks improve the resilience and generalization capacities of security models by mixing various base learners, such as decision trees, neural networks, and support vector machines. This makes it possible to create more potent defense mechanisms against cyber threats. In addition, we investigate how blockchain technology may be incorporated into healthcare CPS to create a decentralized, impenetrable ledger for handling and preserving sensitive data. Healthcare systems may guarantee data integrity, traceability, and auditability

**Corresponding author*: jpimple@stvincentngp.edu.in; pimplejagdish@gmail.com

Parul Dubey, Mangala Madankar, Pushkar Dubey and Bui Thanh Hung (eds.) The Impact of Algorithmic Technologies on Healthcare, (349–374) © 2025 Scrivener Publishing LLC

while also facilitating safe and open transactions among stakeholders by utilizing blockchain-based smart contracts and cryptography approaches.

Furthermore, as a way to maximize the selection of pertinent features for CPS security applications, we present Multi-Attribute Feature Selection (MAFS). MAFS approaches allow for the development of more effective and scalable security models by methodically assessing and choosing subsets of attributes based on their contribution to threat detection and classification tasks. To strengthen CPS security in healthcare, we finally propose a comprehensive system that combines Ensemble Learning algorithms, blockchain-enabled data management mechanisms, and MAFS-driven feature selection methodologies. We show how the suggested strategy works to improve security resilience, protect data confidentiality, and maintain the integrity of healthcare systems in the face of changing cyber threats through empirical evaluation and case studies.

Keywords: Blockchain, ensemble learning, CPS (Cyber-Physical Systems), medical-CPS, Multi-Attribute Feature Selection (MAFS)

16.1 Introduction

One of the main components of a cyber-physical system is user and device authentication (CPS). In a cyber physical system, the interconnectedness of disparate systems and devices leaves them open to cyberattacks. The Internet of Things, blockchain development, and healthcare services are rendered unreachable by the potential for cyberattacks. In the past 10 years, technology and communication have seen a creative revolution. The Internet has spread across many networks in a variety of industries and has a significant impact on every aspect of daily life, especially in the medical profession. Better social and economic outcomes are achieved by the CPS and MCPS systems. Numerous savings have been made worldwide to advance this technology [2]. The tangible elements of the specialized systems take care of important matters like security, dependability, and safety standards, as medical data may be transmitted over social networks and wireless networks. Security presents a significant concern wherever large-scale networks are deployed [3]. Healthcare systems that are based on CPS handle personal data. Significant privacy concerns may still impact these data, even if they came from innocuous wearable sensors. Since most CPS-based healthcare applications employ wireless connections for device operation, security and privacy rank among the most important areas of concern. CPS-based health care applications necessitate robust and secure data links between medical sensors, controllers, patients, and caregivers because they directly involve people. People's ability to utilize CPS-based healthcare apps may be restricted due to misuse or privacy issues [4, 5]. Older safety and protection measures—like modern cryptographic clarifications, sheltering protocols, and secrecy assurance—cannot be used in CPS-based medical systems because of supply limitations, refuge level requirements, and system planning. Strong network safety measures are needed for either short- or long-range communication to reduce the threats outlined above.

Although there are significant security issues with modern wireless networks that can be resolved, CPS-based healthcare applications are not immediately affected by them. The conventional strategy for protecting patient privacy in the healthcare system is under jeopardy due to data leaks and the complex nature of the information. The selection of attributes and information concealing present a challenge to the traditional confidentiality safety techniques. The ability of cyber-physical systems in the health care system to preserve privacy is leveraged in the progress of machine learning. The concept of healthcare data security is enhanced by feature selection that takes into account several factors. The below Figure 16.1 shows the blockchain in healthcare.

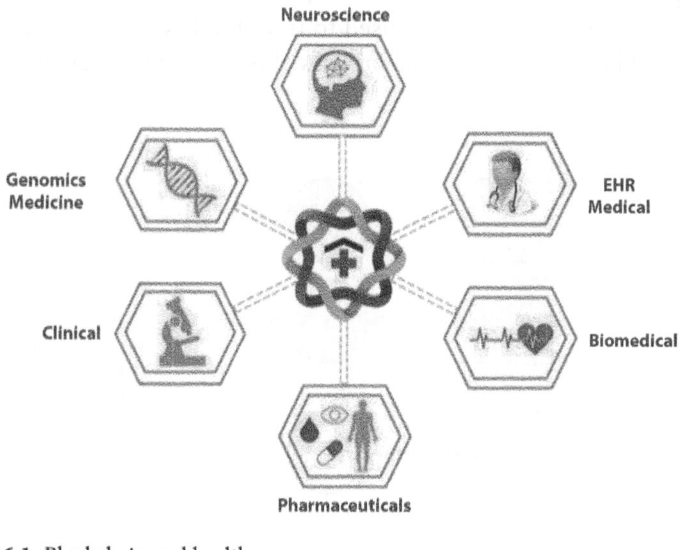

Figure 16.1 Blockchain and healthcare.

Ensemble Learning

A device understanding ensemble processes integrate the knowledge from multiple mastering models to enable more distinct and superior outcomes. The primary benefits of errors in model learning are variance, noise, and bias. The ensemble approaches used in machine learning (ML) help reduce these error-causing elements ensuring the accuracy and balance of ML algorithms. In a similar vein, machine learning ensemble approaches employ multiple models and derive benefits from the aggregated result, which is unquestionably a more accurate prediction than a single model.

16.1.1 Ensemble Techniques

16.1.1.1 Bagging or Bootstrap Aggregating

Variance errors in decision trees are reduced when the "bagging" or "bootstrap aggregating" ensemble method is used. Here, the objective is to generate replacement samples (subsets of the training data) at random. The subsets are then used to train decision trees or other algorithms. Multiple models are combined, which decreases variance, because the average forecast of many models is significantly more reliable and robust than that of a single model or decision tree.

By conforming the residuals of the initial boosting algorithm, data scientists create subsequent algorithms using a boosting ensemble technique, which gives more weight to observations that the prior model mispredicted. The complete data set is used to train the first boosting algorithm. The below Figure 16.2 shows the process of bootstrapped algorithm.

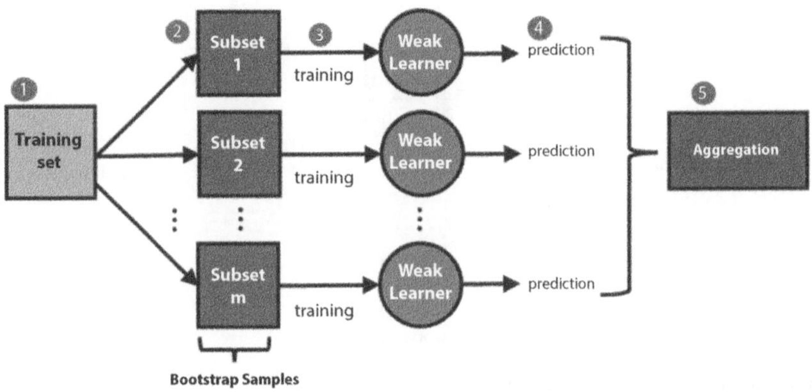

Figure 16.2 The process of bootstrapped algorithm.

16.1.1.2 Random Forest Models

With a small modification, the concept of bagging is applied to random forest area models. When choosing where to divide and how to make selections, bagged choice timber has access to all attainable features. While the final bootstrapped instance result may also differ slightly, each model's records will often break off on the same attributes. As an alternative, Random Wooded Area models randomly select functions to determine the division point. Random forest models feature a degree of variation rather than rending at comparable with attribute at each node for the amount of duration because each tree will split primarily based on numerous properties. This level of differentiation results in a higher ensemble to mixture throughout, which leads to the creation of a more distinct predictor.

16.1.1.3 Stacking

Stacking is a technique for grouping several regression or classification models. Although there are numerous ways to use an ensemble model, bagging and boosting are two of the more used techniques. Several similar models with high variants can be averaged using bagging to reduce variance. To reduce bias while maintaining a small variance, multiple incremental fashions are built upon. Stacking is a special paradigm commonly referred to as layered generalization. Examining the states of various models with a single effort is the goal of stacking. The concept is that there are exclusive approaches to learning problems that allow you to focus on only a portion of the issue and not the overall condition of the endeavor. In this manner, you can make multiple distinct launchers and utilize them as stepping stones, one for every version you come across. Next, a new model is added, and it uses intermediate predictions to identify a matched object.

16.1.2 Blockchain Overview

Blockchain is a disseminated digital ledger that enables peer communities to share records decentralized. Nakamoto *et al.* initially suggested it as a decentralized cryptocurrency. A blockchain is a gathering of blocks that can be connected using cryptographic hashes and timestamps. Every block is visible, searchable, cozy, and unchangeable. The chain grows each time a block is added to its conclusion, and each new block contains the content's hash value from the previous block. Every node is associated with a private key and public key. Consequently, the idea of an asymmetric secret is used by the blockchain network [12, 13]. The blocks are linked to one another by hash. SHA-256 and other cryptographic hash characteristics are used to generate the hashes. This demonstrates the blocks' immutability and anonymity. The transaction is digitally signed using a private key prior to being broadcast on a peer-to-peer network. It provides authentication and transaction integrity. After that, the transaction is made public across the network, and miners gather verified transactions into blocks that are timestamped. For settlement in a dispersed network, the network employs a unique consensus technique that includes, among many other things, proof of labor or evidence of stake. Before being added to a chain of blocks, the blocks are released in a community and confirmed there. Blockchain enables peer-to-peer acceptance. The distributed ledger, consensus, and cryptography constitute the three primary building blocks of the blockchain generation.

16.1.3 Blockchain Technology and Security of Health Data

The fact that the most common application of blockchain technology in the healthcare industry at the moment is data protection is hardly surprising. In the healthcare sector, safety is a big concern. Between July 2021 and June 2022, 692 significant breaches of medical records were reported. The thieves stole bank account details, credit card numbers, data from genetic and medical testing, and more.

Blockchain is the perfect era for data security packages because it can maintain an uncorruptible, decentralized, and transparent ledger of all patient information. In addition, the blockchain is transparent and private, protecting private medical data and identifying each individual through arduous and unrestricted protocols. One more advantage of the decentralized nature of the modern era is the equitable and unrestricted exchange of information between patients, doctors, and other health professionals.

16.1.4 A Health Care Blockchain Model

16.1.4.1 Scalability

A decentralized blockchain for medical records might encounter storage issues and throughput limitations. If built on the Bitcoin blockchain model, every member would need a copy of every health record, which is impractical. Due to the dynamic nature of health data, replicating it for all network members would be bandwidth-intensive and wasteful. Access control mechanisms would be necessary. The proposed medical blockchain would contain an ordered series of health records akin to a library's card catalog listing book locations and information.

16.1.4.2 Data Privacy and Access Security

The user would maintain complete control over their data, with the ability to manage access and permissions on their blockchain. Through a mobile dashboard application, the user could monitor and regulate who queries and updates their blockchain, as well as set access permissions. They would have visibility into access history, including who accessed their blockchain, when, and what data was retrieved. Using the same dashboard, the user could grant or revoke access to individuals with unique identities offering more nuanced control than binary permissions. This flexibility enables the user to establish detailed protocols for access, including authorized users, timeframes, and specific data categories. Importantly, the user retains the option to modify permissions as needed ensuring that access control remains under their exclusive control. These access control limitations would be tightly maintained on the blockchain empowering the user with clear oversight of data collection and sharing practices. The below Figure 16.2 shows the flow of data in the healthcare system.

16.2 Literature Survey

Over the last few years, a researchers has been dedicated to various aspects of healthcare data management, privacy preservation, and security enhancement. Chamikara *et al.* [1] presented a detailed methodology for privacy-preserving distributed machine learning using federated learning techniques. This approach aims to ensure data privacy

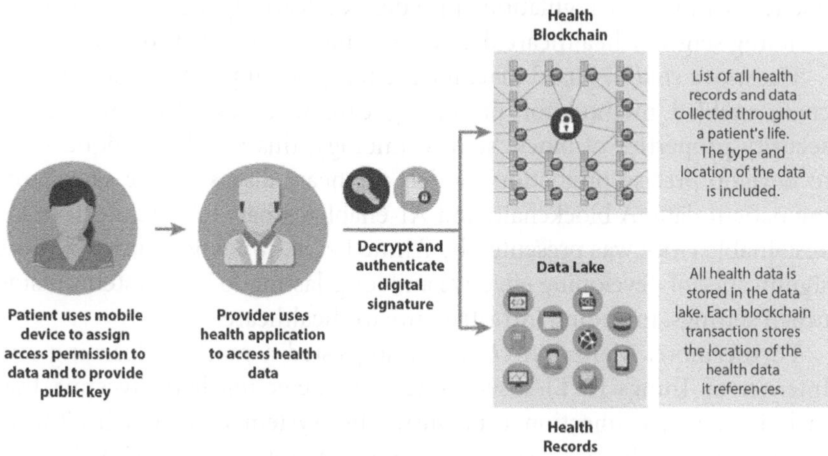

Figure 16.3 The flow of data in the healthcare system.

in scenarios involving distributed machine learning tasks, particularly relevant in healthcare settings where sensitive patient information must be protected. Deebak *et al.* [2] introduced a sophisticated security framework that utilizes chaotic-map-based authentication to ensure privacy preservation in remote point-of-care systems. This framework addresses the growing need for secure remote healthcare interactions, especially in situations where patient data are accessed and transmitted remotely.

Siddique *et al.* [3] explored the intersection of machine learning and healthcare communication, highlighting the potential of machine learning techniques to improve communication processes within healthcare organizations. They discussed various applications, including medical dialog systems and patient communication platforms showcasing how machine learning can enhance healthcare communication efficiency and effectiveness. Aqueveque *et al.* [4] created an innovative approach to privacy preservation specifically for movement analysis systems aimed at home care. This approach addresses privacy concerns associated with monitoring movement and activity patterns in home-care settings ensuring that sensitive patient data remains protected.

In addition, Wu *et al.* [5] suggested a blockchain-based privacy protection technique especially for drone communications enabled by 5G. Their approach aims to enhance the security and privacy of communications between drones and ground stations critical for applications such as medical supply delivery and aerial medical assistance. Truonga *et al.* [6] examined how to protect privacy in federated learning environments and provided advice from the standpoint of the GDPR (General Data Protection Regulation). This research explores strategies to ensure compliance with GDPR regulations in federated learning systems crucial for handling sensitive healthcare data while adhering to data protection laws.

Hasanova *et al.* [7] used machine learning techniques to create a blockchain-enabled method for predicting cardiac illness. By utilizing the security properties of blockchain technology, this novel technique seeks to develop precise prediction models for heart disease while safeguarding patient data. A blockchain and AI-enabled smart IoT architecture for sustainable cities was presented by Ahmed *et al.* [8], who emphasized the significance of developing effective and long-lasting IoT ecosystems inside urban settings, including infrastructure for healthcare.

Furthermore, Mahzabin *et al.* [9] suggested a machine learning and Internet of Things (IoT)-based system for detecting hypoglycemia that includes an auto-injection capability. This system enhances healthcare monitoring capabilities, particularly relevant for patients with diabetes who require continuous glucose monitoring and insulin administration. Kaushik and Kumar [10] demystified quantum blockchain for healthcare and examine how quantum computing might be used to handle patient data, especially in situations when better data security and processing power are needed. Khan *et al.* [11] presented a comprehensive healthcare ledger management system enabled by blockchain and machine learning technologies. This system offers a novel and secure architecture for the medical industry ensuring the truthfulness and privacy of healthcare data. Abbas *et al.* [12] examined the potential applications, challenges, and suggested future directions for blockchain technology in the healthcare industry using lessons from current digitalization trends and emphasizing the necessity of strong privacy protection measures.

Furthermore, in an effort to improve the dependability and security of healthcare information sharing, AlGhamdi *et al.* [13] concentrated on creating trusted IoT healthcare information-based AI and blockchain systems. To solve privacy problems and fraud detection in IoMT applications, Lakhan *et al.* [14] presented a blockchain-based IoMT system for healthcare that is built on federated learning and allows for fraud detection. To protect the security and privacy of lightweight medical devices, Rahmadika *et al.* [15] introduced a blockchain-based privacy preservation strategy for misbehavior detection in lightweight IoMT devices.

To solve the privacy and security issues of cloud-based healthcare systems, Verma [16] created a blockchain-based privacy preservation architecture for healthcare data in cloud contexts. In their discussion of privacy protection and security issues in multimodal machine learning research, Kumar *et al.* [17] emphasized the necessity of strong security protocols in the processing of healthcare data to safeguard sensitive patient information.

Furthermore, Ch *et al.* [18] focused on improving the security and integrity of healthcare systems by proposing a strong cyber-physical system-enabled smart healthcare unit using blockchain technology. In an effort to improve security in IoT healthcare contexts, Ashraf *et al.* [19] proposed Fidchain, a federated intrusion detection system for blockchain-enabled IoT healthcare applications. Puri and Haritha [20] talked on how to use frequency distribution of sensitive information to improve privacy preservation approaches for healthcare data increasing the efficacy of privacy preservation procedures.

With an emphasis on user control over data access and privacy, Pimple *et al.* [21] introduced Medisecure, a blockchain-enabled Ensemble Learning solution for user-controlled single sign-on and privacy preservation in medical cyber-physical systems. In an effort to improve data integrity in healthcare systems, Pimple *et al.* [22] suggested enhancing security measures in cyber-physical systems by deep neural network-based anomaly detection with Ethereum blockchain. Using a hybrid method, Somkunwar *et al.* [23] created a revolutionary human fall detection system with the goal of improving security and safety in healthcare environments. Finally, in an effort to create precise heart disease prediction models, Hasanova *et al.* [24] introduced a novel blockchain-enabled machine learning heart disease prediction mechanism.

16.2.1 Comparative Analysis of the Above Literature Survey

Each of the reviewed papers presents unique contributions and approaches to privacy preservation in medical and healthcare contexts. The literature covers a range of techniques including machine learning, cryptography, blockchain, and more. While each approach has its strengths, it is important to consider the specific context and application requirements when choosing a privacy preservation strategy. The below Table 16.1 shows the comparative analysis of the various research paper.

Table 16.1 Comparative analysis literature survey.

Reference no.	Objectives	Limitations
[1]	Distributed machine learning that protects privacy using federated learning methods	Limited scalability of federated learning approaches; implementation challenges in heterogeneous healthcare systems
[2]	Introducing a security framework for remote point-of-care systems with chaotic-map-based authentication	Lack of real-world validation; scalability concerns in large healthcare networks
[3]	Exploring machine learning applications in healthcare communication	Limited discussion on implementation challenges and scalability issues
[4]	Creating an approach to protect privacy for movement analysis systems aimed at home care	Lack of validation in real-world home-care environments; scalability concerns in large-scale deployments

(*Continued*)

Table 16.1 Comparative analysis literature survey. (*Continued*)

Reference no.	Objectives	Limitations
[5]	Putting forth a blockchain-based privacy protection strategy for communications via drones enabled by 5G	Limited discussion on interoperability with existing communication protocols; scalability challenges in drone networks
[6]	Perspectives on GDPR-related privacy protection in federated learning systems	Limited discussion on practical implementation challenges; generalizability of GDPR regulations to diverse contexts
[7]	Developing a blockchain-based machine learning method to forecast cardiac illness	Lack of extensive validation in diverse healthcare settings; scalability challenges in handling large datasets
[8]	Creating a smart IoT framework for sustainable cities with blockchain and AI enabled	Limited discussion on real-world implementation challenges; scalability concerns in heterogeneous IoT environments
[9]	Putting into practice an IoT- and machine learning-based hypoglycemia monitoring system with auto-injection capability that is connected to blockchain	Lack of validation in real-world medical settings; scalability challenges in handling real-time data streams
[10]	Demystifying quantum blockchain for healthcare	Limited discussion on practical implementation challenges of quantum blockchain in healthcare settings; scalability concerns in quantum computing infrastructure

(*Continued*)

Table 16.1 Comparative analysis literature survey. (*Continued*)

Reference no.	Objectives	Limitations
[11]	Creating a cutting-edge, safe architecture with blockchain and machine intelligence to manage medical records	Limited validation in real-world healthcare systems; scalability challenges in handling large-scale medical data
[12]	Introducing blockchain technology for healthcare: opportunities, challenges, and suggested future developments	Limited discussion on real-world implementation challenges; generalizability of findings to diverse healthcare contexts
[13]	Creating blockchain- and AI-powered trustworthy IoT healthcare information systems	Limited discussion on interoperability with existing healthcare systems; scalability concerns in heterogeneous IoT environments
[14]	Designing a blockchain-enabled IoMT system for healthcare that uses federated learning to protect privacy and prevent fraud	Limited validation in real-world healthcare settings; scalability challenges in handling large-scale medical data
[15]	Putting out a blockchain-based privacy preservation plan for lightweight IoMT device misbehavior detection	Lack of validation in real-world medical settings; scalability concerns in lightweight IoMT device networks
[16]	Presenting a cloud-based blockchain-based framework for healthcare data privacy preservation	Limited discussion on practical implementation challenges; scalability concerns in cloud-based healthcare data storage
[17]	Examining security and privacy issues in multimodal machine learning research for the medical field	Limited discussion on real-world implementation challenges; scalability concerns in multimodal machine learning systems

(*Continued*)

Table 16.1 Comparative analysis literature survey. (*Continued*)

Reference no.	Objectives	Limitations
[18]	Leveraging blockchain technology to design a smart healthcare facility with a resilient cyber-physical system	Lack of validation in real-world healthcare environments; scalability challenges in heterogeneous cyber-physical healthcare systems
[19]	Creating Fidchain, a federated intrusion detection solution for Internet of Things (IoT) healthcare applications enabled by blockchain	Limited validation in real-world healthcare settings; scalability concerns in blockchain-enabled IoT healthcare networks
[20]	Enhancing healthcare data privacy protection strategy through frequency distribution of sensitive information	Limited discussion on real-world implementation challenges; scalability concerns in handling large-scale healthcare datasets
[21]	Creating Medisecure, a blockchain-powered Ensemble Learning method for medical cyber-physical systems that allows for user-controlled single sign-on and privacy protection	Lack of validation in real-world medical settings; scalability concerns in cyber-physical healthcare systems
[22]	Using the Ethereum blockchain to implement deep neural network-based anomaly detection in cyber-physical systems to increase security and improve data integrity	Limited validation in real-world cyber-physical healthcare environments; scalability concerns in Ethereum blockchain-based systems
[23]	Creating a novel hybrid strategy for human fall detection system	Limited validation in real-world medical settings; scalability concerns in deploying the system across diverse healthcare environments

(*Continued*)

Table 16.1 Comparative analysis literature survey. (*Continued*)

Reference no.	Objectives	Limitations
[24]	Presenting a revolutionary machine learning algorithm-based blockchain-based heart disease prediction system	Lack of extensive validation in diverse healthcare settings; scalability challenges in handling large datasets
[25]	Creating a smart IoT framework for sustainable cities with blockchain and AI enabled	Limited discussion on real-world implementation challenges; scalability concerns in heterogeneous IoT environments

16.3 Identification of the Problem

Ensuring the utmost security of patient data is paramount. It necessitates employing state-of-the-art security protocols and validation methodologies to ensure comprehensive encryption and safeguarding of patient data within applications. A meticulous examination of security concerns is imperative for the entire Medical Cyber-Physical System (MCPS). Cloud-based healthcare systems encounter formidable security challenges, including unauthorized data access and manipulation of sensitive patient data stored in the cloud. Consequently, cloud-based healthcare systems and MCPS have to abide with stringent security requirements. Authentication stands as a fundamental prerequisite ensuring robust verification of the identities of healthcare professionals, patients and other system users through reliable cryptographic techniques. Authorization follows authentication guaranteeing that authorized users are granted appropriate access to system resources, with access levels tailored to individual privileges. Non-repudiation is crucial employing cryptographic methods, such as digital signatures, encryption, and time-stamps, to ascertain the authenticity of communications and the legitimacy of patients within the medical system, thereby preventing denial of involvement. Furthermore, integrity and confidentiality measures are imperative ensuring the integrity of received communications and safeguarding against unauthorized alterations of patient data within the healthcare system.

16.4 Objectives

1. Identify Specific Security Challenges: Conduct a thorough analysis of the security vulnerabilities inherent in CPS deployed within healthcare settings, including potential hostile attacks, unauthorized access, and data breaches targeting medical equipment and patient records.
2. Implement Ensemble Learning: Utilize Ensemble Learning techniques to enhance the accuracy of threat identification and categorization in CPS security applications. By integrating various base learners, such as support vector machines, decision trees, and neural networks, aim to bolster the resilience and generalization capabilities of security models against cyber threats.
3. Integrate Blockchain Technology: Explore the incorporation of blockchain technology into healthcare CPS to establish a decentralized and tamper-proof ledger for managing and preserving sensitive data. Leverage blockchain-based smart contracts and cryptography methods to ensure data integrity, traceability, and auditability while facilitating secure transactions among stakeholders.
4. Employ Multi-Attribute Feature Selection (MAFS): Deploy MAFS methodologies to maximize the selection of relevant features for CPS security applications. Systematically evaluate and select attribute subsets based on their contributions to threat detection and classification tasks, thereby enhancing the effectiveness and scalability of security models.
5. Develop Comprehensive Security System: Propose a holistic system that combines Ensemble Learning algorithms, blockchain-enabled data management mechanisms, and MAFS-driven feature selection methodologies to strengthen CPS security in healthcare. Demonstrate through empirical evaluation and case studies how this integrated approach improves security resilience, safeguards data confidentiality, and preserves the integrity of healthcare systems amid evolving cyber threats.

16.5 Proposed Methodology

The authentication process is used by the MCPS approach to get over the constraints on data integrity and continentality. The suggested technique for key authentication makes use of a multi-attribute ensemble approach. The key generation scheme can be constructed differently depending on a number of ensemble classifier properties. It is advisable to thoroughly list all the factors that impact the strategy and evaluate their respective usefulness or value, an extra key that's utilized to generate authentication keys. This particular key is pre-shared by the sender and receiver before the system is even started.

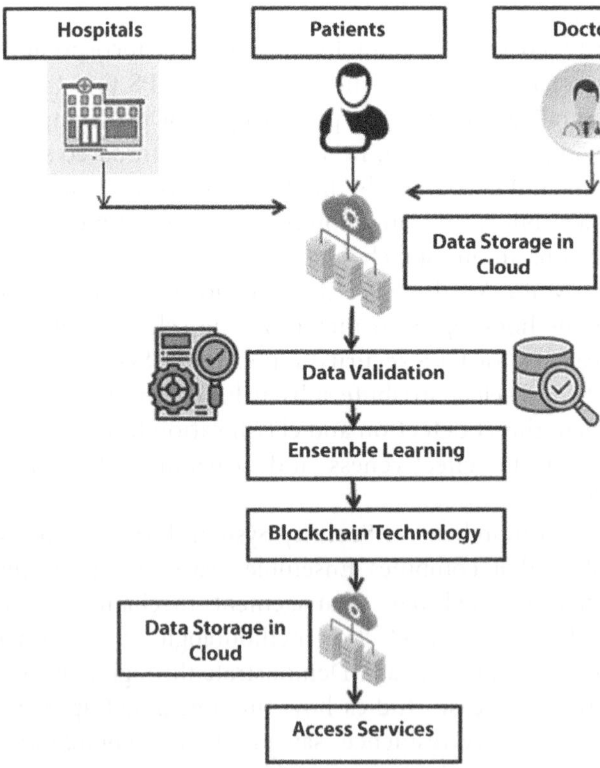

Figure 16.4 MCPS model based on authentication mechanism that is being proposed.

To attain the intended objectives, subsequent actions will be taken:

1. A thorough review of the literature on security assaults and defenses against MCPS-related threats.
2. Examining the several network layer security mechanisms utilized by MCPS.
3. Examining several network layer packet-based attacks.
4. Evaluation of the MCPS security system's machine learning algorithm.
5. Modeling the current techniques.
6. The current security protocol can be improved by utilizing a multiple attribute ensemble classifier.
7. Investigation of the proposed algorithm's performance in relation to different security risks and a measure of the algorithm's resilience.

16.5.1 The Model-Building Procedure Based on the DCNN and Bag of Features

In this section, the methodology for detecting cyberattacks is outlined combining the bag of features methodology with deep convolutional neural networks (DCNN). The bag of features method involves selecting key features from complex traffic data scenarios encompassing both normal and attack instances. This approach allows for the extraction and representation of essential characteristics from diverse traffic data aiding in the identification of patterns indicative of attacks within the network. Deep convolutional neural networks (DCNN) are then employed for the detection of binary data distinguishing between normal and attack traffic. DCNNs are renowned for their efficiency in processing binary data making them well suited for cyberattack detection tasks. Additionally, DCNNs exhibit high data handling capacity enabling them to effectively analyze large volumes of traffic data and extract meaningful patterns for accurate classification. By integrating the bag of features approach with DCNNs, the proposed methodology offers a comprehensive framework for cyberattack detection leveraging the strengths of both techniques to enhance the accurateness and effectiveness of finding systems in complex network environments. Secure cyberspace for preserving cyber data employs blockchain technology, specifically Ethereum-based public blockchain. Ethereum is chosen over other blockchain platforms due to its elimination of third-party involvement in transactions and minimal downtime. The final phase

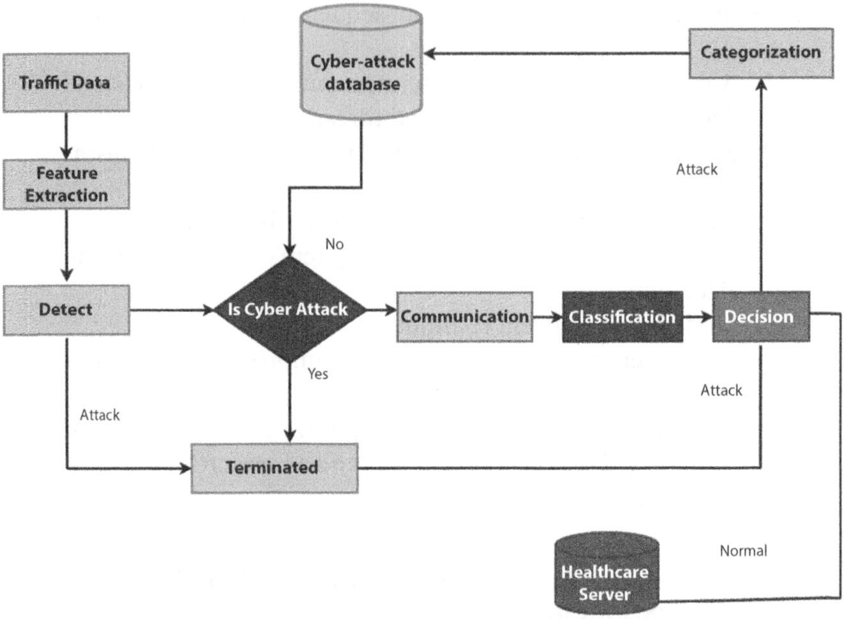

Figure 16.5 Model of cyberattack detection in healthcare system.

involves securely storing the outcomes within a public blockchain driven by Ethereum, as depicted in the algorithm. The processing of algorithm and model is shown in Figure 16.5. The processing of algorithm is described here.

The functioning algorithm is described here, along with the steps involved in building the model using a DCNN and bag of features.

Algorithm

G = group of patterns
SM = vector of DCNN
N = size of sample data
Xi = sample of bag of features
O = mapped data of cluster
V = vector of feature data process
Bf = mapping of features
Wn = weight matric
D = dimension of data
S = sample of set
R = relation of feature data

$B^{\varnothing}$ = adjust matrix
Ac = learning factor
Process
Generates list of features of cyber traffic data for all features of BOF
if (ETH_set >= threshold_set)
Compiled and deployed the process on categorization
The cyberattack data are stored in a block as a transaction.
A unique ID is allotted to the transaction.
Else
The process of training sample as $(X_i \in R^D, y_i \in R)$, i=1..................m

$sample\ of\ input\ (p)$ if $* = V$
$[s^1, \ldots.. s^k] \leftarrow [rand(1,k) \times (p - w)] + 1$
$V \leftarrow n$ vector of neuron
For $i \leftarrow 1\ to\ N\ do$
$O \in C^D \leftarrow S* = V$
$N_*^i \in R^D \leftarrow biase\ of\ O$
$G \in R^D \leftarrow pattern\ N$
End for
Input sample of BF $g_*^1, \ldots\ldots.. g_*^m$
$F_{RBF} \in R^{D \times m} \leftarrow \varnothing([g_*^1, \ldots\ldots.. g_*^m])$ $Adjust\ W$
$W \in R^D \leftarrow BF^{-1}$
$F \in R^d \leftarrow W^T\ \varnothing(G)$

For $C \leftarrow 1\ to\ A_c\ do$ $training\ of\ class\ Cb$
Adjust the cascading process's weight factor.
$CC \in R^{d*} \leftarrow$ relative feature process of SOM
Call kernel function

$$k(x_i, x_j) = \exp\left(\frac{-\|x_i - x_j\|^2}{\gamma}\right), \gamma \in R_+$$

End for
Adjustment matrix $B^{\varnothing}$ of space F mapping of same class

$$B_{ij}^{\varnothing} = \{ \begin{matrix} e^{(-\|x_i - x_j\|^2)}. \\ e^{(-\|x_i - x_j\|^2)}. \end{matrix}$$

16.6 Result and Discussion

The implementation of the multi-attribute ensemble technique within the Medical Cyber-Physical System (MCPS) serves as the cornerstone of its primary authentication design significantly mitigating the risk of data leakage

Table 16.2 Comparative results of DARPA Intrusion Detection Evaluation Dataset of different sets of attributes for detection.

Number of attribute	Methods	Accuracy	Precision	Recall	F-score
5	CML-ADI	98.84	98.87	96.78	97.87
	DIN-V1	97.81	97.87	96.77	95.99
	FFD-CNN	96.82	95.57	95.98	95.87
	BGF-CNN	95.77	95.95	95.88	98.85
	Proposed	99.55	99.15	98.78	99.16
10	CML-ADI	98.75	98.92	97.65	96.91
	DIN-V1	97.74	97.65	97.69	96.89
	FFD-CNN	96.78	95.89	96.95	95.85
	BGF-CNN	95.71	96.68	96.98	98.79
	Proposed	99.45	99.25	98.74	99.26
15	CML-ADI	98.65	98.93	96.75	97.88
	DIN-V1	96.89	97.88	97.18	95.91
	FFD-CNN	96.68	95.88	95.99	95.79
	BGF-CNN	96.67	96.75	95.89	98.89
	Proposed	99.35	99.36	98.91	99.39
20	CML-ADI	98.55	98.85	97.61	96.85
	DIN-V1	96.85	97.84	97.39	95.85
	FFD-CNN	96.74	95.95	96.87	95.99
	BGF-CNN	95.73	96.51	96.91	98.75
	Proposed	99.25	99.46	98.69	99.48
25	CML-ADI	98.45	97.99	96.85	96.79
	DIN-V1	96.79	97.83	96.86	95.75
	FFD-CNN	96.79	96.76	95.97	95.76
	BGF-CNN	95.89	96.98	95.96	98.91
	Proposed	99.15	99.28	98.78	99.55

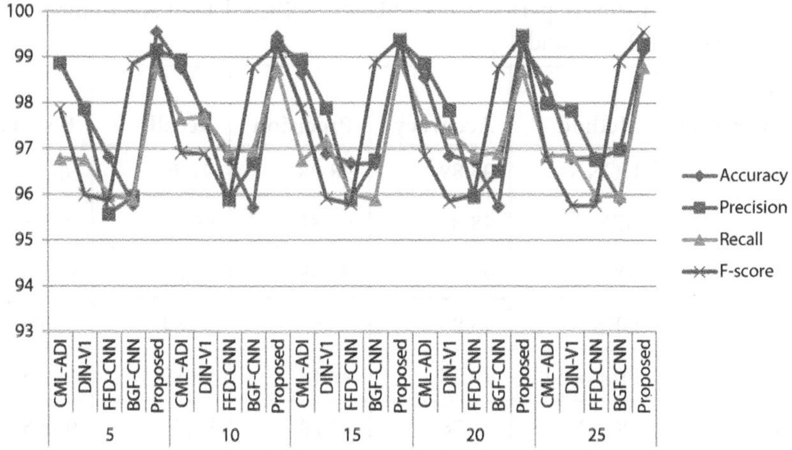

Figure 16.6 Comparative results of DARPA Intrusion Detection Evaluation Dataset of different sets of attributes for detection.

and ensuring a highly secure pathway for information exchange between patients and clinicians. The above Figure 16.6 shows the comparative results of DARPA intrusion detection evaluation dataset of different sets of attributes for detection. Leveraging datasets, such as DARPA Intrusion Detection Evaluation Dataset, which offer a diverse set of attributes for detection, and UNSW-NB15, along with varying numbers of attributes (ranging from 15 to 35), enhance the robustness of the authentication framework. Anticipated outcomes encompass increased resistance to data leakage facilitated by the comprehensive coverage provided by the ensemble technique across different datasets and attribute sets. Additionally, the attainment of optimal forward secrecy, a challenge typically difficult to address with traditional symmetric algorithms alone, is expected to fortify data protection measures. The system will also feature attribute-key validation mechanisms to authenticate user credentials effectively. Furthermore, the integration of advanced technologies into medical practices is poised to improve the communication of healthcare information to patients. The architecture is meticulously developed with a comprehensive understanding of the diverse security challenges encountered by MCPS ensuring a resilient defense against potential threats. By employing individual models to address various security concerns across datasets with different attribute sets, the proposed framework is anticipated to offer comprehensive coverage and effectively bolster the overall security posture of MCPS. Figure 16.7 & Table 16.3 shows the comparative performance of UNSW-NB15 dataset and number of attribute.

Table 16.3 Comparative performance of UNSW-NB15 dataset and number of attribute (15, 20, 25, 30, and 35).

Number of attribute	Method	Accuracy	Precision	Recall	F-score
15	DCNN	95.89	98.98	97.79	95.87
	BPNN	98.87	98.82	96.75	97.75
	RL	97.85	96.98	96.88	95.75
	DBN	96.89	96.56	95.84	95.89
	Proposed	99.25	99.18	98.89	98.75
20	DCNN	95.78	98.78	97.65	96.65
	BPNN	98.91	98.95	9679	96.98
	RL	97.87	96.69	97.75	96.84
	DBN	96.88	95.93	96.76	95.85
	Proposed	99.34	99.22	98.85	98.65
25	DCNN	96.75	98.85	96.78	95.75
	BPNN	98.89	98.85	96.65	96.86
	RL	96.89	96.89	96.86	95.61
	DBN	96.87	94.99	95.59	95.75
	Proposed	99.38	99.28	98.81	98.55
30	DCNN	95.98	98.81	97.87	96.67
	BPNN	98.75	98.89	97.55	96.76
	RL	96.95	96.97	96.76	95.68
	DBN	96.99	95.41	96.96	95.74
	Proposed	99.52	99.35	98.76	98.45
35	DCNN	96.65	98.87	96.89	96.77
	BPNN	98.97	97.99	95.97	96.66
	RL	96.99	95.96	96.89	95.99
	DBN	96.78	95.77	94.46	95.78
	Proposed	99.49	98.99	98.95	99.15

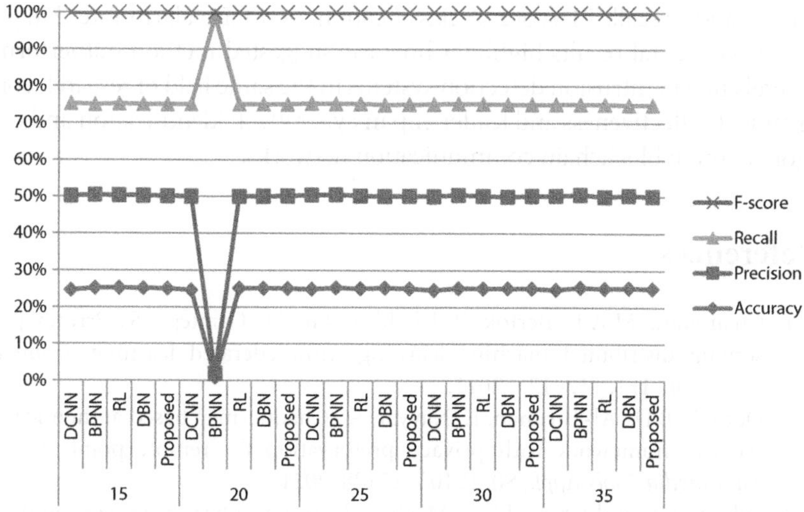

Figure 16.7 Comparative performance of UNSW-NB15 dataset and number of attribute (15, 20, 25, 30, and 35).

16.7 Conclusion and Future Work

This paper presents a state-of-the-art deep learning-based system designed to identify and categorize cyberattacks in blockchain-based communication networks. The system, which consists of three separate subsystems—the feature engineering subsystem, the feature learning subsystem, and the detection and classification subsystem—is painstakingly developed, tested, and validated. As part of this research project, every subsystem is individually developed and then integrated, verified, and validated. With the help of a CNN-based architecture, the suggested system shows remarkable ability to recognize and classify slightly altered cyberattacks that are specific to blockchain networks. This is demonstrated using the DARPA Intrusion Detection Evaluation Dataset and UNSW-NB15 dataset, which include important attacks on blockchain computing.

The algorithm not only displays an impressive 99.3% detection accuracy in identifying anomalous and regular traffic but also demonstrates a 98.2% classification accuracy in dividing blockchain traffic into five different groups. A rigorous fivefold cross-validation procedure is used, with five separate tests for every classification model to guarantee resilience in system validation. To provide thorough insights into system performance, the evaluation process also makes use of confusion matrix parameters (TN, TP, FN, and FP) and computes a number of performance metrics, such as classification precision, classification recall, F1-score of classification, and false alarm rate. Finally, the experimental results highlight how the suggested method outperforms several current intrusion detection systems in the same field of research confirming its effectiveness and leadership in cyberattack identification and categorization in blockchain communication networks.

References

1. Chamikara, M.A.P., Bertok, P., Khalil, I., Liu, D., Camtepe, S., Privacy preserving distributed machine learning with federated learning. *Comput. Commun.*, 171, 112–125, 2021.
2. Deebak, B.D., Al-Turjman, F., Nayyar, A., Chaotic-map based authenticated security framework with privacy preservation for remote point-of-care. *Multimedia Tools Appl.*, 80, 17103–17128, 2021.
3. Siddique, S. and Chow, J.CL., Machine learning in healthcare communication. *Encyclopedia*, 1, 1, 220–239, 2021.
4. Aqueveque, P., Gómez, B., Williams, P.AH., Li, Z., A Novel Privacy Preservation and Quantification Methodology for Implementing Home-Care-Oriented Movement Analysis Systems. *Sensors*, 22, 13, 4677, 2022.
5. Wu, Y., Dai, H.-N., Wang, H., Choo, K.-K.R., Blockchain-based privacy preservation for 5g-enabled drone communications. *IEEE Network*, 35, 1, 50–56, 2021.
6. Nguyen, T. Sun, K. Wang, S. Guitton, F. and Guo, Y., Privacy preservation in federated learning: An insightful survey from the GDPR perspective. *Comput. Secur.*, 110, 102402, 2021.
7. Hasanova, H., Tufail, M., Baek, U.-J., Park, J.-T., Kim, M.-S., A novel blockchain-enabled heart disease prediction mechanism using machine learning. *Comput. Electr. Eng.*, 101, 108086, 2022.
8. Ahmed, I., Zhang, Y., Jeon, G., Lin, W., Khosravi, M.R., Qi, L., A blockchain-and artificial intelligence-enabled smart IoT framework for sustainable city. *Int. J. Intell. Syst.*, 37, 9, 6493–6507, 2022.
9. Mahzabin, R., Sifat, F.H., Anjum, S., Nayan, A.-A., Kibria, M.G., Blockchain associated machine learning and IoT based hypoglycemia detection system with auto-injection feature, arXiv preprint arXiv:2208.02222, 2022.
10. Keshav, K. and Kumar, A., Demystifying quantum blockchain for healthcare. *Secur. Privacy,* 6, 3, e284, 2023.
11. Khan, A.A., Laghari, A.A., Shafiq, M., Cheikhrouhou, O., Alhakami, W., Hamam, H., Shaikh, Z.A., Healthcare Ledger Management: A Blockchain and Machine Learning-Enabled Novel and Secure Architecture for Medical Industry. *Human-Centric Comput. Inf. Sci.*, 12, 1–14, 2022.
12. Abbas, A.F., Qureshi, N.A., Khan, N., Chandio, R., Ali, J., The Blockchain Technologies in Healthcare: Prospects, Obstacles, and Future Recommendations; Lessons Learned from Digitalization. *Int. J. Online Biomed. Eng.*, 18, 9, 144–159, 2022.

13. AlGhamdi, R., Alassafi, M.O., Alshdadi, A.A., Dessouky, M.M., Ramdan, R.A., Aboshosha, B.W., Developing Trusted IoT Healthcare Information-Based AI and Blockchain. *Processes*, 11, 1, 34, 2022.
14. Abdullah, L., Mohammed, M.A., Nedoma, J., Martinek, R., Tiwari, P., Vidyarthi, A., Alkhayyat, A. and Wang, W., Federated-learning based privacy preservation and fraud-enabled blockchain IoMT system for healthcare. *IEEE J. Biomed. Health Inform.*, 27, 2, 664–672, 2022.
15. Sandi, R., Astillo, P.V., Choudhary, G., Duguma, D.G., Sharma, V., and You, I., Blockchain-based privacy preservation scheme for misbehavior detection in lightweight IoMT devices. *IEEE J. Biomed. Health Inform.*, 27, 2, 710–721, 2022.
16. Garima, V., Blockchain-based privacy preservation framework for healthcare data in cloud environment. *J. Expt. Artif. Intell.*, 36, 1, 147–160, 2024.
17. Kumar, S., Chaube, M.K., Nenavath, S.N., Gupta, S.K., Tetarave, S.K., Privacy preservation and security challenges: A new frontier multimodal machine learning research. *Int. J. Sens. Netw.*, 39, 4, 227–245, 2022.
18. Ch, R., Srivastava, G., Nagasree, Y.L.V., Ponugumati, A., Ramachandran, S., Robust Cyber-Physical System Enabled Smart Healthcare Unit Using Blockchain Technology. *Electronics*, 11, 19, 3070, 2022.
19. Ashraf, E., Areed, N.FF., Salem, H., Abdelhay, E.H., Farouk, A., Fidchain: Federated intrusion detection system for blockchain-enabled iot healthcare applications. *Healthcare*, 10, 6, 1110, 2022, MDPI.
20. Puri, G.D. and Haritha, D., Improving Privacy Preservation Approach for Healthcare Data using Frequency Distribution of Delicate Information. *Int. J. Adv. Comput. Sci. Appl.*, 13, 9, 82–90, 2022.
21. Pimple, J.F., Sharma, A., Mishra, J.K., Medisecure: A blockchain-enabled ensemble learning approach for user-controlled single sign-on and privacy preservation in medical cyber-physical systems, in: *International Conference on the Role of AI in Bio-Medical Translations' Research for the Health Care Industry*, Springer Nature Switzerland, Cham, pp. 71–86, 2023.
22. Pimple, J.F., Sharma, A., Mishra, J.K., Elevating Security Measures in Cyber-Physical Systems: Deep Neural Network-Based Anomaly Detection with Ethereum Blockchain for Enhanced Data Integrity. *J. Electr. Syst.*, 19, 2, 105–115, 2023.
23. Somkunwar, R.K., Thorat, N., Pimple, J., Dhumal, R., Choudhari, Y., A novel based human fall detection system using hybrid approach. *J. Data Acquis. Process*, 38, 3985, 2023.
24. Hasanova, H., Tufail, M., Baek, U.-J., Park, J.-T., Kim, M.-S., A novel blockchain-enabled heart disease prediction mechanism using machine learning. *Comput. Electr. Eng.*, 101, 108086, 2022.
25. Ahmed, I., Zhang, Y., Jeon, G., Lin, W., Khosravi, M.R., Qi, L., A blockchain-and artificial intelligence-enabled smart IoT framework for sustainable city. *Int. J. Intell. Syst.*, 37, 9, 6493–6507, 2022.

17

Digitizing Wellness: A Deep Dive Into EHR/EMR Systems

Parul Dubey[1]*, Anansingh Thinakaran[2] and Rajendra Motiramji Rewatkar[3]

[1]*Symbiosis Institute of Technology, Nagpur Campus, Symbiosis International (Deemed University), Pune, India*
[2]*Department of Artificial Intelligence, G. H. Raisoni College of Engineering, Nagpur, MH, India*
[3]*Biomedical Engineering Department, Faculty of Engineering and Technology, Datta Meghe Institute of Higher Education and Research, Wardha, India*

Abstract

This chapter provides an insightful guide on leveraging Amazon Web Services (AWS) for implementing Electronic Health Records (EHR) and Electronic Medical Records (EMR) systems, a key step toward the digital transformation in healthcare. It outlines the critical role of AWS in ensuring scalability, security, and compliance of healthcare data, detailing essential AWS services including HealthLake, S3, Lambda, EC2, and IAM. These tools collectively offer a robust infrastructure for managing sensitive healthcare information, adhering to regulations, and safeguarding patient privacy. The narration extends to exploiting AWS's capabilities in building scalable solutions, harnessing AI for predictive analytics, and integrating various applications to enhance healthcare delivery. Real-world examples underscore the practical benefits and lessons learned from deploying EHR/EMR systems on AWS providing valuable insights for healthcare organizations. Concluding with a proposed AWS architecture for EHR/EMR systems, the chapter highlights AWS's adaptability in meeting healthcare needs, driving innovation, and improving patient care. This guide empowers healthcare providers with the knowledge to transform healthcare delivery leading to a more efficient, patient-centered ecosystem.

Keywords: Amazon Web Services (AWS), Electronic Health Records (EHR), Electronic Medical Records (EMR), digital transformation, healthcare data security, AI and analytics

**Corresponding author*: dubeyparul29@gmail.com

Parul Dubey, Mangala Madankar, Pushkar Dubey and Bui Thanh Hung (eds.) The Impact of Algorithmic Technologies on Healthcare, (375–396) © 2025 Scrivener Publishing LLC

17.1 Introduction

In particular, the widespread use of electronic health record (EHR) and electronic medical record (EMR) systems has revolutionized the way healthcare is delivered as a direct result of the information technology revolution. These digital platforms are leading the way in a number of distinct areas, including the enhancement of patient care, the enhancement of operational efficiency, and the overall paradigm of healthcare delivery. Within this chapter, readers will gain a deeper understanding of EHR and EMR systems, as well as their purpose within the modern healthcare system. Additionally, readers will gain an appreciation for the significant role that AWS plays in the implementation and optimization of these systems.

EHR and EMR systems are the next logical step in the digitization of patient records [1]. These systems improve the accessibility, completeness, and efficiency of patient records. EHRs and EMRs are sometimes used interchangeably; however, there are small but significant differences between the two. Rather than using paper records, electronic medical record systems enable a single practice to maintain a digital record of their patients' medical histories, diagnoses, medications, and treatment plans [2]. This allows the practice to better serve its patients. Systems, on the other hand, take a more holistic approach. They enable the sharing of patient records across a variety of healthcare settings, which enables them to deliver coordinated care and comprehensive health insights. In addition, these systems reflect the characteristics of electronic medical records.

The digitalization of modern healthcare is largely dependent on the use of EHR and EMR technologies. The ability to make better decisions, increase the accuracy of patient data, simplify administrative procedures, and improve workflow efficiency are just some of the many benefits that it offers. This patient-centered approach makes it possible to make treatment decisions that are more informed, to achieve better health outcomes, and to make fewer mistakes in medical care [3]. The digital revolution of healthcare records, which is about more than just making operations easier, is ushering in a healthcare system that is more tightly integrated, more efficient, and more focused on quality.

17.2 Literature Review

The purpose of one of the systematic research [4] was to determine what factors impact healthcare providers' attitudes about the use of EHRs and other electronic health records to raise standards of healthcare delivery in

GCC nations. They combed the Gulf region for main studies that assessed the attitudes of healthcare providers about EHRs and EMRS. For this study, researchers combed through six databases: Medline, CINAHL, Science Direct, ProQuest, PubMed, and Scopus. The databases covered the years 2007–2016. In all, 13 papers were considered for inclusion in this meta-analysis. Perceptions of the systems by healthcare providers can be influenced, for better or worse, by both individual and system-related factors. It is crucial for policymakers to comprehend the influence of healthcare professionals' perceptions of health information technology to guarantee the success of the implementation initiatives. The impact of healthcare practitioners' age, gender, and occupation on their views on e-health technology should be further investigated in future research.

Discoveries and obstacles are part of the process as researchers move through the stages of the EMR Adoption Model developed by the Health Information and Management Systems Society [5]. Involvement, connection building, process management (including teaching and communication), and solution building are all crucial. Clinical risk management integration relies heavily on Failure Mode and Effects Analysis. When it comes to information systems, in particular, conventional project management practices tend to center on the positive aspects. Clinical risk management integration also requires Just Culture. While it is true that every healthcare IT company aspires to be the first to market with groundbreaking solutions, it is equally important to keep in mind the fundamentals. Assuring early and ongoing support from clinician users is a key component of every successful health technology project.

By surveying people about their thoughts and experiences with this tech [6], researchers found out if these internet platforms are going to revolutionize healthcare in the future or if they should look into alternative options. The usefulness, impact on health care, hazards, and challenges of electronic charting technology were examined through peer-reviewed scholarly articles, which were used for secondary research. A poll was used to gather primary data and gauge public sentiment toward electronic charting, its advantages, and its potential for growth in the future. This technology has numerous strengths, a few areas for improvement, and tremendous popular acceptance according to the results of this study. Medical professionals should only plan to employ this technology going forward, and they should work tirelessly to refine and enhance it so that it can revolutionize healthcare.

The use of Hospital Information Systems has grown among hospitals as a means to streamline operations and better serve patients [7]. Despite technology breakthroughs and the significant financial benefits, there are still hurdles to integrating information systems in healthcare. Because of these problems, some medical professionals are reluctant to adopt these systems. In addition, healthcare facilities' operations and the information systems put in place to support them are not always subject to thorough investigation and diagnosis. Thankfully, process mining techniques can optimize company processes, albeit they are usually used after the fact, after the go-live. By suggesting an Enhanced Model to improve upon the current EHR Implementation Lifecycle, this article shows how process mining can aid in the adoption of an EMR/EHR. Not only should process mining not be reserved for post-implementation or post-go-live but should instead be applied appropriately throughout the EHR Implementation lifecycle. Consequently, authors suggest an Enhanced EHR installation lifecycle that incorporates process mining into the testing procedure for the usability of EMRs and EHRs in line with the organization's workflow during other phases of installation. To determine if the suggested approach for implementing an enhanced EHR/EMR is feasible, an experiment is conducted using event logs from an open-source EHR.

The integrated data that comes out of the system [8] not only let doctors and patients see each other's medical history but also uses patients' own health records to see how treatments are affecting their overall health, which means they can give better care. Healthcare data received and streamed from disparate systems can be integrated in real time using data integration techniques including ETL and cloud-based technology. From a unified perspective of integrated EHR and PHR data, it will facilitate the recommendation of high-quality treatments to both patients and providers. Both patients and doctors can benefit from this processed data; the former uses it to prescribe therapies, while the latter uses it for self-care. This technique makes use of cloud computing to efficiently transmit combined data from several healthcare databases.

17.3 AWS and Healthcare Solutions

AWS has emerged as a formidable ally in the road toward digital transformation that the healthcare industry is undertaking. AWS provides a package of services that are tailored to meet the specific requirements of healthcare providers who are deploying (EHR) and EMR systems. These services include a cloud computing platform that is resilient, secure, and scalable. From data storage and processing with Amazon S3 and AWS Lambda to advanced analytics with Amazon SageMaker, AWS provides solutions that assist healthcare businesses in effectively managing their data, adhering to regulatory standards, and utilizing the power of cloud computing to provide superior care to their patients.

The dedication of AWS to security and compliance is particularly relevant in the healthcare business, which places a high premium on the confidentiality and privacy of patient information. By utilizing AWS, healthcare businesses are able to take advantage of sophisticated security features that safeguard patient information and guarantee compliance with regulations such as the Health Insurance Portability and Accountability Act (HIPAA) in the United States [9]. Another interesting point is that Amazon Web Services (AWS) makes improvements in patient care and operational efficiency possible by enabling the deployment of scalable healthcare solutions. These solutions are able to expand in response to the needs of an organization.

Discover the inner workings of EHR and EMR systems, as well as the ways in which AWS can change the digitization of healthcare, and how the organization may use these technologies to provide better patient outcomes while simultaneously reducing costs [10].

17.4 AWS Services for Healthcare

To meet the complicated and ever-changing demands of the healthcare business, AWS provides a range of products and services. The management, processing, and security of the massive volumes of data produced by EHR and EMR systems rely heavily on these services [11]. Read on as researchers explore the primary AWS services that make these procedures possible enhancing the accessibility, security, and actionability of healthcare data. Figure 17.1 shows the AWS services for Heathcare.

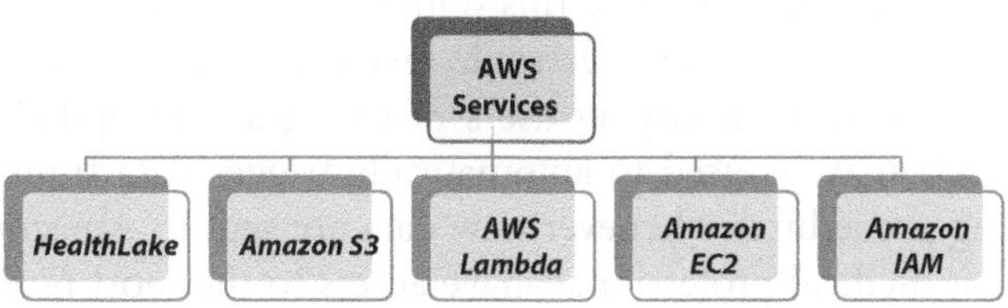

Figure 17.1 AWS services for healthcare.

A. AWS HealthLake

AWS HealthLake is a service that meets the requirements of the Health Insurance Portability and Accountability Act (HIPAA) for processing, transforming, and storing health data in the cloud [12]. It gives healthcare organizations the ability to enter their health data in a variety of formats, and then, it uses machine learning to automatically standardize and index these data. It is possible to apply advanced analytics and machine learning to the data as a result of this technique, and the data will become entirely searchable [13]. EHR and EMR systems are able to merge different patient records into a single, comprehensive database thanks to HealthLake, which provides an alternative to the practice of siloing data. Using these organized data could result in a number of positive outcomes, including improved patient care, better informed operational decisions, and more robust health research.

B. Amazon S3

The Amazon Simple Storage Service (S3) is the storage service offered by AWS that offers object storage that is safe, long-lasting, and highly scalable. Whether it be EHR or EMR systems, it is an appropriate solution for storing and archiving massive volumes of medical data and records. Due to the scalability of Amazon S3, healthcare providers are able to effectively manage the growth of their data without having to worry about the constraints imposed by on-premise storage equipment [14, 15]. Both the confidentiality and the integrity of sensitive medical data may be preserved with the assistance of its powerful security features, which include encryption both while the data is in transit and while it is stored, access control policies, and integration with Amazon Web Services Identity and Access Management (IAM).

C. AWS Lambda

By utilizing AWS Lambda, a serverless computing service, healthcare organizations are able to execute code in response to triggers without the need to provision or manage servers. This solution really shines when it comes to automating workflows for electronic medical records, such as processing data in real time, notifying users of changes, and updating patient data. Lambda may be used to automatically trigger data transformation and loading procedures whenever new data are sent to Amazon S3. This ensures that medical professionals have access to the most recent patient records. Lambda can also be used to prevent information from being lost or stolen.

D. Amazon EC2

Users have access to a cloud computing platform that is scalable through an Elastic Compute Cloud (EC2) that Amazon Web Services offers. The infrastructure that supports electronic medical record apps can be easily scaled up or down by healthcare firms in response to changes in user demand [16, 17]. Amazon Elastic Compute Cloud (EC2) provides a wide variety of instance types to accommodate the diverse workloads that are associated with the processing and management of healthcare data. This variety of instance types includes compute-optimized instances for high-performance computing operations as well as memory-optimized instances for databases that store patient records. The versatility of EHR/EMR applications allows for their hosting to be done at a low cost, while still maintaining responsiveness and availability when it is required.

E. AWS Identity and Access Management (IAM)

When it comes to protecting access to electronic medical record data, Amazon Web Services Identity and Access Management (IAM) is an essential component. The ability to decide who can access their AWS resources and how they can interact with those resources is provided to healthcare organizations. Granular permissions can be granted to individuals based on the principle of least privilege through the use of IAM policies. This allows for the assurance that individuals only have access to the resources and information that are necessary for them to perform their duties. Due to the fact that protecting the privacy of patients is of the utmost significance, the healthcare business places a high value on this. In addition, Identity and Access Management (IAM) has the capability to collaborate with pre-existing identity systems to simplify the authorization and authentication process.

Utilizing these AWS services to increase the functionality, security, and scalability of their EHR and EMR systems can help healthcare organizations improve patient care and operational efficiency.

17.5 Building EHR/EMR Solutions on AWS

For EHR and EMR systems to be able to adjust to shifting loads and maintain their high availability, they need to be resilient and versatile. Using Amazon Web Services (AWS), this section covers methods for constructing scalable and robust EHR and EMR systems. These methods include the utilization of AWS Auto Scaling, Amazon CloudWatch, and integration with other AWS-powered applications.

Strategies for Designing Scalable, Resilient EHR/EMR Systems:

- Microservices Architecture: When utilizing a microservice design, it is possible to construct, deploy, and scale individual components of electronic medical record systems. AWS offers a variety of services, such as AWS Lambda, which is a serverless computing platform, and Amazon ECS (Elastic Container Service), which is a container management platform, to simplify the process of developing and maintaining microservices.
- Multi-AZ Deployment: To guarantee high availability, the most effective method is to implement EHR systems across a large number of availability zones (AZs). This ensures that even in the event of a malfunction in one of the AZs, the system will continue to make use of resources from another AZ to continue functioning. The Relational Database Service (RDS) and Amazon Elastic Compute Cloud (EC2) are two of the many Amazon services that enable deployments to take place across various availability zones.
- Elastic Load Balancing: To increase the application's failure tolerance, Elastic Load Balancing (ELB) is used to distribute incoming traffic among numerous targets, like EC2 instances, in different availability zones (AZs).

Leveraging AWS Auto Scaling and Amazon CloudWatch

- AWS Auto Scaling: AWS Auto Scaling monitors our applications and automatically adjusts capacity to maintain steady, predictable performance at the lowest possible cost. By using AWS Auto Scaling with EHR/EMR systems, healthcare organizations can ensure that they have the right number of resources available to handle the workload. Auto scaling can scale resources up to meet spikes in demand (for example, during public health crises) and scale down resources during quieter periods to save costs.
- Amazon CloudWatch: Through the provision of data and insights that can be put into action, Amazon CloudWatch enables users to monitor applications, react to changes in system-wide performance, and maximize resource use [18]. The integration of CloudWatch with electronic medical record systems enables the gathering and tracking of

metrics, log files, and the setting of alarms based on the performance of the system or faults. This information can be utilized to make decisions about scaling as well as to identify and address problems that may exist within the system.

By delivering comprehensive and integrated services, the integration of electronic medical record systems with other applications powered by AWS has the potential to greatly improve healthcare delivery. Just one example:

- Amazon HealthLake Integration: By integrating with electronic medical record systems, Amazon HealthLake gives healthcare organizations the ability to store, transform, and analyze health data in an environment that is scalable, secure, and compliant. Through its strengths in data analysis and machine learning, HealthLake is able to provide insights into patient care as well as operational efficiency.
- AWS Machine Learning Services: Predictive analytics for patient care are made possible by the integration of machine learning services, such as Amazon SageMaker, with electronic medical record systems. These services allow for the creation of tailored treatment regimens as well as the anticipation of patient admissions.
- AWS Analytics Services: When EHR and EMR systems are improved with the help of AWS analytics services, such as Amazon Redshift for data warehousing and Amazon QuickSight for business intelligence, it is possible to achieve a deeper comprehension of healthcare operations, patient trends, and results.

By creating scalable and robust electronic medical record systems on Amazon Web Services (AWS), healthcare providers can better address the present and future needs of patient care. In addition, this enables them to innovate and enhance the delivery of healthcare by utilizing the whole spectrum of services offered by Amazon Web Services (AWS).

17.6 Innovating with AI and Analytics

As a result of the integration of analytics and artificial intelligence (AI), which will change the analysis and exploitation of patient data for care, the healthcare industry stands to benefit the most from this integration.

AWS provides organizations in the healthcare industry with powerful tools, such as Amazon SageMaker, AWS Glue, and Amazon QuickSight, to assist them in utilizing these technologies. With the use of these tools, electronic medical record systems can be improved with predictive analytics and tailored treatment regimens.

A. Amazon SageMaker

It is possible for data scientists and developers of all stripes to rapidly construct, train, and distribute machine learning models with the help of Amazon SageMaker, which is a fully managed service [19]. SageMaker, when used in conjunction with electronic medical record systems, offers a number of advantages to healthcare institutions.

- Predictive Analytics: Integration of machine learning models generated using SageMaker with electronic medical record systems can help healthcare practitioners enhance the accuracy of patient outcome forecasts. Among the many things that fall under this category are the prediction of disease development, the assessment of the risk of readmission, and the prediction of adverse reactions to certain medications.
- Personalized Treatment Plans: Machine learning algorithms have the potential to discover patterns and make recommendations for individualized treatment plans by sifting through mounds of data from the medical records of patients. One of the potential benefits of this patient-centered approach is that it may lead to improved outcomes and a more efficient utilization of healthcare costs.
- Streamlined Development: The pre-built algorithms, one-click training, and deployment capabilities that SageMaker offers ease the process of machine learning model development. Businesses in the healthcare industry can redirect their attention to innovation and patient care rather than worrying about the complexities involved in establishing machine learning models.

B. AWS Glue

Because it is a fully managed extract, transform, and load (ETL) service, Amazon Web Services Glue makes it simple for customers to get their data ready for analytics and load it [20]. Considering that data pertaining to healthcare is usually fragmented and kept in multiple locations, AWS Glue is able to:

- Integrate Data Sources: Using AWS Glue, it is possible to automatically discover, prepare, and merge data from a wide variety of sources, including clinical databases, lab systems, and electronic medical record systems. It is essential to have this integrated data perspective to conduct comprehensive analytics in healthcare.
- Simplify Data Preparation: The AWSGlue platform makes it possible for healthcare organizations to transform and prepare healthcare data for analysis and machine learning without the need for bespoke programming or additional manual processes.

C. Amazon QuickSight

Using Amazon QuickSight, a business intelligence solution that is hosted in the cloud, it is easily possible to communicate insights to the entirety of the organization. With respect to the medical records:

- Visualizing Health Data: QuickSight allows managers and healthcare professionals to construct and share interactive dashboards, which can help them gain a better understanding of patient care and operational efficiency. These dashboards may be easily included in a wide variety of programs, websites, and portals, which enable them to be accessed from any device.
- Making Data-Driven Decisions: When healthcare organizations have the ability to easily evaluate and interpret health data, they are able to make decisions that are more informed on patient care procedures, resource allocation, and the success of treatment.

Through the innovative application of artificial intelligence (AI) and analytics that are driven by Amazon SageMaker, AWS Glue, and Amazon QuickSight, healthcare organizations have the potential to improve patient outcomes, facilitate the customization of treatment plans, and streamline the delivery of healthcare services. The architecture can use following services in different layers of designing.

1. Data Layer

- Amazon S3: Our primary responsibility will be to serve as the repository for unstructured patient data, which may

consist of documents, photographs, and medical records. Due to its durability, scalability, and security, Amazon Simple Storage Service (S3) is an excellent choice for storing sensitive healthcare data.
- Amazon RDS/Amazon Aurora: Ensure that relational databases have a location where they may store and arrange organized (EHR) data, which may include patient records, medical histories, and diagnoses. The outstanding performance and availability of Aurora ensure that mission-critical healthcare applications will continue to function without interruption while they are in operation.
- Amazon DynamoDB: Provide flexible and adaptive NoSQL database services for real-time analytics and application state data, as well as other sorts of non-relational data that require scalable and high-performance data storage.

2. Application Layer

- Amazon EC2: By acting as a host for the EHR and EMR applications, users may get scalable processing power. Amazon Elastic Compute Cloud (EC2) instances can be configured in an auto-scaling group across several availability zones (AZs) to provide high availability and fault tolerance.
- Elastic Load Balancing (ELB): It is advised that incoming application traffic be distributed among a number of targets, such as EC2 instances and multiple availability zones, to make the application more resistant to failure.

3. Serverless and Microservices

- AWS Lambda: Managing notifications, updates, and interfaces with third-party services and medical records are examples of event-driven processes that can be performed without the need to provision or operate servers.
- Amazon API Gateway: Provide an all-encompassing solution that can manage the creation, release, maintenance, monitoring, and security of application programming interfaces (APIs) of any scale. AWS-hosted backend services and frontend applications are able to communicate in a secure manner as a result of this.

4. Security and Compliance

- AWS Identity and Access Management (IAM): Make sure that only authorized users and services can access sensitive EHR/EMR data by securely managing access to AWS services and resources.
- AWS Key Management Service (KMS): Ensuring the secure protection of patient data in accordance with healthcare compliance regulations involves managing the encryption keys used to encrypt data both at rest and in transit.

5. Monitoring and Management

- Amazon CloudWatch: Keep an eye on our AWS resources by gathering measurements, keeping tabs on log files, and establishing alarms. To keep the EHR/EMR system running well, this is crucial.
- AWS Auto Scaling: Maintain peak performance and cost effectiveness for the application by automatically adjusting the number of EC2 instances in response to changes in traffic.

6. Data Analytics and Machine Learning

- Amazon SageMaker: Using EHR and other EMR data, create, train, and implement machine learning models to do things like forecast patient health outcomes and tailor treatment regimens.
- AWS Glue: Transform data from several sources into an analytically appropriate format; prepare and load data.

7. Interoperability and Integration

- AWS HealthLake: (Optional) Make use of HealthLake's built-in compliance and interoperability features to store, transform, and analyze health data at scale throughout the healthcare ecosystem.

Deploying EHR/EMR systems on AWS is made easier with this proposed architecture, which offers a secure, resilient, and scalable foundation.

By utilizing AWS services, healthcare businesses can guarantee that their her systems can handle the rigors of modern healthcare delivery satisfying patients with top-notch treatment while being in line with regulations.

17.7 Case Studies

Case studies of healthcare companies that have installed EHR and EMR systems using AWS are presented in the following section. Case studies like these demonstrate how cloud-based solutions have the potential to revolutionize healthcare by studying both past triumphs and failures. Additionally, they offer recommendations for future deployments of cloud-based systems.

A. Cerner Corporation's EHR System on AWS
Background: Cerner Corporation, a global leader in healthcare technology, made the decision to host its systems on AWS to improve scalability, dependability, and security.
Implementation: A number of AWS services, including Amazon Elastic Compute Cloud (EC2), Simple Storage Service (S3), and Amazon Lambda, which offer serverless computing, were utilized by Cerner to improve the availability and performance of its EHR systems. The global infrastructure that AWS provides was another factor that made it possible for Cerner to rapidly expand its services to new geographic locations.

Best Practices:

- Scalability Is Key: The capacity to adjust the amount of resources available in response to changes in demand is an essential capability in the healthcare industry, where the amount of data and the patterns of utilization can be highly variable.
- Security and Compliance are Paramount: By employing the built-in security and compliance tools that are accessible through Amazon Web Services (AWS), Cerner was able to fulfill severe regulatory standards and ensure the protection of patient data.

B. Providence Health & Services' Data Analytics on AWS
Background: Using Amazon Web Services (AWS), a large American healthcare organization known as Providence Health & Services developed a data

analytics platform with the intention of improving both the efficiency of patient care and the quality of treatment provided to patients.
Implementation: The Providence organization uses Amazon Web Services (AWS) offerings, such as Amazon Redshift for data warehousing, Amazon S3 for storage, and Amazon QuickSight for business intelligence, to gain a deeper comprehension of the procedures and results associated with patient care. This enabled them to incorporate data from a wide variety of sources, including systems.

Best Practices:

- Integrated Data Is Powerful: Through the discovery of previously undiscovered insights, which is made possible by integrating data from numerous sources into a single platform that is easily accessible, it is possible to improve patient care.
- Leverage Business Intelligence: Instruments, such as Amazon QuickSight, have the potential to transform raw data into actionable insight, which would then make it possible for decision makers to implement improvements that are founded on evidence.

C. Healx's Use of AWS for Drug Discovery

Background: AWS was responsible for powering an artificial intelligence (AI)-driven platform for the company Healx, which focuses on accelerating the finding of treatments for rare diseases.
Implementation: Amazon SageMaker was utilized by Healx for the purpose of developing and training machine learning models, while Amazon Elastic Compute Cloud (EC2) was utilized for scalable computing, and AWS Glue was utilized for data integration. Healx was able to quickly and affordably analyze data from EHR and medical studies, which led to the discovery of potential treatments.

Lessons Learned and Best Practices:

- AI and ML Can Revolutionize Healthcare: The applications of artificial intelligence (AI) and machine learning (ML) have the potential to significantly accelerate the rate at which medical research and therapeutic development are carried out.
- Cloud Computing Facilitates Innovation: As a result of the scalability and flexibility of AWS services, rapid experimentation and innovation in the field of healthcare information technology are now available.

According to the findings of these case studies, the utilization of AWScan enhances EHR and EMR systems, as well as the overall delivery of healthcare. Among the most significant takeaways are the following: scalability, security, integrated data analytics, and the promise of artificial intelligence and machine learning to improve both operational efficiency and patient care.

A number of AWS services that guarantee high availability, security, and scalability must be utilized to create EHR and EMR systems on AWS in a manner that is both resilient and scalable. Data privacy, interoperability, and the capacity to perform data analysis in real time are three of the most essential components of EHR systems. The architecture that has been proposed is an attempt to provide a comprehensive framework that addresses all of these concerns.

17.8 Proposed Architecture Overview

We will propose an AWS infrastructure for EHR/EMR maintenance. We have proposed an architecture based on AWS for real-time patient health monitoring, as seen in the above diagram. The architecture is shown in depth in Figure 17.2.

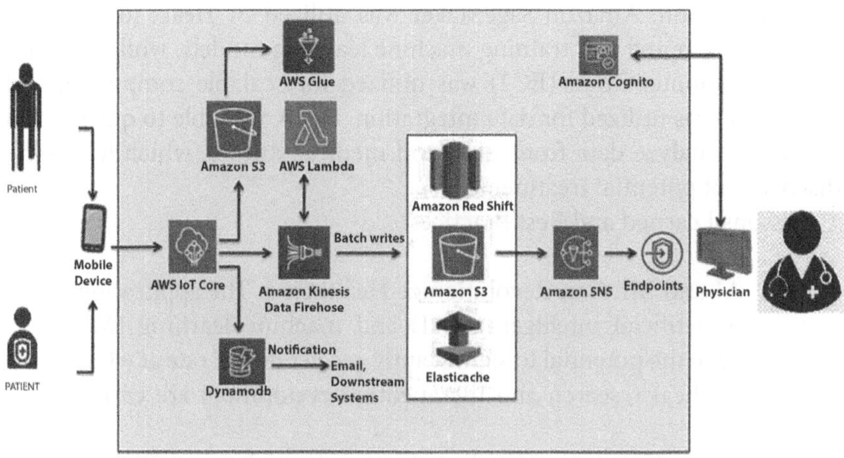

Figure 17.2 Architecture for patient health monitoring with AWS.

This architecture diagram represents a healthcare data processing system built on AWS. Here is a description of the flow and components involved:

1. Patient Data Collection: There are mobile gadgets that patients use to collect data about their health. Wearable technology and mobile health applications are two examples of this type of technology.
2. AWS IoT Core: The devices transmit data to Amazon Web Services' Internet of Things Core, which is a managed cloud service that enables connected devices to interface with cloud applications and other devices in a safe and secure manner.
3. Data Storage and Processing:

    - Data are then forwarded to several services: S3 (Simple Storage Service) from Amazon is being utilized here as a data lake to store the information that has been gathered.
    - Amazon Kinesis Data Firehose: Allows for the ingestion of real-time data streams and the ability to batch the data before sending it to destinations such as Amazon Redshift or Web Services.
    - AWS Lambda: A compute service that does not require a server and executes code in response to events. In the process of receiving data from IoT Core, it may process or filter the data.
    - DynamoDB: One example of a NoSQL database service that might be utilized for the purpose of storing and retrieving real-time data with minimal latency.

4. AWS Glue: An extract, transform, and load (ETL) service that completely manages the process of preparing and loading data for analytical purposes.
5. Batch Processing and Analysis:
   Data are processed in batches, possibly using AWS Lambda for transformation before being written to:

    - Amazon Redshift: An analytics-oriented data warehouse service that may be connected to visualization tools and is used for data analysis.

- Elasticache: A data storage that operates natively within memory and offers real-time analytics capabilities.

6. Amazon S3: Performs the function of a storage place for the data that have been evaluated and can be utilized by a variety of endpoints.
7. Notifications and Access:

    - Amazon Simple Notification Service (SNS): Used to deliver notifications, such as alerts or emails, based on specific data conditions or occurrences. Examples of such notifications include sending texts.
    - Endpoints: Provide end-users, such as physicians or healthcare providers, with data that have been processed using application programming interfaces (APIs) or services.
    - Amazon Cognito: To ensure that only users who have been authenticated can access data, this feature provides user identity and data synchronization information.

8. Physician: The endpoint of the data flow where physicians can access patient data, likely through an application interface that presents the processed and analyzed data allowing them to make informed decisions.

This architecture enables the collection and analysis of patient data in real time, with robust scalability, security, and reliability, illustrating a comprehensive AWS solution for healthcare data management. Deploying EHR/EMR systems on AWS is made easier with this proposed architecture, which offers a secure, resilient, and scalable foundation. By utilizing AWS services, healthcare businesses can guarantee that their EHR systems can handle the rigors of modern healthcare delivery satisfying patients with top-notch treatment while being in line with regulations.

17.9 Conclusion

This chapter delves into the implementation of electronic health records (EHR) and electronic medical record (EMR) systems using Amazon Web Services (AWS) emphasizing AWS's pivotal role in modernizing healthcare. We have unpacked the essentials of EHR and EMR systems, their benefits for healthcare providers and patients, and AWS services that bolster their implementation, such as HealthLake, S3, Lambda, EC2, and IAM. These services ensure scalable, secure, and compliant healthcare solutions meeting the complex demands of healthcare data management. Key sections highlighted the importance of compliance and security leveraging AWS's robust framework to protect patient data and adhere to regulations like HIPAA. The narrative on building scalable solutions and harnessing AI and analytics with AWS showcases the potential for enhancing patient care and operational efficiency.

Real-world case studies have provided insights into successful EHR/EMR implementations offering lessons learned and best practices. Additionally, the proposed AWS architecture offered a comprehensive blueprint for deploying these systems underscoring AWS's adaptability to healthcare needs. In essence, transitioning EHR and EMR systems to AWS represents a significant advancement toward an integrated, efficient healthcare system. This chapter offers healthcare providers a foundational understanding of how to navigate the digital transformation of healthcare highlighting the journey toward innovation, improved patient outcomes, and operational excellence in a rapidly evolving sector.

References

1. Dubey, P. and Dubey, P., Expand Patient Care with AWS Cloud for Remote Medical Monitoring, in: *Next Generation Healthcare Systems Using Soft Computing Techniques*, pp. 137–148, Jul. 2022, doi: 10.1201/9781003217091-10.
2. Dubey, P. and Tiwari, A.K., Solution Architecting on Remote Medical Monitoring with AWS Cloud and IoT, in: *Advanced Technologies and Societal Change*, pp. 189–202, 2023, doi: 10.1007/978-981-99-0377-1_12.
3. Dubey, P., Chhabra, G.S., Bhattacharya, R., Singh, T.G., Enhancing the Performance of Traditional Hadoop Using AWS with EMR Approach. *Des. Eng.*, 2021, 8, 571–580, 2021.
4. Alanazi, B., Butler-Henderson, K., Alanazi, M.R., Factors Influencing Healthcare Professionals' Perception towards EHR/EMR Systems in Gulf Cooperation Council Countries: A Systematic Review. *Oman Med. J.*, 35, 6, e192–e192, Oct. 2020, doi: 10.5001/omj.2020.85.
5. Parker, M. and Partridge, B., Management and Leadership Distinctions Required at Stages of Maturity in an EHR/EMR Adoption Model Context, in: *Mobile Medicine*, pp. 79–102, Sep. 2021, doi: 10.4324/9781003220473-7.
6. Newton, J.Z., *Int. J. Transpers. Stud.*, 34, 1–2, 172–186, Jan. 2015, doi: 10.24972/ijts.2015.34.1-2.172, https://digitalcommons.ciis.edu/cgi/viewcontent.cgi?article=1079&context=ijts-transpersonalstudies.

7. Asare, E., Wang, L., Fang, X., Enhancing EHR Implementation with Process Mining. *J. Phys. Conf. Ser.*, 2356, 1, 012025, Oct. 2022, doi: 10.1088/1742-6596/2356/1/012025.
8. Bateja, R., Dubey, S.K., Bhatt, A., Integration of EHR and PHR leveraging cloud services for approving treatments. *Int. J. Health Sci.*, 4940–4959, Oct. 2022, doi: 10.53730/ijhs.v6ns8.13322.
9. Tawalbeh, L., Muheidat, F., Tawalbeh, M., Quwaider, M., Abd El-Latif, A.A., Edge enabled IoT system model for secure healthcare. *Measurement*, 191, 110792, Mar. 2022, doi: 10.1016/j.measurement.2022.110792.
10. Cloud-based Healthcare data management Framework. *KSII Trans. Internet Inf. Syst.*, 14, 3, 1014–1025, Mar. 2020, doi: 10.3837/tiis.2020.03.006.
11. Dubey, P., Tiwari, A.K., Raja, R., *Amazon Web Services: the Definitive Guide for Beginners and Advanced Users*, Bentham Science Publishers, USA, 2023, [Online], Available: http://books.google.ie/books?id=rQbgEAAAQBAJ&printsec=frontcover&dq=Amazon+Web+Services:+the+Definitive+Guide+for+Beginners+and+Advanced+Users.+Bentham+Science+-Publishers.&hl=&cd=1&source=gbs_api.
12. Dubey, P. and Raja, R., *A Beginners Guide to Amazon Web Services*, CRC Press, New York, 2024, [Online], Available: http://books.google.ie/books?id=MPTkEAAAQBAJ&printsec=frontcover&dq=A+Beginners+Guide+to+Amazon+Web+Services.+CRC+Press.&hl=&cd=1&source=gbs_api.
13. Dubey, P. and Tiwari, A.K., Cloud Integration in the Educational Sector Using Amazon Web Services. *2023 Third International Conference on Advances in Electrical, Computing, Communication and Sustainable Technologies (ICAECT)*, Jan. 2023, Published, doi: 10.1109/icaect57570.2023.10117739.
14. Dubey, P., Dubey, P., Sahu, K.K., A Guide to Cloud Platform with an Investigation of Different Cloud Service Providers, in: *Big Data, Cloud Computing and IoT*, pp. 37–51, Feb. 2023, doi: 10.1201/9781003298335-3.
15. Dubey, P., Mahalle, A.V., Deshmukh, R.V., Sawant, R.S., Data Processing Methodologies and a Serverless Approach to Solar Data Analytics, in: *Multimedia Data Processing and Computing*, pp. 116–134, Sep. 2023, doi: 10.1201/9781003391272-10.
16. Dubey, P. and Tiwari, A.K., Unveiling AWS Spot Instance Trends: An Empirical Illustration. *IETE J. Educ.*, 1–11, Feb. 2024, doi: 10.1080/09747338.2024.2319036.
17. Dubey, P. and Tiwari, A.K., AWS Spot Instances: A Cloud Computing Cost Investigation Across AWS Regions. *Int. J. Intell. Syst. Appl. Eng.*, *12*, 1, 01–10, Dec. 2023.
18. Dubey, P., Dubey, P., Sahu, K.K., Deep Learning-Based Serverless Image Handler Using Amazon Web Services, in: *Software Engineering Approaches to Enable Digital Transformation Technologies*, pp. 25–41, Sep. 2023, doi: 10.1201/9781003441601-3.

19. View of Based on an analysis of Amazon S3, real service simulation techniques are used to study the latency performance of distributed storage systems, https://jomaar.com/index.php/jomaar/article/view/5/5.
20. Dua, I.K. and Patel, P., Monitoring flood using Amazon SageMaker geospatial capabilities, Feb. 2024, Published, doi: 10.36227/techrxiv.170831574.41596325/v1.

18

Harmony in Healthcare: Implementing an AI-Powered Biometric System

S. Sharmila[1]*, M. Nirmala[1], Somasundaram Devaraj[2] and M. Menagadevi[3]

[1]Department of Biomedical Engineering, Dr. N.G.P. Institute of Technology, Coimbatore, Tamil Nadu, India
[2]School of Electronics Engineering, Vellore Institute of Technology, Vellore, India
[3]Department of Computer Science and Engineering, Malla Reddy University, Telagana, India

Abstract

With the advancement of modern technologies, the healthcare business is increasingly shifting toward a more personalized smart care model. This shift is being driven by a number of causes, including improvements in digital health, artificial intelligence (AI), data analytics, and wearable technologies. Artificial Intelligence (AI) and the Internet of Things (IoT) are the enablers of SmartCare approaches. An appropriate pattern of the patient, these technologies collect and analyze data from people receiving treatment. However, relying heavily on IoT devices to collect continuous data expands attack surfaces and necessitates high-security measures. To reduce the vast number of attack vectors, equipment and patients must be verified. The biometric authentication method has been seen as a potential tactic in these circumstances. This study presents an AI-based multimodal biometric authentication model for single and group-based user devices that increase protection against the traditional single-modal approach. AI-based biometric systems have a lot to offer the healthcare industry, but it is important to solve privacy and security issues, including data security and compliance when adopting such systems. Strong security precautions and ethical considerations are crucial to safeguard patient data and preserve public confidence in medical procedures. AI-based biometric systems in healthcare have the potential to significantly improve patient care, reduce errors, increase security, and advance medical research. To preserve

**Corresponding author*: sharmila.s@drngpit.ac.in

Parul Dubey, Mangala Madankar, Pushkar Dubey and Bui Thanh Hung (eds.) The Impact of Algorithmic Technologies on Healthcare, (397–420) © 2025 Scrivener Publishing LLC

patient data and sustain trust in healthcare practices, strong security measures and ethical concerns must be implemented.

Keywords: Biometrics, machine learning, personalized healthcare, internet of things, smart aging, cybersecurity

18.1 Introduction to Biometric System

An electronic framework that employs unique physiological behavioral traits of people for authentication, identification, or verification is called a biometric system. A person's identity is established by these distinctive characteristics, that involve hand geometry, voiceprints, iris patterns, face features, and fingerprints, with behavioral patterns like typing rhythm or stride [1, 3]. These traits are detected, recorded, and transformed by the system into digital data so that they can be compared or matched with templates that are kept in a database [2]. In place of more cumbersome and unsafe techniques, like credentials, biometric technologies are made to precisely verify or authenticate a person's identification. Biometric systems, which are typically connected with identification and security, are finding extensive uses in the medical industry. To precisely identify people, these systems make use of distinctive physiological or behavioral traits like voiceprints, iris patterns, fingerprints, and even DNA. By guaranteeing safe patient identification, advancing access to medical information, increasing diagnosis accuracy, and optimizing overall patient care, biometric technologies in healthcare provide a revolutionary approach [2, 3]. Healthcare providers can reduce identification errors, accelerate administrative procedures, and guarantee the appropriate patient obtains the right care by incorporating biometric technology into medical settings. This is a huge advancement in the nexus of technology and healthcare improving not just the effectiveness of medical care but also patient safety and anonymity.

18.2 Types of Biometric Systems

The computerized method of identifying a person or individual based on their physiology and observable characteristics is called biometrics [4]. Many businesses and organizations utilize biometrics these days for access control and identification. Humans are involved in biometric calculation traits. Biometrics allow the identification of physiological traits such as body form and fingerprints. The main objective is to improve security and

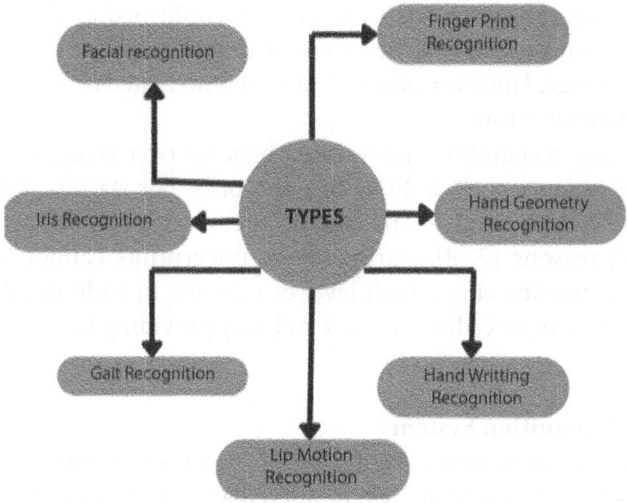

Figure 18.1 Types of biometric systems.

offer practical and efficient authentication [6]. This provides readers a thorough knowledge of biometric technologies by recording their development from primitive uses to the complex systems of today, shown in Figure 18.1.

A. Fingerprint Recognition

One of the earliest and widely utilized biometric technologies is fingerprint recognition. Each person's fingerprint is distinct due to the minute characteristics, complex ridge patterns, and ridge features found on the fingertip. The characteristics of the optical, capacitive, or ultrasonic sensors are stored by the fingerprint recognition system [5, 8]. To generate a biometric template—a digital depiction of each fingerprint's distinct features—the captured fingerprint picture is processed. Several phases are involved in the fingerprint recognition process. The person's fingertip is first put on a fingerprint scanner, which is a feature of gadgets including laptops, cell phones, and access control systems. The fingerprint picture is captured by the scanner using either an optical or capacitive sensor. The captured picture experiences several preprocessing, such as thinning, binarization, and enhancement [3]. The picture quality is improved, and precise fingerprint detail is extracted with the aid of these methods.

A database's stored templates are compared with the extracted points. The fingerprint templates of authorized persons are pre-registered in the database [8]. Advanced algorithms are used to compare the stored templates and the collected fingerprints analyzing how similar they are. The person is given access or has their identity confirmed as the authorized user if their fingerprint matches a template that has been saved within a reasonable range. However, access is denied if no match or if the similarity is not sufficiently strong.

Fingerprint recognition has various benefits over traditional authentication techniques such as PINs or passwords. For starters, fingerprints are unique to each individual, making them extremely trustworthy for identifying reasons [7, 8]. Furthermore, fingerprints cannot be readily reproduced guaranteeing a high level of security. In addition, the fingerprint registration procedure is quick and easy providing for a smooth user experience.

B. Facial Recognition System

Facial recognition systems are a type of biometric technology that has gained popularity due to its use in surveillance and protection, authentication, and a variety of sectors. As a result of its potential to improve security and ease, this technology has received a lot of curiosity and acceptance in a variety of industries [8]. Face recognition requires a number of stages to complete. First, a picture or video of a person's face is captured by a camera or sensor. This picture is then analyzed to identify and extract facial information such as the distance between the eyes, nose shape, and facial contours. These characteristics are known as face landmarks [7, 8]. Following the removal of face features, they are turned into an algebraic model known as a facial template.

To verify or identify a person, the captured face template is compared to a database of stored templates. This database contains pre-registered face templates of approved people. The comparison is carried out utilizing powerful algorithms that examine the similarities between the captured template and the stored templates [8]. If a captured face template matches a stored template within an acceptable threshold, the individual is confirmed or recognized. This allows users to get entry to a secure location, unlock a device, or carry out other approved tasks. Access is prohibited if there is no match, or the similarity is less than the threshold.

Systems that recognize faces have several benefits [6, 7]. First of all, because each person's facial characteristics are distinct, they are extremely trustworthy for identification. Furthermore, remote face recognition processing makes non-intrusive and simple authentication possible [4, 8]. Furthermore, the technology may improve security in a number of contexts, including identity verification, access control, and law enforcement. Privacy, security, and prejudice problems also should be addressed.

C. Iris Recognition System

Iris identification is a biometric technique that uses distinctive patterns seen in the iris of the human eye to identify individuals. Unique characteristics, including radial and circular patterns, furrows, and freckles, can be seen on the iris, the colorful area that surrounds the pupil. Even among identical twins, these traits are very unique, which makes iris recognition a reliable and safe biometric identification system [1, 9]. The unique and consistent characteristics of iris patterns allow iris recognition systems to achieve high accuracy and low false acceptance rates.

It takes many processes to recognize an iris [8, 10]. The iris and eyelids are detected by the system after the pupil's position has been determined. Eyelids and lashes are examples of superfluous pieces that are filtered away as noise. The distinct patterns present in the iris are subsequently retrieved and transformed into a mathematical template and may be used for identification or confirmation by evaluating it to alternative templates.

Iris recognition systems use infrared light to collect photographs of the eyes. The iris enables clear imaging of the iris patterns since it is transparent under infrared radiation [10]. The recorded photos are then analyzed to extract the iris patterns and provide a comparison template. The great uniqueness of iris patterns is one of the primary benefits of iris recognition. Even among identical twins, the chances of two irises being the same are exceedingly rare [8, 10]. In addition, the iris patterns are stable throughout time, which means they do not alter considerably with age. Iris recognition is therefore a dependable and long-term biometric authentication mechanism.

D. Handwriting Recognition System

Handwriting recognition is also known as Handwriting Character Recognition (HCR) or Handwritten Text Recognition (HTR). It is a sophisticated technology that interprets and converts handwritten text into digital, machine-readable forms [12]. The idea is to facilitate a smooth transition from traditional pen and paper to digital platforms. Handwriting recognition requires numerous important procedures. First, the system uses a specialized sensor, such as a camera or scanner, to capture a picture of the handwritten text. This image is then preprocessed to improve its quality, which may include techniques such as noise reduction and image enhancement [11, 12]. The machine then extracts important picture characteristics. Stroke direction, curvature, and spatial interactions between distinct portions of the characters are examples of these properties. Feature extraction is a crucial step since it assists in expressing handwritten characters in a form that is recognized by algorithms [10].

Once the characteristics have been retrieved, the system use classification algorithms to determine the most likely character for each input picture [12]. This can be accomplished using approaches such as support vector machines (SVM), hidden Markov models (HMM), or deep learning models. To select the closest match, the system compares the extracted characteristics to a database of known characters or patterns. Handwriting recognition systems have limitations. Because handwriting styles vary, developing systems that can reliably identify a wide range of handwriting can be difficult. Environmental variables like noise, smudges, and distortions can also have an effect on accuracy [11, 12].

E. Hand Geometry Recognition System

Hand geometry recognition is a type of biometric technology that utilizes the geometric features of a person's hand [1, 3]. This system measures different characteristics like hand size, finger length and width, and the distance between specific landmarks on the hand. It has been in use since the late 1980s and is known for its distinctiveness, which is derived from the overall shape and proportions of the hand, including finger length and width, palm size, and the placement of key landmarks like fingertips and valley points [6, 12].

During the process of enrollment, a scanner captures three consecutive images of the hand. These images are then analyzed and measured to generate a template that represents the unique characteristics of the user's hand. The images are taken from different perspectives, including the front, back, and palm. The captured images are combined to create a three-dimensional representation of the hand [11]. The template includes measurements of finger length and width, palm size, and the position of important landmarks such as fingertips and valley points.

Once a claim is submitted, the system compares the hand image captured at that moment with the template that was created during the enrollment process. The system generates a verification template from the captured image and matches it against the enrolled template. A similarity score is generated, and depending on the system's predefined threshold, the claim is either accepted or rejected [10, 11]. Hand geometry recognition offers several benefits, including non-intrusiveness, low rates of false acceptance and false rejection when appropriately calibrated and maintained, and user friendliness. Nevertheless, it also has limitations. Unlike fingerprints or iris patterns, hand geometry is not as distinct, and there may be resemblances between individuals, particularly among family members.

F. Gait Recognition System

Gait recognition is a type of biometric technology that utilizes the unique characteristics of an individual's walking patterns. By analyzing factors, such as rhythm, stride length, and body movements during walking, gait recognition creates a distinct gait signature for each person [12, 13]. This technology is based on the understanding that each individual has a distinctive walking pattern that can be differentiated from others. The Gait recognition system involves several steps. First, data acquisition is performed by capturing a video footage of individuals walking. This can be done through cameras strategically positioned in public spaces or specialized sensors in controlled environments. The captured video is then preprocessed to improve quality and extract important information [14]. Techniques, like noise removal, image stabilization, and background subtraction, are used to isolate the walking subject.

The video frames that have undergone preprocessing are examined to identify the distinctive traits that define an individual's walking pattern. These traits encompass factors like the angles and movements of different body parts, the timing and rhythm of the walk, and other spatial and temporal parameters. The identified traits are then converted into a suitable format for further examination and comparison [12, 15]. This may involve encoding the traits as numerical values or employing more complicated representations like gait energy images (GEIs), which capture both the spatial and temporal characteristics of the walking cycle [15].

To analyze and classify the extracted features, machine learning algorithms, like support vector machines (SVM), hidden Markov models (HMM), or deep learning models, are utilized. These algorithms compare the extracted features with a database of known gait patterns to find the most similar match [14, 15]. Using the classification results, the gait recognition system then identifies and authenticates the individual by linking their gait pattern with their identity. This can be achieved by comparing the extracted features with stored templates or by calculating similarity scores between the observed gait pattern and the known patterns in the database [13, 15].

G. Lip Motion Recognition System

Lip motion recognition is a type of biometric technology that focuses on analyzing the movement and patterns of the lips to identify and authenticate individuals [4]. This technology takes into account the specific characteristics of lip motion, such as shape changes, gestures, and dynamics, to create a unique biometric signature. It operates on the principle that each person has a distinct way of moving their lips during speech or specific gestures making lip motion a reliable method for biometric identification [16]. Lip motion recognition systems utilize cameras or specialized sensors to capture high-resolution facial images, with a specific focus on the area surrounding the lips. The captured video frames or images undergo preprocessing to improve quality and extract relevant data. Techniques, like noise removal, image stabilization, and normalization, are employed to address variations in lighting and camera angles [8, 17].

The video frames or images that have been preprocessed are examined to identify features that reflect the distinct qualities of an individual's lip motion. These features may encompass the shape, movement, and dynamics of the lips while speaking or making facial expressions [7, 15]. Various machine learning algorithms, including support vector machines (SVM), hidden Markov models (HMM), and deep learning models, are utilized to analyze and categorize the features that have been extracted. These algorithms compare the extracted features with a database of preexisting lip motion patterns to find the closest match. Using the classification results, the lip motion recognition system can confirm the identity of an individual by linking their lip motion pattern to their identity [16]. This can be achieved by comparing the extracted features with stored templates or by calculating similarity scores between the observed lip motion pattern and the known patterns in the database.

18.3 Biometrics in Healthcare Application

The biometric technology is a computerized object identification and authentication. In this biometric technology, the individuals are recognized based on some features present in an individual. In ancient days, the Egyptians and Babylonians are known for the usage of biometrics with the help of fingerprint features for person identification [18]. Then, the Chinese use this technology for enhancement of their business transaction and for payment security using their handprints [19]. Due to some technological revolutions, biometric technology get upgraded by scanning the various unique features of an individual. Today, biometric technology integrated with IoT and AI enhance the privacy, security and safety measures in various domains like data storage sectors, automobile industry, healthcare, industrial workplaces, employee, and industrial safety measurements [17, 21].

A. Involvement of Biometrics in Healthcare

In the field of healthcare, biometric technology involves various parts like Administration, Patient Monitoring, Patient Identification, Medicine Prescription, Data Analysis, Sample Analyzation in laboratories, and Telemedicine, which play a role in the identification and access provisions to authorized persons that lead to the enhancement of the quality of healthcare and patient safety. Over the entire field of healthcare, biometrics plays a vital role in providing quality healthcare [21].

The involvement of biometrics in healthcare, mentioned below, is due to some technical revolution in biometric technology. The features of identification, communication, authentication, and access provision are upgraded due to the integration of IoT and AI.

1. **Handprint Recognition System**
   The handprint technology was used earlier by the Chinese, Egyptians, and Babylonians for their business safety and transactions [3, 6]. Following the FBI, industrial sectors and healthcare use this technology for storage of data, privacy, safety, and security [23]. In this method of handprint recognition, the individuals' prints are stored in the database priorly for identification. Once the individual's handprint or fingerprint is updated, those fingerprints are known as referral templates [20, 22]. At the time a user uses the biometric input fingerprint template, it is compared with a pre-existing fingerprint template, which is stored in a device. At the time of comparison, if the result is positive, the person gets access to a respective area. This handprint recognition system is mostly used in prohibited areas and also provides an information about a person using the results of biometrics [21].

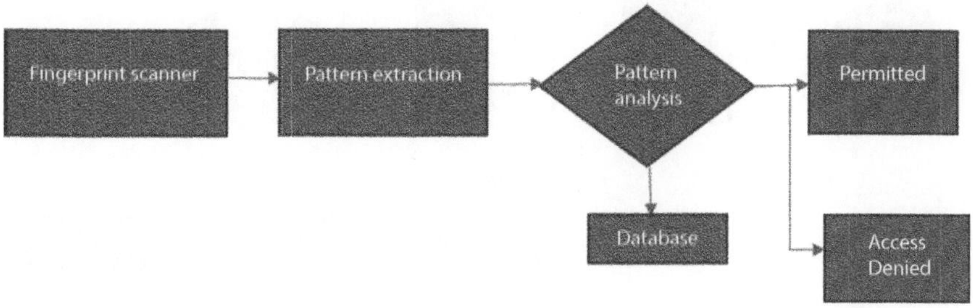

Figure 18.2 Fingerprint recognition system.

The role of the finger or handprint recognition (shown in the Figure 18.2) in the field of healthcare is to provide appropriate information about a patient and identification of an employee and patient. Primarily, the biometric technology using the finger or handprint is applicable to all the minor and major levels in the perspective of administration [18, 22] because each staff working in the healthcare or hospital is monitored using this technology, along with the process of identification, which plays a role in safety security measures in healthcare by identifying the correct person to perform a specific task by pre-defined inputs.

2. **Facial Recognition System**
The facial recognition system is an upgraded fingerprint recognition system. In this system, the facial features are used for identification [12, 17]. Based on the algorithms of pattern and pattern extraction, facial recognition is performed. The facial pattern analysis is a process of determining a face pattern of an individual by calculating the size of the nose, distance between the nose and eye, distance between the eye and eyelids, structure of the nose, and so on [21].

By comparing the fingerprint recognition system, the facial system has more amount of performance in both security and safety due to accurate measurements between those parts leading to the approval of the appropriate person.

3. **Iris Recognition System**
The iris recognition system is a type of system used for highly confidential sectors in which the iris of the eye is used as an input. This type of recognition process is more efficient than the others. The method used in this recognition process is by

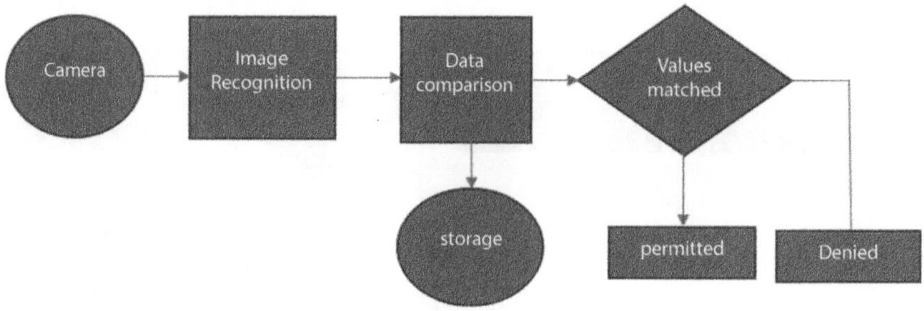

Figure 18.3 Pathway of face authentication.

sense and movement of the iris of an individual was shown in the Figure 18.3. The individual's eye movements are scanned and converted as a template [16, 19]. This type of template is slightly different compared to the handprint or fingerprint templates because the iris template stores both the structure and movement of the iris. These types of system are preferred for highly confidential sectors like FBI data storage sections, financial and administrated sections of industries, and patient database section of hospitals. The major importance of this system is that it permits an individual's input at the time the eyes are alive. So, it is preferred than the other methods.

B. Voice and Signature Dynamics

The voice and signature dynamic system, which works based on pre-stored data, is a comparison between pre-stored data and input data [24] in which the pitch of each tone and curvature of signature are noted based on the pre-stored data.

The abovementioned are types of biometrics, which involves various sectors. The biometric system in healthcare systems plays an important role in privacy, security, and safety [22]. The biometric systems, which help in healthcare, are mentioned below.

- Let us start with the administration purpose [25], where the biometric technique is used for identification of work in their specific field and which also permits a specific worker in a rare area.
- The administration is responsible for collecting the entire workers' fingerprints, and they are classified based on their restricted area or limitations of the worker. The workers workplaces are closed using biometric doors [22]. Once the appropriate worker punches on the biometrics, a process is undergone. If the biometrics match, the doors are opened; if they do not match, the doors remain closed.
- The fingerprint biometric system is also applicable to patients [23]. Based on the fingerprints, the patient's details are shown.
- The facial recognition system was mainly used by some higher-position administrators in which facial recognition data are maintained by the database of an organization [16, 22]. Due to the presence of a certain technology, an appropriate person gets involved in a specific task.

- Facial recognitions are used in telemedicine, machine calibration, and as key for certain lock settings. It is a quick identification of a patient in an emergency, for security and safety purposes [15, 16].
- The iris recognition system is a major system used in sectors like patient, employee, and administrators. In certain sections, only persons of higher rank are allowed [15, 19]. This system is more sensitive and provides more safety and security.
- The iris recognition system is specifically used in data storage, server maintenance, account locker unit, documentation area, medicine storage unit, and so on. For these areas, the iris recognition methods are essential because the above-mentioned need more security [21].
- The voice and signature dynamic analysis is helpful in verifying whether an information is true or false. The voice and signature recognition system helps mainly in the field of telemedicine as the remote medicine system can generate and transmit fake details [13, 22].
- The voice recognition technique receives the voice of a user and is compared with a predefined one. The technique makes sure that the pitch of both voices are the same; then it allows access to the user [18, 21, 23].
- In the field of healthcare, biometric technology plays a major role in security and safety.

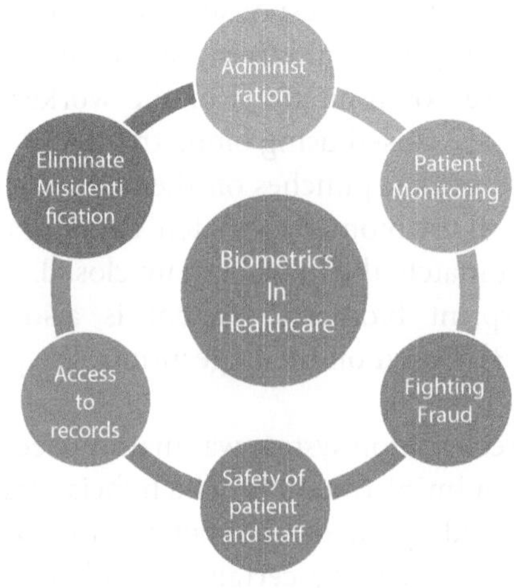

Figure 18.4 Role of biometrics in healthcare.

- Due to the presence of numerous authentication processes, problems that occur in this field can be minimized by providing appropriate information [14].

18.4 Biometric System for Monitoring and Disease Diagnosis

Biometric systems are cutting-edge technologies that identify and verify people based on their distinct physical or behavioral traits [13, 16]. Because these traits are hard to fake or duplicate, biometrics are an effective tool for security and customization.

A. Biometric System Types

- **Facial Recognition:** Identification of people by facial traits is known as facial recognition; used for airport security, surveillance, and authentication (such as unlocking iPhones) [18].
- **Iris Recognition:** Examines the distinct patterns found in the colored portion of the iris; excellent precision and non-intrusive; utilized for border control and security institutions [16, 17].
- **Voice Recognition:** Evaluates vocal qualities (tone, pitch, etc.); utilized for speaker verification, voice assistants, and phone banking [19, 25].

B. Behavioral Biometrics

Behavioral biometrics examines behavioral characteristics, such as typing speed and gait, and increases security without needing specific user intervention. Unique physiological or behavioral traits, such as voiceprints, iris patterns, or fingerprints, are used by biometric systems to identify or authenticate people. These systems are extensively employed in many different applications, such as border control and smartphone unlocking, since they simplify access management and improve security [11, 22].

For a number of reasons, early illness diagnosis and ongoing surveillance are essential.

1. **Treatment Effectiveness:** Early illness detection frequently enables more effective treatment, which may reduce complications and enhance overall results.

2. **Lower Healthcare Costs:** When illnesses are discovered early on, less extensive and expensive treatment may be required, when they are discovered at an advanced stage. Additionally, it can lessen the general strain on healthcare systems.
3. **Better Quality of Life:** Early diagnosis enables timely treatment increasing the likelihood of controlling or curing illnesses. This lessens the intensity of symptoms and improves a person's quality of life.
4. **Prevention of Consequences:** Early diagnosis offers the chance to treat and control illnesses before they worsen averting potential consequences in later stages.
5. **Public Health Impact:** By limiting the transmission of infectious illnesses and enabling early therapies for ailments with potential outbreaks, early detection generally improves public health.
6. **Patient Empowerment:** Real-time tracking of health parameters made possible by continuous monitoring enables people to take charge of their health and makes wise lifestyle decisions.
7. **Research and Development:** Research into improved treatment choices and preventative measures is facilitated by early diagnosis, which advances medical knowledge and technology.

It is critical to improve treatment efficacy, lower healthcare costs, raise patient empowerment, prevent complications, address public health issues, and promote technological and scientific developments in medicine [22, 25, 27, 29].

C. Conventional Techniques for Diagnosing and Tracking Diseases Encompass Many Approaches

1. **Clinical Examination:** To create a diagnostic impression, physicians examine patients physically, inquire about their symptoms, and study their medical history.
2. **Laboratory Tests:** Analysis of physiological fluids, such as blood, urine, and others, can provide important details about a patient's health [30]. Tests for infectious diseases, cholesterol, and blood counts are frequently performed.
3. **Imaging Techniques:** By providing comprehensive images of inside structures, X-rays, CT scans, MRIs, and ultrasounds can identify and track a variety of illnesses.

4. **Biopsy:** To identify diseases, like cancer, tissue samples are taken and examined under a microscope.
5. **Electrocardiogram (ECG or EKG):** This diagnostic tool assesses the electrical activity in the heart to assist in identifying cardiac conditions.
6. **Blood Pressure Monitoring:** Monitoring regularly aids in the detection of hypertension and other cardiovascular issues.
7. **Physical Measurements:** Taking baseline health measurements, such as taking your temperature, pulse, and breathing rate, is important [22].
8. **Symptom Observation:** Doctors evaluate patient-reported symptoms to find trends that point to certain illnesses.
9. **Endoscopy:** This procedure allows doctors to see inside the body and detect abnormalities in organs, such as the digestive system, by inserting a flexible tube equipped with a camera. Even if they work well, these conventional techniques might not be as good at early detection and real-time monitoring, which emphasizes the necessity for additional contemporary techniques and technology [20, 21].

Biometric systems are applied in the medical field. Biometrics provide safe and precise patient identification lowering mistakes in medical records and improving the integrity of healthcare data. Biometric identification techniques, such as iris or fingerprint scanning, improve data security and privacy while simultaneously streamlining patient record access [14, 19]. This increased level of identification accuracy helps to guard against medical identity theft, guaranteeing that people receive the treatment they need while enabling smooth, safe interactions throughout the healthcare system. In addition to increasing productivity, biometric system integration in healthcare is essential for protecting private patient data and enhancing patient safety.

D. Examining the Use of Biometric Systems in the Diagnosis of Disease
Although identity verification is the main use of biometric systems, they may also be applied to the detection of diseases through a variety of creative means:

1. **Remote Patient Monitoring:** Biometric sensors can track a patient's blood pressure, heart rate, and temperature continually giving medical personnel access to real-time

information. This makes it easier to identify abnormalities or changes in health markers early on [2, 27].

2. **Gait Analysis:** Biometric systems have the ability to examine a person's gait, or walking pattern, to identify irregularities that may be a sign of musculoskeletal or neurological conditions [3, 20].
3. **Voice Analysis:** Variations in speech patterns may be a sign of a number of illnesses, including cardiovascular or pulmonary problems. The examination of biometric speech patterns has the ability to diagnose diseases early [12, 16].
4. **Facial Recognition for Health Indicators:** You may use facial biometrics to scan your face for illness indicators by analyzing its aspects. For example, certain disorders might show up as variations in the color or texture of the skin [19].
5. **Analysis of Palmprints:** Distinctive characteristics in palmprints can be used to find markers linked to particular illnesses. The potential of palmprint biometrics in the detection of illness is still being investigated [18].
6. **Iris Recognition for Health Monitoring:** Iris scans are useful for more than simply identifying people; minute alterations in the iris may provide information about specific medical issues, therefore serving as a possible means of diagnosing disease [13, 17].
7. **Biometric Data Fusion:** Combining various biometric characteristics—such as voice, facial features, and fingerprints—can produce a thorough health assessment for each person. Examining these profiles can help identify trends that point to underlying medical conditions [10]. Even if these applications show promising result, it is crucial to remember that a lot of them are still in the research and development stage. Early detection, monitoring, and individualized healthcare methods might be possible with the integration of biometric technologies in illness diagnostics leading to more effective and efficient healthcare systems [18].

E. Analyzing How Biometrics Fit Into Ongoing Health Monitoring

Because biometrics provide precise and up-to-date data, they are essential for continuous health monitoring [26]. They also improve overall health management and tailored healthcare. Biometric sensors can continually monitor a variety of physiological and behavioral factors, which helps to provide a more thorough knowledge of a person's health state.

Important Facets of Their Work Consists of the Following:

1. **Real-Time Data Collection:** Vital health measurements, including heart rate, blood pressure, temperature, and activity levels, may be continuously collected thanks to biometric devices. These real-time data provides a dynamic picture of a person's health enabling timely action in the event of abnormalities [19, 30].
2. **Early Health Issue Detection:** Ongoing monitoring makes it easier to identify anomalies or modifications in biometric patterns that might point to possible health issues. By taking a proactive stance, prompt medical action is made possible, which may stop illnesses from worsening.
3. **Personalized Healthcare:** Biometric information offers a unique perspective on a person's health enabling customized medical actions [14]. Both patient outcomes and treatment efficacy may be enhanced by this individualized strategy.
4. **Chronic Disease Management:** Ongoing observation is especially important for those with long-term illnesses [28]. Healthcare professionals can modify treatment routines as necessary to the tracking and management of ailments including diabetes, cardiovascular diseases, and respiratory problems made possible by biometric technologies.
5. **Behavioral Biometrics for Mental Health:** Assessment of mental health is aided by the ongoing observation of behavioral biometrics, such as stress levels and sleep patterns. Identifying possible mental health problems and creating effective therapies are made easier with the use of this information [24, 27].
6. **Remote Patient Monitoring:** With the use of biometric systems, medical professionals may keep an eye on patients from a distance, particularly those who are recovering from surgery or chronic illnesses. In addition to reducing the need for frequent hospital visits, this encourages patient autonomy.
7. **Data Integration for Comprehensive Health Insights:** Combining several biometric metrics offers a comprehensive picture of a person's health. Integrating information from several sources, such as heart rate, sleep habits, and physical exercise, provides a more thorough picture of general wellbeing.

Issues that must be carefully considered are data security, privacy, and the interpretation of intricate biometric data patterns. Biometrics in health monitoring is expected to grow as technology develops resulting in a more proactive and individualized approach to healthcare [10, 14]. The application of biometrics in healthcare has enormous potential to improve efficiency and results in continuous health monitoring and early detection allowing for prompt treatments. By increasing the efficacy of therapies, this proactive strategy improves patient outcomes and helps move healthcare away from reactive to preventative. Healthcare professionals may optimize treatment regimens for individual patients by customizing treatments based on the unique insights obtained from biometric data. Furthermore, biometric-enabled remote patient monitoring eases the strain on the healthcare infrastructure enabling more economical management of chronic illnesses and more effective use of available resources [26]. Biometrics in healthcare stands to improve patient care quality, increase efficiency, and shift the paradigm toward a proactive and patient-centered healthcare system. Innovative uses for biometric systems in illness diagnostics are possible, especially when it comes to early detection.

Biometric sensors provide real-time data gathering on a range of physiological and behavioral factors through continuous health monitoring. Anomalies underlying health concerns can be detected early on by examining patterns and variances in biometric data such as heart rate, temperature, stride, or even speech [9]. Alterations in biometric patterns might indicate the beginning of illnesses such as respiratory, neurological and cardiovascular. In addition to streamlining the identification process, the use of biometrics in illness diagnosis allows for proactive healthcare measures that may enhance patient outcomes by preventing the course of the disease and initiating treatment early [24]. A notable development in healthcare practices is the capacity of biometric systems to offer a dynamic and continuous health profile, which improves diagnosis accuracy and promptness.

In disorders where fast intervention greatly improves outcomes, early identification is especially important. One prominent example is cancer, where a timely diagnosis significantly improves prognosis and lowers the need for intrusive, lengthy treatments. For cardiovascular illnesses, early detection of symptoms and risk factors enables prompt medical intervention or lifestyle changes to avoid future heart attacks or strokes [29]. When it comes to infectious illnesses, early diagnosis is especially crucial to allow for quick containment measures and lower the possibility of broad epidemics. A lot of diseases, including cancer, heart problems, and infections, highlight how crucial early diagnosis is improving treatment outcomes and overall patient health [12, 30].

There is a great deal of promise for transforming healthcare procedures through the use of biometric technologies in illness monitoring and diagnosis. The utilization of distinct biological identifiers enhances precision and efficacy while enabling healthcare practitioners to provide more tailored and prompt therapies [11, 18]. To guarantee the correct application of biometric technology in healthcare, however, ethical issues, data security, and patient permission must be carefully negotiated. To fully realize the potential benefits of ongoing breakthroughs, cooperation among technology developers, healthcare providers, and regulatory agencies is essential [21].

18.5 Future Direction of Biometrics in Personalized Care

Personalized medicine and healthcare systems of the future healthcare biometrics is seeing a significant expansion in its applications, and many different healthcare areas are using this technology [2, 3]. Healthcare biometrics are predicted to have a big influence on the healthcare sector in the upcoming years because of its accuracy, convenience of use, and non-intrusive nature. Biometric technology is expected to become a crucial component of healthcare systems throughout the globe due to the continuous advancements in wearable technology and customized treatment. The advent of innovative technology has brought about a significant shift in the healthcare sector in recent years. Healthcare biometrics is one of the most cutting-edge and exciting technologies that have become popular in the sector [22]. This amazing technology recognizes people based on their distinct physiological and behavioral characteristics using sophisticated techniques including voice recognition, facial and fingerprint identification, and more. Ensuring patient data security and protection is the main goal of healthcare biometrics. The market for healthcare biometrics is expanding quickly right now, and in the next years, it is anticipated to keep growing. Expanding usage of biometrics in healthcare, several healthcare systems throughout the world now use healthcare biometrics [21].

The National Health Service (NHS) in the United Kingdom employs biometrics to confirm patient identities lowering the possibility of fraud and medical mistakes. The Aadhaar system in India utilizes fingerprints to confirm people's identities facilitating quicker access to healthcare services [18].

Biometrics is employed in clinical studies to guarantee data integrity and accuracy. Participant's identities may be confirmed using biometric data, such as fingerprints and face recognition, which make it simpler to track their progress during the trial.

Also, by tracking people's movements using GPS and face recognition, biometric data may be utilized to track the spread of illnesses like COVID-19. Healthcare biometrics is finding a wide range of uses, and the industry is adopting this technology. Healthcare biometrics is transforming the field from remote patient monitoring and access control to safe and precise patient identification. Healthcare procedures are being streamlined, and the security and privacy of electronic health records (EHRs) are being improved by technology. Healthcare biometrics are predicted to have a big influence on the healthcare sector in the upcoming years because of its accuracy, convenience of use, and non-intrusive nature. Advancements in biometrics in healthcare research and development are still being conducted in the relatively new subject of healthcare biometrics to maximize its potential.

Wearable biometric devices is one such advancement. Healthcare practitioners may get real-time data from these devices using their ability to monitor vital indicators including blood pressure, heart rate, and temperature [16, 29]. The necessity for in-person hospital visits can be decreased using these data to diagnose and treat patients remotely. As a real-time example, in April 2021, Fitbit introduced the Fitbit Luxe, a wearable fitness tracker. The gadget monitors heart rate, stress, exercise, sleep, and other health indicators. With a color AMOLED display, phone and text notifications, and access to guided breathing sessions, it has an elegant and sophisticated appearance. The use of biometric data to tailor treatment is another significant advancement. Healthcare providers can create individualized treatment programs using biometric data to identify patients who are at risk of developing specific illnesses [23].

Patient's biometric data indicate that they are at risk for diabetes, and a customized diet and exercise regimen can be recommended to lower that risk. The Apple "Gero Health Span" mobile application is one instance of a product that uses biometric data for customized treatment. It combines biometric data and artificial intelligence to forecast a person's biological age and likelihood of contracting age-related illnesses [21, 29]. With continuous advancements in customized medicine and wearable technology, biometric technology is poised to become a crucial component of healthcare systems around the globe. Additionally, biometric technology can increase healthcare services' accessibility, especially in isolated and underdeveloped locations. Healthcare providers may monitor patients' health remotely by utilizing biometric data, which eliminates the need for in-person visits.

- **The Verdict:** For medical treatment in the healthcare sector, biometrics is revolutionary since it offers safe and precise patient data access. Global healthcare systems are expected to include biometric technologies as wearable technology and tailored treatment continue to advance. Biometric information may also be utilized to enhance healthcare service accessibility and track the development of illnesses like COVID-19. We should anticipate notable advancements in patient outcomes and healthcare quality as technology development. Biometrics, which uses distinct physiological and behavioral characteristics to identify a person, is going to be extremely important in healthcare systems.
- **The Current State of Healthcare Biometrics:** To identify people based on their distinctive characteristics, healthcare biometrics uses sophisticated techniques including voice, face, and fingerprint identification. Securing and safeguarding patient data are its main goal. Notably, biometrics is already used by the National Health Service (NHS) in the UK to confirm patient identification lowering the possibility of fraud and mistakes [18]. The Adhaar system in India uses biometrics to identify citizens making it simpler for them to get healthcare services. Clinical studies also benefit from the use of biometrics, which confirms participant identities and maintains precise data integrity. It uses GPS tracking and face recognition to help monitor the spread of diseases like COVID-19.2.
- **Remote Patient Monitoring:** Even when a patient is far away, biometrics allows for continuous monitoring of their health parameters and vital signs [11, 19, 22].
- **Access Control:** Secure access to electronic health records (EHRs) and other private medical data is guaranteed via biometric authentication [24]. Ensuring precise patient identification lowers medical errors and improves the general quality of care. Biometrics simplifies administrative tasks, like patient check-in and checkout procedures, by streamlining processes.

- **Improved Security and Privacy:** Biometrics improve security and privacy by taking the place of conventional techniques [28].
- **Wearable Technology:** Biometrics will become naturally integrated into daily life as wearable technology continues to advance. Biometrics will be crucial to personalized medicine to customize care according to patient attributes [22].
- **Accessibility:** Biometrics can improve healthcare accessibility, especially in remote and underserved areas [4, 16].

Biometric technology will soon be a standard feature of healthcare systems all over the world due to continued advancements in wearable technology and personalized medicine. Additionally, biometric technology can increase healthcare services accessibility, especially in isolated and underdeveloped areas. Technology concludes, biometrics will continue to improve patient care, data security, and the effectiveness of healthcare systems.

References

1. Palma, D. and Montessoro, P.L., Biometric-based human recognition systems: an overview. *Recent Adv. Biom.*, 27, 1–21, 2022.
2. Liebers, J. and Schneegass, S., Introducing functional biometrics: Using body-reflections as a novel class of biometric authentication systems, in: *Extended abstracts of the 2020 chi conference on human factors in computing systems*, 2020, April, pp. 1–7.
3. Kaur, N., A study of biometric identification and verification system, in: *2021 International Conference on Advance Computing and Innovative Technologies in Engineering (ICACITE)*, 2021, March, IEEE, pp. 60–64.
4. Arora, S. and Bhatia, M.P.S., Challenges and opportunities in biometric security: A survey. *Inf. Secur. J.: Global Perspect.*, 31, 1, 28–48, 2022.
5. De Keyser, A., Bart, Y., Gu, X., Liu, S.Q., Robinson, S.G., Kannan, P.K., Opportunities and challenges of using biometrics for business: Developing a research agenda. *J. Bus. Res.*, 136, 52–62, 2021.
6. Ryu, R., Yeom, S., Herbert, D., Dermoudy, J., The design and evaluation of adaptive biometric authentication systems: Current status, challenges and future direction. *ICT Express*, 9, 1183–1197, 2023.
7. Kaur, N., A study of biometric identification and verification system, in: *2021 International Conference on Advance Computing and Innovative Technologies in Engineering (ICACITE)*, 2021, March, IEEE, pp. 60–64.

8. Priesnitz, J., Rathgeb, C., Buchmann, N., Busch, C., Margraf, M., An overview of touchless 2D fingerprint recognition. *EURASIP J. Image Video Process.*, 2021, 1–28, 2021.
9. Omran, M. and AlShemmary, E.N., An iris recognition system using deep convolutional neural network. *J. Phys. Conf. Ser.*, 1530, 1, 012159, 2020, May.
10. Ak, T.A. and Steluta, A., An iris recognition system using a new method of iris localization. *Int. J. Open Inf. Technol.*, 9, 7, 67–76, 2021.
11. Altwaijry, N. and Al-Turaiki, I., Arabic handwriting recognition system using convolutional neural network. *Neural Comput. Appl.*, 33, 7, 2249–2261, 2021.
12. Singh, H., Sharma, R.K., Singh, V.P., Online handwriting recognition systems for Indic and non-Indic scripts: a review. *Artif. Intell. Rev.*, 54, 2, 1525–1579, 2021.
13. Пуріш, S.V. and Лобачев, M.V., Gait recognition methods in the task of biometric human identification. *Вісник сучасних інформаційних технологій*, 6, 1, 13–25, 2023.
14. Hnatiuc, M., Geman, O., Avram, A.G., Gupta, D., Shankar, K., Human signature identification using IoT technology and gait recognition. *Electronics*, 10, 7, 852, 2021.
15. Mathivanan, B. and Perumal, P., Gait recognition analysis for human identification analysis-a hybrid deep learning process. *Wireless Pers. Commun.*, 126, 1, 555–579, 2022.
16. Srilakshmi, K. and Karthik, R., A Novel Method for Lip Movement Detection using Deep Neural Network. *J. Sci. Ind. Res.*, 81, 06, 643–650, 2022.
17. Handa, A., Agarwal, R., Kohli, N., A multimodel keyword spotting system based on lip movement and speech features. *Multimedia Tools Appl.*, 79, 27, 20461–20481, 2020.
18. Sodhro, A.H., Sennersten, C., Ahmad, A., Towards cognitive authentication for smart healthcare applications. *Sensors*, 22, 6, 2101, 2022.
19. Wells, A. and Usman, A.B., Privacy and biometrics for smart healthcare systems: attacks, and techniques. *Inf. Secur. J.: A Global Perspect.*, 33, 1–25, 2023.
20. Balaji, S. and Rahamathunnisa, U., Multimodal Biometrics Authentication in Healthcare Using Improved Convolution Deep Learning Model. *Int. J. Artif. Intell. Tools*, 32, 03, 2340013, 2023.
21. Singh, A.K., Anand, A., Lv, Z., Ko, H., Mohan, A., A survey on healthcare data: a security perspective. *ACM Trans. Multimidia Comput. Commun. Appl.*, 17, 2s, 1–26, 2021.
22. El-Bendary, M.A., Kasban, H., Haggag, A., El-Tokhy, M.A.R., Investigating of nodes and personal authentications utilizing multimodal biometrics for medical application of WBANs security. *Multimedia Tools Appl.*, 79, 24507–24535, 2020.
23. Punithavathi, P. and Subbiah, G., Digital Healthcare Security Issues: Is There a Solution in Biometrics?, in: *Research Anthology on Securing Medical Systems and Records*, pp. 17–30, IGI Global, Hershey, PA, 2022.

24. Bilal, B.O.R.A., Emanet, A.E., Elmaci, E., Kandaz, D., Uçar, M.K., Hybrid AI-based Voice Authentication. *Turk. J. Forecast.*, 7, 2, 17–22, 2023.
25. Zhang, L. and Yang, J., A continuous liveness detection for voice authentication on smart devices, arXiv preprint arXiv:2106.00859, 2021.
26. Alsaadi, I.M., Study on most popular behavioral biometrics, advantages, disadvantages and recent applications: A review. *Int. J. Sci. Technol. Res.*, 10, 1, 15–22, 2021.
27. Finnegan, O.L., White III, J.W., Armstrong, B., Adams, E.L., Burkart, S., Beets, M.W., Weaver, R.G., The utility of behavioral biometrics in user authentication and demographic characteristic detection: a scoping review. *Syst. Rev.*, 13, 1, 61, 2024.
28. Silat, S. and Sadath, L., Behavioural biometrics in feature profiles-engineering healthcare and rehabilitation systems, in: *2021 International Conference on Computational Intelligence and Knowledge Economy (ICCIKE)*, 2021, March, IEEE, pp. 160–165.
29. Dargan, S. and Kumar, M., A comprehensive survey on the biometric recognition systems based on physiological and behavioral modalities. *Expert Syst. Appl.*, 143, 113114, 2020.
30. Abdulrahman, S.A. and Alhayani, B., A comprehensive survey on the biometric systems based on physiological and behavioural characteristics. *Mater. Today: Proc.*, 80, 2642–2646, 2023.

19

Investigating the Revolution of Healthcare Application with Intense Comparisons and Case Study

Amudhavalli P.[1], S. Urmela[2], Vishnupriya G.[3], N. Gopinath[4]*, R. Anandh[5] and Lyndsay R. Buckingham[6]

[1]*Department of Computer Application, B.S. Abdur Rahman Crescent Institute of Science and Technology, Chennai, India*
[2]*Department of IT, Sathyabama Institute of Science and Technology, Chennai, India*
[3]*Department of Computer Science and Engineering, Easwari Engineering College, Chennai, India*
[4]*Department of CINTEL, SRM Institute of Science and Technology, Kattankulathur, Tamil Nadu, India*
[5]*Department of CSE, Vel Tech Rangarajan Dr. Sagunthala R&D Institute of Science and Technology, Chennai, India*
[6]*TEFL, Universidad Pontificia Comillas, Madrid, Spain*

Abstract

Big data, Internet of Things (IoT), and cloud computing (CC) have all contributed to the advancement of digital twin technology as a precision tool. In addition, simulation is significant in healthcare, particularly in studies on medical activity prediction, medical resource allocation, and medical pathway planning. Digital twins and healthcare will be combined to create a novel and efficient way to provide elder healthcare services that are quicker and more precise. Nonetheless, two major obstacles remain in the precision medicine era: how to accomplish personal health management for senior patients throughout their lives and how to integrate medicine's physical and virtual worlds to create proper, competent healthcare. The digital twin healthcare paradigm proposed in this paper can be applied to a cloud-based healthcare system. This novel, comprehensive, and expandable personal health management system works in a cloud environment to track, identify, and forecast many elements of a person's health through wearable medical

**Corresponding author*: gopinathit14@gmail.com

Parul Dubey, Mangala Madankar, Pushkar Dubey and Bui Thanh Hung (eds.) The Impact of Algorithmic Technologies on Healthcare, (421–446) © 2025 Scrivener Publishing LLC

devices, among other gadgets. It is especially beneficial for older people. DTH aims to establish links and convergence between medicine's virtual and physical realms. The result is implementing a DTH model and proposing and investigating a unique idea known as digital twin healthcare (DTH). After that, a DTH reference architecture is built using DTH, and the leading enabling technologies are looked at. Finally, a real-time supervision case study is presented, and the viability of several application scenarios is discussed.

Keywords: Internet of Things, big data, digital twin, healthcare, cloud computing

19.1 Introduction

With the widespread availability of telemedicine services and the expanding array of health and lifestyle management tools (diet monitors and activity trackers, for example) on the market, there is a marked increase in the demand for and expectations of better quality healthcare [1]. Digital services benefit patients and doctors in modern medicine by collecting data, facilitating clinical communication, enhancing medication efficacy, and facilitating more effective treatment delivery. The launched Industries 4.0 program marked the start of the digital transformation process that now impacts every industry, including health. Modern ICTs (information and communication technologies), including big data analytics, CC, AI, and IoT comprise its foundation [2]. DT-based technologies are mainly utilized by engineering and industrial firms and regarded as pro-medical innovations to enhance public health management and therapeutic outcomes. The components of a digital twin are digital representations of physical assets that permit data sharing in real time across the physical and digital domains because of bidirectional connections. A digital twin can accomplish many tasks by utilizing these data, such as supervising and managing the physical counterpart or forecasting its future actions [3].

Several DT applications to the healthcare industry have been proposed in the past 10 years. Hospitals can be made more efficient by virtualizing their physical areas and organizational procedures or by modeling clinical processes or an individual's physiological, genetic, or lifestyle choices that facilitate tailored care and enhance the treatment of illnesses. Therefore, the human HDT, aiming to digitally replicate characteristics associated with human anatomy, genetics, physiology, and lifestyle, is the impressive DT technological applications [4]. Though there are a few examples in the field of cardiology, the creation of human DT in its early stages and much work need to be done before they are used on a larger scale to enhance people's health. Conversely, when integrated into public health management protocols, DTs' planning, optimization, and monitoring capabilities can be leveraged to improve population-level health [5].

However, the majority of the scientific literature still concentrates on the application of DT technology to the treatment of disease and to avoid it, frequently excluding other possible uses for the technology connected to health (such as surgery). Identifying a general solution for executing a digital twin is challenging because academics only offer high-level explanations for creating one. On the other hand, practical, real-world applications (like "SIMULIA Living Heart") do not provide enough information to achieve this goal [6]. The COVID-19 pandemic, which the globe has been dealing with since early 2020, has forced governments and public health organizations to work extremely hard at tracking and containing infections and providing medical treatment for patients. Similar to the discovery of novel vaccines and medicines, managing mass processes like screening and immunization and monitoring infected individuals, even in such a critical situation, implementing viral containment measures has been and still is of the highest importance [7, 8]. DT technology for social distancing in the workplace effectively contains the virus and limits its spread. This is the specific subject of this research. Academic and professional environments have employed digital twins to assess the effects of social separation; nonetheless, a recurrent issue in digital twin research is this: no information about the implementation architecture is accessible. A reference architecture still needs to be included even though a few academics have concentrated on the components required to create a digital twin [9, 10]. This study makes three contributions:

This work concentrates on applying DT technologies in the medical field. It categorizes the diverse array of DT applications into four groups accounting for additional prospective applications for digital twins in surgery; in contrast, previous studies have mainly concentrated on their use for preventive medicine. Furthermore, you suggest a universal design for digital twins that might act as a roadmap for DT-based application development. It combines the functional elements of the DT into a six-layer architecture, in particular, facilitating seamless bidirectional flow between the digital and physical realms and implementing various services made possible by the DT's capabilities. In addition to social distancing monitoring, DT can be installed using the recommended design to provide queuing inspection, person counting and tracking, and desk occupation supervision. DT has been applied in a genuine work setting to guarantee a safe return to the job following the pandemic and trauma prediction. It was created with a universal approach to architecture.

This is how this chapter is set up. A concise formal description of Section 19.2 presents a digital twin and a summary of the most current studies on digital twins in the healthcare industry and their industrial applications, all based on a classification system centered on case studies. An architectural reference for digital twin systems is covered in Section 19.3. In conclusion, Section 19.4 presents a case study of DT, including various data about its features, technologies utilized to implement it, and its evolution in healthcare applications. Section 19.5 summarizes our findings and suggests the following paths.

19.2 Digital Twin

In 2003, the digital twin (DT) notion was introduced [11]. Digital twins have been interpreted and researched by numerous academics to date. One definition of the term currently in common usage states that a DT is a comprehensive system that integrates several scales, physical models, and probabilities. It uses appropriate physical models, sensor, history, and appropriate data to replicate behavior and characteristics accurately [12]. A digital twin is composed of virtual and physical things and related data. The following factors are listed in the description of the digital twin:

(1) **Real-Time Reflection:** To maintain real-time mapping of physical things, it is essential to incorporate several types of physical object data.
(2) **Interaction and Convergence:** It coexists and changes in tandem with physical items during their complete existence.
(3) **Iteration and Evolution:** The iterative virtual model can optimize and describe actual items.

The digital twin is mainly utilized in manufacturing, real-time equipment monitoring in industry, product life prediction, and product design and service management [13]. Furthermore, to our knowledge, technical reports or research articles that explain the use of digital twins in conjunction with medical technologies have yet to be published. DT can significantly impact the medical field due to its practical use in the industrial field. For instance, it can allow researchers to conduct drug trials and testing on virtual patients to lower medical personnel risks and expenses. Furthermore, doctors or other medical professionals do not need to see patients in person according to the digital twin paradigm. In Table 19.1, by utilizing various dynamic real-time data from DT models, they can

Table 19.1 Comparison of DT applications in the healthcare system.

References	Applications	DT characteristics
[15]	Utilizing mechanical models enables researchers to explore how the effectiveness of Cardiac Resynchronization Therapy (CRT) is influenced by mechanisms operating at the cellular level and across entire organs	This approach was employed to forecast a patient's likely reduced response to CRT treatment and to establish new criteria for selecting suitable patients
[18]	The HeartFlow Analysis integrates data from CT scans with artificial intelligence, CC, and evaluational physiology	Non-invasive prediction test assisted physicians in determining how blockages affect blood flow to the heart
[21]	They utilized DT technology in infarct-related ventricular tachycardia field	It enhanced ablation by identifying patient-centric optimal efforts before the clinical process
[24]	Heart navigator tool merges CT images into a comprehensive patient's heart anatomy	It offers real-time 3D insight toward device positioning during surgery simplifying the planning process in advance
[27]	To create diagnostic tools, they constructed a DT model incorporating head vibration and blood flow dynamics	Assessing *in vivo* vibration toward virtual data to discern the carotid stenosis severity from a human face video
[33]	The body's DT was developed using dynamic equations and pressure control methods that rely on pressure reflexes	It can produce extensive data on alterations in blood pressure and blood flow
[35]	They derived a rupture risk model via multi-variate logistic regression using CT images	The model determined multi-dimensional parameters identifying vessel length, age, and pressure loss coefficient as significant risk factors

(*Continued*)

Table 19.1 Comparison of DT applications in the healthcare system. (*Continued*)

References	Applications	DT characteristics
[39]	Pharmaceuticals transitioned to DT technology in production processes enabling them to provide groundbreaking therapies globally	DT models have the potential to streamline pharmaceutical processes enabling realistic predictions of input–output outcomes for biochemical reactions
[40]	Siemens collaborated with the pharmaceutical industry to develop DT enhanced by AI, IoT, and various technologies	Manufacturing process saw enhancements through the implementation of physical, DT models, specifically designed to address challenges related to efficiency and production
[42]	It is developing DT that customizes settings to evaluate system usage and glycemic results on a personalized level	This marked the inaugural showcase of DT's ability to administer insulin pump therapy through automation and customization effectively
[44]	They combined agent and multi-agent system technologies with DT for trauma patient management	This represents the pioneering utilization of agent-based DT in severe trauma cases leading to the implementation of personalized management strategies
[46]	They developed DT that amalgamated scientific data with clinical information	It facilitated drug research, biomarker identification, development of tests, screening processes, and optimization of clinical trials
[48]	The model was constructed based on complete blood circulation system that automatically adjusts its calibration according to individual patient parameters	DT model was showcased for its ability to predict postoperative portal hypertension by estimating hepatic flow rate

diagnose illnesses, recommend courses of action, and use model iteration online to maximize therapy alternatives. Medical device-manufacturing organizations can do structural life forecasts, device management, and real-time monitoring [14]. Through DT models, patients' physiological conditions can be monitored in real time by the DT, who can then instantly provide the information to the patients or their informal caregivers.

19.2.1 Digital Twin in Healthcare

The medical industry's relationships between individuals, healthcare facilities, and commercial or insurance companies are intricate. Moreover, due to the complex and unpredictable nature of the existing healthcare systems, which may be conceptualized as a network of interconnected systems, it is exceedingly challenging to study the behavior, patterns, and healthcare principles using real-life scenarios which shown in Table 19.2 [14]. Thus, modeling deals with healthcare systems. In particular, medical research can be made more flexible, medical hazards can be decreased, and expenses can be saved using simulations in the medical field, like those utilized to create medical auxiliary equipment and medical surgery training. Healthcare education through clinical trial simulation, business process simulation, resource allocation optimization, virtual reality, and healthcare mechanics, among other simulation techniques, are currently the main focus of research in healthcare simulation [15]. Service models, behavioral guidelines, and wise decision making throughout the healthcare system need to be examined more in the vast majority of healthcare simulation platforms and systems to enable the quick creation of realistic healthcare simulation scenarios. The lightweight micro-service technological advancements combined with cloud computing allows speedy completion of simulations about cloud healthcare network evolution, resource allocation, treatment and diagnosis, disease prediction in CC environment, and business model. We can use these simulations to increase the effectiveness and quality of medical services offered in a DTH-based cloud healthcare system [16, 17].

19.2.2 Implementing DT in the Healthcare Sector

Accurate multi-science, multi-physics, and multi-scale simulations are now more straightforward to perform thanks to the advancement of IoT and CPS technologies that use data from physical models, sensor data, and their operational history. Using sensors to provide real-time parameter data into digital models from medical devices, simulation verification and dynamic adjustment can be completed quickly, for instance, when treating patients.

Real-time health monitoring and the anticipation of medical equipment breakdowns are made possible by introducing digital twins into the healthcare industry. The concept of DT Healthcare (DTH) is introduced next, building on Grieves' definition of a digital twin [18]. With DT technology and multi-science, physics, and scale model capabilities, it is a revolutionary medical execution method enabling a medical procedure that provides prompt, precise, and adequate medical care. The three primary components of DTH are virtual objects, physical objects, and healthcare data. An external factor (weather, social behavior, government policy, etc.) influencing the patient's health, medical equipment, wearable technology for the elderly, medical equipment, or a system comprising some unit objects may be considered the physical object. In that sequence, the virtual objects are the models of wearable technology, medical equipment, digital persons, external factors, and digital systems [18]. Healthcare data comes from a multitude of sources, including diagnostic data from external systems or medical equipment, wearable device data from real-time monitoring, history data and records, digital model data from the simulation, and service data from platforms that link virtual and physical worlds [19].

There are four primary phases in the DTH operating system. Advanced modeling approaches or tools should be used to construct precise digital twin models connected to the physical entity objects [20]. Assuring real-time interaction among physical and virtual commodities requires health IoT development and mobile internet technologies that facilitate second-party data linkage. Third, rapid execution and calibration guarantee the model's accuracy and confirm the simulation. Fourth, model evolution should be done continually based on the needs and natural conditions to refine and repeat the DT models. Better solutions for senior healthcare services are offered by feeding and returning information from DT models to the actual objects and service systems. Hospital administration, design, and patient care are two other application areas in which the DTH can be used [21]. Several viable options are investigated in virtual settings before scheduling and executing fundamental changes like organizing beds and staff schedules, simulating surgeries, and conducting virtual medication tests with the DTH, as in Figure 19.1. For example, medical professionals can find diseases early on, test out different treatments, and get ready for operations more effectively using a digital twin of the human body. As new facilities and innovative medication therapies are planned, hospital staff members without a DTH must rely solely on their domain expertise and fundamental analysis while they watch for results [22]. DTH can lower risks and save expenses by predicting issues before they arise in patients.

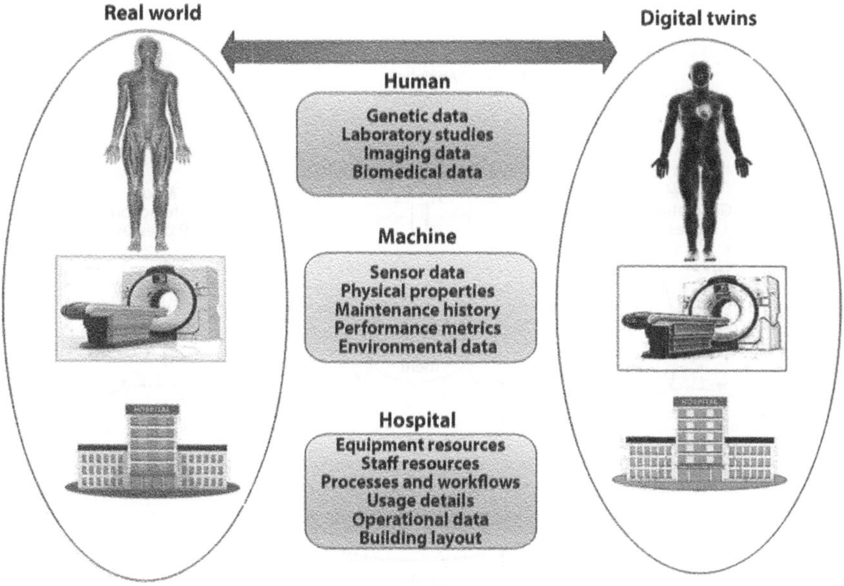

Figure 19.1 Integrate DT in healthcare.

19.2.3 Components Related to Digital Twin

What is the DTH-based operation mechanism if the physical item is a system that can provide seniors with critical messages and real-time monitoring? The primary DTH system components shown in Figure 19.2 are a digital object, healthcare DT data, physical object, external elements, and a cloud healthcare service platform. The system's primary engine is the DTH data and outside influences [23]. External elements, like social policies and the weather, influence the health and decisions of patients. These factors not only affect the cloud healthcare service platform's decision making but also impact the digital simulation. The system's internal driving forces include the data from physical objects, digital objects, services, external factors, and their fusion. Real-time status information, behavioral information, environmental information, and other information from physical items are all managed and analyzed by the DTH database in addition to service data, evaluation data, model and simulation data, connection and interaction data, including additional data from digital items from cloud-based platforms for healthcare services.

1) Physical Object: Mostly made up of actual individuals, the physical object also includes wearable sensors connected to actual people, instruments, and

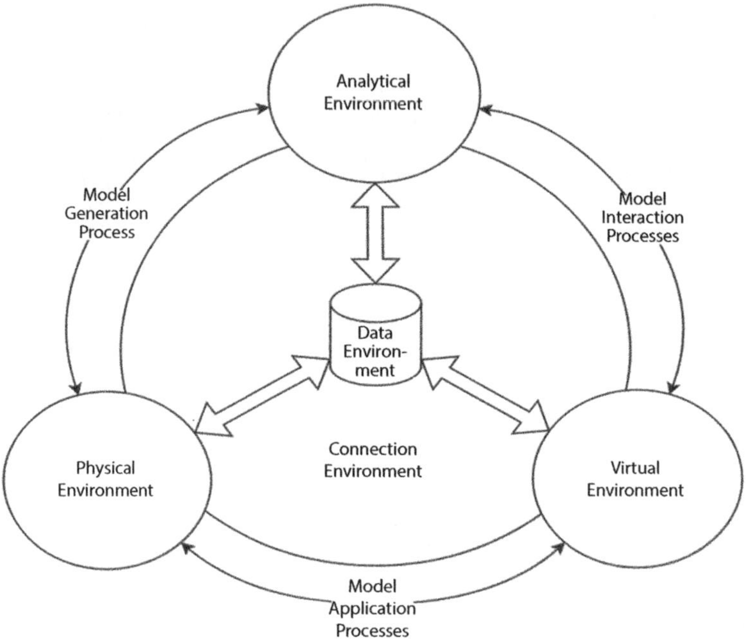

Figure 19.2 DT components.

supplementary medical equipment. In addition, these units can interact and establish connections with one another. Wearable technology and a range of cutting-edge medical diagnostic and scanning tools can be utilized to collect multi-source data, both static and dynamic, about physical persons. Physical people provide data from these unit components with real-time access to a virtual world, and the virtual space uses those data to transmit commands to the physical people in real time. Accessing data is challenging because data from many devices may be transferred via disparate communication protocols and interfaces. Therefore, it is essential to establish a standard interface and protocol to facilitate integrating data and sending it to the online environment [24]. The protocol is then changed for use with various medical equipment connection modes and actual individuals once orders are passed from the virtual world to the data interface. The orders address medical equipment and physical individuals carried out [25].

2) Virtual Object: The virtual object model modeling method is demonstrated. This modeling technique uses wearable technology to track the patient's physiological condition and alert users about emergencies or prescription reminders. An information model about the patient's age, sex, genetic information, and PHR is first created to explain their age and PHR.

The sensor provides physical qualities or physiological information to develop the sensor model. These attributes include prompt, alert, and type index [26]. The following behavioral models are then created to describe the actions of the aged, including their medicine behaviors (taking a prescribed amount of pills or not) and their crisis behaviors (stopping breathing or collapsing). Last, models of restrictions, deductions, and association rules are created to summarize domain knowledge and facilitate the abovementioned models' evaluation, reasoning, and prediction. It is possible to formulate the DTH model as follows:

$$DTH_{PDes} =< P_{Attr}, Phy_{data}, EF, Sym, Sol > \tag{19.1}$$

Name, gender, age, and PHR history are among P_{Attr}'s data. Basic information about an individual's health is derived from these statistics. Electrocardiogram (ECG), body temperature, blood pressure, and other medical data from medical sensors are the core components of phy_data. Elderly medical issues or unexpected diseases might be caused by external factors, such as weather, natural disasters, or political choices, which EF represents. As determined by the DTH model, patient symptoms are denoted by Sym, and Sol describes the optimal remedy for those symptoms as determined by the DTH model [27]. Furthermore, verification, validation, and accreditation (VV&A) must be rigorously carried out in modeling and simulation to ensure that the models are accurate and correct. Model evolution is finally

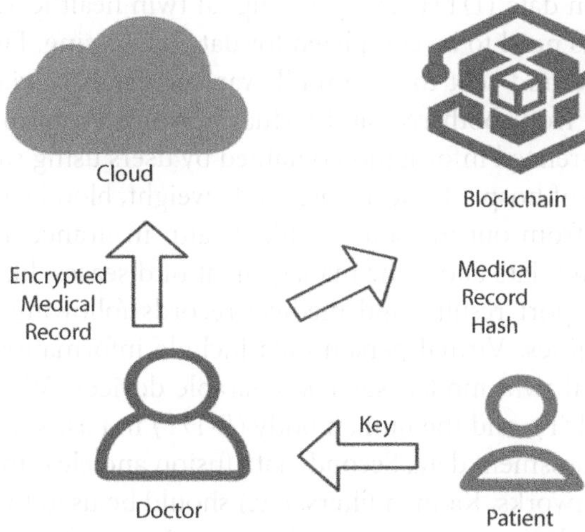

Figure 19.3 Cloud privacy and storage for DT.

carried out in parallel, and models operate in tune with tangible objects via calibration process. The improved models offer accurate evaluation, prediction, and optimization for the operational processes. Figure 19.3 shows the evidence of diagrammatic representation of cloud privacy and storage for DT.

3) Cloud Healthcare Service: Requests for things like real-time monitoring, crisis alerts, illness diagnosis, prescription reminders, medical treatment plan pathways, and management are made by physically present people. To accomplish early warning or disease prevention based on the patient's physiological condition, the surroundings, and other pertinent information, these activities demand a prompt, ideal response in real time. As this is going on, demands from virtual individuals call for plans, data mining, testing, and providing more resources to aid in the optimization and development of the model. These requirements or jobs can be broken down into smaller assignments that concentrate solely on a particular issue and comprise algorithmic and model selection in the cloud healthcare service [27]. The service platform then chooses appropriate sub-services from the candidate services combining them to create a full service available to both real and virtual users. If everything goes according to plan, these services are composed to finish the assignment and operate in the service monitoring mode. Before being executed on actual people, the services are sent to models of virtual people for validation. Utilizing wearable technology or their smartphones, patients can directly choose the services they wish to get. A public or private cloud environment can be used to construct the cloud healthcare service platform.

4) Healthcare Digital Twin Data: Physical objects, virtual objects, services, and their fusion data (DTH) comprise digital twin healthcare data. Three primary actions need to be completed for data processing. First, information is gathered and sent to the middleware or database via adapters or data interfaces from both real and virtual persons. Physical people data include health-related information obtained by users using wearable technology outside of hospitals, heart rate, body weight, blood sugar, or blood pressure; data from outside sources, like health insurance and consultation records; and data about the management of diseases, like test results, imaging and report results, and medical records following diagnosis in healthcare facilities. Virtual person data include information in connection with digital twin models such as wearable devices (W-DT), medical equipment (E-DT), and the human body (B-DT) in terms of model, simulation, and assessment data. Second, data fusion and cleaning techniques (e.g., neural networks, Kalman filters, etc.) should be used to merge physical and virtual data to guarantee the data's consistency [28]. Consolidated data are kept in a standardized format in the cloud platform's data center.

Table 19.2 DT in cloud-based healthcare systems.

References	Description	Findings
[5]	Cloud-based model for attaining healthcare services to elderly people	DT merged with data sources and sensors to track patient's health and individual therapy. ML approaches employed to predict patterns and trends in executing patient's health Generating real-time notifications and feedback to acquire healthcare professionals
[11]	Merging DT with system agents for accessing patients from remote location	DT is utilized to acquire patient's data based on behavior Provisioning multi-agent system to examine and monitor DT actions Providing individual solutions for elderly care based on data acquired. To test system with positive outcomes
[13]	Merging DT with system model and learning approaches for healthcare data initialization	DT is utilized to acquire patient's data based on behavior Provisioning multi-agent system to examine and monitor DT actions using ML approaches Providing individual solutions for elderly care based on data acquired. To test system with positive outcomes
[15]	Comprehensive model for examining digital twin applications in healthcare sectors	DT is employed for monitoring patients, treatment, and diagnosis Issues rely on privacy; security is also discussed DT technology has the efficiency to revolutionize healthcare by providing individual care
[17]	Generating health-based DT for precision medicine	Generate accurate and secure healthcare information-based monitoring Potential use of health-based DT in precision medicine like prediction, planning, research Healthcare monitoring on potential transformation

This stored data and AI algorithms make predictions and diagnoses available through healthcare services like monitoring, data mining, and prescription reminders [29]. The data created during the service are ultimately returned to the real and virtual worlds to deliver valuable knowledge and enhance the DTH models.

19.3 Case Study—Healthcare Applications

This subsection will discuss a prospective mode of healthcare in the future. DTH integrates environmental factors (including weather), senior citizens (with wearable monitoring devices), medical facilities (with healthcare resources and capabilities), a relevant mirror virtual model, and DTH data in this application scenario. The DTH data consist of digital healthcare records (blood pressure, body temperature, etc.) from healthcare facilities, virtual data (temperature, wind speed, etc.) from digital models, and real-time physiological data of senior citizens from their wearable intelligent gadgets [29, 30]. When the data have been fused, these will be relocated to the healthcare cloud service center. The scheduling of resources, supervision, and early warning services are especially covered below. An early warning system, the virtual supervision process module will receive data from healthcare records, physical sensor data of older patients, and external environmental parameters, including temperature change, wind speed, and road surface status. A DTH simulation scenario will be created using modeling techniques taken from the C-DTH simulation service. After that, a rapid simulation based on a virtual model can be finished, and the healthcare regions, elderly patients, and caregivers will receive the simulation's results.

Furthermore, machine learning techniques to iterate the virtual DTH model can anticipate dangerous occurrences like falls. The crisis early warning system will then be fueled by the signals from these potentially catastrophic events. Thus, to promptly arrange medical resources or take any necessary emergency action, the relevant healthcare facility, patient, and caregiver will be notified. To enable the delivery of emergency care, the precise location of the patient will be ascertained upon confirmation of a crisis. The supervision system acquires updated data like BP and blood oxygen levels. Multiple evaluations and simulations of the virtual model are planned. After optimization, the virtual model recommends the medication dosage based on PHR data and the senior patient's electronic medical record system. It also prompts the caregiver to keep an eye on the health of the elderly patient. Third, based on the physical characteristics of senior patients and meteorological variables, the resource optimization service identifies which diseases are more common during each season. Healthcare staff and equipment will be prearranged for planning reasons to meet the highest demands of senior patients. The DTH mechanism can gain from the cloud healthcare simulation service's quick simulation scenario building to raise the standard and efficiency of healthcare services [31, 32].

Study 1: Using an online ECG device, users can use the cloud platform and verify the viability of a real-time supervision service for older people. A local PC configures its server address before using the included Wi-Fi module to contact the network via the ECG device. Subsequently, it uses the TCP protocol to transmit data to the cloud server. Second, when the data have been pre-processed and delivered to the C-DTH platform [33], it needs to be submitted to DTH for forecasting and analysis. Following data processing, the medication reminder module recommend actions to them via display device when any strange phenomena concerning the patient occur. Two volunteers participated in our experiment, imitating abnormal and normal heart rhythms. Figure 19.4 displays the experimental procedure and outcomes. The real-time monitoring demand is sent to the C-DTH platform server. After data processing based on patient ID, PHR, and gene type, the DTH model produces results suggesting one person had arrhythmia. The medication reminder service was turned on at that point. With an intelligent terminal, this service provides patients and their caregivers with pharmaceutical suggestions, like "Antiarrhythmic medications are recommended to help balance your heart rate." The patient's physical and genetic conditions determine the amount of drugs to be taken. For instance, a volunteer was reminded to lower the dosage of the medication fluorouracil because their gene type, rs 67376798, is associated with DPYD TA [34, 35].

Furthermore, the service recommended avoiding Clopidogrel because they possessed the gene type CYP2C19−2/∗2, which influences this medication. This feature indicates that the platform's DTH-based personalized drug delivery is possible [36]. The system dynamics modeling method was also used to simulate the interactions in an emergency between emergency patients and regular patients in hospital wards, which are made possible by the scheduling and optimization services offered by the C-DTH platform. This made it possible to confirm whether scheduling and optimization services for older people were feasible. A hospital's financial capability must be investigated using services for simulating DTH models and dynamic data in real-time, as many older individuals require emergency treatment due to external conditions like high temperatures. This model illustrates

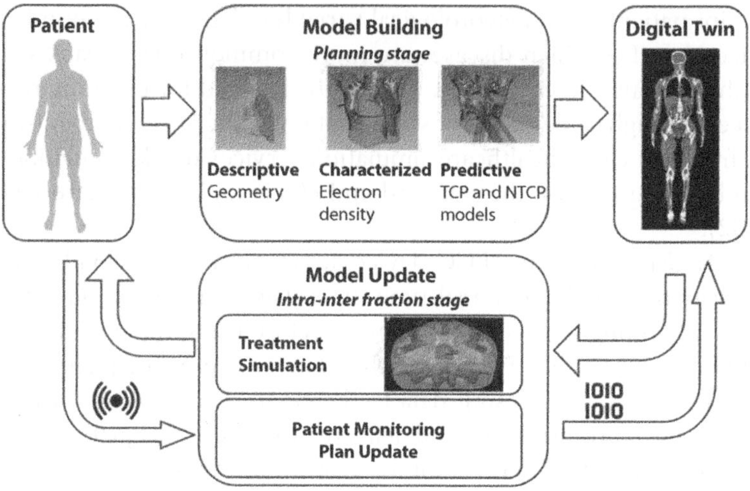

Figure 19.4 Model building based on healthcare.

the interaction among patients scheduled for hospitalization due to bed difficulties and ER patients. As a default option, the hospital's overall size determines the bed's reception capacity. The horizontal axis shows time units, and the vertical axis shows quantity. There were 200 and 200 beds in this trial. The results of the simulation are shown in Figure 19.5.

The figure shows how many hospitalized patients are scheduled to be admitted, as indicated by the variable EmergencyAdmitRate; the purple line shows how many emergency patients are admitted; and the blue line shows how many beds are available for scheduling, as indicated by the variable ScheduleElectiveAdimssions. The number of senior emergency patients rises due to external variables, like high temperatures, raising the need for hospital beds. These circumstances necessitate large hospitals and communities with treatment capacities [36]. With the help of this experiment, decision makers may optimize the distribution of medical resources by adjusting the number of beds and reception capacity via the platform's simulation module. This will help medical leaders in their endeavors to improve the construction and administration of hospitals [37].

Study 2: In line with expectations, in this work, which contains a case study regarding the use of DT technology to deal with health-related procedures with huge communities, researchers further examine and categorize DT applications and present a generalized architecture for DT implementation. The presented case study, "DigitalTwin," illustrates how DT is used in digital public health management. It was created to guarantee that workers

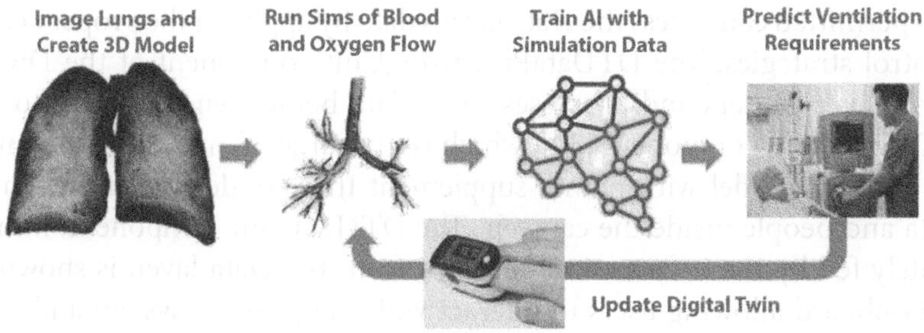

Figure 19.5 DT in COVID-19 monitoring.

could safely return to their jobs during the COVID-19 pandemic. To be more precise, the cafeteria service of the industrial site in Naples is digitally replicated and is known as DigitalTwin [38]. During the 2 h that the meal service is offered, it was intended to regulate the movement of people. With 350 people consuming food at once during the first shift at the canteen, which provides over 100 cold lunches and 1,000 hot meals daily, the company had to implement special containment measures to abide by COVID-19-related regulations. The majority of these strategies dealt with monitoring social separation. The canteen is an excellent case study for testing the planning and execution of a sophisticated congestion rate-monitoring apparatus that uses the digital twin's simulation and prediction capabilities. In addition to forecasting future congestion based on the elaboration of real-time data, the system is used to optimize mitigation tactics under various congestion scenarios. Researchers shall detail the digital twin system's design in the following sections, discussing each component of the suggested DT architecture.

Sensor data are sent via PoE + switches to an aggregator part fastened to the Physical layer sensors. The Connectivity layer comprises bi-directional HTTPS connections, through which the data are sent from the aggregator to the data layer. As previously stated, transmitted data only include anonymous person identifiers, each person's spatial coordinates, and any alarms that may eventually be generated (for instance, when a group of people get exceptionally close to one another and stay together for longer than a set period). Personal identification information is not contained in transmitted data. A non-relational MongoDB database serves as the DataStorageUnit representation of the Data layer, while data from the Physical Twin layer are collected via a custom DataManagementUnit component. Every communication is encrypted using the HTTPS protocol to guarantee security standards, and only employees whom the organization has permitted can access the Data layer's data by applying the proper access control strategies. The DTDataProcessingUnit component of the Digital Twin layer gathers and processes these data before sending them to the DTModelUnit component [39], which is in charge of managing a geometric canteen model with point's supplement that are derived from sensor data and people inside the canteen. The DTHMIUnit component, immediately fed by the information obtained from the Data layer, is shown as a dashboard allowing users to interact with the physical system and view its current state. The lengths of time between the points that symbolize the workers in the canteen are computed. The coordinates of those points are elaborated by the DTCognitiveUnit component. It also calculates the average time a person spends in a line within a specific time range and extracts different data regarding the overall occupancy of the various areas. Last, if pre-established thresholds for interpersonal distance are surpassed, for example, the EventSourceUnit component is in charge of transmitting alerts and messages to the Physical Twin layer [40].

One unique Social Distancing Monitoring program, which makes sense to be on the Service layer, is the source of the alarms. However, DT offers much more than just social distancing monitoring. Predictive analysis, a real-time representation of the entire canteen population, takeout area, and surrounding area at that precise moment, as well as data on table occupancy (unoccupied, fully occupied, partially occupied, and in need of cleaning), conveyor status, and availability, are all included in their offerings. To be more precise, we now employ a straightforward analytical model to forecast the degree of congestion shortly (over the next 3 h) by tracking the journey times of the various queues over a specified (adjustable) time range. This information may benefit maximum distribution and space usage and raise the general caliber and die. The procedure of serving canteen food is depicted in the activity diagram shown in Figure 19.6. The canteen undergoes an initial temperature check (entry control activity) before allowing an employee to enter. Should the temperature rise above 37.5°C, the employee must vacate the building and follow the protocols (exit due to temperature activity); if not, they may proceed into the canteen area. The employee must continuously enter the building and use the entrance (D0) screen for available seats (check occupancy activity) [41, 42]. If there are not enough seats in the canteen, the staff member has to leave the area and return later (exit and try a later activity). Staff members can go to the first section of the standard line for both parties if the canteen is not yet filled (activity: get in standard line), choose their favorite dish, and go to the right side of the line (activity: choosing menu).

At the designated time, the person is attended to by employees who provide meal service (provide food and drinks). Afterward, they can select a seat from the options on the D2 screen, take it, and start eating (find a spot to sit and engage in activities). Consulting the D3 display after the meal requires checking the conveyor belt status to avoid crowds. The tray must be removed from the table and put on the conveyor once the meal is finished (check conveyor status activity). The worker leaves the tray on the conveyor belt and leaves the canteen.

Study 3: Specific medical uses are the focus of case studies. According to one study, a digital twin can replicate each patient's unique coronary artery to help with stent design and placement. Another case study focuses on the application of digital twins in trauma surgery and advancements in the management of tibial plateau fractures following surgery. These examples demonstrate that virtual twins can aid in surgical planning and decision making [43]. Monitored health: digital twin technologies can diagnose and track specific systems' conditions. For example, electric vehicle motor condition monitoring has been done using it. More complex satellite systems may find identifying errors and monitoring system health easier. Population and public health: combining information from multiple sources, allowing targeted interventions, and offering individualized care, digital twin technology can promote precision public health.

Additionally, it can support managing aging populations' health and the supply of healthcare services for older people. Ultimately, improved patient care, tailored medical care, remote monitoring, surgical planning, and system health management could come from using digital twin technologies in the healthcare sector. Further study and development are needed to fully realize the potential advantages and address problems such as data security and privacy. Remember that this is still a very young subject. Customized medicine refers to the ability of medical practitioners to imitate and modify medical procedures to meet each patient's unique demands by building a virtual patient replica with digital twin technology [44]. Medical practitioners can get genetic data about a patient using digital twins' lifestyle and medical history to create personalized treatment plans. In addition to improving patient outcomes, this reduces the likelihood of adverse effects.

Healthcare Products: Manufacturers can improve the performance and aesthetics of their medical gadgets by creating virtual replicas of the products utilizing digital twins. With digital twins, manufacturers may collect performance data on medical devices to optimize maintenance schedules and identify any problems. In addition to improving patient safety, this reduces downtime [45].

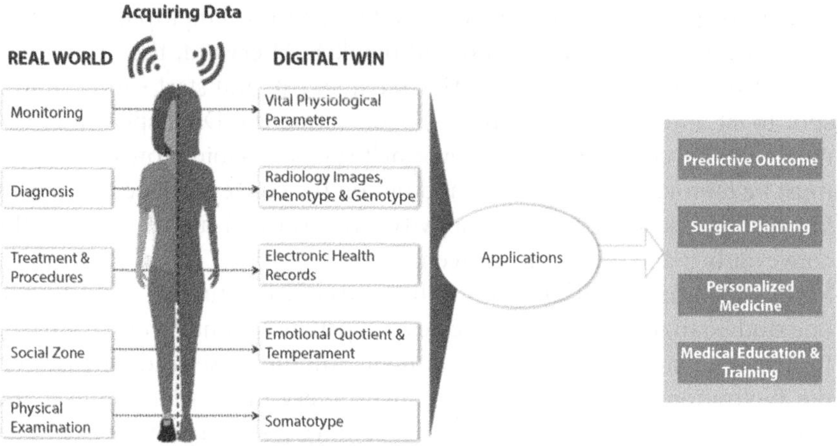

Figure 19.6 Real-time scenario of healthcare monitoring.

Planning and Simulation of Operations: Using digital twins to model and plan operations, surgeons can minimize risks and streamline processes. Healthcare practitioners can reduce the possibility of adverse effects and improve patient outcomes by simulating surgical procedures and assessing the outcomes before surgery. A virtual replica of the patient's anatomy is created to accomplish this. Medical personnel can watch a patient remotely with digital twins, which allows them to check their health in real time and take necessary measures. Establishing a virtual patient image allows medical staff to monitor vital signs, medication compliance, and other health markers. Hospitalizations are decreased, and early intervention is made possible [46].

19.4 Future Research Ideas

Qualitatively speaking, the case study under discussion shows that the suggested architecture is successful in providing direction for the creation and deployment of a digital twin by highlighting the various features that are required to construct generic services that are highly flexible and modular [47]. Assessing twin's performance from a quantitative perspective becomes intriguing as the canteen's capacity is increased. This evaluation should account for limitations on the minimum physical distance that can exist between any two individuals as well as the maximum capacity of the canteen. Every sensor has a fixed coverage area when positioned at approximately 3 m. There is no requirement for a higher resolution; therefore, even if each sensor produces four frames per second, the backend program only updates people's positions once every second. Through multiple experiments, researchers discovered a relatively consistent lag of 4 s between the elaboration from the back end and the display visualization of a social distancing violation event [48]. In these experiments, the number of individuals within the sensor-covered area was increased from 1 to 30 (i.e., two persons per square meter).

The amount of on-board elaboration that the sensors do is independent of the number of individuals in the frame. Then, the refresh rate is barely affected by it, so it stays below a certain threshold to prevent problems. Twin has robust scalability features; thus, we can draw this conclusion. In summarizing our conversation, it is noteworthy that the knowledge gained from working in the canteen can be transferred to different environments. For instance, if we look at the railway industry, the people movement coming and going from the canteen is comparable to what happens at a station [49].

Similarly, lines for various food items can be compared to those for ATMs, and table occupancy can be compared to train seats. The advantages of using the DT paradigm would logically increase in such a situation if it was discovered that an enhanced system model could capture not just geometric but also behavioral characteristics. Incorporating a behavioral model into DigitalTwin would allow for the simulation of various scenarios to determine the best arrangements for the table layout, placement of menu lines, and employment of service and cleaning personnel to minimize wait times and prevent congestion. One possible approach to describe the process seen in Figure 19.6 is to create a discrete-event simulation model (formally represented by a Stochastic Petri Net, for example) and feed the model with real-time data from accessible sensors. A comparable strategy that models the COVID-19 immunization procedure has been developed to reduce patient waiting times. This approach simulates several scenarios and identifies the best solution. It is possible to temporarily activate an additional line for dinner service when it is hectic and then deactivate it when the congestion has been cleared [50], for example, using real-time simulation to handle various operational circumstances dynamically.

19.5 Conclusion

The most ambitious and intricate uses of this new Industry 4.0 technology are in the healthcare sector, where digital twins are used. Despite the growing attention from the scientific community and enormous potential, there still needs to be a reference design and a recognized description. Based on the reviews, the application of DT in the healthcare sector was the first step in our work. Four main categories were distinguished: i) digital therapeutics (DTs) for patient care, ii) digital therapeutics for medical practice for doctors and surgeons, iii) digital therapies in the pharmaceutical sector, and iv) digital treatments for managing public health. Researchers suggested a DT conceptual architecture based on the information obtained from the corpus of recent literature. It produced DTH, the digital twin of an industrial facility run in the context of COVID-19 and trauma programs. Its accepted architecture was designed to control the movement of individuals and keep an eye on social separation. It intends to search for a generalization of security levels and connections in our upcoming work. Furthermore, companies must advance toward practical solutions addressing privacy and security issues while considering the moral and legal ramifications. Ultimately, researchers intend to include a behavioral model in digital twin for process optimization by modeling many scenarios and identifying superior solutions.

References

1. Yeh, L.Y., Chiang, P.Y., Tsai, Y.L., Huang, J.L., Cloud-based fine-grained health information access control framework for lightweight IoT devices with dynamic auditing and attribute revocation. *IEEE Trans. Cloud Comput.*, PP. 99, 1–13, 2015.
2. Porambage, P., Braeken, A., Gurtov, A., Ylianttila, M., Spinsante, S., Secure end-to-end communication for constrained devices in IoT-enabled ambient assisted living systems, in: *IEEE 2nd World Forum on Internet of Things*, Milan, pp. 711–714, 2015.
3. Banka, S., Madan, I., Saranya, S.S., Smart healthcare monitoring using IoT. *Int. J. Appl. Eng. Res.*, 13, 15, 11984–11989, 2018, ISSN 0973-4562.
4. Perumal, K., and Murali M., A survey on internet of things: case studies, applications, and future directions. *Internet of Things: Novel Advances and Envisioned Applications*, pp. 281–297, 2017.
5. Guadagni, Y. *et al.*, RISK: a random optimization interactive system based on kernel learning for predicting breast cancer disease progression, in: *Proceedings of the 5th International Work-Conference, IWBBIO*, Spain, Granada, 2017, April 26–28, pp. 189–196, 2017.
6. Ambrogio, A.D., Gaudio, P., Gelfusa, M., Luglio, M., Malizia, A., Roseti, C., Marsella, S., Use of integrated technologies for fire monitoring and first alert, in: *Proceedings of the International Conference of Information and Communication Technologies, AICT 2016*, p. 1, 5, 2017.

7. Boella, G., Di Caro, L., Humphreys, L., Robaldo, L., Rossi, P., van der Torre, L., Eunomos is a legal document and knowledge management system for the Web that provides relevant, reliable, and up-to-date information on the law. *Artif. Intell. Law*, 24, 3, 245–283, 2016.
8. Zhang, D., Zhou, L., Nunamaker, J.F., A knowledge management framework for the support of decision-making in humanitarian assistance/disaster relief. *Knowl. Inf. Syst.*, 4, 3, 370–385, 2002.
9. Abiodun, M.K., Awotunde, J.B., Ogundokun, R.O., Misra, S., Adeniyi, E.A., Arowolo, M.O., Jaglan, V., Cloud and big data: a mutual benefit for organization development. *J. Phys. Conf. Ser.*, 1767, 1, 012020, 2021.
10. Adebiyi, M.O., Arowolo, M.O., Olugbara, O., A genetic algorithm for prediction of RNA-seq malaria vector gene expression data classification using SVM kernels. *Bull. Elect. Eng. Informat.*, 10, 2, 1071–9, 2021.
11. Mutlag, A. *et al.*, Enabling technologies for fog computing in healthcare IoT systems. *Fut. Generat. Comput. Syst.*, 90, 62–78, 2019.
12. Jara, A.J., Zamora, M.A., Skarmeta, A.F., Drug identification and interaction checker based on IoT to minimize adverse drug reactions and improve drug compliance. *Pers. Ubiquit. Comput.*, 18, 1, 5–17, 2014.
13. Chiuchisan, G., Using Internet of Things concepts, an approach of decision support and home monitoring system for patients with neurological disorders. *WSEAS Trans. Syst.*, 13, 1, 460–469, 2014.
14. Gopinath, N. and Prayla Shyry, S., Enhancing the cloud security using side channel attack free QKD with entangled fuzzy logic. *J. Intell. Fuzzy Syst.*, 43, 6, 8359–8369, 2022.
15. Shamim Hossain, M. and Ghulam, M., Cloud-assisted industrial Internet of things (IoT)-enabled framework for health monitoring. *Comput. Netw.*, 101, 192–202, 2016.
16. Bhatia, M. and Sood, S.K., Temporal informative analysis in smart-ICU monitoring: M-HealthCare perspective. *J. Med. Syst.*, 40, 8, 1–15, 2016.
17. Gupta, S., Lipika, G., Abhay, K.A., A novel framework of health monitoring systems. *Int. J. Big Data Anal. Healthcare (IJBDAH)*, 6, 1, 1–14, 2021.
18. Uddin, M.S., Jannat, B.A., Suraiya, B., Real-time patient monitoring system based on Internet of Things, in: *2017 4th International Conference on Advances in Electrical Engineering (ICAEE)*, IEEE, 2017.
19. Dey, N., Ashour, A.S., Bhatt, C., Internet of things driven connected healthcare, in: *Internet of things and big data technologies for next-generation healthcare*, pp. 3–12, Springer, Cham, 2017.
20. Rahmani, A.M. *et al.*, Exploiting smart e-Health gateways at the edge of healthcare Internet-of-Things: a fog computing approach. *Fut. Generat. Comput. Syst.*, 78, 641–58, 2018.
21. Arowolo, M.O., Adebiyi, M.O., Adebiyi, A.A., Olugbara, O., Optimized hybrid investigative-based dimensionality reduction methods for malaria vector using KNN classifier. *J. Big Data*, 8, 1, 1–14, 2021.

22. Vahidi Farashah, M., Etebarian, A., Azmi, R. *et al.*, An analytics model for TelecoVAS customers' basket clustering using an ensemble learning approach. *J. Big Data*, 8, 36, 2021.
23. Vahidi Farashah, M., Etebarian, A., Azmi, R. *et al.*, A hybrid recommender system based on link prediction for movie baskets analysis. *J. Big Data*, 8, 32, 2021.
24. Xiao, F.F. *et al.*, Artificial neural networks forecast PM2. 5 pollutions using air mass trajectory-based geographic model and wavelet transformation. *Atmos. Environ.*, 107, 118–28, 2015.
25. Al-Khafajiy, M., Webster, L., Baker, T., Waraich, A., Towards Fog Driven IoT Healthcare: Challenges and Framework of Fog Computing in Healthcare. *ICFNDS'18*, Amman, Jordan, June 26–27, 2018.
26. Gopinath, N. and Shyry, S.P., Secured: quantum key distribution (SQKD) for solving side-channel attack to enhance security, based on shifting and binary conversion for securing data (SBSD) frameworks. *Soft Comput.*, 27, 18, 13365–13372, 2023.
27. George, A., Dhanasekaran, H., Chittiappa, J.P., Challagundla, L.A., Nikkam, S.S., O.A., Internet of Things in health care using fog computing. *2018 IEEE Long Island Systems, Applications and Technology Conference (LISAT)*, 2018, 10.1109/LISAT.2018.8378012.
28. Mutlag, A.A., Ghani, K.A.M., N., A., Mohammed, M.A., M., O., Enabling technologies for fog computing in healthcare IoT systems. *Future Gener. Comput. Syst.*, 90, 62–78, Jan. 2019.
29. Negash, B., Gia, T.N., Anjanpour, A., Azimi, I., Jiang, M., Westerlund, T., Rahmani, A.M., Liljeberg, P., Tenhunen, H., Leveraging Fog Computing for Healthcare IoT, in: *Fog Computing in the Internet of Things*, A. Rahmani, P. Liljeberg, J.S. Preden, A. Jantsch (Eds.), Springer, Cham, 2017.
30. Ullah, K., Shah, M.A., Zhang, S., Effective ways to use the Internet of Things in the field of medical and smart health care, in: *2016 International Conference on Intelligent Systems Engineering (ICISE)*, pp. 372–379, 2016.
31. Cedillo, Sanchez, C., Campos, K., Bermeo, A., A systematic literature review on devices and systems for ambient assisted living: Solutions and trends from different user perspectives. *Int. Conf. eDemocracy eGovernment (ICEDEG)*, vol. 1(1), pp. 59–66, 2018.
32. Murabet, A., Abtoy, A., Touhafi, A., Tahiri, A., Ambient assisted living systems models and architectures: A state of the art survey. *J. King Saud Univ. Comput. Inf. Sci.*, 1, 1, 1–10, 2018.
33. Woo, M.W., Lee, J., Park, K., A reliable IoT system for personal healthcare devices. *Futur. Gener. Comput. Syst.*, 78, 626–640, 2018.
34. Aktas, F., Ceken, C., Erdemli, Y.E., IoT-based healthcare framework for biomedical applications. *J. Med. Biol. Eng.*, 15, 1–12, 2017.
35. Guo, W., Xiong, N., Vasilakos, A.V., Chen, G., Cheng, H., Multi-source temporal data aggregation in wireless sensor networks. *Wirel. Pers. Commun.*, 56, 3, 359–370, 2018.

36. Wan, J., O'Grady, M., li, M., Alaqi, M., Time-bouned Activity Recognition for Ambient Assisted Living. *IEEE Trans. Emerg. Top. Comput.*, 3, 1, 1–14, 2018.
37. Hallfors, N.G., Alhawari, M., Abi Jaoude, M., Kifle, Y., Saleh, H., Liao, K., Ismail, M., Isakovic, A.F., Graphene oxide: Nylon ECG sensors for wearable IoT healthcare—nanomaterial and SOC interface. *Analog Integr. Circ. Sig. Process.*, 1, 1–8, 2018.
38. Varatharajan, Manogaran, G., Priyan, M.K., Sundarasekar, R., Wearable sensor devices for early detection of Alzheimer disease using dynamic time warping algorithm. *Clust. Comput.*, 6, 1–10, 2017.
39. Romero, L.E., Chatterjee, P., Armentano, R.L., An IoT approach for integrating computational intelligence and wearable sensors for Parkinson's disease diagnosis and monitoring. *Health Technol.*, 6, 3, 167–172, 2016.
40. Özgür, Bromuri, S., Sindlar, M., van derWeide, T., Pelaez, E.A., Schaechtle, U., Alves, B., Zufferey, D., Rodriguez-Villegas, E., Schumacher, M.I., Stathis, K., COMMODITY 12: An intelligent e-health environment for diabetes management. *J. Ambient Intell. Smart Environ.*, 5, 5, 479–502, 2013.
41. Xia, Zhu, Y., Sun, X., Qin, Z., Ren, K., Towards privacy-preserving content-based image retrieval in cloud computing. *IEEE Trans. Cloud Comput.*, 6, 1, 276–286, 2018.
42. Xia, Xiong, N.N., Vasilakos, A.V., Sun, X., Epcbir: An efficient and privacy-preserving content-based image retrieval scheme in cloud computing. *Inf. Sci.*, 387, 195–204, 2017.
43. de Almeida Mendes, daSilva, I.C.M., Ramires, V.V., Reichert, F.F., Martins, R.C., Tomasi, E., Calibration of raw accelerometer data to measure physical activity: A systematic review. *Gait Posture*, 61, 98–110, 2018.
44. Gopinath, N., Enhanced cloud security protocols for data protection in the Internet of Healthcare Things (IoHTs) using Entangled Fuzzy Logics, 2022.
45. Garcia-Ceja, Galvn-Tejada, C.E., Brena, R., Multi-view stacking for activity recognition with sound and accelerometer data. *Inf. Fusion*, 40, 45–56, 2018.
46. Lee, and Kwan, M.-P., Physical activity classification in free-living conditions using smartphone accelerometer data and exploration of predicted results. *Comput. Environ. Urban Syst.*, 67, 124–131, 2018.
47. Hui, and Zhongmin, W., Compressed sensing method for human activity recognition using the tri-axis accelerometer on a mobile phone. *J. China Univ. Posts Telecommun.*, 24, 2, 31–71, 2017.
48. Cheng, Feng, D., Shi, X., Chen, C., Data quality analysis and cleaning strategy for wireless sensor networks. *EURASIP J. Wirel. Commun. Netw.*, 61, 1–11, 2018.
49. Cheng, Su, Z., Xiong, N., Xiao, Y., Energy-efficient node scheduling algorithms for wireless sensor networks. *Inf. Sci.*, 329, 2, 461–477, 2016.
50. Cheng, Xiong, N., Vasilakos, A.V., Yangy, L.T., Chen, G., Nodes organization for channel assignment with topology preservation in multi-radio wireless mesh networks. *Ad Hoc Netw.*, 10, 5, 760–773, 2012.

Index